LEIGH HUNT'S POLITICAL AND
OCCASIONAL ESSAYS

LEIGH HUNT

LEIGH HUNT'S

Political and

Occasional Essays

EDITED BY

LAWRENCE HUSTON HOUTCHENS

AND

CAROLYN WASHBURN HOUTCHENS

WITH AN INTRODUCTION BY

CARL R. WOODRING

1962

NEW YORK AND LONDON

Columbia University Press

The frontispiece of Leigh Hunt is
from a print, by an unnamed en-
graver, after a pencil drawing by
Wageman, made at the request of
Vincent Novello when Hunt left
prison, February 1815. In the
Louis A. Holman Collection, Keats
Room, Houghton Library, Harvard
University. Reprinted by permis-
sion.

Library of Congress Catalog Card Number: 62–7206

Printed in the Netherlands

For STELLA HOUTCHENS McCLASKEY

and ORA PICKETT HOUTCHENS

with gratitude and affection

PREFACE

THE present volume is the third in a series projected some years ago, including *Leigh Hunt's Dramatic Criticism* and *Leigh Hunt's Literary Criticism*, published by the Columbia University Press in 1949 and 1956. The essays of which it consists have not hitherto been reprinted, with the exception of one which appeared in a Manchester newspaper, and for all practical purposes have been inaccessible to the student of the period. Even before Hunt and his brother John established the *Examiner,* the source from which many of these essays are taken, they had learned from experience that impartial theatrical and literary criticism would find enthusiastic popular support. They rightly concluded that the same kind of unbiased political criticism would be equally well received. Hunt never left anyone in doubt about what he stood for in matters concerning the many phases of parliamentary reform in which he was interested, and his political idealism was essentially unique for its day. Borrowing a phrase from Pope, he insisted that "Party is the madness of many for the benefit of a few" and he printed the statement as a motto beneath the title of each weekly *Examiner.* He demanded that all measures of reform and correction which the journal supported should stand strictly on their own merit, not on their identity with any political party or faction. With this ostensibly neutral and impartial approach to the complex problems concerning parliament, Hunt declared himself against all forms of political conservatism, yet in spite of his avowed disinterest he became the chief of the anti-Tory journalists. He advocated causes which parliament had long since either ignored or openly opposed, such as the freedom of the press, abolition of slavery, Catholic emancipation, aid to the Irish, and popular education — to name only a few. George III seems to have epitomized the "intellectual inferiority of parliament to the demands of the age" in his own classic declaration: "I will have no innovations in my time." The several occasional essays re-emphasize Hunt's wide range of interests and his versatility as a man of letters.

We wish to express our gratitude to those whose help and cooperation in the preparation of this work have been invaluable. In particular we are indebted to President John D. Millett, the late Provost Clarence W. Kreger, and the Faculty Research Committee of Miami University for making possible a Summer Research Fellowship to aid in the later stages of our project. We are also grateful to Mr. Leland S. Dutton, Librarian of Miami University, to the officials of the Library of the State University of Iowa for use of material from the Luther A. Brewer Collection, to the University of Illinois Library, to the British Museum, and to the Houghton Library at Harvard University. We should also like to express our indebtedness to Professor Louis Landré of the Sorbonne, whose monumental two-volume work, *Leigh Hunt (1784-1859): Contribution à l'histoire du romantisme anglais,* has been an invaluable source in our study, and, finally, to Professor Carl R. Woodring for his lucid and scholarly treatment of Hunt as a political essayist.

Miami University   L. H. H.
Oxford, Ohio   C. W. H.
April, 1962

CONTENTS

LEIGH HUNT AS POLITICAL ESSAYIST

by Carl R. Woodring

LEIGH HUNT AS POLITICAL ESSAYIST

I

POLITICAL BACKGROUND

On the day after Christmas, 1808, an unpunctual "hundred a year" clerk in the War Office submitted his resignation to the Secretary for War. He had been made clerk some three years earlier as the result of political patronage. From his aplomb in resigning, he might have been a general who had just buffeted Napoleon. He defined the situation he was leaving as one "in which a sound freedom of thinking and speaking is liable to mistrust and misrepresentation." Here in a nutshell was James Henry Leigh Hunt, known to his fiancée as Henry. He was completing his first year as editor, and with his brother John as coproprietor, of the *Examiner,* one of "the Radical Sunday newspapers." His freedom of speaking in the *Examiner* was so much more than mistrusted that during the previous week the Attorney General had filed an ex-officio information against him for a libel on the Duke of York, Commander in Chief of the British armies (the Royal Duke of York who stands on his head, high atop his commemorative pillar, in Thackeray's cover-drawing to *Vanity Fair*).

In 1808 the Tory Cabinet was headed by the antique Duke of Portland, and in 1809 by Spencer Perceval, thought by Coleridge — but certainly not by Hunt — to be the greatest statesman of the age; from Perceval's assassination in 1812 until 1827, the Earl of Liverpool gave his name and his "arch mediocrity" to a Ministry that yoked the somewhat liberal and very witty George Canning with Canning's chilly, efficient enemy, Lord Castlereagh, the chief director of military policy and foreign affairs until his suicide in 1822. With Whigs for his personal friends, the Prince of Wales had been thought to favor removal of the political disabilities of Irish Catholics; yet his ascension as Regent in 1811 not only left the Tories in office, but soon consolidated their power. Although personally bitter, the official Whig opposition led by Lords Grenville, Grey, and Holland desired no extreme changes in the state. Among the independent, individualistic, and divided Radicals, rash Sir Francis Burdett gained the widest popular following; Sir Samuel Romilly's attempts to revise the barbarous criminal code best represented the Benthamite "Philosophic Radicals" who were to found the *Westminster Review* in 1824; and Samuel Whitbread, a radical Whig who often spoke for the merchants of London, revived a faction for peace that had been dormant since 1803.

Hunt, more than most of his countrymen, fretted over wars outside Europe, especially in India, where the relentless mopping up by the Wellesley brothers, completed in 1805, was begun again in 1813, with the initial task, as an English historian of the twentieth century puts it, "to reduce the Gurkhas of Nepal . . . to the state of friendly alliance." To offset murder for the benefit of the East India Company, Hunt could watch with hope the stirrings against foreign tyrants in Italy, Greece, and South America. As for Central Europe, every English liberal and internationally minded nationalist suffered for Poland; but Napoleon, as well as Britain's "allies," Russia (which opposed France for seven of the twenty years of Britain's war) and Prussia (which opposed France for a total of six years), played rough games with Poland as the ball.

In 1808 Napoleon controlled most of the Continent. Recently, at Tilsit, he had purchased the subserviency of Russia, Prussia, and Denmark. In 1809 he stilled Austria. Except for a sudden, unannounced assault on Copenhagen in 1807 and a disastrous expedition across the English Channel to Walcheren in 1809, George III's Ministers concentrated on such economic retaliation as the blockades announced by the Orders in Council, which led disagreeably to war with the United States from 1812 through 1814. Meanwhile, however, Napoleon's activities in the Iberian Peninsula so roused the spirit of nationalism and the theorists of self-determination that all

English Romantics, both the young rebels like Shelley and Byron and the older patriots like Coleridge and Wordsworth, united in condemnation of the Convention of Cintra, which they interpreted as betrayal of the valiant people of Spain. For most Englishmen, Sir Arthur Wellesley lived down Cintra several years before he became Duke of Wellington in 1814 and finished Napoleon near Brussels the following June.

During the crucial years before and after Waterloo, domestic life writhed under the coercive thumb of Viscount Sidmouth. Byron spoke in the House of Lords against the penalty of death thrown up to discourage "Luddite" rioters from smashing machinery and burning textile mills, where they worked long hours for less than the cost of gin. Combination Acts made criminal, until their repeal in 1824, not only bargaining but even meetings to discuss the conditions of work. Subsequent to the Corn Law of 1815 and other Acts by which landowners protected rents and prices, several bad harvests stirred the poor to such frenzy as Sidmouth and near-starvation allowed them. Parliament opened in 1817 to a loud chorus of rioters. In fear of revolution, the Government sustained in 1819 the local magistrates responsible for the "Peterloo Massacre" at Manchester, where cavalry rode into a crowd gathered to petition for manhood suffrage; immediately, Ministers passed through Parliament the despised Six Acts, which restricted public assembly and outlawed unauthorized marching, taxed Radical newspapers, forbade seditious literature, and improved the already effective methods of arrest without warrant and confinement without trial.

The recurrent scandals among the Royal Dukes, and especially the attempts of "Prinny" to divorce his official wife, Princess Caroline, now seem farcical; or, at the furthest stretch of seriousness, they seem to be convenient breaches for the Opposition to assault. Despite the original temptations to ridicule and caricature, however, the royal transgressions were morally repugnant and financially abhorrent to the social classes represented and addressed by the Hunts.

More forcefully outside Parliament than within it, the

traditional rights of Englishmen — and some newly imagined rights — gained heroic champions: the radical journalists William Cobbett, William Hone, Richard Carlile, Thomas Wooler, and others. Hone and Carlile took interest in reprinting Thomas Paine's antitheistic as well as his republican writings; but the Government feared equally, and for similar reasons, both irreligion and disaffection from monarchy. The Hunts were trying for a more dignified version of Cobbett's *Register*; Carlile and Wooler sought to be more democratic in tone than the *Examiner*. Cobbett, long in opposition but basically conservative, despised placemen, pluralists, fundholders, landlords, and Methodists as virulently as Hunt did. Wooler, the Ministers had reason to believe, was as ugly-spirited as the title of his most effective periodical, the *Black Dwarf* (1817-1824). Despite their sustained vigor and frequent vulgarity, these editors, like the rowdy orator Henry Hunt, urged no violent revolution, but peaceful methods of securing Parliamentary reform. ("Orator" Hunt, indeed, did not discourage violence.) The editors did not seriously propose, like the followers of Thomas Spence, that all land be nationally owned; they did not stress the "one idea" of Robert Owen, to reorganize factories and factory communities for the welfare of the workers. In tone, they were hard pressed for greater stridency than the *Morning Chronicle*, edited for the Whigs by James Perry. Aside from their violent language of demagoguery, their crime was to encourage the working classes to hope for that universal suffrage which the aristocracy, gentry, and wealthy householders hoped to avoid. Against them were erected such buffers as the *New Times*, edited by John Stoddart, and *John Bull*, assigned to Theodore Hook on its establishment in 1820. Into this arena of vituperation the belletristic and somewhat urbane *Examiner* was called.

II

LEIGH HUNT BEFORE THE CHARGES OF LIBEL

With irony almost Voltairian, Hunt told in the *Examiner* and later in his *Autobiography* how he had first ventured into verse with the topic of the Duke of York's great victory at Dunkirk, which he later discovered to be just another of the Duke's defeats. He followed these trusting verses, however, with some to "learned Horne Tooke," a craggy individualist who had opposed the party of the Crown since the days of Wilkes. It is to experiences of his childhood and to inheritance from his West Indian and American ancestry that the *Autobiography* persuasively ascribes his sensitivity to suffering in others, and his spirit of political martyrdom. He and the brothers associated with him in the *Examiner*, he said, "inherited the power of making sacrifices for the sake of a principle." His mother descended from a line of republicans; from the lax independence of his father, Leigh had a very early remembrance of prison, where indebtedness had cooped his father with ugly, drunken malefactors. Had Hunt not signalized such episodes and affections of childhood, we should have sought them out in order to prove the child a father to the man. As he has signalized them, we can either burrow under them in search of unconscious infantile frustrations or accept them for the unusually acute observations that (to this one reader) they seem to be.

Along with the other half-charity boys at Christ's Hospital, Leigh read English history; the most thorough analyst of Hunt and his works, Louis Landré, attributes to the school the man's admiration for such martyrs and servants of liberty as Algernon Sydney, Lord William Russell, and Andrew Marvell. Perhaps a political student should follow Stephen F. Fogle (*Leigh Hunt's Autobiography: The Earliest Sketches*, University of Florida Monographs, No. 2, 1959) in noting the possessive, protective, and courage-building aspects of Leigh's romantic schoolboy friendships. The greatest tribute to Christ's Hospital in the *Examiner* lies implicitly in Hunt's repeated attacks on the manufacture, by "the more fashionable schools" of Eton and Westminster, of tyrants and slaves, as demonstrated in Canning's clique. Leigh studied, at first without pleasure, the periodical essays of Addison, Steele, and Swift. His *Juvenilia* of 1801 mixed with its Spenserian and Ossianic strains a conventional defense of Freedom and the Swiss against French aggression. This convention he could have learned in or out of school.

From his most imposing relative, Benjamin West, president of the Royal Academy, he caught a respect for Bonaparte, which was not dissipated in 1802 when the timid and rather cowardly boy joined a regiment of volunteers then parading in the courtyard of Burlington House. Marianne Kent, who married Hunt in 1809 after an interrupted engagement of six years, has disturbed Hunt's biographers because she unsettled most of his later friends and appalled several besides Byron; yet a student of Hunt's politics will find her a milliner's daughter who encouraged her Henry to follow his political conscience (as Montaigne suggested) up to the fire, and into it (without Montaigne) if duty called.

As the dramatic critic for his brother John's *News*, 1805-1807, Leigh practised independence to the point of refusing the free tickets customarily provided by the theaters. When to the evaluation of actors and his clerkship in the War Office he added political editorship at the beginning of 1808, he possessed scarcely a political work, according to his later memory, and knew from close study only the two compact volumes of Jean Louis de Lolme, entitled *The Constitution of England*, and the more extensive commentaries of Blackstone.

This apology for little history and less law does not sound propitious for a reader of the *Examiner*. From its inception until November, 1820, except during the worst stages of recurring illness and occasional literary business outside London, Leigh Hunt was the general editor and the "Political Examiner" who wrote the front page under that heading. Of the three brothers (Robert wrote on art), only Leigh referred

"NEW ROADS TO THE TEMPLE OF FORTUNE"

Hunt, in the central panel of a caricature in the Scourge, *1811*

Reprinted by permission of the Pierpont Morgan Library

to himself editorially as the Examiner. He wrote the comments on foreign intelligence — frequently on the lack of foreign intelligence — that occupied a column or so between the masthead and the printer's hand, or Indicator, by which he identified his essays and paragraphs. Except for his two years in prison, he normally wrote the "Theatrical Examiner"; otherwise, most of his contributions, both regular and supplementary, were in some way political. In an average Examiner, nine of the sixteen pages are concerned with politics and "domestic economy." A later "Political Examiner" may extend to five pages. For embarking as navigator, Hunt represents himself as equipped with two books and no training in sextant or barometer.

Soon, however, as citations in the Examiner show, he utilized treatises and tracts by Swift and Bolingbroke; by seventeenth-century republicans like Sydney, Milton, and Andrew Fletcher; by Jeremy Bentham, other Philosophic Radicals, and the Edinburgh Reviewers; and by such current disputants as Henry Maddock, Burdett's answerer in 1810, and Francis L. Holt, whose conservative Law of Libel (1812) afforded little comfort to the Hunts. Noticing Swift's high praise, Leigh reread Utopia, but More's narrowness in religion made him prefer the heroism of Alfred, Hampden, the Antonines, Sully, and L'Hôpital. He took just pride in defying insular prejudice by frequent reference to Voltaire as the chief deliverer of mankind from the tyranny of intolerance. Voltaire he read for himself, at least as far beyond Zadig and Candide as the Dictionnaire philosophique. But admiration for the character and interests of Bentham could not really drive him through the barriers of Bentham's thought and style. Machiavelli and the Tractatus of Spinoza, starting points for many of Hunt's poetic contemporaries, lay beyond his goal as a political journalist. And events quickly moved the goal nearer to his inclinations.

Alexander I of Russia is pragmatically considered in the first two pages of the Examiner; he returns often in later weeks, either alone or in company with other mediocre, stagnantly supreme monarchs. Hunt's second Political Examiner, with the ironic title "Meekness and Modesty of the Jamaica Planters," answers spokesmen of the slave trade. His initial boldness was limited to external affairs. Not at all explicitly for Parliamentary reform, the Examiner's earliest domestic pronouncements are against narrowness of party. But such chance circumstances as Hunt's view from the bottom of the War Office and the current debates on royal and reversionary grants — to which we must add a costly war interrupted only once in sixteen years — catapulted the *Examiner* out of its place in the shade. From a humanitarian belief that the suffering of the poor required retrenchment in public generosity to the idlest of the rich, as well as from patriotism and common sense, Hunt pronounced the necessity of military reform, which meant first of all removal of the Duke of York. Agreeing that York was no field general, historians concede less grudgingly than the Hunts that his considerable — and within limits dedicated — administrative talents improved the army. More to the point, the Royal Duke apparently saw no link between military promotion by favoritism and purchase, instead of by merit, and the army's sixteen years of expeditionary disaster; but young Hunt, not uniquely, concluded from Napoleon's victories that fewer irregularities of promotion made for a better army, and he said so. By saying so he precipitated those legal episodes which require prolonged examination in any study of Hunt's political writings.

III

THE FIRST THREE INFORMATIONS

The story of the Hunt trials is generally said to begin with a pamphlet of mid-October in which Major Denis Hogan strongly insinuated, through a recital of his own experiences, that officers normally secured promotion by payment to a Cooke, a Creswell, a Clarke, a Sinclair, or a Carey. With mock innocence the *Times* supposed these to be "some Generals of whom we have never heard," but ballad-mongers knew them as names borne by the Duke's mistresses. For quoting Hogan's pamphlet, or commenting on it, the Hunts and some twenty-five other editors and publishers received notice that the Attorney General had filed a charge of libel against them. In the midst of these charges, in the Crown Rolls of the King's Bench, you can find one William Horseman, laborer, charged with sticking up an advertisement of Hogan's *Appeal*. (Public Records Office, K.B., Hilary 49th Geo. III 1809, Pleas, Docket Roll 35.) But William Horseman is named as publisher on the title page of A *Letter to His Majesty: The Bandogs*, which attacked all the Royal Dukes except Kent late in 1808. The *Examiner* was aboveboard in a war of subterfuge.

Even in the usual accounts, Hunt did not quite wait for Hogan. On August 21 he had warned the Prince of Wales against evil companions; on September 25 he had denounced Wellesley's part in the Convention of Cintra under the heading "Military Delinquency"; on October 9 he deplored the possibility of York's assuming the command in Spain as infinitely worse than Wellesley's return there. To contrast with "Military Delinquency," he headed his four full pages on the Hogan affair "Military Depravity." Thereafter, until Waterloo (not merely Hunt's in 1813 but Napoleon's in 1815), he publicly contrasted his own and his brother John's probity and continence with the known, disgraceful, and disgusting absence of these virtues from the Duke of York and *his* elder brother, the Prince.

But it was not simply in for a penny, in for a pound. After initial moderation, Hunt had been inveighing since February with all the fervor of honest indignation and inexperience. His seventh Political Examiner had attacked a Royal Grant to the Duke of York. At the end of March the *Examiner* had been much occupied with the case of General Whitelocke, who was cashiered by court martial for giving cowardly orders in an unsuccessful assault on Buenos Aires. Hogan first threatened the Duke with exposure in late August, but Hunt had asked on April 10 what would become of the armies "if ever they are commanded by a Chief, who shall be deaf to all but his favourites" and "shall take it into his head to maintain his mistresses upon the sale of commissions." He was taking more seriously than other editors, or at least with earlier daring, the charges against the Duke in such scurrilous pamphlets of the last several months as *The Bonne Bouche of Epicurean Rascality; Dedicated to the Worst Man in His Majesty's Dominions*. One of these pamphlets, *Mentoriana*, referred in its subtitle to "Meretricious Influence" and pondered hypothetically the sad result "if your Royal Highness (which God forbid) should resign the chaste pleasures of the nuptial bed for the wanton embraces of a harlot, *and permit her to prostitute your patronage, in return for the prostitution of her person*." Perhaps many readers of the *Examiner* (sales passed 2,200 by November) regarded the case of maintaining mistresses as hypothetical, but suspicious Ministerialists would have been alerted from April 10 for blackmail or libel.

By October, when the *Times* was shriller against the Duke than the *Examiner* was, the stakes were high: the forces in Spain must be saved from imminent command by a royal general so inept, cried the *Times* on October 6, so inept that his return to the field could have been suggested only through "the pertinacious insolence" of the Court. The impulse of Hunt's attacks on the Duke had been moral more than patriotic, but patriotism and practical politics were suddenly gathering momentum together. Because of the Convention of Cintra, Hunt believed that the Ministers, sinking into disrepute, could not last another month. Certainly he hoped to expedite by his writings the expulsion of both the Duke and the Ministers.

It seems necessary to review here the legal hazards that faced Hunt during the years of competing intrigue and collision between the *Examiner* and the sons of George III. The Crown could avoid submitting its charges to a grand jury by having the Attorney General file ex-officio informations instead of indictments. As a second annoyance, authors, editors, and printers so charged underwent the expense of preparing a legal defense. Until his actual conviction in 1812, it was about the expense that the Examiner complained. At first Leigh might have wished naïvely for a trial by jury, but John would have known better. However perplexed, most jurymen felt a deep loyalty to the Crown, feared Napoleon, trusted the court, and obeyed the dictates of the law. The Crown had two more specific reasons for confidence in trial juries, especially in Middlesex cases. First, the truth was no excuse — that is, counsel for the defense was not permitted to introduce evidence that the statements alleged to be libelous were true in fact. This gag on truth seemed to Hunt both immoral and absurd. As a second advantage to the Crown, special jurors could be chosen by an appointee of the court from among gentlemen notably loyal. In short, they were nominated by the Government. Some special jurors held appointment under Ministerial control, and all of them could be well paid as long as their decisions encouraged the court to retain them on the panel. As Bentham pointed out in *The Elements of the Art of Packing,* one sufficiently purchased special juror could wear down the other eleven, whose interests would be less intense than his, until they agreed to a verdict of guilty. Most contemporary analysts of the system agreed that the talesmen, chosen on the spot when a full panel of jurors failed to appear, were "qualified by the Crown" just as the special jurors were "esquired by the Crown" (*State Trials,* XX, 687). "Esq." after a name indicated availability for the special jury. According to John Hunt's report on the choice of jurymen for his trial in 1823 (*Examiner,* May 18), the petty constable put "Esq." by whatever name he liked.

In trials for libel against the Crown, the prosecutor spoke first, the barrister for the defense second, and the prosecutor again third and last — except for the judge's charge to the jury. In the first decades of George III's reign, the Lord Chief Justice left to the jury only a decision on the fact of writing, printing, or publishing. Even after Fox's mollifying Libel Act of 1792, the judge determined for the jury whether the statements in question, no matter how true, did or did not constitute a libel. Thus Lord Ellenborough's attitude toward the Hunts was scarcely less important than the Duke's and the Prince's. Personally, said Bentham, he had rather be tried by Star Chamber with no jury at all.

No more fully or forcefully than other opposition papers did the *Examiner* of October 23, 1808, quote and moralize upon Hogan's pamphlet, *An Appeal to the Public and a Farewell Address to the Army*. Nor did the Attorney General, Sir Vicary Gibbs (so humorless and caustic he was known as Sir Vinegar), treat the Hunts as any different from the rest when he kept the threat of prosecution dangling over their heads. But some of the waspish spirit of Tom Paine had entered Hunt, as it had his fellow-libelers Hone and Carlile. Informed that the Duke of York had set on the Attorney General, but unaware that Gibbs counseled against prosecution (because it would not stick — B.M. *Add. MSS.* 38,243, ff. 1, 50), Hunt taunted Gibbs almost weekly as "a peevish little Personage," or, in a lighter tone, as one "in whose accomplished curls and taking ways nestle and sport all the little loves and graces of law." Back in the days of Wilkes, liberals had argued that public morality must be distinguished from private morality; in heart and soul against such a distinction, Hunt eventually had to tell readers of the *Examiner*, on March 10, 1811, that Sir Vicary was of good private character.

As a critic of politics and the theater, Hunt boasted again and again that he knew no actors and no politicians. Yet he had private sources of information, and the two or three politicians he knew were just enough to make him more biased than if he knew dozens. The Duke of York scandal provides an instance. The Hunts were saved from trial by the smelly Parliamentary hearings, which resulted — despite a declaration of innocence "on the honour of a Prince" — in the Duke's resignation of command. Their chief savior was Gwyllym Lloyd Wardle, Burdettite M.P., who moved the investigation and fought it through. Wardle had first become aggrieved against the army command in his capacity as contractor for uniforms. Like Cobbett, Hunt repeatedly asked his

readers not to share the contumely spread against Hogan and
Wardle. He continued to urge suspension of judgment even
after it became clear that Wardle had entered into close
financial league, if no other, with Mary Anne Clarke, the
mistress who admitted selling the Duke's influence. Later, in
his *Autobiography,* Hunt remembered that "neither then, nor
at any time, had I the least knowledge of Colonel Wardle";
but he had an appointment to meet Wardle on March 1, 1809,
at the scurrilous height of the hearings (*My Leigh Hunt
Library: The Holograph Letters,* ed. by Luther A. Brewer,
Iowa City, 1938, p. 41). Hunt could have made the later
statement from forgetfulness; similarly, his bitter memory of
the sentencing in 1813 fixed almost at once on the wrong
judge, and when he declared that he "never saw" Sir Vicary
Gibbs he must have meant that he never saw him without his
wig. I would not charge Hunt with lying about Wardle; but
he was not an innocent bystander.

To call down a second information, the *Examiner* of October
1, 1809, declared the advisers of George III so wretched that
the sovereign who succeeded him would have an almost un-
precedented opportunity to become "nobly popular." Hunt
clarified his statement somewhat in December, in the Preface
to *An Attempt to Shew the Folly and Danger of Methodism,*
but the chief business of the Government was to silence such
periodicals as the *Examiner.* In the information, repeating
Hunt's most obnoxious sentences under six distinct counts,
Sir Vicary charged John and Leigh with "most unlawfully
wickedly and maliciously devising designing and intending
as much as in them lay to bring our said Lord the King and his
Administration of the Government of this Kingdom into great
and public hatred and contempt among all his Liege Subjects."
(See the *Keats-Shelley Memorial Bulletin,* no. X, 1959). In
general, the passage cited as a libel created soreness by attacking the King indirectly through his "mutilated Administration."
The *Examiner* of December 3 ridiculed the information for
revealing the Ministers' excessive tenderness toward their own
charred reputations. Again Hunt had hoped to bring down the

shaky Government. Sir Vicary first prosecuted the publisher and printer of the *Morning Chronicle,* on February 24, for reprinting the sentence that named the King, apparently in the belief that conviction of the Hunts would follow automatically. When the jury acquitted James Perry and his printer, the call for *The King* vs. *the Hunts* brought Sir Vicary to his feet: "My Lord, I withdraw that."

About the time of this "nobly popular" libel, the *Examiner* began to meddle in an almost totally forbidden topic: military flogging. Over his usual signature, on November 19, 1809, Leigh publicly informed a correspondent that "no officer has the least military right or pretence whatever" to flog a soldier for such a cause as that reported by the correspondent: marrying without the commanding officer's consent. On September 2, 1810, he reprinted an article headed "ONE THOUSAND LASHES!!," written by John Scott for the *Stamford News* of John Drakard. As the article not only condemned military flogging but noted that Bonaparte's armies were the better for being unflogged, Sir Vicary brought in a third information. Being as always "malicious seditious and ill disposed persons," the Hunts were charged with "devising and intending to injure the Military Service" by attempting to "excite discontent and disaffection" in the minds of soldiers and to "deter the other liege Subjects" from entering the said army.

As the barrister to speak for them on February 22, 1811, the Hunts chose Henry Brougham, a political maneuverer who for four years had been pamphleteer and manager of the Whig press and now sat in the House of Commons for a pocket-borough of the Duke of Bedford's. Brougham's masterly defense of the Hunts, asking the jury to decide "whether an Englishman still enjoys the privilege of freely discussing public measures," founded his popularity among Radicals. Despite the presence of two special jurors and ten talesmen, he won the case for the Hunts. Even more, he won despite a distortion of facts in Lord Ellenborough's summing-up, which contained such rhetorical questions as whether the "irritating detail" of the libel were not "inflammatory discussion which overpowers

reason." As a final obstacle, Ellenborough concluded his charge
to the jury: "It is not peremptory on me — but it is generally
expected — that I should state my opinion: — I have no doubt
that this libel has been published with the intention imputed
to it; and that it is entitled to the character which is given to
it in the Information" (*State Trials*, XXXI, 414).

In his own summings-up for the *Examiner*, noting that 1808,
1809, and 1810 each closed with a legal action, Hunt had
mocked the Attorney General along with (other) "corrupt
placemen" and "mean princes." He lost no time in deriding
Sir Vicary in the *Examiner* of February 24 for the third failure
to convict. Hunt had higher claims as a gentleman by birth
than several of the Quarterly Reviewers who scoffed at him
and his "Cockney School" of letters; yet there is presumption
in his stern chastening of the Attorney General's and the Lord
Chief Justice's procedures, language, and inconsistencies in
the courtroom. For especial pride of the kind that goes before
a fall, notice the Political Examiner of December 24, 1809,
which advises Ellenborough to be more severe in his moral
judgments. Hunt would have seemed still more presumptuous
on the occasions when he passed on to his readers the gist of
rumors that Gibbs and Ellenborough were both of decent
private character. Yet his insistence upon the public significance of private vices and virtues, as well as his hearthside
chattiness, required him to convey whatever information he
had concerning the domesticity, sobriety, and charitableness
of the men who judged him officially. And his success thus
far tempted him further.

IV

CONVICTION AND IMPRISONMENT

Affecting to worry at the end of 1811 because the Attorney
General had filed no information against the *Examiner* that
year, Hunt asked with pert irony, in the Preface to the annual
volume, whether his writing had become slavish enough to

deserve such neglect. Distrusting the Whigs, Hunt had not been extremely concerned when the Regent retained the Tories in office, but rumors that reinstatement of the Duke of York was imminent led the Examiner to recall on May 19 that the Prince, although he "has had his follies and his vices also," had never, like the Duke, "publicly degraded himself." Two weeks later, with the Duke reinstated, Hunt lost at once his last illusion and his temper. Implying that the King's insanity was hereditary, he called the Duke "one of the most imbecile persons existing" and declared it charitable to believe that the Prince acted from "a native imbecility — an inborn rickettiness of mind." So unpopular was the reinstatement that the Government chose not to act against these words. But from June, 1811, neither side could have turned back until the Hunts landed in jail. Leigh attacked "the present and future character of the Prince Regent" in October, in the third number of the *Reflector*.

In the Political Examiner of March 8, 1812, entitled "Princely Qualities," he represented himself as trying desperately but unsuccessfully to think of a single example of the Prince's generosity, magnanimity, or patriotism, even though by severe effort of the imagination he became the Prince and went the rounds of the known mistresses (indicated by initials). His conscience then asked him why, as Regent, he had turned out of doors his particular friends (the Whigs); "I referred him," says Hunt-as-Prince, to my debts and "to a particular 'Book' in my library." The Government could have regarded the reference in the last phrase as a threat. Before events had made him the Regent's Prime Minister, Spencer Perceval had drawn up and had printed a full record of the "Delicate Investigation" by which Caroline of Brunswick, the Princess of Wales, had been acquitted of the Prince's charges of adultery. This work, known as "The Book," had been suppressed, and frantic efforts had been made to recover any escaped copies. The Prince's staff at Carlton House had an important question to answer: Did the Examiner have a copy in *his* library?

"A FREE BORN ENGLISHMAN! THE PRIDE OF THE WORLD!"

Both the central figure and the date, April 19, 1813, suggest that George Cruikshank had Hunt in mind.

Angrily, Hunt next charged the Prince's advisers with basest treachery for their betrayal of the Irish Catholics. In his seventh successive weekly attack, on March 22, Hunt issued a challenge that the Prince Regent's Government could not in honor ignore. Verses addressed to the Prince in the Ministerial *Morning Post* had contained the following typical lines:

> To Honour, Virtue, Truth, allied —
> The Nation's safeguard and its pride;
> With monarchs of immortal fame
> Shall bright Renown enrol thy name.
> Adonis! in thy shape and face,
> A lib'ral heart and Princely grace
> In thee are seen combin'd . . . .

As Hunt's dancing destruction of these sentiments has been often reprinted, we must omit most of its sprightliness here and give only his thundering summary. What reader of the ridiculous *Morning Post* could imagine, the Examiner asked, "that this *delightful, blissful, wise, pleasurable, honourable, virtuous, true,* and *immortal* PRINCE, was a violater of his word, a libertine over head and ears in debt and disgrace, a despiser of domestic ties, the companion of gamblers and demireps, a man who has just closed half a century without one single claim on the gratitude of his country or the respect of posterity!" John Forster is supposed to have said (according to Gosse in the *Athenaeum*, March 23, 1889) that Charles Lamb had a hand in writing this libel, but probably Lamb's part in the campaign did not extend beyond a few epigrams and the poem of March 15 that distinguished the "Prince of Whales" from other "Monsters of the deep."

Brougham saw at once that it would take more than eloquence to keep the Hunts out of prison. Leigh continued to write as if either he felt he had gone too far to adopt tardy caution, or — and this seems to be his tone — he could not imagine himself imprisoned. An April 19 he objected that only "the indolence of a feeble Prince," who rose "from a sluggish and bloated bed at noon-day," could justify the appointment of Colonel McMahon (a "domestic," said Hunt)

as Privy Counsellor and Private Secretary to the Regent at
£2,000 a year. The next day he received notice that the
fourth information had been filed against John Hunt "and
another."

Maneuvering began at once, as it would with the Regent
and the Government on one side and Brougham on the other.
Rumors persisted during the rest of 1812 that the Hunts could
and would avoid conviction by threatening publication of
"The Book." Many of the details lie beyond our present reach,
because the lack of system at Carlton House allowed documents to be destroyed by both accident and design, and most
of the pertinent papers that survive are yet withheld from
the public. The trial was called for Saturday, June 27, but
"Six Special Jurors only attending," as the *Times* reported on
Monday, it was postponed "for defect of Jurors" or, in the
words of the official plea roll, "In Default of the Jurors aforesaid who came not to try in form aforesaid" (K.B. 28/442,
Roll 22). Whatever the reason, delay must have been welcome
to William Garrow, who had that day been named Solicitor
General and given charge of the intricate, delicate, and royally
guided chore of prosecuting the Hunts. Previously attorney
general to the Prince, Garrow was more lenient than Gibbs
but also, according to *The Dictionary of National Biography*,
more ignorant of "abstruse branches of the law." Nearly silent
before June 27, Hunt took heart from the postponement. On
July 3, Lord Holland brought before the House of Lords a bill
to deprive the Attorney General of the power to prosecute
through ex-officio informations. The bill lost, but the Examiner
soon regained the habit of crowing with the sunrise every
Sunday. He broke into indecorous volubility against the Prince
and his cronies in the weeks immediately preceding December
9, the second and final date of the trial.

Not sufficiently handicapped by his denunciations of the
royal family, Hunt took an infallible road toward infuriating
the man who would judge him. Perhaps it did not matter, for
Ellenborough had a strong "courtly zeal," a notoriously bad
temper, a general and "quite frightful" contempt for the anti-

Ministerial press, sour memories of the Hunts' acquittal in 1811, and a marked distaste for their counsel, Brougham. In addition, he had a particular craving to serve his Prince. Just before the trial was first called, he had sought through the Regent a bishopric for his brother, and he desired other "good things," as Hunt called them, for various kinsmen (B.M. *Add. MSS.* 38,248, ff. 39-41, 45; Historical Manuscripts Commission, *Dropmore Papers*, 1927, X, 125, 252, 321). In the address to Ellenborough on December 6, reprinted in the present volume, Hunt denounces as corrupt his Lordship's appointment to the Privy Council. Did he hope thereby to intimidate his irascible judge, to enter a legal wedge (on Brougham's advice) for later maneuvering, or merely to prove that he had more courage than Cobbett, who had whined when in danger? In Cobbett or another rival journalist, Hunt would have regarded such daring as exhibitionist and mercenary: sales of the *Examiner* rose to 10,000.

When the day came, it was clear that Garrow had prepared the ground carefully. Of the twelve special jurors, four were described in the *Examiner* as holding "Situation under Government" and a fifth as "Employed by the Government Offices"; in a pamphlet of 1813, *The Prince of Wales v. The Examiner,* a sixth is identifed as "India Pensioner." In the next unpleasant surprise, Garrow had the alleged libel read to the jury and announced that he was reserving his argument until he knew whether Brougham would "urge any of those topics, or endeavour to enforce any of those arguments, which may have been urged in other places, with a view to excite a premature impression and create a prejudice." Brougham assured the court that the ugly rumor was false: he would give no detail of "printed, though unpublished slander." The line he actually followed has been called a line of beauty by lawyers who have studied it; nonetheless, it may seem to a layman, as it seemed to the judge, to wander rather far from straight logical progression.

As Brougham proceeded, Ellenborough was at first hasty and later hot in interruption. Garrow explained pedantically to the jury how legal method must and would lead to instruction by the Chief Justice against Brougham's illegal methods. In conclusion, to the astonishment of the Hunts, Ellenborough declared Brougham's client to be "a libeller with a bold front," one who had produced "a foul, atrocious, and malignant libel," and declared Brougham himself to be "inoculated with all the poison of his publication, and the principles from which it proceeded." In his anger, Ellenborough unfortunately defended adultery as sometimes venial, too hastily called the payment of heavy damages for adultery a "misfortune," and inadvertently repeated Hunt's argument that the loyalty of a people required that the heads of government be of good personal character. Ellenborough meant reputation, but Hunt meant *character*. After some hesitation, the foreman of the jury delivered the verdict of guilty, and the Hunts awaited sentence with a greatly increased sense of their own virtue.

Yet the rumor that Brougham might reveal previously unpublished slander cannot have been wholly false. Professor George D. Stout's account of the collisions between the Hunts and the State, in *The Political History of Leigh Hunt's Examiner* (St. Louis, 1949), an account generally precise beyond all cavil, does not quite make it clear that Brougham was ready to place in Hunt's hands, with the connivance of Princess Caroline, either shortly before the trial or immediately after it, selected papers intimately concerning the Prince and Princess. In *The Diary of a Lady-in-Waiting* (ed. by A. F. Steuart, London, 1908), Lady Charlotte Bury placed as if of November, 1811, a letter to the Princess from "one of the most celebrated men of this day." The year was 1812, for the writer advised the publication of letters corroborating the Princess, "accompanied with a *proper narrative*, which I have engaged a most unexceptionable person to write as soon as required, namely, Mr. Hunt." Of course, the celebrated man who engaged Leigh Hunt was Brougham, as he makes clear in one of his two letters to Earl Grey dated November 25, 1812, (*The Life and Times of Henry Lord Brougham*, 2nd ed., Edinburgh, 1871-72, II, 170). These were among the transactions that led Hunt to write in the Political Examiner of March 7, 1813, "of the famous *Book*, or rather *Books* (for there are two of them)," and to append a footnote: "We take this opportunity of saying, that we have seen only *extracts* from these intended publications."

Perry of the *Morning Chronicle* was reportedly ready to promise the support of the Whig press if the Hunts published "the Genuine Book" as compiled by Perceval. Both before and after the trial, Carlton House offered release from the sentence of imprisonment if the Hunts "would abstain in future from commenting upon the actions of the royal personage." Leigh wished to imply that the offer had originated either with the Regent or with his personal secretary, Colonel McMahon. Brougham wrote to Grey that one offer came "almost directly" from McMahon. The actual intermediary may have been William Knighton, whom cruel chance had made the physician of both the Regent and the Hunt family when the trial began. This identification seems the more likely because Hunt insisted, in an account reprinted in *Lord Byron and Some of His Contemporaries* (2nd ed., 1828, II, 237), that "his Royal Highness has not one more zealous or liberal on his behalf" than the intermediary. Constrained by the Prince, Knighton ceased his direct treatment of Hunt, but sent a friend to care for the frequently ill prisoner and his family. He kept a bad conscience in the matter, as his diary shows, but Leigh remained grateful for previously free treatment and generous financial aid: it is Knighton to whom the Examiner refers on August 19, 1821, as the cause of his own (temporary) abstinence from ridicule of George IV. But John, under the name of "Charles Fitzpaine," slashed away. (See *Holograph Letters,* ed. by Brewer, pp. 66, 91; *Letters of George IV,* III, 478; *Brougham and His Early Friends,* London, 1908, III, 18; Hunter P. McCartney, "The Letters of Leigh Hunt in the Luther A. Brewer Collection: 1816-1825" [microfilmed dissertation, University of Pennsylvania], Philadelphia, 1958, pp. 67-69.)

On February 3, 1813, Lord Ellenborough pursued his severe

charge with a harsh sentence. In the words of the official record, the sentence required that John and Leigh "pay a Fine to our Sovereign Lord the King of Five hundred pounds of lawful Money of Great Britain and be Imprisoned for the Term of Two Years now next ensuing the said John Hunt in the House of Correction in and for the County of Middlesex and the said Leigh Hunt in the Common Gaol in and for the County of Surrey and that each of them . . . do give Security for his good behaviour for the space of five Years to be Computed from and after the end and Expiration of the said two Years (that is to say) each of them in the Sum of five hundred pounds with two sufficient Sureties in two hundred and fifty pounds each and . . . be each of them kept in safe Custody in Execution of this Judgment and until he shall have paid the said Fine and given such Security as aforesaid." In the briefer words of an official marginal gloss, "Let them be Taken."

Honorably enough, John and Leigh, with the concurrence of Marianne, refused all compromise and conditional mitigation, even when a conscience-stricken juror offered to pay the fines. Rather foolishly, they refused once more, as they had previously refused, subscriptions to be raised from such well-wishers as Sir John Swinburne; later, but too much later, Hunt appealed to Brougham and other patrons for the aid he had declined when it was offered. For a time they lost full financial control of the *Examiner*. Both honorably and foolishly, Hunt borrowed a large part of the required funds from publishers (Gale and Fenner), as an advance on writing he would do thereafter. He thus made doubly sure that his earnings, for the rest of his life, would strive in vain after the wave of his debts until they finally broke on the shore, the debts first, the earnings behind. It should be said here, in connection with the fines and with Hunt's acceptance of alms from a surgeon very close to the Prince, that Dickens treats him unjustly in the caricature of Harold Skimpole, in so far as Skimpole practiced languor and Hunt merely preached it while he wrote even harder than Dickens or Trollope; but it should be said also that Hunt traded on his failure to sense financial obligation from the time of his marriage, and not merely from the time of his imprisonment.

Readers of the *Examiner* had been promised that in the event of imprisonment the Hunts would enjoy whatever comforts they could obtain. The promise was fulfilled. Although it took much protestation, cash, and serious illness, Leigh achieved a two-roomed bower with books, paper flowers, a real cherry tree, his family, and evening visitors — all too famous to need description in detail. He suspected that the separation from John resulted from the Government's malignancy in revenge, but of course the chief aim was to reduce their efficiency in issuing the *Examiner*. Louis Simond, a Franco-American Tory, had marveled in his *Journal of a Tour and Residence in Great Britain during the Years 1810 and 1811* to find Cobbett pouring "his torrent of abuse as freely as ever" from Newgate, with "punishment for what is done, and liberty to do the same again." We are to take this anomaly as a contradiction dictated by the Constitution and accepted by the Crown, rather than as hesitancy or deliberate leniency. The Regent, as Knighton testifies, was in the full flower of an urge to persecute the Hunts and all who upheld them. So odious would Hunt's name seem to have become that royalists attacked in print by him appealed to Carlton House for pensions (*Letters of George* IV, II, 69).

V

HUNT'S LATER POLITICAL WRITING

Edmund Blunden has pictured Hunt as numbed by his imprisonment. It could be argued cogently that he never regained quite the same political zest again. During one of his several illnesses he ceased to sign political articles with his indicator hand. When disease let him up, distaste kept him off, and the messenger frequently relaxed while Leigh grew nervous over subjects not then very interesting to him. In a rebuttal against Cobbett on August 20, 1815, more than six

months after his release from prison, he admitted that he and
his brother had not knowingly risked a second imprisonment.
During the next year his enthusiasm for politics nearly expired;
the Political Examiner of May 26 called upon other editors to
admit as frankly as he did that political topics lacked interest.
But famine, distresses, and Luddite riots awakened his humanitarian sympathies, and Caroline of Wales soon requick-
ened his concern with the Hanoverian dynasty.

By 1819 he felt more intensely about political acts than
about political writing. He edited the *Indicator*, 1819-1821,
as a literary "Companion" rather than as a political pointer.
To offset Leigh's laxity, John had begun to give readers more
of himself. On July 23, 1820, under his pseudonym of Fitzpaine, John attacked George IV, ridiculed Queen Caroline,
and libeled the House of Commons as "containing a far greater
portion of Public Criminals than Public Guardians." Beneath
the rhetoric, he was merely saying that the unreformed Parliament corrupted the Constitution. In Parliament, Castlereagh
declared the clause libelous. The Examiner (Leigh) at once
denied Castlereagh's right so to declare in that place, and
thereby made certain that an information would be filed once
the Queen's trial for adultery was out of the way. At the
suggestion of John, lest they both be again imprisoned, the
Editor announced on November 19 his obligation "to rest himself a little." From John's conviction on February 21, 1821,
until Leigh departed toward Italy in November to edit the
Liberal with Byron and Shelley, the indicating hand appeared
less and less frequently in the *Examiner*. For official purposes,
John was now sole proprietor.

Until now they had been joined in endeavor and martyrdom; hereafter their good will toward each other met with
inevitable thorns. Shelley drowned; Byron came to agree with
friends like Moore that the *Liberal* (and the vulgar leech Hunt,
too, if it came to that) be left to die. After another year in
prison, John suffered again, as publisher of *The Vision of
Judgment*, by harassment, conviction, a fine of £100, and
sureties of good behavior for five years. He has been called a

tradesman for his obduracy in arguing that Leigh renounced his share in the *Examiner* by yielding to the siren call of Italy. But his impatience and strain, delayed through much of Leigh's financial irresponsibility, began when Leigh started trusting Brougham and Shelley at points where John recommended distrust. And very probably Leigh's severest unspoken charge against Byron, in later years, was the severance of loving brothers — a charge so little just that it could not have become fully conscious; but I speculate, and somebody besides John had to be blamed. John's son Henry, the first culprit chosen, quickly proved too slight intellectually, but also too amicable, to bear the load.

As Hunt announced in the Preface to the *Liberal*, "the connexion between politics and all other subjects of interest to mankind having been discovered, never again to be done away," he was ready to present his liberalities within such "amenities" as poetry, tales, and essays. Leaving the formal political essay to Hazlitt, he bent himself to defense of Byron's abuse of the late King in *The Vision of Judgment*, to regret at the excesses of Tory reviewers, and to justification of religious heterodoxy among the liberal poets in exile. His intemperate response suggests that he was especially galled by the apparent unity of the English press in lamentation that the brilliant Lord Byron had yoked himself with a dull Cockney. Otherwise, Hunt molded his own illiberalities for the liberal cause into such poems as "The Dogs," "The Monarchs, an Ode for Congress," and the separately published *Ultra-Crepidarius; A Satire on William Gifford.* Despite illnesses and an agreement to write for the *New Monthly Magazine,* nonpolitical essays trickled from his pen into the *Examiner* until 1825. To aid his increasing unconcern, Castlereagh's death in 1822 brought to the Government the liberal force of Canning, William Huskisson, and the younger Peel.

As editor of the *Companion* during the first half of 1828, Hunt made no attempt to regain his radical sting. Instead, as if Canning had not died the previous August and left Wellington supreme, Hunt reports his pleasure at the new liberality of Tory government: "We find ourselves in a very new position — that of being ministerialists, if not absolute courtiers." He pauses to quarrel with Hazlitt's assertion that Burke loved truth, but will not quarrel seriously with expensive additions to Windsor Castle. He still prefers the progress of industry and tolerance to misery and "miserable Methodists." Nevertheless, although the Duke of Wellington stands against removal of the Test and Corporation Acts, a report of his sincerity gives Hunt "an inclination to like him." Of political theory there is none in the *Companion,* but when Wellington dropped from the Cabinet its efficient Benthamite Tory, Huskisson, Hunt could hope that the Duke would not turn out after all "a mere soldier"; he waited a month before generalizing with an innocent air: "The moment soldiers come to direct the intellect of their age, they make a sorry business of it." He could exempt only George Washington.

Louis Landré, who read Hunt a century later as carefully as Luther Brewer collected him, found a resurgence of vitality in the *Tatler,* 1830-1832, and Hunt regarded himself there as Junius Redivivus. But his political excitement remained well below the national average in the months surrounding passage of the Reform Bill. Distraught Wordsworth felt that the ship of state had been navigated "into the breakers, where neither Whig nor Tory can prevent her being dashed to pieces." Those who belittle Hunt for his stridency in 1811 should praise him for keeping his head in 1831 when all about were losing theirs. Hunt spoke politically both to and for the middle classes; he felt only as a humanitarian for the laboring poor. The Reform Bill of 1832, taken with the laws for tolerance that preceded it, satisfied for some years his basic political needs. Even his masterly Preface to *The Masque of Anarchy,* with its skilled explanation of Shelley's poetic patience as "the deposit of many impatiences," reveals his acquiescence. Shelley's poem, he says, "advises what has since taken place, and what was felt by the grown wisdom of the age to be the only thing which *could* take place."

From the blithely melioristic *Leigh Hunt's London Journal,*

1834-1835, he excluded all politics in order to "assist the enquiring, animate the struggling, and sympathize with all" by the unpolitical method of putting "more sunshine into the feelings of our countrymen, more good will and good humour." He wished to encourage in his readers "a greater *habit* of being pleased with one another and with everything." In part the uncritical benevolence of these years came from the search for enough popularity to pay his debts. This aim encouraged his highly unusual procedure: he reined his journalism toward poetry and drama, and let his political passions gallop in verse. Just now, in 1835, it was *Captain Sword and Captain Pen,* a pacifist poem that gives narrative movement to the allegorical method of *The Masque of Anarchy* and uses with force some factual narratives earlier drawn upon by Southey and Coleridge. Inflamed by his own poem and freed from the necessity of popular appeal, Hunt added a Postcript to attack more explicitly Sir Robert Peel's "barely civil" Government, which had been made military by the presence of Wellington and made ineffective by the presence of other involuntary reformers.

Given charge of the ailing *Monthly Repository* in July, 1837, he promised to be "an ardent Reformer, without thinking it necessary to mistake brick-bats for arguments." He felt no unfairness in flinging debris at the aristocracy as a class, and he tried to be frugal in tossing an occasional flower toward the young Queen. He declared for household suffrage, secret ballot, and national education. He was still impetuous enough to explain Lord Durham's reputation as a Reformer in three contradictory ways within three months. Yet he was now confessedly "anxious to stipulate for the tranquillity and good of all," and nothing he wrote on current events equals in vigor his retrospect of armed raids by the Political Examiner. At the deathbed of the *Repository,* he confessed that he could no longer serve with his pen the good cause he had once served by his sufferings. Although he strove patriotically during the next decade to make himself available to the Queen by writing one "funny volunteer Laureat-Ode" after another, it was his sufferings, rather than his writings, that Lord John Russell acknowledged when he secured a Civil List pension for Hunt in 1847. The phrase just quoted (from the *Correspondence of Henry Crabb Robinson with the Wordsworth Circle*) came from a prejudiced observer, son-in-law to the official Laureate; but most readers would agree that the Hunt who was anticipating Martin Tupper as a kind of shadow laureate, however lingering his love of liberty, contrasts somewhat grotesquely with the champion of latter-day Puritan ideals who had challenged the "Guelphs" weekly in the *Examiner*. After 1821 Hunt continued as a superb public taster of literature, plumbed still deeper as a critic, rose to popularity as a poet and dramatist (with *A Legend of Florence*, enthusiastically received in 1840), achieved lasting importance as a translator, and kept the boundaries open between journalism and literature. For the student of Hunt's political writings, however, there is no substitute for the *Examiner*.

VI

GENERAL PURPOSE AND PRINCIPLES OF THE *Examiner*

The Political Examiners were works of passion, weekly intelligence, and education. Hunt began with political emotions and prejudices, the desire to instruct, a stock of ideas, imagination, and a motto from Pope — not, as Hunt at first believed, from Swift: "Party is the madness of many for the gain of a few." Events and the printer's messenger came so fast that ideas were often not in stock; it took imprisonment to give Hunt one hour a day with books of politics, law, and history. Meanwhile, current events and exuberance kept readers thoroughly involved.

The Examiner frequently declared the importance of restoring to political writing a "philosophical spirit." By this spirit he did not mean political theory or a fixed platform. Rather, he meant that he intended to apply traditional Ciceronian morality to political questions. As he wrote in the Preface intended for the first volume, "The essence of philosophy is the cultivation of common reason." The Examiner would be idealistic in that he would deplore the spirit of money-getting and all economic combat within the nation. Hunt was thinking also of the freedom of Voltaire and other *philosophes* from superstitious fears. The Examiner would not fear scare-words, such as "Jacobinism." As a Constitutional meliorist, he would stand his ground if the *Morning Post* called him a Jacobin.

The deepest implications of his call for a philosophic spirit can be found in "New Features of the War" (February 28, 1808), where he deplores the loss of "gentlemanly candour" and the rise of international propaganda, invective, and other ungenerous devices of psychological and economic warfare. Not only the contemptible Napoleon, but the English themselves have been reduced to "wretched and malicious" warfare "with the very sick, with the very hospitals of our enemies." For a time in this essay Hunt turns to an argument of expedience, against rousing the indignation of the enemy and friends of the enemy. But he returns again to higher philosophy: "Must we, instead of fighting nobly and fairly with a fellow-creature, exercise some diabolical art which in the midst of his sufferings shall make him turn his own hand against himself?" He could not approve a total war in which the Emperor of the French scribbled propaganda for the *Moniteur*. Nor would Hunt write mere propaganda against the French.

Most of all, he felt that journalism in London needed a "philosophic" editor uncompelled to support a particular party. Every other editor, he was convinced, wore the leg irons of a partisan. As dramatic critic, he had always tried to avoid prejudicial acquaintance with actors and managers. As political editor, he wished to remain independent of funds from those seeking place as well as those in place. In effect, he wished to remain free to criticize. By the "philosophic spirit," in sum, he meant freedom to criticize all parties. For this purpose he had in mind especially the Tories in power and the official Opposition of the Whig noblemen seeking place.

If Hunt was prejudiced in his belief that the Tories feared art and intellect, he nonetheless had nearer evidence than the failure of Ministers to appoint as official painter either his relative West or his friend Haydon: every *Examiner* bore a stamp, threepence halfpenny until 1815, fourpence thereafter, which represented a direct "tax on knowledge." And their desire to imprison him certainly showed a failure of Ministers to appreciate truth.

At times, of course, Hunt engaged in partisan politics of a seemingly narrow and elementary kind. An unsigned Political Examiner of October 18, 1812, predicted Brougham's victory in the current election at Liverpool; after his defeat, the Political Examiner of November 1 explained that Liverpool was not a free borough like Westminster after all, but was largely closed. This analysis of Liverpool's partial rottenness originated in a private letter from the defeated candidate himself, and would never have come up had Brougham won the election. But Brougham, like Hunt, represented causes rather than party; as Hunt saw it, he just happened to be going Brougham's way. It needs saying that Hunt's ideal, for himself and his readers, was independence, not vapid nonpartisanship. He had no use for those who took no side because they took no thought, the "inert mass" that included "the lowest order of peasantry, — the most of mere fashionable, light-reading, dressing folks, — the inferior clergy — the inferior mercantile class — and the idle and luxurious rich."

Above all, he wrote on November 21, 1813, the Examiner purposed "to keep a jealous watch on that national spirit and character, which is beyond all other resources, in maintaining the safety and predominance of a country." On Christmas Day, 1814, he related more directly to the individual reader this purpose of preserving the "PUBLIC SPIRIT, popularly and properly so called, which priding itself on the independent exercise of a sturdy common sense, and judging inflexibly of every thing by one obvious standard of right and wrong, tends to keep the community in proper condition, as a whole, by teaching every one to feel and assert his own political value,

as an individual." With the perspective of years, he remembered the chief policy as reform of Parliament, or return to
the "Constitution," by which he meant returning to the high-
road taken from the Settlement of 1689 until George III began
his encroachments upon the powers of Parliament. All this is
implicit in Hunt's plan to teach the individual reader to "assert
his own political value."

Implicit also, perhaps, are the interests of the middle classes,
such as opposition to the Napoleonic Wars partly on the
grounds of their heinous cost in high taxes. During one of
Leigh's illnesses, his brother Robert denounced "the income
tax, that worse than Egyptian exaction" (May 1, 1808). On
commencing the quarterly *Reflector* in 1811, Hunt announced
explicitly a public policy that had been left implicit in the
more popular weekly: "to reform, to retrench, to restore the
just harmony between the three divisions of the state." From
the three estates of lords, clergy, and commons, the divisions
of the state had come to be given usually as King, Lords, and
Commons; but Hunt probably had in mind a division of the
nation into Crown, Parliament, and people. Without the
people, there could be no national spirit and character to
maintain. Let it be said, parenthetically, that the opposition
to a national debt was not merely either fear or frugality. Both
the Radical bourgeois and the nonradical could see that the
creation of fundholders gave the Crown another method of
purchasing loyalty. Objection to fundholders was objection to
increase of Crown power.

These general principles of the Hunts might be taken as
popular among the trading classes. Paradoxically, although
Farington the diarist thought the *Examiner* had a greater sale
than any other paper at the end of 1812, as an independent
weekly in opposition it had to adopt the tone of the radical
minority. And yet it adapted that tone, for London tradesmen
as much as for Cockney poets. In a tradition given dignity by
Charles James Fox, Hunt frequently shaped his editorials in
the form of addresses to the electors of Westminster. The
voters of Westminster, which included artisans as well as

tradesmen, could then be expected to petition Parliament on
the issues raised by Hunt and his colleagues of the Whig and
radical press. In the context of journalism before the Reform
Bill, the word *radical* implied uprooting in an indirect way;
not necessarily even the way of the demagogue in inciting the
masses to uproot, but dangerously enough (the Tories thought)
in encouraging or rousing the demagogues. Robert Southey
made just this accusation in 1816 (reprinted in *Essays Moral
and Political*, 1832): "Marat and Hebert followed in the train
of Voltaire and Rousseau; Mr. Examiner Hunt does but blow
the trumpet to usher in Mr. Orator Hunt in his tandem, with
the tri-color flag before him ..." Privately Southey suggested
to Lord Lonsdale that Cobbett and Mr. Examiner Hunt should
be transported, since imprisonment failed to check their
virulence.

Although his role as encourager of public spirit made Hunt
sometimes inflammatory, it kept him away from what he called
"the more skilful but drier investigations of domestic economy."
He was completely innocent of statistics. Sure that nearly
every Englishman would feel a conviction, or at least a moral
uneasiness, about retaining as the commander in chief a profligate consorter with vulgar courtesans, he granted "one man
against ten thousand perhaps being in favour of the Duke."
The percentage seems unlikely. He left agricultural economics
to Cobbett. In season and out, his tone was intimate. He was
personal, confiding, seldom hesitant, never ashamed — except
of the past. Gaiety and indignation bubble and boil within
the *Examiner* in close proximity. Hunt seems to have thought
of his pointing signature originally as an offer to shake hands
with his readers. Even fatigue or boredom becomes a state the
reader is asked to share with the editor: for one day, to blazes
with the Court and Whitehall; for today, walk with the Examiner from Hampstead toward Hendon — languorously, "leafily."
The readers' memory of such candor must have been very
persuasive on days when the Examiner might otherwise have
seemed a quibbler and a hot partisan.

Although no republican, Hunt was a vigorous and effective

opponent of caste. Talent and genius, and he would add integrity and character, defy the bars of class distinction. He
wrote as an angry young bourgeois declaring to the aristocracy
and others who were privileged and established that individuals of the middle classes possessed valor, probity, taste, and
creative talent. Simultaneously he entreated the more numerous among his readers to allay money-getting and acquire
valor, taste, and learning. Much was then made, and has been
made since, of Hunt's egotism, of what Lockhart in *Blackwood's Edinburgh Magazine* called his "extravagant pretensions." But a moment's attention to the complacent scorn of
Lockhart and his fellow anonymous bludgeoners will expose
a greater evil than egotism against which Hunt railed, the
more pernicious "we-gotism" of a few, empowered by the
weight of the past to proscribe and exclude. The contest required vanity, and Leigh Hunt had it. Less often than most
persons in his situation, however, did he betray his cause
by appeal to the facts or pretenses of his or Shelley's or
Brougham's ancestry. He wanted talent acclaimed wherever
found. Hunt is honored most widely as the first promoter of
Keats and Shelley, but against the Tory newspapers he waged
battles for Keats before Keats was even apprenticed as apothecary. Finding politics distasteful, he continued to fight as a
humanitarian. What Albany Fonblanque wrote of stern John
Hunt he could have written almost as truly of tenderer Leigh:
"His faults lay on the side of tenacity and prepossession: when
he had taken up a cause or a quarrel, it was hard to alter his
view of the merits by fact or argument; and he was sometimes
misled, by his sympathy with the weaker, to fight the battle
not really of the more righteous, but of the worsted party."

VII

LIBERALISM UNDER LIMITED MONARCHY

Hunt's easily aroused humanitarianism did not deprive him of ideas and principles in politics. His eighth Political Examiner, "On the Naval Dominion of Great Britain," applies in an interesting way the antithesis between nature and art. Consummate art, he says in conclusion, "has made France the mistress of the Continent; but nature herself has conspired to render Great Britain the mistress of the Ocean." In an anti-Ministerialist, the theme called for a charge that the bounty of nature deserved better servants. Hunt does not neglect this charge. He does, however, rise above it, patriotically by explaining in what sense Great Britain does and must rule the sea, and intellectually by arguing that nature has been assisted, and must continue to be assisted, by British industry. Art, then, is here that assiduity of the British people that has produced the industrial revolution. Britain must maintain her right of search at sea (where no original rights of property exist) in order to restore national justice to the Continent. Hunt achieves a similar success with concepts and argument whenever he is not weary, ill, overly excited, or choked with fresh data.

Among the principles passing by, he sought out the empirical rather than the Utopian. He rejected the abstract system-building of the French revolutionaries. He reserved his praise for mixed government in the form of limited monarchy. True Whigs, he said (April 1, 1810), were "for monarchy but not for tyranny, for the nobles but not for monopoly, for the people but not for licentiousness." Nevertheless, despite his distrust of abstract Utopias, the limited monarchy that he envisioned was an ideal, dependent upon his belief that any king who wished to be virtuous could be so, that a king (like any man) needed only to choose rightly to be unselfish, just, and generous.

Divine right was an exploded superstition. Nor did Hunt

wish mixed government for the benefit of kings or noblemen. On the whole, he does not seem to have expected right choices from the aristocracy; they alone were past preaching to. The French Revolution had made him wary of reference to "the Majesty of the People," but an idea of popular sovereignty is discoverable in his discussions of reversionary grants: all royal funds came ultimately from the people, who gave that the king might be generous in turn, not merely to those nearest to him in blood, but to his whole British family. Hunt believed enough in the sovereignty of modest householders to desire very little power left to the House of Lords. In his view (March 19, 1809), Parliament should be "the *representative* of the great, active, efficient, and enduring part of the nation, the People." He is not trying here to distinguish a free representative from an instructed delegate, although a reformed Parliament might deserve freedom of decision. His ideal would have been a legislature of London tradesmen familiar with Italian poetry.

Hunt thought that he valued monarchy and deplored democracy because decorum accompanied the one and vulgarity the other. But the office of kingship did not in itself contain much dignity for him. To the jury about to convict the Hunts, Ellenborough pointed out that "he who holds the office, as well as the office itself, should be held in public estimation." Leigh agreed that the holder should be esteemed; therefore, he should be estimable. Ellenborough would have been much surprised had he realized the true problem: Hunt could not believe that the office itself conferred dignity; monarchy merely afforded the opportunity for an example of virtue and grace.

Hunt, as far as he could tell, stood ready to admire the person who was the king. On the less delicate subject of foreign monarchs, however, he makes his opposition to legitimacy quite clear. In the first column of the first *Examiner,* before the Attorney General had tried to make him shy, he referred to "sovereigns, who are mere men walking, like the Arabian traveller, in a kind of sunny mist, that renders the

appearance gigantic." Ambitious though he was, Napoleon
had done good in ending the feudal system and holding a
mirror before the paltry kings of Europe. For more than
twenty years the Opposition had decried Britain's degenerate
allies; Hunt continued the practice with vim. According to the
Autobiography, the *Examiner* in 1815 "had a hopeful and
respectful word for every reigning prince" except George IV.
If so, the good word is hidden under vituperation. The Allied
Sovereigns at the Congress of Vienna represented "imbecility
meditating injustice." Instead of Napoleon's virtues, which
they uniformly lacked, they had one to offer: hereditary rank.
Like Napoleon, they were usurpers; unlike him, they were
degenerate. If Czar Alexander offered some improvement on
his predecessors, the Prince of Austria did not. Ferdinand VII
of Spain, as described in an unsigned article of January 15,
1815, was "an infatuated despot," hypocritical, foolish, ungrateful, cruel, and mean. Earlier, in accepting a suggestion
of the *Edinburgh Review* that a "mixed monarchy" be established in Spanish South America, Hunt had warned that
Bourbons must be excluded; and he had countered with the
suggestion (July 1, 1810) that Francisco Miranda, the Spanish-
born revolutionary, be installed locally as Inca.

Hunt upheld the idea of kingship, we see, not because the
nineteenth century had witnessed an Alfred on a throne somewhere, but because a King Alfred was possible; even more he
upheld the idea of restricted kingship because he approved
of Englishmen and their ways. He wished to retain the limited
monarchy for its aesthetic and moral value to the national life.
The editorial remarks in the *Examiner* of October 22, 1809,
which have been quoted to show his dislike of republics, are
unsigned and appeared when Leigh was too ill to write the
Political Examiner; yet they probably represent him fairly.
A few months later he assured readers that Englishmen did
not need a republic similar to the United States any more than
they needed a Robespierre; he so concluded because of "the
known ill-temper, vulgarity, and discord of all unmixed republican forms of government." Apparently he considered it more

dignified to have an aristocracy to accuse of stupidity, vice, and venality than to have commoners brawling among themselves.

To be just, Hunt feared tyranny in any form, whether from despots, oligarchs, or mobs. Machiavelli's admiration for the republic of Venice was a strong influence in Hunt's day, as Wordsworth witnesses; but for Hunt (September 11, 1808) the states of Holland and of Venice had consisted "of a hundred little tyrants," and should not be restored. A less avid reader of history than Byron or Wordsworth, Hunt did not feel vehemently about the past, either for it like Burke, or against it like Dickens. As for the future, his frequent writings in support of Robert Owen seem to have come from enthusiasm for Owen's urgent desire to improve the lot of workers in the factories, and perhaps in part from personal acquaintance, rather than from endorsement of Owen's plans for a socialistic reorganization of society. As Louis Landré says in his great work on Hunt, Owen's idealism and spirit of charity found an echo in Hunt's heart.

Although he would pass in almost any English company as an idealist, Hunt had a streak of pragmatism as well as a Romantic distrust of abstract schemes. Would you not expect him, as a Romantic, to place his trust in the particulars of individual experience? He lived up to that expectation. Even an appeal to "the wisdom and virtue of our forefathers," in the Preface to the second year's *Examiner*, contains within it an appeal to experience: "Every day, therefore, an enlarged and frank manner of treating politics, with reference to nothing but experience and common sense, becomes more and more approved and useful: we see, that the corruptions even of a good cause cannot prevail against the industry and genius that may adorn a bad one . . ."

Hunt went far beyond any of the major Romantic poets in welcoming the Utilitarianism of Jeremy Bentham. He went much further than Hazlitt, although he accepted less easily than Hazlitt the associational psychology, the theory that the mind is a complex of associations with pleasure and pain, on

which Utilitarianism based its doctrine of the greatest good
for the greatest number. He could not go all the way, but
he went a great distance. Within the second month of the
Examiner, he observed in Benthamite terms that "the common
comforts of common men are, after all, the great end of the
greatest statesman." For the Examiner, one assumes, this point
was reached partly by way of humanitarian sentiment. No
reader of Hunt's nonpolitical essays fails to see that for him
the moral sense and the aesthetic sense seemed to be in closer
alliance than the moral and the utilitarian. In hedonism, where
Hunt comes closest by principle to such utilitarians around
him as Brougham and his brother John, he differs most in
temperament: unlike Bentham, he sets poetry considerably
above pushpin. He regards poetry, music, the plastic arts,
and a rural outing as ends, not means.

Yet Hunt became the first effective spokesman in the popular press for the Utilitarians. Why? How important was the
role of chance? It was the practical problem of writing his
weekly bit on politics, and even more it was the insistent
stirrings of the Attorney General, that drove him to read
Bentham's *Fragment on Government* and *Traité de Législa-
tion.* Their agreements on the need for Parliamentary reform
led Bentham in 1812 to correspond, visit, and invite Leigh to
dine at his home, the Hermitage. Soon he had the opportunity
to call on Leigh at Horsemonger Lane Gaol. Thereafter, he
appeared in the *Examiner* as the greatest living philosopher.
Leigh Hunt's London Journal regularly filled out its columns
with an "admirable maxim" or a "profound and noble remark"
from Bentham's posthumous *Deontology.* Meanwhile, Hunt
had been willing to support in spirit, and occasionally by
analysis, the legal reforms proposed by Bentham and Romilly.
For an example of learned-sounding analysis, see the Political
Examiner of May 29, 1808, "Upon the Necessity of a Reform
in the Criminal Law of England." He found nothing to object
to in Romilly's bills. The sympathy in aim was not chance.

Hunt admired Bentham, Owen, Burdett, Brougham, and
Romilly because each was a reformer in a time of retrogres-

sion. In his years as political journalist, Parliamentary reform meant advance on two fronts: first, the redistribution of seats, in order to recognize the new industrial concentrations of population and to abolish pocket boroughs by which a few families dominated both Houses; second, extension of the franchise. The first was intended to correct abuse of the Constitution; the second represented the new democratic idea at least as far as giving to the middle classes political power commensurate with their economic power. The Radicals, both Philosophic and Chartist, spoke also for further extension of the franchise, payment to Members of Parliament, secret ballot, and annual or frequent Parliaments. No reformer spoke for exactly what happened in the boroughs through the Bill of 1832: uniform franchise for householders of a £10 annual rent, which actually disenfranchised working-class voters of Westminster. Although the Bill greatly restricted "the oligarchy of Boroughmongers," Hunt might have written in 1833 as he did in 1818 of "the Intellectual Inferiority of Parliament to the Demands of the Age," if logical consistency were one of the demands. The fluctuating price of the *Examiner* itself, from sevenpence to tenpence, demonstrated the impermanence of a £10 suffrage.

In keeping with his friendly reception of the Utilitarians, Hunt avoided the usual Romantic renunciation of John Locke. More typically than Byron and Shelley, who each in his own way looked with awe into the mystery of man, Hunt embodied the rational faith of their title, the *Liberal*. Of liberal beliefs descending from Locke, as listed conveniently by John H. Hallowell (*Main Currents in Modern Political Thought,* New York, 1950), Hunt held every one: the spiritual equality of individuals; the essential rationality and goodness beneath the human will; the inalienability of the individual's rights to life, liberty, and property; the contractual nature of the relationship between the individual and the state; law, as an embodiment of reason, expressing itself through the agreement of individual wills and under freedom and responsibility of the individual to follow his own conscience "in all spheres of life (political, economic, social, intellectual and religious.)"

Currently, as a first public step toward expansion of the individual in full realization of his potentiality, it seemed necessary to meet the stifling advance of royal power through rotten boroughs, pluralities, excessive taxation, and purchased loyalty. An editor who kept firmly in mind this aim did not need to discuss political ideas in the Aristotelian sense with his readers.

VIII

ROMANTIC INTERESTS

Mistakenly, the Romanticism that was somehow detonated by the French Revolution has been identified sometimes with revolt and sometimes with organic, conservative, or totalitarian reaction. The Romantic movement in the arts can be associated with political fervor, and with a search among fundamentals; but it should not be directly identified with any particular political complexion. Yet it is interesting, whether ideologically useful or not, to observe the matter of Hunt's essays in relation to such Romantic predilections as political morality, nationalism, hero worship, and sentiment.

We may be sure that "every schoolboy" in Hunt's day knew the Roman republican axiom that a nation's freedom depends upon the virtue of its people. But Hunt took no chances. On September 11, 1808, the Examiner lamented the failure of his age "to discover that one nation has generally reduced itself to an humiliated state, before another can trample on it's freedom." To blame national disaster on the mistakes of party instead of on national immorality was to lack philosophy. In October he defined the necessary Roman virtue as containing "both courage and morality, both strength and goodness of heart." If you regard Hunt as a reader and thinker, you may say that his moral emphasis lay on Roman republican frugality; if you are inclined to find him thoughtless, you may say that he made instinctive bourgeois objections to luxury and extravagance. One of the most common words in the Political Examiners is *profligacy*. George III's sons (except one) are profligate, Napoleon is profligate, and the stupid monarchs of Europe are profligate: choose among Austria, Russia, Prussia, Spain.

Hunt apologizes several times in his *Autobiography* for the "nonsense and extravagance" of the Examiner in imputing bad motives to his opponents. Apology was due. A writer in the first number of the *Scourge; or, Monthly Expositor of Imposture and Folly*, although friendly to Hunt's cause, castigated him for the impertinence of denying talent to the party of Burke and of T. J. Mathias, the then-admired satirical author of *The Pursuits of Literature*. Sir Denis Le Marchant, secretary to a statesman — Brougham — who claimed much credit for the Reform Bill, recorded his disgust at Hunt's claim that persecution had fertilized the soil: "Yes, we worked this revolution," said Hunt at Bulwer's in 1832. "The country has forgotten, but the sediment has made the edifice" (*Three Early Nineteenth Century Diaries*, ed. by A. Aspinall, London, 1952). Despite Le Marchant's reaction, we may wonder if Hunt had not come a long way from his earlier view that he had succeeded because his persecutors were evil.

On the subject of character Hunt was often a bore. With the fourth information hanging over him, he denounced Sheridan and the Prince on June 21, 1812: "Character! Character! To character we must come at last, — to common, private, everyday habits, we must come at last, for all that produces a nation's welfare or misery . . . ." Insistent though he was, his consistency on this score compels admiration. He was glad, for example (December 10, 1809), to see the debate on the Walcheren Expedition, in the Common Council of the City, not a debate on "common expediency," as it would have been over such issues as the balance of trade, but a debate concerned with "the test of moral sentiment."

The standard sermon on political morality by a Christian humanist — by Coleridge, for example — called upon the whole congregation to depart from the ways of evil lest God exact retribution. In Hunt's version, the mass of the congregation could be congratulated on their upright behavior and natural virtue. For Hunt, the issue of morality came near to being a conflict between classes. It could be said of governments (April 26, 1812), "as it has been of authors, that nobody can write them down but themselves." And, "no people, we are persuaded, will ever be secure against the most humiliating causes of overthrow, — such causes as have lately taken dreadful effect in France and Spain, — unless the moral sense of the many can be freely and formidably expressed against the profligate insensibility of the few." Consequently, he could not consent to privacy for the vices of public men. Furthermore, as he had argued in the first year of his editorship (October 23), "there are very rarely any such things as the private vices of public men; the action may be private, but the effect is almost sure to be public." Given the habits of the Examiner and of most newspapermen, the effect was indeed almost sure to be public.

It may be objected additionally by moralists that the public effect Hunt complained of was often, at the point of contact, economic, that it was once more a question of high taxes. Yet Hunt kept in mind the morality of the nation as a whole, as he shows in the essay of January 10, 1813, "On the Censorial Duties of the Press with Regard to the Vices of the Court." Remedy had to be taken to preserve the people from contagion. Espying no Nero or Commodus in the Court, the Examiner did not suppose that because the adulterous Marquis of Headfort was a Lord of the Bedchamber every Englishman would surrender to the French. "But we do suppose, that by the loose example of a Court, the region immediately about it becomes soft and relaxed; and that by downward gradation into the other walks of life, a general thaw may take place in our principles, which shall take away the freshness and vigour of the national feeling . . . ." Here, therefore, rose the duty of the Examiner to libel the Prince and go to jail, so that the English people might hold taut their fiber and thereby defeat Napoleon.

Concern over individuals among the responsive *Volk* did as much as belief in organic union with the land to promote the strong new religion, national self-determination. Byron, although not much of a patriot, held to nationalism, and felt annoyance at Napoleon's lust for imperial expansion. Indebted partly to the Encyclopedists and other *philosophes*, in this matter as in others, Hunt like Byron turned his regard for national independence into internationalism. To use his own word, he was a cosmopolite. He felt and denounced in the Congress of Vienna a disregard for the rights and interests of such smaller nations as Poland, Norway, Italy, Spain, and poor Saxony, with a piece of her soil "malignantly torn away" (March 12, 1815). In Italy, as unpublished letters in the British Museum reveal, he went to unusual trouble to get news, intended for the *Liberal*, from Mavrokordatos and other Greek revolutionaries. (The *Examiner* settled, on February 1, 1824, for an account from Trelawny, "an excellent Englishman now in Greece.")

Hunt thought of his translations as serving in the cause of international good will. Opposing the kind of geopolitics that would declare the people of certain areas restricted in creativity, he objected in the first article of the *Reflector* to J. J. Winckelmann's thesis that England was too cold-climated for the fine arts. Instinctively he distrusted the current anthropological distinctions concerning race. In contrast with Thackeray, who charged against the Regency that a gentleman then could consort with Negro and Jewish boxers without forfeiting his place in society, Hunt opposed the doctrines of inferior race. On August 4, 1811, in "Negro Civilization," he went further than he could find books to prove, and in subsequent correspondence (with Haydon) reluctantly gave up the ground of physical equality; but he continued to argue with spirit and sanity that distinguished men like Toussaint L'Ouverture had to be accounted for.

Against Winckelmann he had reacted as a patriot, and the name of Benjamin West, P.R.A., appears prominently in his refutation. When not on guard, in fact, Hunt could appear as insular as a snail. A few pages after deriding Sheridan for enslaving himself to red liquor "in a polished country" (April 2, 1809), he noted in an editorial that the King of Sweden had acted rashly "in the usual way of the less polished nations of Europe." Or notice in the essay "French Fashions" the good-humored inference that outrageous hats and dresses originated in the deficiencies of women who had the misfortune of birth across the Channel. Nevertheless, when his evaluations of France and French culture are placed against those of Wordsworth, Coleridge, Dickens, or Tennyson, it will be seen how fair, balanced, and informed he was.

Few of his compatriots were free enough intellectually to admit, as he could, that the French Revolution had "shaken up and reinvigorated the sources of thought all over Europe." Hunt's mixed and varying judgments on Napoleon form a fascinating but complicated subject, studied in some detail by Professor Landré and more thoroughly, along with the judgments of the *Edinburgh Review,* in a doctoral dissertation by Ahmad Hasan Qureshi (*Dissertation Abstracts,* 1959, XIX, 2604). It would be equally instructive to have a close chronological comparison of Hunt's assessments with those of Byron. Some of Byron's best political poetry, it will be remembered, was written with recent numbers of the *Examiner* close at hand. A believer in Napoleon's opportunities rather than in his personality, Hunt moved gradually toward disillusion, with forecasts of the astute valuation in his essay "Progress of Liberal Opinion, and What Becomes the Highest Ambition Accordingly" (*Companion,* May 14, 1828) and of the summary rejection of Napoleon in the *Autobiography.* His much severer disillusionment with the Congress of Vienna, however, made him feel for several intermediate years that Napoleon was far less poisonous to humanity than the Bourbons were. When Metternich and Castlereagh forced him to choose, he chose Napoleon.

B. R. Haydon, who tried steadily to rescue Hunt and Hazlitt from Radical aberration, wrote from Paris in June, 1814 (holograph in the State University of Iowa): "I am convinced,

my dear Hunt you might make a fine Article on Buonaparte's
secret closet — and all that has been thought of *there* — *there*
he revelled in dreams of Dominion & conquest, of murder &
blood and when his mind & imagination were fired with a
sort of bloody, gleamy splendour, perhaps sent for the Empress!" It tells something of Hunt's attitude toward Napoleon
that summer, and more of his editorial methods and his taste,
that he inserted the "gleamy splendour," without the Empress,
at the proper place in Haydon's pseudonymous account, which
he published in the *Examiner*, with extensive modifications,
at the end of August: "Here he revelled in visions of dominion
and conquest; and when his imagination was fired to a gleamy
splendour, he rose, filled with high designs — his frame fevered!
— his mind in a blaze! — Perhaps at such moments he resolved
on the murder of D'Enghien! — perhaps, on the gigantic
enterprise against Russia!" (Haydon's son, incidentally, in
1876 Bowdlerized the impressive phrase into "gory, gleaming
splendour.")

Hunt fits the Romantic pattern well enough in his praise
of the noble living and the noble dead. His lists of English
heroes begin, like Wordsworth's and Coleridge's, with Alfred,
Shakespeare, Milton, Sydney, Hampden, Marvell, Harrington,
and Selden. To these he almost invariably added Richard
Steele, as the chief exemplar of metropolitan gentlemen. With
Hampden standing at the head of England's country gentlemen, Steele spoke and acted for "her gentlemen and fine
writers." In a tribute to the late Samuel Whitbread (July 9,
1815), Hunt showed his reforming spirit more clearly by
having Whitbread stand for England's "traders and men of
acquired substance, who love their country still better than
their gain." As a footnote or appendix to such lists, the *Examiner* treats Shelley, often anonymously, as a young man of
great political wisdom who will yet startle the nation as he
has already startled a few. Unlike Byron, Hunt exercised great
restraint in offering as ideals the patriots of classical Greece
and Rome. This was one of the several points at which he kept
politics and poetry separate. In any case, his admiration for

Roman virtue found little reason to go beyond the English transplantation. Although he paid many tributes to Voltaire, he never found a way of listing him among the lights of England. Cosmopolite though Hunt was, his stream of history fed into London.

Surveying the "State of the Civilized World at the Close of the Year 1812," he found England (he should have included Ireland) in current possession of the abolitionist Thomas Clarkson; of Maria Edgeworth, instructive novelist and personal friend (to whose work of "beauty, knowledge, and utility," *Patronage*, he devoted two Political Examiners in 1814); of Bentham and Romilly; and of Joseph Lancaster, the planner of a monitorial system in elementary education, supported by the Dissenters in rivalry with the almost identical system of the Anglican Dr. Bell. A few years later he would have added Robert Owen; occasionally he noticed the oldest Radical, Major Cartwright.

Unquestionably, although Hunt's candor made the most avid Burdettites doubt it, the Examiner admired beyond all other living politicians Sir Francis Burdett. It has been said that Hunt regretted publicly such actions of the baronet as (1) the publication in Cobbett's *Register* of an open letter denying the right of the House of Commons to imprison arbitrarily a free Englishman, and (2) encouragement of the mob that resisted a commitment of Burdett himself to the Tower. To the contrary, the unsigned account in the *Examiner* of April 15, 1810, suggests very little regret, and Leigh's own remarks then and in successive weeks contain no regret at all, except in behalf of the statesman "who is every day more beloved by the honest, because every day he becomes more hateful to the dishonourable." Twenty-seven years later, in the *Monthly Repository*, Hunt wrote humorously of this attachment to Burdett as if it had been a kind of puppy love; but it was a serious attachment indeed in 1810; as he knew, it altered his status as an editor without allegiance to party, even though there could be no question of venality. The most serious disagreement came on May 10, 1812, after Burdett had spoken against the use of troops to quell riots; troops or not, the *Examiner* favored "security of property and life."

Brougham gradually replaced Burdett as "the greatest independent Reformer." Much closer to Hunt, courting him with suggestions and aid, Brougham had a genuine interest in literature and an interest apparently genuine in the welfare of his clients. A very large book could be written on Brougham and the *Examiner*. Sometimes artfully, sometimes openly, sometimes bluntly but confidentially, he suggested subjects or provided facts. The surviving correspondence, in the British Museum, shows how he would praise an essay, as on abuse of Poland, soon thereafter convey more ammunition, and subsequently encourage repeated firing at the same targets. Correspondence with him was invaluable, because he could often tell Hunt what both Whigs and Ministers intended to do next. In return, he got value as well as loyalty from Hunt. He was always warmly supported in candidacy for office. As attorney for Caroline, he knew that he could count on the insertion of whatever his tactics required. Perhaps he knew also that John Hunt was getting a little sick of so much Brougham.

Despite these commitments, however, Leigh like John gave his first allegiance to causes rather than men. In praise of Parliamentary debates on the income tax and a standing army (March 3, 1816), he gave Brougham and Burdett only their just place along with Tierney, Folkstone, and other "Ministerial Opponents, whether Whig, Reformist, or otherwise." He did not grovel before living heroes.

Although Hunt's humanitarianism was alien neither to his political Radicalism nor to Romantic individualism, it belonged to that softening of the heart first made evident in the writings of Addison and Steele. The *Examiner* makes much, indeed, of such antiaristocratic topics of the *Spectator* as the inhumanity of dueling. The meeting between Castlereagh and Canning in 1809 made objections to dueling notably partisan, as they had been several times during the ministry of Pitt, but social and philanthropic censure remained. Leigh thought that his humanitarianism came intellectually from Voltaire; besides its basis in his own temperament, it came also through those Methodists he so despised. In answer to John's objection that his system was "ultra-sentimental," he explained himself as meaning only that "when the case *was* such an urgent one, and a bed was *necessary,* a man should rather give up his own than run the risk of the sufferer's not having *any at all*" (*Holograph Letters,* p. 163; McCartney, p. 292).

The *Examiner* was more often humanitarian than politically ideological. Although Leigh and John were charged three times with libel against members of the royal family, where the ultimate issue could be regarded as misuse of tax money, the fourth information lodged against them jointly, that concerning military flogging, had political allies in Burdett and Brougham but must be distinguished as humanitarian in them as well. The Examiner defends the trading classes, above all the small shopkeepers, those not very successful at making money: but in this defense also the humanitarian impulse is strong. His representation of the commercial classes stops morally far short of the slave trade.

In February, 1820, according to judicious historians, the bloodthirsty "physical force" Radical, Arthur Thistlewood, conspired to blow up the whole Cabinet. On the first of May he and four accomplices were executed. To a reader of standard histories, it comes as a surprise to find Leigh Hunt defending these "alleged conspirators" as in fact pitiable paupers "driven to desperation in unconstitutional times." The same Christian gunpowder, he notes, was used equally without warning against the residents of Copenhagen — by Government. That the *Black Dwarf* and other Radical weeklies made similar defenses of mad Thistlewood and his twenty wretched companions does not prove large conspiracy or disaffection; it merely shows that most of the Radical editors had a broad streak of rash and sentimental humanitarianism. Knowing very little of how laborers lived, Hunt wished to feel with them and forgive all.

His defense of these Cato-Street conspirators shows how

courageous Hunt could be made by sympathy and a sense of becoming public protector to "desperate men, desperately poor." After their execution, Cobbett took up the subject for the first time. In the *Register* of May 6, through the device of a newsletter to his son in New York, he began by denouncing the daily press, which had condemned without a hearing the men now executed:

In these vehicles they had continually been described as *murderers, assassins, blood-thirsty monsters,* and as every thing calculated to excite public hatred against them; while no man, who had the smallest regard for his own safety, dared to utter a syllable, tending to stem this torrent of cruel calumny; or even to hint at the *possibility* of the calumniated persons being innocent of wicked intention. At last, however, they are *dead;* and we may now, surely, be permitted to relate, to peruse, to remember, and to think of, their *dying declarations.*

Hunt, as one seeming to lack "the smallest regard for his own safety," had tried from February 27, when the first word of alleged conspiracy had reached him, to stem the torrent by refusing, as he put it, to beg the question of guilt. Ministers, he knew, were guilty of aggravating wrongs. On April 30, two columns from the news that William Clement of the *Observer* had been fined £500 for publishing an account of the trials of Thistlewood and Ings, the *Examiner* published a summary of Thistlewood's protest at the time of his sentencing. Cobbett greatly exaggerated the silence of Radicals.

However sentimental, Hunt's humanitarianism belonged to his insistence upon tolerance, in the rational tradition from Locke. It was the converse of the distaste for Calvinism that made him write in June, 1808, when the Catholic petition for suffrage was rejected: "I do not contend that the Catholics should be admitted to the highest offices of state, but I contend at the same time that known Methodists should not be admitted to them either." Like Locke, he wished to exclude bigots from power over the defenseless.

Inexperienced as Hunt was, the thirsts of Radicalism, Romanticism, humanitarianism, and journalism took him down many streets. He informed Marianne in June, 1808, that he had been "studying vaccine inoculation, which has now become a political question." Everything did. At midyear in 1814 he publicly declared the three choice topics to be Poland, Africa, and universal education; apologetically, therefore, he entered upon the topic of military torture, and in later weeks apologized as he turned from Poland to report on the Prince Regent's mistreatment of Caroline and of the Hunts. In his defense before Ellenborough in 1812, Brougham listed ten topics with which the *Examiner* had been occupied — without mentioning India, the "stupidity of the present War," or the necessity of reform in a corrupt Parliament. Early in 1816 Hunt provided a sort of prospective table of contents for the year by listing under eight headings the evils his readers could expect from the new Parliament. In fact, the provision of lists became an organizational device in several later essays, but the next week usually brought a topic not previously accounted for except under such general headings as reform or religious tolerance. Tolerance was not merely a topic, it was a standpoint and a livelihood.

IX

HUNT AS ANTAGONIST

"The definition of a true patriot," wrote Hazlitt in the *Examiner*, "is *a good hater*." In his view Castlereagh and Eldon were good-natured; the Examiner was not. The patriotic spokesman for tolerance, according to Hazlitt, will be intolerant not only of tyranny and intolerance, but of all who tolerate intolerance. To highlight the heroes, there must be antiheroes. It is not chance that the Examiner shares with Junius many of his sources (for example, Lolme), topics (popular sovereignty, freedom of the press), and axioms (writers cannot *cause* public evils). In style he does not achieve Junius' urbanity. In style of vituperation he has closer kin among journalists of his own day. Each of Hunt's enemies is superlative, or near it, "one of the meanest and most impudent of mankind." But in idea of exposure and in courage to be right his acknowledged master is Junius. He also studied Swift. It is to be noted further that political pamphlets by Hunt's English idol, Steele, reveal great skill at cold-blooded contempt.

One duty of a party in opposition is to expose, and a reforming minority necessarily has continuing doubts about those in power. Hunt's political essay on February 9, 1817, begins rather typically: "The Ministers and other corruptionists . . . ." By 1828, in *Lord Byron and Some of His Contemporaries,* he expressed an altered view: the state of society makes him object still to the controlling circumstances, but he no longer blames the "individuals who are the creatures of those circumstances." Twenty years earlier, not satisfied with taking on all Wesleyans, the Duke of York, the Prince of Wales, and the King's Ministers, he had reached out rather priggishly to whack ancient Horne Tooke, with incidental damage to Burdett, and to thump the Whig bookseller Sir Richard Phillips, with advantage only to his own moral superiority. No, to charge him with mere priggishness is unfair; in both attacks he has an ideal of political and commercial integrity, and by exposing Phillips he soothes a known victim of the bookseller's chicanery.

Within eight months his antilist of "quacks," who had promised much and performed little, expanded to include Scott, Wordsworth, Thelwall, Godwin, Holcroft, Erskine, the elder Kemble, Samuel Jackson Pratt, and as many more. Reacting against praise of Pitt as he later reacted against praise of the Regent, he tried to prevent exhumation of the inventor of the income tax and of the policies of alarm, the minister who taught Sidmouth to silence opposition by suppressing civil liberties; Hunt spoke because false idols should be destroyed at the moment of erection. With distrust of the place-seeking Whigs and open contempt for such vices as wine drinking, he took instant advantage of R. B. Sheridan's two words against the motion of censure on the Duke of York. Like Byron, Hunt was often generous in reversal, as on the poetry of Wordsworth. Because of Sheridan's fidelity to the Prince, he delayed his inevitable reversal toward the aging shadow of a playwright and orator. Brash, heedless, and even cruel in his remarks, he thawed at last to write appreciatively, probably with some influence from Byron, "The Late Mr. Sheridan" (July 14, 1816 — reprinted in *Leigh Hunt's Literary Criticism*, ed. by L. H. and C. W. Houtchens, New York, 1956).

To quarrel with writers who quarrel with you belongs to the conduct of periodicals, whatever their subject. What clearer reason for quarrel than politics? It was bad enough in the *Examiner's* eyes for a free editor to sell his mind to a party; it was considerably worse to cling, like the *Morning Post*, "to every corruption of the constitution with as rank and sleepy a pertinacity, as a bat to his winter dungeon." He could be very prickly over small errors, especially if they appeared in the *Times*, then far from being London's foremost or most accurate newspaper but independent enough to exasperate Hunt by zigging just when he zagged. It is a pleasure to note that he also took occasion to praise other papers, the *Times*, Cobbett's *Register*, the rather unsavory *Independent Whig*, *Bell's Weekly Messenger*, and especially, among others, the *Champion*, edited by John Scott with contributions by Thomas Barnes — later editor of the *Times*, formerly schoolfellow at Christ's Hospital and now friend.

Without investigating Hunt's quarrels with the *Morning Post, Courier*, or other Tory organs, we can note some of the impulses in his frequent spats with William Cobbett, whose political views were not greatly unlike Hunt's. The important thing at first was to draw attention to himself in a field where other writers were already established. By jabbing at Cobbett, he obtained free advertising in Cobbett's replies and stimulated the interest of his own subscribers, whether or not these were conscious aims. He proved his independence, and he served pride by setting his own Radical anger off from the vulgarity of Cobbett's. It was even more important to distinguish himself from one of Cobbett's allies, Orator Hunt — who incidentally regretted later that he had mistakenly supported

Cobbett against the Examiner (Robert Huish, *The History of . . . Henry Hunt*, London, 1836, I, 394). At bottom, of course, Hunt simply disliked Cobbett, or rather Cobbett's public image. Hunt was impulsive; Cobbett was quixotic.

In 1812, in addition to his other reasons for quarrel, Hunt strengthened himself for martyrdom by deriding Cobbett's shuffling efforts to avoid it. They did not quarrel always or completely. Hunt was ready enough to defend the *Political Register*, that is, Cobbett, along with the *Statesman*, the *Morning Chronicle*, and the *Edinburgh Review*, against disparagement by the *Times* (January 15, 1809). After years of renouncing Henry Hunt as a vulgarian and demagogue, he began after Peterloo to declare the orator a nonconspirator whose rights as an Englishman were being arbitrarily abridged. Meanwhile, Cobbett had made himself once more objectionable by diatribes against Burdett.

If Leigh's attacks were occasionally grounded to his own person, as against Holme Sumner for intimating that Hunt rested without complaint or reason for complaint in the Surrey jail, more often he attacked on principles, moral or political or both. He and John had various political objections to the Earl of Moira in 1813 and to the Wellesleys from beginning to end. Before Tennyson arrived, the Duke of Wellington had little but abuse from poets — even from Wordsworth. From his record in the *Examiner*, one might think that the family name of Wellesley had been mistaken for the Methodist name of Wesley. But Leigh began the Wellesley record in India, with "their fetterings of the press, encroachments on territory, and imprisonments of dying Nabobs." Back in Europe, in 1807, Sir Arthur had been involved in the highhanded raid on Copenhagen. Next, the dubious Convention of Cintra. At home the repeatedly titled Wellington stood with Pittite Tories; abroad he led a corrupted army for the benefit of corrupt and corrupting monarchs. Grudgingly Hunt admitted from time to time that Wellington could not fail to rank with "the proudest names in our military history." Always, nevertheless, the general advanced in blood and in nepotism. "The WELLESLEY family," said the *Examiner* of December 3, 1809, "in time will be enabled to carry on the business of the state without any other assistants."

Associated as it is with two particularly notorious reviews of Keats and Tennyson, the name of John Wilson Croker does not sweeten literary history. Besides writing for the hated (by Hunt) *Courier* and *Quarterly Review,* he "happened to be" First Lord of the Admiralty. The one serious effort to rehabilitate Croker the reviewer, by Myron F. Brightfield, avoids any reference to Hunt's side of the exchanges between them — avoids, that is, explanation of a phrase in Croker's review of Hunt's *Foliage:* "whatever he may think or say of us." What Hunt had said most recently (February 15, 1818) may be read among the essays now collected.

The case of Castlereagh requires special handling. Were it not fundamental to any explanation of Hunt's work in the *Examiner,* what is required would have to be called a prolonged digression. With very little circumlocution, from 1809 steadily until Castlereagh's suicide in 1822, Hunt declared him a corrupter and seducer of minds, a political dealer in seats and places, a selfish and heartless ignoramus, a toady to monarchs, and a traitor. Shelley and Byron were more metaphorical, but no politer.

Now, it has proved much too easy to say that the Romantics based their politics upon emotion and a convenient scarcity of information. To rescue Castlereagh from Romantic opprobrium and "the Whig view of history," revisionists currently point out how much Castlereagh, unloved by all the poets, strengthened the foreign policy and the diplomatic position of his country in relation to the Continental powers. By the contemporary evidence, which Hunt and the major poets judged and did not misjudge, Castlereagh began a notorious career when he supervised, if he did not actively administer, an unremitting and bloody suppression of the Irish: and he born in Ireland. To explanation by recent historians that he probably did not know how bloody his administration was, his contempo-

raries have already answered that his whole career was
marked with signs of hypocrisy oddly combined with unconcern about public condemnation of his acts. Scrupulous
defenders have mitigated this charge, but have not denied it.

He affected indifference to public opinion; but he just
happened to have a copy of the *Examiner* in his hand in the
House of Commons on July 25, 1820, when he suggested that
the Attorney General file an information for libelous breach
of privilege. This offhand action resulted in the second imprisonment of one of his critics, John Hunt. In the *Examiner*
of August 6, Leigh made the just point that Castlereagh, in a
properly constituted Parliament, would have had no opportunity to address the Commons on this or any other issue.
Where is the historian who wishes to live without rank or
franchise in Castlereagh's England?

Castlereagh defended the most oppressive domestic legislation of two centuries. It mattered little to contemporaries
that officials who carried out this legislation were humane in
temperament and baffled because the poor acted so wickedly
and ungratefully. That Castlereagh's expertness lay abroad
made it seem no more admirable to the Hunts that he explicitly
promoted sorrow at home—as if a father whose business took
him among brothels should be excused for ordering his children
beaten on the grounds that he lacked the opportunity to study
children. The Romantics had no doubt that a circuit of brothels
was a rather polite description of Castlereagh's business with
the Continental monarchs. That he added technical ability of
the highest diplomatic kind to his vigilance and large budget
fails to invalidate Byron's classification of him as an "intellectual eunuch." Wilberforce, who did not have volcanic fire in
his veins, declared Castlereagh as cold-blooded as a fish.
Hunt would not have nominated him for the chancellorship
of Cambridge.

Somewhat contradictorily, to be sure, the poets described
him as totally without creative force but joined other critics in
holding him responsible for the stupid war with the United
States in 1812. He had character enough to provide contra-

dictions himself. Contrary to his usual policy of concealing from the people his methods, aims, and results, he withheld only the secret clauses of the Treaty of Paris from the otherwise public knowledge of his opposition to, and contempt for, Italian nationalism. C. K. Webster (*The Foreign Policy of Castlereagh*, London, 1925) defends his hero on the ground that Lord William Bentinck overstepped his authority in promising Genoa her ancient freedoms. But knowledge of Bentinck's indiscretions would not make Castlereagh's gift of Italian cities to Austria and Sardinia more palatable to Romantic believers in nationalism. Nor did his diplomatic efforts to restrain Russia and other interested powers from encouraging Greek revolt against Turkey represent that behavior toward Greece regarded by Byron, Shelley, and Hunt as ideal.

Most modern historians of diplomacy seem to agree that it was Castlereagh's duty to endorse the despotism and aggrandizements of the legitimate and restored monarchs of Europe in order to get from them either the diplomatic terms that Britain's power and accomplished peace made just or the next best terms he could achieve. But Hunt, himself a poet of some ability and wisdom, wrote in Castlereagh's day as a believer in poetry, imagination, and individual man. Humanists of today — including historians — should see that it was not only the impulse of Hunt and the poets, it was also their duty, to uphold the highest human values and political ideals on which they were agreed, including a few on which they and we disagree. Beyond the unimpeachable standards of bare justice, freedom from abject servitude, and an occasional meal for every body, Shelley no doubt raised against Castlereagh a standard of democratic utopianism that many intelligent humanists will not accept today. But pointing to the selfless industry with which Castlereagh matched his diplomatic skill against Metternich's inadequately answers the charges of Hunt, Moore, Byron, and Shelley, and the judgments of Coleridge and Wordsworth, that he was an effective tool at home and abroad against the axioms of the open society.

In a broader view, a series of works, of which the most

persuasive is *A World Restored,* by Henry A. Kissinger (London, 1957), credits primarily Metternich and Castlereagh with the stability of Europe from 1815 to 1914. Not only could the Romantics regard such stasis in no other way than as pathological in a world that must change or burst; the Romantic would also regard the Italian, Greek, Hungarian, and Polish victims of this stability as analogous to laborers asked to enjoy the stability of 1799. Further, those who identify and praise the architects of European stability must now look toward Africa and Asia to see the world problem of which that stability has become one cause. Attention to the Romantics is well rewarded if we learn from them that opponents of revolution can desire nothing more suicidal than stability.

In *Marianne Thornton* E. M. Forster made a plea for another Tory of the Romantic period, Wilberforce, that can be extended to Castlereagh as well: however he is condemned philosophically, the man of history who acted for his fellow men should, at the very least, be freer from our opprobrium and our moral disapproval than the thousands unknown to us because they consumed in private comfort. What needs to be established beside Forster's astute maxim, as applied to Castlereagh and his critics, is this: although subsequent historians need not, on balance, condemn Castlereagh's role in British history, liberals like Hunt were right to make a literature of condemnation from what they knew; would have been right to condemn all that the greatest industry could have enabled them to know; would be morally right if their roles and his were transferred into the context of today; and by their roles have strengthened the effectiveness of literature today and tomorrow. Imaginative literature and conscience, at their greatest, face issues, cruxes, dilemmas, not facts.

X

FORM AND STYLE

The *Examiner* distinguished itself from other Radical periodicals, such as the *Independent Whig* and the *Black Dwarf*, partly by a less violent tone, but more especially by serious attention to imaginative literature, theater, and fine arts. Hunt published verse not only as William Hone did, for parody and satire, but because he liked poetry; Shelley, Keats, Byron, Wordsworth, and Hunt seemed to be poets worth publishing. He tossed off songs on topical matters: Walcheren, the death of General Moreau, Ellenborough, Southey as Laureate, or a notorious response — *"Non mi ricordo"* — by an Italian witness against Caroline. Like other editors who enjoy having subscribers, he published verse by correspondents, political and nonpolitical.

To our advantage, he held seriously a theory similar to that in a letter written to him by Shelley in 1819: Dante, Petrarch, and Boccaccio, said Shelley, were "the productions of the vigour of the infancy of a new nation — as rivulets from the same spring as that which fed the greatness of the republics of Florence and Pisa, and which checked the influence of the German emperors"; in contrast, the inferior Tasso and Ariosto wrote when "the corrupting blight of tyranny was already hanging on every bud of genius." Agreeing that national vigor and great poetry occur together, and believing also that Dante and Petrarch helped give vigor to a free nation, Hunt wished to identify and encourage the Petrarchs of his own day in England. In turn, poets had a duty to defend the general freedom of the press. A scholar seldom wrong, Kenneth N. Cameron (*The Young Shelley*, New York, 1950), has described Shelley's letter of March 2, 1811, to the Examiner as a plan for uniting Reformers against Tories and Foxite Whigs. Not partisan in that sense at all, the letter describes a plan of mutual indemnity for authors, editors, and perhaps hotheads like Orator Hunt against prosecutions for libel. The supporting documents have been lost, but the plan must have included a pool of funds for legal defense and fines, as well as a method of standing together to fight. Poets and libelers had to plot together.

The tone of the *Examiner* is not that of astute plotters. As a journalist Hunt could not have had greater inspiration than the idea that he and his readers could do better than stand together: they could sit together. Departments like "Table Talk" and "The Round Table" were begun from Hunt's sense that he and his readers, whether they were also correspondents or not, chatted together every week as acquaintances. His habit of confiding publicly all his aches and joys, his rips and repairs, has been described by Edmund Blunden. It is the habitual style of the Examiner.

As Hunt recalled in the *Autobiography*, he attempted "a fusion of literary taste into all subjects whatsoever." In the Prospectus to the *Reflector* he noted that politics were "exhibiting their re-action upon literature, as literature in the preceding age exhibited its action" on politics. His practice belied this chronological division; he made literature act on and in politics. And in discussing Hunt's political writings it has been necessary to refer frequently to essays collected in *Leigh Hunt's Literary Criticism,* where they belong. Not only did he introduce politics into essays on other subjects — how could he discuss for long Byron, Southey, Moore, or Wordsworth without reference to politics? — but he also introduced literary interests into political editorials. He made his points in imaginative ways. He objected as an Englishman to a Royal Grant out of the Droits of Admiralty; he also objected in behalf of the English language to there being any Norman *Droits* in England at all. He played with phrases used by the Ministers. Rather fortunately, he was less successful than Cobbett at inventing phrases that he could repeat *ad nauseam.* Unfortunately, he lacked both the vigor and the knowledge of detail that enabled Cobbett to maintain a salty spray of inventive phrase: "the Rich Ruffians of Coventry," or "preserve Old Sarum."

In invective, all the editors except Cobbett were almost equally matched. But none could live by invective alone. To observe some differences and similarities between Hunt and other political journalists of his day, not scientifically but conveniently, we can place side by side a few paragraphs on similar subjects. As all the writers had a variety of tones and devices, credit should be given more to similarities among the passages than to their differences.

When the Stamp Office threatened Cobbett with prosecution for unpaid duties in 1817, he fled to the United States. Wooler, in the *Black Dwarf*, went to his high generalizations and Cobbettlike italicized sarcasm:

Our posterity will consider we should have been the faithful guardians of their freedom: and if our fears surrender it, we are morally responsible for the loss we shall have occasioned. But though our self-called general has fled — has left his place unoccupied — we perceive that happily there is no consternation among the champions of reform: — not another has deserted his post: — not a private will surrender his arms: — In such a cause, every man is competent at once to *lead* and to *act*. Nature, that teaches us the value of liberty, will supply the means of securing it. It is not *tactics*, or *discipline*, that we need; let the mechanical assassins of despotism have recourse to tuition in the art of murder; the sons of freedom are always competent to their own defence.

.   .   .

Corruption, says our runaway, has put on her armour, and drawn her dagger. Well! and when [*for* what?] then. Have we not ARMS too? And must we *throw them away*, when she advances to the contest, after we have been brandishing them before her eyes so long. Who expected that such a hydra-headed monster as the corruptions of the day would fall without a struggle! If Mr. Cobbett did, we will venture to say that he was the only man who could be so foolish; and it explains the secret of his former *apparent courage. He thought there was no danger!*

Hunt, anxious to declare Cobbett wrong in principle without once more damning his motives, turned from Cobbett's own common idiom to urbanely mild inversions of syntax and quiet rhetorical progression:

He goes to America, he says, because he cannot continue to write in support of the claims of the people without the certainty of getting into a dungeon, and because he can continue to write in support of them elsewhere, and therefore does best to go thither. But in the first place, *why* cannot he continue to advocate the claims of the people, as well as others? He was, to be sure, liable to the unresponsible and German despotism of the Suspension of the Habeas Corpus Act, and so are all of us; so is every writer, whether answerable otherwise or not, who sits down to write a single paragraph, and may be discovered to be the author; but do all these persons, or even the best known among them, conclude themselves justified in ceasing so to write and to remain?

Eschewing the emphasis of an answer, Hunt left the rhetorical question and moved on. It is fifteen years before Cobbett will reach Parliament, but only three years before Hunt will wish him there. In the last paragraph on Cobbett's flight to America, Hunt makes a psychological diagnosis, involving, just as typically, a contrast:

The same deficiency that makes Mr. COBBETT see nothing great in SHAKESPEARE, makes him see nothing grand in the risking of sufferance. When MILTON was abroad and heard of the troubles in his country, he was anxious to return and share the grandeur of the danger; — when Mr. COBBETT thinks he sees danger coming, he feels nothing but the thing itself, and is only anxious to argue himself to a distance from it. When MILTON, in his old age, — blind and solitary, felt himself surrounded by dangers, he retreated into the glories of epic poetry, and thought only casually of his triumphant enemies; — when Mr. COBBETT was in prison he could only regret his freedom, and make himself doubly uncomfortable with an eternal feeling of resentment.

Wooler, like most of the Radical writers, has drenched himself in Paine, as his homely metaphors reveal. Hunt has studied the simplicity, repetition, and rhythms of Addison, Steele, Goldsmith, Johnson, and the essayists of the *Mirror,* the *World,* and the *Connoisseur.* He has also read Cobbett — and Milton.

At the beginning of 1822, when Cobbett had returned to his anvil, he proposed that the distresses in the county of Norfolk and elsewhere be solved by a demand from farmers that rents be abated. With its self-satisfied laziness of metaphor, *John Bull* reacted on March 10. Its tone of security in alliance with Government (and with the new method of indictment for libel through the Constitutional Association) may serve to suggest the mixture of complacency and threat by which the Ministerial *Morning Post* and *Courier* had repeatedly incensed Hunt:

It will be seen that the excessive cheapness of provisions, the plenty which abounds, and the mildness of the season, have occasioned something like rioting in the county of NORFOLK.

A very sensible sort of proclamation has been issued by the Magistrates of that county, the wisest part of which, is the warning to—*beware of bad advisers.*

We have our eyes upon the part of the country *infected*; and we would suggest to *those persons who have an influence,* that their *best* and SAFEST plan will be to use it in *moderating,* rather than *exciting* a disposition to insubordination.

We are perhaps more intimate with the politics and politicians of the eastern counties than the worthies we allude to imagine. We trust we shall see them at their post, using every effort *to keep the peace;* — it will be better for them if they are: for, if their *indiscretions* are not cognizable by HIS MAJESTY'S ATTORNEY-GENERAL, they may be, by JOHN BULL — and we give them this fair warning.

Cobbett had given his own threat, in the *Weekly Register* of January 5, a wider range. As usual, he had converted the plenitude of Elizabethan prose into conversation:

I am firmly persuaded, and, indeed, I know, that the threatening storm *might* be averted, but, I am far from thinking that it *will,* seeing that *the two factions* divide the powers of the press between them, and seeing, that, if this base, servile, corrupt and all-stupifying press prevail, there will and there must arise a state of things, which with *Six Acts* before my eyes, I will not venture to describe. However, this I will say, that, in my opinion, the question, the awful question, whether the winding up of the drama shall be gentle or fierce, peaceful or bloody, depends simply on this: whether, before it take place, *the House of Commons be, or be not reformed.*

Since the "big, blustering, hypocritical," and "despicable,

place-hunting" Whigs agreed with the Tory Ministers that impoverished tenants ought to be required to pay whatever rent they had contracted for, Cobbett warned with his normal exaggeration on May 25:

> We have only to add to this Malthus's *refusal of parish relief,* in order to give English Landlords a right, a *legal right,* to rob of the last farthing, to strip stark-naked, and to throw down on the highways to die with hunger the whole of the tenants of the country.

Besides agricultural detail, Cobbett maintains superiority over Hunt in one other accomplishment even yet: he keeps us laughing. Otherwise, Hunt should regain and hold the higher place in political literature.

It could be argued that Hunt lacked imagination concerning political reality. A case should be made that, just as he could not imagine in advance what imprisonment or a sudden access of financial responsibility would be like, so he could not imagine the motives of a Duke (whether York or Wellington), a Perceval or Castlereagh, a Burdett or Brougham, or even a Cobbett. Nearly all his political essays spring from immediate external suggestion. Even his slight but pertinent theorizing awaits the occasion. To some extent, these deficiencies result from his candor and innocence. To a greater extent, they do not exist, but merely appear to exist because he fortunately could not bring himself to concentrate on either practical politics or abstract theory. He was no philosopher. His success and his value depended upon his acting instinctively as a middle-class man of letters observing public affairs.

Praise of his instincts should not be carried to a point of absurdity; in general, the longest among his later Political Examiners are the best, because they were not written on Saturday while the boy stood by in wait for copy. By his own testimony, the editor of the *Examiner* followed a sort of manic-depressive curve. Either he had serious spells of sickness, as his physicians believed, or he was a hypochondriac, as charged in the *Scourge.* Aside from illness, he had two problems more awkward than any others: his readers' ever-potential boredom with politics, and his own. He dealt thoughtfully with both problems.

For his readers, he achieved some variety by his spirit of tolerance, which rose from much deeper within him than his antagonisms. This tolerance cannot be shown briefly in a better way than by quoting Thomas Barnes, who inserted a friendly postcript — when the imprisoned editor was not looking — at the end of his series on notable figures in the House of Commons: "I must be allowed to return you my grateful acknowledgments for the candour and liberality with which you have frequently, in the course of these articles, given publicity to opinions which were at variance with your own." This tribute could not have been sent with any honesty at all to Cobbett or Wooler.

Fortunately for Hunt, the job of political essayist had a certain variety built into it. Certain conventional forms had grown up, such as point-by-point rebuttal, lists of political or social horrors, addresses to prominent persons or groups of persons, and above all — though I had never thought of it until I read the *Examiner* steadily for several weeks — obituaries, or rather character-sketches of the recently dead. Thus we have the eulogy to Whitbread, the tribute to Sheridan, the treatment of Ellenborough (deceased) as a victim of false education, the carefully negative report on Queen Charlotte, the black-bordered obituaries of Caroline and Napoleon, and the apology for not enclosing within a border the fair but firm death-notice of George III. Within such conventional forms Hunt almost always rose above his weekly average. Every few months, by lifting himself and his readers out of the atmosphere of weekly debate, he destroyed all awareness of convention with lively snatches of imagined dialogue, now in the spirit of the inquisitorial Ministers, again to parody the ignorant indifference of people who ought to be concerned. Cobbett used dialogue disputatiously; Hunt used it imaginatively.

As if to forestall boredom by the natural ebullience of his literary imagination, he began in the first number a series entitled "Miscellaneous Sketches upon Temporary Subjects," which was to consist mostly of political fantasies. In the first, Napoleon called his cabinet together to dispose of all the kings and then by balloon to take over the universe. In the second, Napoleon had indigestion from devouring mankind. In another, a visit was made upon Talleyrand and Napoleon by Conscience, but the Emperor ran him through and burned him. Later in the year Hunt thought up the Ancient and Redoubtable Institution of Quacks. Soon afterward the original series came to an end.

The imaginative device, or characteristic, or release, had only begun. *Jeux d'esprit* belonged to Hunt's political life. In the second number of the *Indicator,* he described the *Examiner* as his "tavern room for politics, for political pleasantry, for criticism upon the theatres and living writers." Landré translated the middle phrase as *"railler ses adversaires politiques,"* but Hunt also used his political pleasantries to rally himself. A good example of this lightening of the heart can be seen in the present volume in the story of the old gentleman with bad stewards, under the title, "Reform Not to Be Expected from the House of Commons." Rather similar is his account on June 6, 1819, of a remarkable politician named George Court Place Burroughs Middlegent Parish Bull. His fanciful way with Napoleon continued through July 28, 1816, when he provided comic dialogue between Napoleon and the daughter of his host at St. Helena, Miss B., who would like to beat Napoleon — for money — at cards.

Once embarked along this road of pleasantry, Hunt was bound to make stops with the Oriental craze apparent in scattered works by most of his favorite writers of eighteenth-century France and England. The sixth Political Examiner, against reversionary grants, ends:

A simple Chinese might exclaim "Pigtail of the Great Fo! If these English give pensions to infants just born, what must they give to their deserving men!" But one of their literati, that is to say, one of their noblemen, would be more likely to exclaim "Head of CONFUCIUS! If these English give pensions to babies for no reason in the world, if they enrich a mere substance, and bestow rewards almost upon what is not, how is it that their poets, their philosophers, and their learned men have so often died of neglect."

Note the adroitness of his satiric observation that in China the noblemen are literati. A similar adroitness can be observed within the forensic parody in the essay "Deliverance of Europe," September 11, 1808.

Building on two rough efforts of early 1813, he captured Hone and many other lovers of quaint satire against the Regent, at the beginning of 1816, with his "Account of the Remarkable Rise and Downfall of the Late Kan of Tartary." Of famous works known to him, his technique does not closely resemble that of any tales and essays by Voltaire, Montesquieu, Marmontel, Goldsmith, or even a nearer analogue, the *Letter from Xo-Ho* by Horace Walpole. Hunt's Oriental parables are more specifically political than any of these, more in the tradition of journalistic attack, more narrowly allegorical in application to prominent persons and events. So much of the fun has gone out of these pieces that even their influence on *The Cap and Bells* by Keats seems to pass unobserved.

Often the Political Examiners took the form first suggested by the editorial, the speech, or the debate in Parliament that excited their creation. Rarely did Hunt organize them as expanded syllogisms or other structures of logic. Both the imaginative and the conventional methods of organization, referred to in earlier paragraphs, may be regarded to some extent as escapes from the difficulty Hunt had in arranging ideological argument. On the other hand, mischance frequently prevented him from rounding out a strong discussion of topics on which he had something worth while to say. In consequence, many lopsided Political Examiners contain neat or vital passages. Like most of the familiar essays of the Romantic period, Lamb's and Hazlitt's as well as his own, Hunt's political pieces best achieve organic unity when they center in a single emotion — indignation, the rare joy of a victory, or the anger of disappointment.

XI

In a list of subscriptions for the benefit of Hone, appended to a pamphlet with the title *Trial by Jury and Liberty of the Press*, in 1818, the sum of five pounds from John and Leigh Hunt bears a legend: "not what they would, but what they could." Leigh might have attached this legend to his work for the *Examiner* in almost any week during which he felt relatively free from observation by enemies. To apply the somber words of Haydon, to which Hunt was more entitled than the painter, he had sought to benefit his country "by telling the Truth to Power."

His importance to the silver stream of journalism has been affirmed many times. It would be hard to overestimate the practical value of a periodical that informed and stimulated Shelley and Byron in Italy and Élie Halévy in Paris a century later. Michael Roberts (in the *Review of English Studies*, vol. XI, 1935) found that Hunt's answer to the *Edinburgh Review* in 1810 anticipated by two years, and more satisfactorily, the liberal solution of the Hampden Clubs in bringing together the democratic wing of the Whigs in Parliament and the more moderate Radical reformers. In collecting (and abridging) some thirty-five Political Examiners in 1928, R. Brimley Johnson attributed Hunt's general importance to three principles: "resolute personal independence, constant and full recognition of the responsibilities of his position, an instinctive discernment of popular understanding and taste."

Hunt had the will, then, and he found the way. Historians of the British press — Andrews, Knight Hunt, Fox Bourne, Escott, Aspinall — have recognized the great significance of the Hunts' audacity for the continuing freedom of the press. It was not merely their sacrifice under legal restraints, it was the tone of independence and candor week after week. Insubmissive, they nevertheless avoided the bellicosity and recklessness of Cobbett. Their quieter intransigence was more useful in shaping a tradition for the middle-class press of mounting power than the intemperance of Cobbett's "flame-colored epithets."

We can test for ourselves the clarity and progression of Hunt's prose. But on the magnificent influence of the brothers, a younger contemporary of theirs provides the best witness. After mentioning John and Leigh in an essay on Hazlitt, at mid-century, P. G. Patmore continued: "I cannot let slip this occasion of testifying my belief, that the wholesome and happy change that has taken place in our political and social institutions since the period above referred to, and is still in happy progress, is owing in no small degree to the excellent individuals just named; for I verily believe that, without the manly firmness, the immaculate political honesty, and the vigorous good sense of the one, and the exquisite genius and varied accomplishments, guided by the all-pervading and all-embracing *humanity* of the other, we should at this moment have been without many of those writers and thinkers on whose unceasing efforts the slow but sure march of our political, and, with it, our social regeneration as a people mainly depends" (*My Friends and Acquaintance,* London, 1854, III, 101).

Patmore hit just the note to please Hunt. To say that the movement of society upward and onward was irreversible and that Hunt had given it a necessary thrust would have been as satisfying as if Patmore had paraphrased "Abou ben Adhem," with the freedom of their friend Hazlitt, to say that Hunt had written himself into history (may his tribe lead all the rest!) "as one that loves his fellow-men."

Primarily historical rather than appreciative or exegetic, this Introduction has done little to suggest our great indebtedness to Professor and Mrs. Houtchens for extending their harvest, selection, and annotation of Hunt's essays into this third volume: political and occasional.

LEIGH HUNT'S POLITICAL AND OCCASIONAL ESSAYS

ON THE SEPARATION OF RUSSIA
FROM THE BRITISH INTEREST

January 3, 1808

The very credulity of the English arises from their virtues.[1] They mistake novelty for merit, professions for deeds, and mere cunning for disinterestedness; they leap over little obstacles and little objections to grasp at what they imagine a noble character, and when they discover it to be a mere phantom, are ready to cross themselves, like Papists, at the mistake. Yesterday, the Emperor Alexander[2] was a charming prince, a very resolute, thinking, and wise prince, but above all, a most magnanimous prince: it is in the nature of things, that all our allies should be magnanimous. To-day, nobody can be sufficiently astonished at the weakness and folly of this great man; one politician hopes he will return to a sense of his duty and true interest; another begins to think that we owe his loss to the present Ministry; and a third wonders how he could be deluded from us when the Ministers treated him so well. Thus it is, that for want of a little philosophy, mankind are always pursuing a thousand conjectures. They forget, that the same passions and petty follies influence powerful states and feeble individuals, and in spite of everlasting lessons, they will not be persuaded of that unfortunate but incontrovertible truth, that there is no real disinterestedness in any government relatively considered. If they knew a little more of human nature they would know a little more of sovereigns, who are mere men walking, like the Arabian traveller, in a kind of sunny mist, that renders the appearance gigantic. Frederick of Prussia owed his most violent fits of royal passion to indigestion; his courtiers and his physician hardly dared to approach him during his disorder, however short its continuance was likely to be; and if his Generals had known the true origin of some of his harshest commands, the poor

peasants, who humbly asked why their villages were destroyed, might have been answered, "His Majesty's ragout dis-
agreed with him yesterday." And yet after this, we are
astonished how Alexander could have forsaken us! We forget,
that weakness of mind is a thousand times more pernicious
in a sovereign than weakness of body, that it has no intervals
in which sound reason acts for itself, and that in an absolute
monarch, paradoxical as it may appear, it acquires a kind of
monstrous strength which wisdom in vain opposes. In short,
the Emperor of Russia is a very weak man, and we should
have thought so always, had he not been our ally. The Empress
Catherine, whom all the world knows to have been disappointed in her family, looked on him in his younger days as a
prince of mere good nature, and it was for this reason she
wished him to have ruled in preference to her son Paul, whom
she looked upon as a savage: she had encircled her grandson
with men of abilities, and she thought it better that men of
abilities should rule a good natured monarch, than that a mere
barbarian should rule them. Napoleon however has found his
way into the Russian councils, and wherever his influence
gains admission, he shews how well he can rival the Satan of
Milton, and "make the worse appear the better reason." What
has been the political life of the Emperor of Russia? He was
the ally of England because he thought her alliance was to
his interest, he meets the French in battle, is beaten, drinks a
bottle of wine with that 'upstart' and 'usurper' his enemy, and
separates from his English ally because he thinks the French
one more to his interest. If our wonderers could be informed
by Napoleon of the whole secret of the conferences at Tilsit
and of all the astonishing influence which turned the head
of Alexander, he would give them the precise answer of the
celebrated Leonora Galligai, when she confessed to her judges
the magic with which she was supposed to have influenced
Mary de Medicis:[3] "My magic," said she, "was the exercise of
that power, which strong minds always possess over weak
ones."

The Declaration of our Ministry, in reply to that of the

Russian Emperor, is not only written with classical spirit, but upon the whole is a very argumentative refutation of the pretexts of Alexander. One cannot but lament at the same time, that it should have condescended to use that old political talk about disinterestedness, which it renders so ridiculous in the Russian Emperor. There never was "a war undertaken by Great Britain *solely* for the purpose of maintaining Russian interests against the influence of France." To maintain Russia against France is to weaken or at least to obstruct the power of the latter, and this obstruction is evidently to the interest of England. I am afraid also, that no argument, upon the principles of right and wrong, can reconcile the attack upon Copenhagen to sound reason.[4] I would not assault the authors of that enterprise with all the noisy reproach, which has been rung in their ears: it becomes a thinking person to do justice to the motives of a set of men, that is, to the more active part of the Ministry, who hold a laborious responsibility for their country, and who carry into their councils the respectability of private worth. But these Ministers themselves insist not on the actual dereliction of the Danes, but on its future probability; nay, they do not so much insist upon this even, as upon the probable compulsion by which the French would have driven Denmark into hostilities against us. It must be confessed, that it is a hard thing to punish an innocent man now, lest he should be guilty hereafter; and it is certainly still harder to punish him, lest he should hereafter be compelled into error. The plea of necessity cannot be admitted without an acknowledgment, neither honourable nor true, of essential weakness in our own country; and those politicians, who so gaily set moral principles aside to gain a favourite end, forget that common honesty and common sense are the true grounds of all policy whatsoever. Shall we address the Deity and say, "Thou hast given us reason to discern right from wrong and to enable us to do justice to every body, but we beg leave to set this divine gift aside just now for a certain small end."

In the mean time, I am ready to do justice to the manly spirit with which the Ministers have dissipated the pretensions of Russia. That sudden fit of protection, which inspired the Emperor Alexander to draw his sword for Prussia, and which terminated, like all other fits, in mere impotence, is certainly more likely to have originated in the Emperor's own efforts of interest than in his ardour for this country; and if it did not, the Protector of the North and the Guarantee of the Germanic Constitution did very little honour to his ancient *magnanimity*. His Imperial Majesty would persuade us, that a man does not defend his neighbour's house from fire for reasons of neighbourhood, of natural pity, and of strong self-interest; but because he has been requested by a certain house at a distance, which is connected with his neighbour by family and by trade. Catherine would have used more specious logic than this.

There are in fact one or two proceedings on the part of Russia, which would almost have justified Great Britain in declaring war against the Emperor Alexander. His transfer to France of the Ionian Republic, of which, in the usual mock-heroic style, he had called himself the solemn Protector, was a meanness that might have been regarded with mere contempt; but his concealment of the Tilsit articles of peace, and his utter abandonment of Prussia at a time when she was ground into the dust, exhibited all that want of candour, firmness, and integrity, which is a hundred times more dangerous in a friend than in an enemy. The weakness however of a shrub makes it bend to one wind as well as another: Alexander may turn to us again when he is no longer propped up by French interest, but let us beware of leaning upon him as a fast friend. The man who has betrayed one friend, will betray fifty.

At any rate, let us cease to wonder at the changes and the follies which a mind naturally weak can exhibit. It is the part of weakness to wonder, not to be wondered at: and I dare say, when the Emperor considers his quarrel with England, his hugs with France, his legionary ribbon, and his new acquaintance, the immaculate M. Caulaincourt,[5] he does not know what to think of his own magnanimity. If we must wonder at the Emperor of Russia, in the name of common sense, let us wonder at him just as we wonder *what it is o'clock*, or *whether it will rain*, or at any other wonderful thing not at all wonderful.

A LETTER OF STRONG ADVICE TO HIS ROYAL HIGHNESS THE PRINCE OF WALES ON HIS CHARACTER AND CONNECTIONS

August 21, 1808

Let not Princes flatter themselves. They will be examined closely in private as well as in public life; and those who cannot pierce further, will judge of them by the appearances they give in both. To obtain true popularity, that which is founded in esteem and affection, they must therefore maintain their characters in both; and to that end neglect appearances in neither, but observe the decorum necessary to preserve the esteem, whilst they win the affections of mankind. — That which is here recommended to princes, that constant guard on their own behaviour even in private life, and that constant decorum which their example ought to exact from others, will not be found so difficult in practice as may be imagined, if they use a proper discernment in the choice of the persons whom they admit to the nearest degrees of intimacy with them. A Prince should chuse his companions with as great care as his Ministers. If he trusts the business of his state to these, he trusts his character to those, and his character will depend on theirs much more than is commonly thought. General experience will lead men to judge that a similitude of character determined the choice, even when chance, indulgence to assiduity, or good-nature, or want of reflection had their share in the introduction of men unworthy of such favours. But in such cases, certain it is, that they who judged wrong at first concerning him, will judge right at last. Bolingbroke's *Idea of a Patriot King*.[1]

How is it, Sir, that a man cannot address your Royal Highness without winning the reputation of a satirist?[2] If he is serious with you, reproof is unavoidable; and if he is flattering, his praise becomes the bitterest of mockeries. Even those who could attempt sincerity in speaking well of you, must have recourse to miserable compliments on your person and manners: your parasites dare not look beyond your surface: poetry itself will not venture to speak of your temperance, your charity, or your justice. A new birth-day dress affords your admirers the luckiest excuse for panegyric: a good leg and a gracious smile must suffice them instead of a good life and a commanding virtue; and the Heir of the British Crown becomes a puppet of wax-work, moulded by women and finished by the tailor.

Do not be alarmed, Sir, when I happen to mention your tradesmen. I have neither inclination nor time to rake up from pamphlets and from prisons the stories of men you have distressed, of debts you have never paid, and of mistresses you have. The People of England, Sir, would have forgotten these things long ago, had you forgotten them yourself; and it is the object of the present letter to warn you against their continuance. It must be confessed indeed, that a desertion of your old habits and old friends is not extremely probable, when we see you recalling to your favour the very persons whom the nation had almost hoped you had forgotten; but the less probable it becomes the more necessary it will be, and the more need you will have of honest and fearless admonition. Your Royal Highness recollects the saying of the poet,

A fool at forty is a fool indeed:[3]

but without meaning to apply the maxim to you in its most decided sense, you must recollect also that you are already six years older, and to all appearance not a jot the wiser than you were at forty. For God's sake, Sir, turn your face round from the infatuations of your past life, and look forward a little. You have told us over and over again, that you wished to be beloved by the nation and that you would never be despotic. Sir, you never can be despotic in the strict sense of the word, whether you would or not: the People have not sufficient respect for your talents or your integrity to be cheated into slavery under you, and I am willing to believe that you have too great a *respect* for them to attempt it; but if you thus abhor despotism, why are you a slave to your habits; why do you indulge in a style of living, which may impoverish your People as much as the most avaricious tyranny? Extravagance in a king very often leads him into tyrannical proceedings, for princes who are not very delicate in the application of money will not be very scrupulous in obtaining it. The first step which led Charles to the scaffold was a proceeding of this kind arising from his extravagance; and his extravagance, Sir, was of a more excusable nature than yours for it was of a less selfish one: it threw away money upon state-matters and not upon mistresses, horses, and fine clothes. It was his son Charles the Second, whose extravagance, in proportion as it was more selfish and wanton, rendered him a more odious tyrant than his father; it was Charles the Second, who owed more to his People as well as his creditors than any king before him, and whose vile pleasures made him neglect the latter and sell the former to their enemies. This man, it is true, was not brought to the block but it was only because the people were too tired of bloodshed; his memory suffers a continual execution in the justice of posterity. Extravagance then, Sir, is not the way to shew your hatred of despotism; and as to gaining the love of your country, you must first shew you can suffer for her sake and renounce the pleasures that interfere with her happiness. To this end, your Royal Highness must take care not to identify the People about you with your country. You must not live for a political party or for a wine party; you must have nothing to do with profligate soldiers who are helping to ruin their country, however well they may talk of defending her: you must not listen to professed drunkards and swindlers, however witty they may be upon claret and creditors: and you must positively shut your ears to all titled lawyers, who disregard the common ties of society, however proudly they may exhibit their knowledge of the laws. I have no doubt that your Royal Highness is one of the pleasantest of companions, that you can be gay and kind to all about you, and that you can drink your wine with the greatest applause. I do not accuse you of want of good nature, simply considered; I am willing, if the papers please, to acknowledge the radiance of affability that perpetually sparkles about you, and to believe, that whenever you make a bow, you only stoop to conquer. But is this the sum total of the value of a British Prince? Is it his whole ambition to be a pleasant fellow at a dinner, and an enchanting one at a ball? Does he place his chief glory in enlivening the featherbed sensibilities of Mrs. Billington's [4] aspect, or in lifting into gaiety the downward bloat of Sheridan? [5]

Sir, whatever my illustrious brothers, the Editors, may tell you, posterity will be very apt to call your good nature and your affability very worthless ornaments, unless you are just before you are good natured, unless you pay industrious men with something more solid than smiles. Your birth-day may have been a very splendid affair; you may have attacked a host of fashionable hearts at the review; and after unsettling the faculties of those about you with your affability, you may have clenched the universal conquest with your golden stirrups and your diamond star: but had every body reason to be satisfied with the gorgeousness of this appearance! Did you leave nothing for your friends and your dependants to regret, when you pranced away to the spectacle, like the Prince in the Arabian Tale, darting a new sunshine about you? Really, Sir, this frivolity, to consider it in no other light, is beneath a man of your age.

Cannot your Royal Highness forget for a few moments the miserable parasites who drink your wine and laugh at your anecdotes? Let posterity have some good anecdotes to relate of yourself. They will do you more honour, even though they may be told with only half the grace. If remonstrance can be of any service to you, you may see that there *are* people who can be bold in your cause. I am endeavouring to gain a difficult reputation, that of the honest Editor of a Journal; and if those real enemies, who call themselves your friends, make a merit of never giving you advice, it becomes every man in my situation to be content with advising you as a friend though he may be regarded as your enemy. Your Royal Highness may be assured, that men who think and speak as I do, will be the first to hail your virtues, and to defend a generous and just Prince to the last drop in their veins. A career is now opened to you infinitely more glorious than that of our warlike neighbour, for self-conquest is what he cannot attain. A King who at once rules himself and reigns over a free people is the greatest of monarchs. Regain the elevation, Sir, you possessed, when you were a happy and an innocent youth, when neither your good appearance depended on dress nor your comfort on forgetfulness. You are destined to be high on the balance, but when you slip so often and weigh it down, your inferiors gain an elevation by your descent; and instead of looking up to you, the people look down on your head with a dangerous superiority. Dismiss therefore from your presence these idle and dissipated men, who would reduce you to a level with themselves. Patronise the arts for themselves rather than their professors; admire a good singer, but never condescend to talk with a common prostitute; go to the theatre for a witty play, but pass not your time with a drunkard however facetious; his sense makes his vices more monstrous: if wit will not flow without wine, it is at best a poor compound and wants the true fluency. Spend not whole mornings in chatting with tradesmen about the turn of a hat or the cut of a waistcoat: it is beneath you, Sir, or any gentleman; and in proportion as the enraptured mechanic spreads abroad the fame of your affability, he diminishes the reputation of your common sense. Turn away with contempt from those ever-grinning minions, who doat on all you say and all you do, who affect to admire your generosity in disregarding such addresses as the present, and who call your worst errors the foibles of a generous heart. The first instance of generosity you could give to the public would be to sacrifice these dastards to your country; the second to commence economist; the third to take home your Royal Consort. It must be better I should think, for a man of gallantry, even to endure a wife, than to be reproached with slavery to a regardless mistress. Nobody would expect all this to be done at once; but if your Royal Highness values the opinion of the whole nation, you will do something of it directly. People flattered themselves a little while ago, from your comparatively secluded style of living, that you had prepared to meet the wishes of the country; but your birth-day companions have disappointed them. Alas, Sir, of what can princes be made, when they require so little to make them idolized, and will not be so! A little prudence, a little self-command, a little self-respect, and your name might obtain a real lustre in comparison with the princes of the day. But what is its brilliancy at present? It is a mere cypher, flourishing on the caps of your soldiery or glittering over the tradesman's door upon birth-days. It is a delusive light, borrowed from your ancestors and misleading your followers; an *ignis fatuus* which rises out of the graves of the departed, to wander and to make wanderers.

Rise, unhappy Prince, rise ere it be too late from the dreams that weigh upon luxury and disturb your faculties. Flattery is not the language of your real friends. Wine is not the Lethe in which you will forget your errors and your cares. Be just, be temperate, and forget every thing in the happy tears of a forgiving people.

> I am, Sir, with the best intentions,
> Your Royal Highness's most devoted
> Friend and Fellow-subject,
> THE EDITOR.

DELIVERANCE OF EUROPE

WHAT THE DELIVERANCE OF EUROPE MEANS.
CHARACTERISTIC TOUCHES OF ITS MONARCHS.
THE EDITOR'S PROFESSIONS OF INDEPENDENCE.

September 11, 1808

There are people who talk of the downfall of Bonaparte
and the deliverance of Europe as if the two circumstances
were indisputably the same.[1] They seem to imagine that when
he is overthrown, a kind of millenium will arise on earth; that
things, in returning to their old channel, will flow with a
delicious peace and purity; that every man in short will be
free and every nation happy. These men forget that the overthrow of one tyrant is not the destruction of all, and that
governments have in general much more to fear from themselves than their enemies.

I have no inclination whatever to lament the degeneracy of
the times, which are in some respects much better than any
preceding age, but I think there never was a less portion of
philosophy in our political writers than at present. They look
upon the circumstances and changes of the world with so
partial an eye, that they account for every event upon the
most petty causes of party: their minds are so nearsighted,
that they can behold but a few minute objects at once, and in
poring over little dates and disturbances they are unable to
look abroad upon the world, to seek for the changes of things
in the vast revolutions of the human mind, and to discover
that one nation has generally reduced itself to an humiliated
state, before another can trample on its freedom. These are
the politicians, who unable to look or to move out of their
little sphere, are so tenacious of the prejudices of their circle,
of the privileges of their mental dungeon: the least attempt to
lighten their darkness renders them irritable, and makes them

shut their eyes with an impatient weakness that cannot bear
the light. These are the patriots, who confound national prejudices with patriotism; who cannot bear to hear an enemy
praised; who attribute all the misfortunes of their country to
its external enemies or to a mere existing party; who think
every war necessary, provided the French are its objects; who
call any stupid and selfish ally *magnanimous*; and who in
their zeal to forget what are called little corruptions in
their government and to exaggerate every corruption in another, are always flattering the vices of the state and literally
killing their country with kindness.

On the other hand, there are politicians who take quite a
different though quite as narrow a view of the charge of
ignorance and corruption upon the opposite party, attribute
the principal humiliation of Europe to the sole genius of the
French Emperor. These men, who are of a more enthusiastic
turn of mind, are also more inconsistent than their opponents,
for while the latter are blind to their country's errors and
therefore have the excuse of ignorance on their side, the
former inveigh against the folly and corruption of the government without seeing that the real talents of our neighbour
naturally decrease in value proportionably to the folly and
corruption of his competitors; they will have all his opponents
to be fools, and yet he must shew consummate wisdom in
defeating them, and they are guilty of an enormity against
reason and against their professed love of freedom, in railing
against the best existing constitution in Europe, however
corrupted it may have become, while *at the same time* they
are wishing success to a man who would exterminate liberty
from the face of the earth.

All this prejudice arises from the want of a little philosophy,
from the want of a love of truth on truth's account, and from
a vanity which few men will acknowledge even to their own
hearts, that of maintaining an old opinion at all events. Wherever there have been violent political disputes, they have
proved that the truth has nothing to do with extremes: its
force is truly centripetal and the moral as well as the natural

philosopher may say that whatever is stable and accordant with the true harmony of things tends directly to a centre.

The misfortunes of Europe are originally owing neither to the errors of party in this single country nor to the talents, great as they are, of the French Emperor. They are owing to the corruptions of the several states, and to various political tyrannies similar in their origin to that now exercised by Bonaparte, though weakened by age and rendered contemptible by sloth and ignorance. The tyranny of France will come to the very same end, when the talents and freshness of the French Revolution shall be corrupted by the gradual influence of court and party interest, when tyrants shall have become stupid and contemptible, and the people not possess one intoxicating cause of self-glory to keep them in spirits and hinder them from thinking. Europe therefore must be delivered, not only from the French Emperor, but from itself, not by the death of one tyrant, but by the purification of many bad and tyrannical governments. It always seems to me, that Providence has placed us in an age of wretched kings in order to give a lasting lesson to slavish minds and to shew the nothingness of mere royalty. The only mystery is, how any common reasoner can wonder at the successes of a man of talent when the opponents are so supremely weak, how he can wonder at the thraldom of the Continent when its princes are bound in their own ignorance and its nations in their own tyranny.

I forget what facetious nobleman it was, who, bold enough in common but bashful in the senate, laid a wager that he would make a speech in the House of Lords, and upon the strength of two or three bottles made that memorable and pithy oration against impeachers, which consisted of producing an example and then saying, "And you see, my Lords, what became of him." But it produced a great sensation, as the French say, for it consisted of the best logic in the world, the logic of fact. I think I may fairly exercise the same mode of reasoning upon the subject of the present *"noble race of potentates."* I have only to fancy myself replying to the speech of a Noble Lord, now living, who in a manner little to be expected either from his talents or way of thinking reprobated the little respect which has been shown by some of the public papers to the existing Princes of Europe.

In the first place, my Lords, there is the Emperor of Austria,[2] who ought still to have been Emperor of Germany if his common sense had permitted him. — This Prince, my Lords, could never divest himself of the military prepossessions of his house; so he directed his army in person though he was some hundred miles off, and waged war against the French with a closet-faction instead of a field-officer; and your Lordships see what has become of the Emperor of Austria.

Then there is the Emperor of Russia, my Lords, a very magnanimous prince — that is to say, when he was on our side. This great man is weak enough to be ruled by every Ambassador that can reach him, especially after having received a beating from the said Ambassador's master: he once presented the novel sight of a despot fighting for the liberties of Europe, but his natural dulness was too powerful for him and he is now fighting against them — and your Lordships see what has become of the Emperor of Russia.

Then, again my Lords, there is the King of Prussia,[3] a very amiable man, except that he has attempted to cheat both friends and foes and is a little given to prevarication. The King of Prussia, my Lords, is the petty tyrant of a worn-out state who wished to beat the tyrant of a young one, and your Lordships very well know what has become of the King of Prussia.

Fourthly, my Lords, there is the King of Denmark,[4] who it must be confessed — but if your Lordships please, I'll drop the King of Denmark.

Well, my Lords, then there is the Pope of Rome, who anointed Bonaparte with holy oil, and after being his slave till this very moment suddenly began to question his master, and your Lordships know what has become of the Pope of Rome.[5]

Then, my Lords, there are the States of Holland and of Venice, consisting of a hundred little tyrants, my Lords; I need not say any thing of them, but will conclude with King

Charles of Spain, a very stupid and worthless old gentleman, and his son King Ferdinand, whom I will not teach to despise his father by calling him any better. These two personages, my Lords, are manifestly the most stupid, corrupt, and coward-ly princes in Europe, and I believe your Lordships pretty well know what has become of King Charles and King Ferdinand.[6]

In short, to drop my oration, if the deliverance of Europe means the destruction of all tyranny, that is, not only Bona-parte's tyranny, but the whole pandemonium of corrupt courts, interests, and factions, I coincide with all my soul in the honest ardour of those who cry so loudly for it: but if it merely means the restoration of *the noble race of Potentates*, with all their suite mental and bodily, if it means the restoration of corrupt courts, of senseless and profligate princes, and of prejudices that do nothing for the people but render their slavery sacred, I really think that Europe is already delivered as much as ever she can be, or to borrow a phrase from the ladies, that she is already as well as can be expected.

I foresaw, when I adopted my political motto, that my professions of independence would raise not only mistrust but malevolence, and that he who is of no party, is by turns caressed and abused by all parties. The event has proved as I expected. People cannot imagine how an Editor can be neither Pittite nor Foxite, and as if they had not had enough of Pittites and Foxites already, are determined he shall be one or the other whenever they please. If I praise consistency and rail at place-hunters, then the Foxites shake their heads at me: if I dislike war and remonstrate against new alliances, then the Pittites shake theirs. I was a very good Windhamite[7] till I differed with General Whitelocke;[8] an excellent Burdettite till I mentioned the words "credulous young man;" and a very promising Wilberforcite till I laughed at the Methodists. It is infinitely amusing, but piteous too, to see the regard which all party men have to relative instead of positive opinion: a Foxite will rejoice, not that you wish to have no placemen in par-liament, or in other words to have nothing but the constitution, but that you like Mr. Fox and hate the Pittites: a Pittite on

the other hand will rejoice, not that you know any thing about
Mr. Pitt, but that you like him at all events and hate the
Foxites. If I must give my creed, it is simply this — The truth,
the whole truth, and nothing but the truth; the constitution,
the whole constitution, and *nothing but the constitution*. I can
admire the talents of an illustrious scoundrel without ap-
plauding his ambition, and lament the errors of the state
without wishing to live under any other: in short, I will flatter
neither my country nor its enemies, and the distinction which
I make between the corruptions of the British constitution and
the corruptions of the French, is precisely the same which
I make between the errors of a good man and the vices of a
profligate.

FRANCE AND ENGLAND

November 19, 1809

The present age, however it may affect our interests, is unquestionably a brilliant period in the history of the world.[1] Great as it has been in arms, it promises, at the return of peace, equal greatness in arts; and to survive such an age — to be handed down in despite of its conquerors to posterity, when all the little great, the Percevals and the weak princes, have been silently swept away, is a thought almost sufficient to inspire the soul of mediocrity itself. I mean not to pay homage to the renown of mere conquest or to the vices of conquerors; Napoleon in his gusts of passion, Caesar in his brothel, and Alexander in his drunkenness, are equally as contemptible, as in their indifference of bloodshed they are detestable: ambition so degraded and unfeeling is but the keeper of a huge charnel-house; and when the poet talked of it as

The glorious fault of angels and of gods,[2]

he should have added, that it converted those angels and gods into devils. But Alexander the friend of Aristotle, Caesar the cultivator of literature and the overcomer of difficulty, and Napoleon the patron of arts and annihilator of corrupt monarchies, are worthy of accompanying the poet and the philosopher to immortality; and it must be allowed, with all the weakness of mankind in admiring their destroyers, that posterity will not place a conqueror in the rank of great men, unless he exhibit some great quality of the mind, beyond a brutal inflexibility. Timour and Jenghis are considered but as lucky and frightful barbarians: Charles the 12th,[3] with all his contempt of danger and wonderful successes, has obtained no title but that of a splendid madman; and the overthrowers of Rome itself are remembered only as the lightning from heaven, which comes to flash, to execute, and to vanish.

The first great features, which will engage the attention of posterity in looking back to our time, are the empire of Napoleon and the facilities or obstructions he experienced in obtaining it. The former will naturally remind them of the Roman; the latter will awaken very different reflections, in which we have a peculiar interest. The Roman empire, during the ages of its genuine strength, was bounded by the Atlantic on the West, the river Euphrates on the East, the Rhine and Danube on the North, and the deserts of Barbary on the South. To the possession of this empire, besides all the facilities it will give to unbounded conquest from the state of the modern world, is Bonaparte rapidly hastening. On the North indeed he is beyond it; on the West he will be complete master in three months; on the East he is already inclosing Turkey with Poland and his new Illyrian provinces; and the South, containing the states of Barbary, only waits for the settled master of the European Continent to yield at the first attack. Add to these, his influence in remoter Asia and over the whole civilized north of the Continent, and the Romans themselves might admire a conqueror who, in surpassing them in ambition, has reason also to surpass them in hope. Whether his successors will be able to keep his acquisitions, is another question: many natural causes, particularly the barbarism of the surrounding nations, operated both as a check and a protection to the empire inherited by Augustus: his successors quietly obtained or fought with each other for the whole dominion; and the strength of the empire was not dissipated by those independent divisions, which lost the conquests of Alexander and of Charlemagne. The *causes* of French empire are the most interesting subject, for they involve every effect which a nation like ours has reason to fear. These are very different from the causes of Roman conquest, and should make Europe blush for her civilization. Barbarism, with its vices and its virtues, was the only formidable obstacle through which the Romans had to cut their way to dominion, and while their civilization and discipline rendered them irresistible to the vices of barbarism, they met with enough of its virtues to give dignity to their prowess. How direct has been the reverse with the enemies of France! Equal to her in civilization, originally superior in discipline, with their long reputation to sustain, and at last their very independence to preserve, they have nevertheless displayed all the weakness of barbarism without making a single use of experience. Some of the very countries which the Romans conquered with difficulty from their savage possessors, have fallen, in the height of their civilization, at the first attack. Such are the German countries west of the Danube; the most renowned provinces of Spain; and the wretched nation of Portugal, once celebrated by the title of the warlike Lusitania. Yet even these are not sunk lower than Rome herself, the mistress of them all. Perhaps the bitterest satire that can be cast on this once all-powerful city, is the feeling which hinders a writer from indulging in declamations on her fate: — pity itself has become common-place on the subject.*

Ask a Contractor the cause of these changes, and he will answer "The ambition of Bonaparte;" ask a Courtier, he will say "The ambition of Bonaparte;" ask a Minister, and he will still say "The ambition of Bonaparte;" ask a King, and he will impatiently say "Nothing *but* the ambition of Bonaparte;" —

---

* Yet one may well stop, in the midst of one's contempt, to admire the native artifices by which Italy managed so long to maintain the form of dominion when the reality had been lost for ages. First, it obtained empire by the perfection of the military art; when it lost this, it assumed and gained a dominion over the minds of mankind by superstition; the Pope, from becoming the Caesar of the religious world and conquering all sorts of barbarians by the force of terror, became in time the arbiter of the temporal Caesars; and it may be said that the very corpse of Roman power still sat on the throne of the Vatican, ruling almost as mightily, when it could do nothing, as when it enjoyed its glorious faculties. When this ghostly power began to be disputed, Italy still reigned the mistress of arts, as she had been of arms: no longer the forceful conqueror, she yet subdued the nations with her song; her laws of harmony won the implicit obedience of the artist as well as musician; and Raphael and Michael Angelo are to this day the acknowledged princes of painting. Nay, when the sovereign arts have at last divided their residence among various countries, and nothing but the name of Rome survives, Fortune, as if she still lingered from very habit near her former residence, has selected from a little Italian island, directly opposite her beloved city, a new Favourite to work her imperial will, and subdue the nations.

but ask an impartial observer, and he will say "The corruption of Courts." The ambition of Bonaparte sprang out of the facilities that presented themselves to such a man; but the corruption of Courts was at its height when he was a child, and is the sole, putrid and deadly fountain of all the bloodshed that has deluged the Continent. Had Bonaparte left Spain to herself, she would soon have committed suicide from nervous exhaustion; her limbs could no longer have borne their own feelings; and where the King was an idiot, and his first Minister an ignorant favourite living upon that idiotcy, what was to be expected from a Court already worn out with debauchery—or from a people already ruined by that Court? God forbid I should defend his atrocious as well as contemptible arts against the Spanish monarchy: he shoud have left it to Jovellanos[4] and its other enlightened men to see what they could do for its regeneration; but whenever Bonaparte's ambition is mentioned in terms of abhorrence, it is but an etiquette due to such monarchs as Charles of Spain, and Ferdinand of Naples,[5] &c. &c. that court-corruption should have the precedence in our detestation. In fact, had this corruption not existed, or had it even existed but to half its extent, it would have required a miracle from heaven to account for the elevation and triumphs of this extraordinary man.

Posterity then will know where to look for the true causes of these wars; and it will most assuredly brand them with infamy. But shall our enemy, thus brightening his fame by contrast, be handed down to future ages at the expense of England herself? To England, posterity will look either as the consummator or eclipser of this man's glory; and shall we continue to add to his beams by assisting his course over countries where he dissipates in an instant every thin cloud of opposition, and bursts forth in the full heat of meridian triumph? — To England posterity will look; and shall we, confessedly the most moral nation in Europe, with the example of a thousand illustrious forefathers to inspire us, consent to creep on in petty corruptions at home, and petty intrigues abroad, and petty compromises with our hopes and fears, till at last we grow sufficiently corrupt and timid to become the prey of our rival? The apathy of this nation, in suffering the present despicable Ministry to rule a moment longer without petitioning the King for their removal, is the worst sign for its independence that has appeared for years. The business of Walcheren[6] is the common theme of execration; yet we ourselves, we, the people, who suffer from these fooleries and fatalities, do nothing towards their prevention; we seem to think there is no such thing as the right of petitioning the Throne, that Ministers cannot be removed, and that if a pugdog were to be Premier, it would be the sole business of our lives to wait on the snarling and craving puppy like the vilest of slaves. England wants a man of a great mind at its helm; it wants, not a man who will do nothing but cram his conscience with places, and then go to church to sleep off or to pray off the surfeit, but a man, truly highminded; a man above all place and above all *politics*, as they are called; a man with one avowed principle and object of action, *this* an inflexible integrity, and *that* a preservation of his country; a man, in short, as full of disdain as the great Chatham for those vermin and bloodsuckers the Jobbers, and as deaf as our *enemy* to the importunities of his friends for this *little* office and that *small* department; for how is he who cannot withstand the soft voice and cringing of his friends, or his uncle's friends, or his wife's brother's nephew's friends, to stem the progress of a great conqueror? Common sense laughs us to scorn, if we think so for an instant. "Well," say we, "but who is such a man? Where is he? How is he to be made Minister?" So saying, we sit down and have no more to say, except when the income-tax-gatherer knocks at our door, and then we cry out, "Ah, this is a terrible evil;" or except when Bonaparte's invasion of us is mentioned, and then we exclaim, "Ah, perhaps he *may* come indeed." But the time is past for these gapings and groanings, so unworthy of Englishmen; and unless we get rid of our apathy, we shall soon get rid of more guineas and more fine armies. It was well observed the other day, that an individual has no right to plead his inability to do any thing *as* an individual: individuals compose bodies, and bodies do every thing: a body obtained for us our Magna Charta; a body settled the Bill of Rights; and a body, animating other bodies, may restore to us all our blessings by procuring Reform. If we trust to our insular situation or to our navy, we trust to a certain extent very justly; but as worms can eat through the hardest wood, so corruption can render the best arms of no avail. On such a land indeed, and with such a navy, pure political *honesty* would be to us a wall of adamant; and this, I firmly believe, is as little to be obtained without Reform, as Reform is without individual exertion. Whatever be our fate, to this age posterity will look as to the last rivalry of character between England and France. If we go on as at present, and value neither our character with our children's children nor *their* happiness, then France decidedly wins the palm in the greatest contest she ever fought with us; — but if we reform and rouse all our faculties, driving Corruption from the land as we would the most fatal of the enemy's spies, then shall our comparative glory shine upon posterity, like the sun compared with a comet, and history will still say, "France is a nation of brilliant eccentricity; but England is one illustrious family of freemen and philosophers."

DINNER IN HONOUR OF
"THE IMMORTAL PITT"

Hic petit excidiis urbem, miserosque Penates,
Ut gemma bibat.   VIRGIL, Geor. Lib. 2. v. 505.[1]

For cities given up to fierce ambition,
And things at home in terrible condition,
We drink this jewel of a politician.

June 3, 1810

In some countries, and with certain common orders of
people, the mode of paying tribute to departed excellence is
by a natural and unobtrusive grief, by indulging in quiet recollection, and forgetting the little passions and struggles that
agitate mankind.[2] But if you lose a "great man" in England,
there is an universal recipe for sorrow as well as joy, which
will enable you to shew your affliction in the liveliest manner
possible, without at all interfering with your pleasures: nay,
so accommodating a contrast does it furnish to the usual modes
of being afflicted, that it obliges you to be sociable and even
provokes an excellent appetite: — the reader is aware that I
can mean nothing but a Public Dinner, — a medium of expression that would have been worthy the pen of a Voltaire, so
various are its powers, so complicated and full of contrast its
sympathies. If the object of grief is a very great man—a departed Statesman for instance — the sorrow must be very great,
and therefore the dinner is great in proportion. This is always
the case with the very melancholy entertainments in honour
of Mr. Pitt's memory: their historians pique themselves as
much on relating the good cheer as the solemnity, and with
very good reason. Not to be profuse on such an occasion and
run up a long bill would be to show that the friends of that
great man did not appreciate his talents; and though there

might be more grief of another kind were there less eating, yet eating and drinking do very much assist in the production of real tears, and in this respect our great men agree with those of Abyssinia, who count it highly honourable to take mouthfuls that bring the water in their eyes. Everybody therefore eats at least as heartily as he grieves, and by the fondness which is manifested for the several dishes, one would suppose that they were emblematical of the fine qualities of the "illustrious Statesman:" — the fish of his deep research, the fowl of his vigilance, the birds of his excursive genius, the beef of his English vigour, the turtle of his high credit in the City. — Dr. Young, Petrarch, or Simonides himself, in comparison with these Anniversary-men, had but a poor taste for the "luxury of woe."

Such was the Dinner given on Monday last in commemoration of Mr. Pitt's Birth-day, — Mr. Williams, East India Director, in the Chair. My friend the *Post* is not so amusing as he was last year in his account of the solemnity, for he has attended a little more to his English; but he is still grave enough to be droll. He tells us in his commencement that "decorum and unanimity were the order of the day, and the loyal and" (what is more, the) "*orderly* sentiments entertained and expressed by every person present, formed a striking and brilliant contrast to those of the rude and mischievous factions with which the public sense has of late been so much insulted." Of the "striking" part of the contrast, the reader will have a very good idea when he hears that among the company were Messrs. Perceval and Canning, my Lords Castlereagh, Clancarty, and Melville, Sir Vicary Gibbs, Mr. Charles Yorke,[3] &c. &c. — and of the "brilliant" part he will have a lively sense in reading, among others, the names of my Lords Eldon, Mulgrave, and Mountmorres, Sir Charles Price, Sir Anderson, Sir James Pulteney, Sir Wm. Curtis,[4] &c. In short, never was seen a finer shew of state-cattle, comprehending Mr. Pitt's "servile herd of imitators," the Ministry, — the Boroughmongers, noble and ignoble, — the Barterers of Conscience for Title, — the Placemen and Pensioners, — the Jobbers, the Con-

tractors, the time-serving Lawyers, the Parliamentary Delin-
quents, the Public Defaulters, and all those who received
favours from Mr. Pitt or expect to reap profit from lamenting
him.

> Ambubalarum collegia pharmacopoiæ,
> Mendici, mimi, balatrones, hoc genus omne
> Mæstum ae sollcitum est cantoris morte Tigelli,
> Quippe benignus erat.   HOR. Sat. 2. Lib. 1 (1-4)

> The school of all those who can play to some tune,
> Each parasite, beggar profess'd, and buffoon,
> All mourn for his death as a common disaster,
> For sure never breath'd such a bountiful master.

After enumerating the persons who composed this "most
respectable" assembly, — "most respectable," says the historian
with his usual climax, "for rank, consequence, talents, and
wealth," he immediately passes on to the toasts after dinner,
— an unpardonable hurry, of which I have before complained.
The commemoration is a dinner, and we have a right to know
all about that dinner, — who paid the most voracious respect to
its subjects, — who spoke in praise of the flummery, and who
of the calf's head, — what sentimental Contractor shed tears
from the united effect of melancholy and the mustard, — who
drank to whom, a most important and curious piece of specu-
lation, — what true things Mr. Perceval said, — what pathetic
things my Lord Castlereagh, — what brilliant things Sir William Curtis, — and what dignified things about the Reformists,
Mr. Canning. These matters are left to the imagination, and
indeed though a shorthand description of them would be interesting in one point of view, it would tell us little that we
may not conceive. Public dinners are all pretty much of the
same cast, that is to say, very stupid. He who expects to find
in them —

> The feast of reason and the flow of soul,[5]

will meet with nothing but a feast of turtle and a flow of
gravy; — all the soul he shall discover will be in the waiter,

and all the reason he shall hear will be the reason why rooms
are hot when they are crowded, and why hares eat better with
their heads on.

The cloth being removed, and the King's health "*drank* with
every demonstration of enthusiastic loyalty," such as boldly
standing up for him, exerting the lungs for him, and shedding
the last drop of the bottle for him (loyal souls!), the Chairman
gave, "the immortal Memory of the late Right Hon. William
Pitt," which "was accordingly drank in reverential silence," —
a mode with which nobody can quarrel, as the less that is said
on such a subject the better. The President then, who it seems
has as good a taste in poetry as in politics, requested that ever-
to-be-lamented poet Mr. Fitzgerald [6] "to favour the company
with the recital of his *admirable* "Independent Tribute," every
line of which was received with the most *electric* enthusiasm."
— One can easily imagine the shock. Mr. Fitzgerald is an unfortunate middle-aged Gentleman, who being ambitious of
poetical fame, has forsaken the quiet corner of a Lady's Magazine to rhyme and rant in the political world, and accordingly
he fastens himself upon a public dinner now and then, to lift
his muse into notice, just as Sinbad in the Arabian Nights tied
himself to a piece of beef in order that the eagles might carry
him away with it out of the valley. Here he gets a seat among
the "great men," and being warmed with a little praise and a
little more port, begins singing and spouting forth his smoke
like a tea-kettle. His eulogies of Mr. Pitt are sometimes unlucky, and sometimes unseasonable. Of this foreign policy he
tells us, that —

> — *Till* his plans by Austria's fate were cross'd,
> The liberties of nations were not lost; —

that is to say, that till his plans failed, they were successful.
The praise of his disinterestedness with regard to money is
just; but what does Mr. Perceval say to it? — Mr. Pitt, who
manifested a contempt for good letters during the whole of
his administration, is properly rewarded by having such a poet
as Mr. Fizgerald. — After another customary toast or two,

somebody gave, "May the Principles of Mr. Pitt ever animate the Councils of Great Britain;" — in other words, may the Habeas Corpus be suspended when the Minister pleases, may we do as much for France as we can, and may Taxation and Jobbing leave not a guinea in the people's pocket. This toast, so consolatory to the Ministers and so hopeful to the Contractors, was "drank," says the accurate *Post*, "with *more* than three times three, — perhaps we should not much err if we said *nearly* nine times *nine*, — amidst the most extatic bursts of applause we have ever heard on such an occasion." The mourners must have been in a pretty "orderly" cue by this time, and very well prepared to join in the chorus of a new Song which followed, called "Pitt the Patriot's Name," written "expressly for the commemoration" by Mr. Fitzgerald. Then came "The Independence of Parliament; may it ever be equally secure from the power of the Crown and the violence of Factions." — The reader may wish to have seen between these two enemies, the Corruptions of the Aristocracy; but the author of the toast was perfectly right: he knew that the corruptions of the Aristocracy were now identified with the Parliament, and that to wish for security against them would be flying in the face of the House of Commons. The health of the London Anti-petitioners was then given " with rapturous applause," and the City-Baronets, in spite of the beef and pudding, rose to return thanks; a little jeu-d'esprit about factions and rallying round the Constitution, ending with that epigrammatic touch, "salvation of the country," was accordingly delivered by Sir William Curtis, who was happily succeeded by a song called "the Independent Man." The Anti-Revolutionists of Middlesex met with the same honours, and acknowledged them with equal brilliancy through Mr. Mellish,[7] who said something about victory, loyal men, and being at his post. This was followed by the toast and some of "the Pilot who weathered the Storm," a pleasant piece of fiction written by Mr. Canning, shewing how we were all rescued from the storm by Mr. Pitt, though we are now in the midst of it. "The Landed and Commercial Interests of the Country," were next toasted, and incontinently roused up Mr. Beeston Long, Banker, who said (luxurious soul!) that "he could not *deny himself* the pleasure of giving the health of a Right Honourable Gentleman present, who was pursuing a course of administration which he considered well calculated to promote and unite the landed and commercial interests of the country." He therefore gave "the Right Honourable Spencer Perceval," to the infinite satisfaction of that orthodox and worthy Reversionist, who amidst bursts of applause rose to say, — that he was at a loss what to say. However, he assured the company, that the sole object of himself and his colleagues was to follow in Mr. Pitt's steps, though "at an humble distance." The public burdens, the loss of allies, and Walcheren, sufficiently demonstrate the main part of this piece of information; and the "humble distance" is an exquisite touch, considering that Mr. Perceval is Prime-Minister; and that he and his colleagues continue in office in spite of all sorts of disasters. The glasses were then filled to "Lord Wellington and our gallant Army in Spain and Portugal," which produced the Glee of "Britons, strike home." — (For *strike* read *come*.) After a few more customary toasts, the company being warmed into a comfortable carelessness, and glad of any excuse for a bumper, ventured on the health of the Ex-minister Canning, which was followed by great applause and then by as great a silence in expectation of a speech; but whether that Gentleman felt himself disconcerted by the honours of Mr. Perceval who had tricked him, or by the presence of Lord Castlereagh who had exposed him, or by the recollection of certain high hopes expressed by him at the late Anniversary respecting the alliance of Austria, the company found that he had slipped from under his laurels, and gone away. For this disappointment, after another toast or two, our impartial and jolly mourners consoled themselves by making as great a noise in favour of Lord Castlereagh's health, who said, that he "felt deeply," but informed them twice over that he could not "express himself," — an incapability which, considering the lateness of the hour, was very readily pardoned.

But human glory has an end, and so have dinners. "Shortly after this," says the dignified but smug *Post*, "the greater part of the company left the room highly gratified with a scene, which, though in fact principally as it was intended to be a festival of the heart, and a commemoration and a confirmation of a man and of measures that constitute the safety of Britain, was at the same time, by the care of the Stewards, and the exertions of Messrs. Hall and Co., keepers of the tavern, as superb and elegant an entertainment as could possibly be provided for so large a company. The dinner, dessert, and wines, were in quality, and in the manner of serving, admirable and *satisfactory* in the highest degree." — Thus concludes the patriotic historian, with a noble climax, and a puff for Messrs. Hall and Co. — a conclusion perfectly characteristic both of the dinner and its designs, for the end of your "loyalty" is nothing but the enjoyment of good things. The Reformists, to be sure, are an annoyance, but then the dinner is "admirable;" — the loss of Pitt is a terrible thing, but then how "satisfactory" the wines!

PROPOSED MONUMENT TO LOCKE

June 10, 1810

More than twelve months, I believe, have now elapsed since a Subscription was commenced for the erection of a Monument to the illustrious Locke.[1] For this purpose it was calculated that about a thousand pounds would suffice, and contributions have been invited by promises of engravings and medals representing the Monument. It appears however from the Advertisements in the Daily Papers that so far from being yet complete, the Subscription is little more than half full. We raise contributions for persecuted club-spouters, and for women of doubtful character, but we can afford nothing in honour of the sage who shed such a noble radiance on the human intellect and on the fame and freedom of the English character. What is it that hinders us from doing justice to such a man? He has been dead long enough to surmount the effects of ignorance, of envy, and of bigotry; he has raised our reputation in a manner at once the most innocent, most useful, and most sublime; he taught us to think for ourselves, and in so thinking to act for all mankind; it was he and the great Newton, who put to flight the dreams of former ages and opened the eyes of man to the true consciousness of his powers: even our rival neighbours could not but worship the radiant hands that dispersed their own philosophy; and shall we refuse honours to one of them? Newton, who taught us to look upwards and contemplate the glory of nature, has his monument as he ought to have; his fame was too immediate in the eyes of his countrymen to be overlooked. Locke, who taught us to look inwards and contemplate ourselves, did us more good though with less grandeur of effect, and has no monument but in the glory he bequeathed us. It is not necessary perhaps to his reputation that he should have any other; — but it is very necessary to ours.

That the present Administration[2] should take up so laudable a matter, is not to be expected: — men who have no regard for their own proper fame, who waste the powers of the country in the most frivolous manner, who do every thing to cripple the freedom of thinking, and in fine, who think to no purpose but a bad one, can care little about the memory of Locke; besides, they will tell you that they cannot afford a few hundreds for the sake of dead merit, when they have so much to do for the reward of living; that is to say, pensions to bestow on their creatures, thousands to throw over the rocks and precipices of Spain, £20,000 a-year to furnish to the Marquis of Buckingham for writing his name, and the use of £40,000 a-year to entrust to my Lord Arden[3] for the same laborious piece of virtue. It signifies nothing that one twentieth part of a sinecure would do honour at once to Locke and to the nation: every body knows that it is not at all necessary to care for Locke or the nation, whereas it is absolutely indispensable that a statesman should be enabled to have forty hams stewed down to make him a little sauce. — But if the People of England regard these things in the proper light, they will rather thank the Government for surrendering up to them exclusively the attainment of so easy and true an honour. It used to be the praise of Englishmen, that on all such occasions they could act nobly for themselves, pay their own unassisted tribute to excellence, and prove to surrounding nations that their Philosophers had indeed done them good and rendered them grateful. — It is true, our character for thinking is not so famous as it used to be: our passions have for years past been too much called into play; and in yielding ourselves to political quacks, who have been weakening us while they professed to cure, our temper and good sense have been injured together, and even a returning consciousness of error will torment us long before it will re-invigorate. But we have many and great blessings still, and for these we must still be grateful. "Aye," cries the Pittite, "to the great Minister who saved you out of the wreck of nations:" — "Aye," cry the busy getters of wealth, "to us who enable your government to carry on the war:" — "Aye," cry Mr. Perceval and his colleagues, "to us who oppose Bonaparte wherever he moves and keep you afloat till *something turn up.*'" * "No," says the man of common thinking, with a sigh and a bitter smile, "not to any one of these, — neither to the great Minister who did us the favour not to destroy us — nor to the getters of wealth, who enable the Government to impoverish us — nor to Mr. Perceval and his colleagues, who fight because 'something may turn up' — but to the wise and exemplary teachers who came before them — to the philosophic and foresighted men who saw that England's greatness was to be preserved only by the maintenance of sound thinking and of a jealous liberty — to the sages, who by the union of all that is great in precept and in practice left us their wisdom to instruct and their virtue to inspire — to Alfred, to Hampden, to Sidney, to Holt, to Somers, to Addison, to Chatham, to *Locke.* They who teach us to think best, teach us to act best: and they who teach us to think and act best, teach us to live longest and freest.

It is to Locke — I do not say to Locke only, but it is to that admirable man chiefly — that English thinking has owed its freedom from jargon, from ostentation, from superficiality. The father, though not the perfecter, of definition, and the great recommender of a system of reflection at once *conscientious,* modest, and profound, there is no profession, no mode or object of learning, no mental accomplishment or personal virtue, to which he has not been of incalculable service. We are naturally too apt to refer our blessings as well as misfortunes to things or men before us; but philosophy, of all other social greatness, is that which leaves the best and most lasting influence behind it, and is acting for us long after the philosopher is dead. It is his good spirit left upon earth to counteract the baneful glories of the ambitious and the warlike, and to whisper to the mind even amidst the shouts

---

* Mr. PERCEVAL's words and argument too, when he got nearly a million of money from Parliament, the other day, to maintain "the struggle" in Portugal.

of multitudes and the blasts of the trumpet, that there is *something* infinitely nobler than all this.

Thus there is not a day passing over our heads, in which we do not reap some solid advantage from the influence, however unacknowledged at the moment, of such men as Locke. We say to ourselves, when thinking — "This thing we see clearly," and we thank our education, or the improved state of society, for being able to see so clearly: — it was Locke who so much assisted that education and that improvement. We say to ourselves when thinking, "Thank God! nobody can deprive us of our freedom of opinion, or even dictate to us inquisitorially:" — it was Locke who asserted for us that freedom of opinion, that liberty of speech and conscience. We say to ourselves, when thinking, "France, by the help of weak opposers, has risen to a great pitch of worldly glory; but after all, the spirit of her society has not a particle of that independence which is still preserved in England:" — it was Locke, who in teaching us to distinguish false glory from true — it was Locke, and such men as himself, who, in teaching us to give up our mental liberty to no man, taught us to give up our personal liberty to no man; but to prefer even the consciousness of independence to a slavery however worshipful. — To such a man as Locke, therefore, every Englishman owes love and reverence, and not even Nelson himself, though he died on the waves bequeathing triumph to his countrymen, deserves a more glorious acknowledgment of their gratitude, than he who, dying in solitude and in silence, with no glories about him but the anticipation of heaven and the meek sublimity of departing virtue, bequeathed to his countrymen the love of what is rational.

I know nothing of the persons who have set on foot this laudable subscription; but there is no reason to doubt their motives, and there is every reason to admire and recommend their undertaking. What I have said on this subject is owing from me as a public writer, and as one to whom, in the midst of political bustle and political follies, the very thought of Locke is as refreshing as it is useful. Much more might be said on such a subject, and infinitely better: but those who think and feel as Englishmen should, it will be sufficient to have *reminded* of their illustrious countryman, and to those who do not, declamation would be equally as useless on my part as it would be unworthy of the subject. Let us be wrought up to enthusiasm — let our faculties be artificially roused by "pomp and circumstance," when we would admire the slaughterers and enslavers of mankind: — it is upon the strength of our reason only — upon the calm strength of reason and gratitude — that we should pay unadultered homage to their preservers and deliverers.

CONTINENTAL PRINCES

September 23, 1810

Some time ago a Nobleman rose up in the House of Lords, and with a pettiness little expected from a man of his Lordship's connexions, views, and accomplishments, expressed great indignation at seeing the Crowned Heads of the Continent treated with disrespect in the newspapers.[1] Whether or not his Lordship principally alluded to this paper, which had expressed much indignation of an opposite kind, I cannot determine; but certain it is, that incalculable mischief has arisen from paying those Crowned Heads too much respect; and a journalist should be anxious to save his countrymen, first from the vice of praising folly and exciting its drivelling efforts, and second from the mortification of being compelled to revoke these praises or the shame of continuing them against conviction. The above noble lord may have been, for aught I know, at the old court of Spain, and may have suffered his faculties to be overwhelmed by some smirking attentions from a personage infinitely less respectable than himself; but why should we like imbecility, because we disapprove ambition? Why should we set up a kind of opposition homage to folly and worn-out despotism, because our enemy is a man of talents and a formidable despot? Persons, who give in to these errors, naturally fall into all sorts of inconsistencies. They denounce one tyrant because he reigns over Frenchmen, and flatter another because he happens to be a Russian; they lament the downfall of the Pope, and abuse the Irish for being of his communion; they talk of the necessity of men of talents in office, and stir up the continental dotards against France; and they execrate Bonaparte as an usurper with the very same lips which blessed and encouraged the Empress Catherine when she made a shew of resisting the French armies! In all this there is neither virtue nor policy. Follies

and crimes do not become amiable or odious as they attach
to this or that person: wherever they are, and whatever shape
they wear, they injure the cause of sound freedom, and it
becomes an Englishman not only to oppose them when
acknowledged enemies, but to *discountenance* them, by every
means in his power, when pretended friends. To denounce
the ambition of Bonaparte is perfectly rational, is just and
patriotic, nay is absolutely incumbent on all who would prove
their respect for virtue; but then, it is quite as just and as
necessary to denounce the follies and vices of those who give
this ambition its opportunities, — who prepared the Continent
for its last blow, and who would nevertheless still claim our
sympathy and good word. Half the miseries of the Continent
are owing to bad Ministers; and from what do bad Ministers
arise but from foolish Kings?

When Bonaparte began to develop his ambitious plans
against Europe, the state of continental Royalty was truly
deplorable. From North to South, the crowns were upon heads
manifestly unfit to wear them. It seemed as if Providence
itself had smitten them with prophetic weakness; or as if, by
intermarriages and hereditary infirmity, the whole race was
debased and exhausted. In Russia reigned a lunatic,[2] who
belaboured people with his own hands for not saluting him
and for wearing a round hat; the King of Denmark[3] was an
idiot; the King of Sweden[4] exhibited, to say the least of it,
marks of a very fantastic mind; the German Emperor and the
King of Prussia were men of flat mediocrity, — and the petty
Princes of Germany, with the exception perhaps of the Elector
of Bavaria,[5] fondly wrapped themselves up in that little self-
sufficiency so peculiar to their rank and nation; the Pope was
as weak in mind as in power; the Queen of Portugal was a
lunatic, and her Son the Regent[6] a devotee; the King of Spain
was a dotard despised even by the loyal Spaniards; and to
sum up this appalling list, the King of Naples, his brother,
spent his time in shooting partridges and contending with
watermen. Posterity will look back with astonishment to an
era so fatal and so unparalleled.

Of these Princes of the first class, two are since dead, two have been utterly despoiled of their influence, and five have been driven from their thrones; but amidst so many and such fearful warnings, have themselves or their successors shewn at any time a promise of better government, a dawning ray of intellect or of enlarged feeling indicative of better days? Not one, with the exception of the present King of Denmark, who remained neuter as long as he could. To the frantic Paul of Russia has succeeded the great boy Alexander, who is like a tawdry servant driving a huge unmanageable coach which threatens every minute to break down with him; * — the King of Sweden has been displaced to make way for an old man,[7] who quietly receives an heir from the French, and who will be displaced in his turn; — the German Emperor, encouraged into a succession of useless coalitions but never into one necessary piece of reform, sits peaceably down as the father-in-law of his enemy, and, according to the court-gazettes, takes an interest in his son's conquest of Spain; — the King of Prussia perhaps can no longer do any thing, if he would; — the Prince Regent of Portugal has gone to America to preserve what he can of superstition for the benefit of those who come after him; — the representatives of the King of Spain call out for liberty and enslave the press; — and King Ferdinand of Naples passes his time in mending fowling-pieces and in execrating the French for having interrupted his sports. †

* This Monarch, whom we call pusillanimous whenever he inclines towards the French, and magnanimous whenever he looks towards us, is vain of his person, the turns and graces of which he displays by every possible mode of attitude and tight clothes. It is said that when he presented himself before the French Emperor on the raft at Tilsit, Bonaparte exclaimed with a theatrical gesture of admiration, "The Belvidere Apollo." This piece of French policy, though likely enough to succeed, may well be doubted as uncharacteristic of Napoleon: but the story serves to shew the light in which the understanding of this magnanimous Russian is held.

† There are one or two characteristic stories of this Prince, with which the public may not be acquainted. The reader may rely upon them as coming from the most incontrovertible source. When his Majesty was driven from Naples, and had reached the coast of Sicily in safety, he bethought himself of certain near and dear friends who had been unfortunately left behind, and he commanded, with an agitation proportioned to the danger, that some person

It is as well to recall these things to mind now and then, lest Ministers should continue to deceive us about persons who still *struggle* against the subjugation of the Continent; and lest, at no great distance of time, they should demand the aid of our purses and persons in assisting some one of this lamentable list against *other* enemies in *another part of the globe*. Persons of the least unprejudiced reflection would imagine such dynasties should be suffered to expire when they will not mend; but in spite of all the miscries they have wilfully brought upon their subjects and upon their allies, there are people, who with as much ease as if they were taking boxes at a theatre, talk of securing places in America for Charles of Spain and his Son Ferdinand, and the *Edinburgh Review*[8] has given an opinion in favour of this melancholy drollery. What! Is it not enough that *one* Prince of the old bigoted stock is there already, and must we think of transplanting more bigotry, more folly and misfortune, into the New World, as if it had not suffered enough already? For pity's sake, let us give up these hopes, as barbarous as they are impossible, and let one part of the world at least escape the shackles of France. Legitimate stupidity will do it as little good as illegitimate ambition.

---

should go back instantly at the risk of his life and bring them over. These friends were his dogs and fowling pieces, which after much difficulty and hazard were brought away in triumph, and received with tears of exultation by their fond master. His Majesty, it is well known, has always been a great, though not a very magnanimous sportsman. He hunted the gentler quadrupeds with great spirit, and brought down pheasants with still greater eclat; but he had no great affection to any danger on such occasions. One day however he could not resist the temptation of hunting a new animal that had been procured for him, — the buffalo. After taking a few little precautions, such as choosing his station near a tree, and entrenching himself behind a *fence* over which he was to fire at the said buffalo, he boldly waited for the beast, which was gently driven by the spot; but whether the buffalo had a French cast of countenance, or the fence appeared not quite so snug as might be wished, certain it is, that his Majesty did neither more nor less than climb up with great vigour into the above-mentioned tree, from which, in due time, he was helped down by his attendants, saying at the same time to the English Ambassador, "Many persons, Chevalier, have a strange antipathy, you know, to particular animals, such as eats and badgers; but for my part, I *find* that my antipathy is to the buffalo!" What a glorious ally have we Englishmen! And what a formidable rival has Murat!

ON CERTAIN TERMS MAGNANIMOUSLY
APPLIED TO THE FRENCH RULER

September 30, 1810

There is no publication more desirable than a summary of Bonaparte's actions and character,[1] written by some well-informed and temperate person, who could abstract himself from the influence of the times, and regard his subject as a curiosity of which, like the researches of the antiquarian or the anatomist, his principal object would be to make a *report* for the public instructions. Such a production is by no means impossible, but it is hardly to be expected for two very simple reasons: first, because the persons most likely to have an unprejudiced judgment on the occasion are of a middle, plain thinking class, not likely to become authors; and second, because the whole remaining mass of society is at present too much interested in the subject. In times like these, every body almost is, one way or other, a politician; and the very circumstance that should induce people to an unprejudiced estimate of Bonaparte's character, disables them from attempting it. They all agree that it is necessary to have a thorough knowledge of him, and then they all proceed to fix on some individual parts of his character and represent each of them as the whole. Those who have suffered by his progress to empire are, of course, not likely to do him justice; on the other hand, those who see him punishing the persons they despise, are apt to give him too much credit; the blustering affect to undervalue him in order to get noticed themselves; the admirers of external character and imposing effect talk of nothing but his "glory"; the politicians who exalt the Percevals and Wellesleys profess to be shocked at his hypocrisy and ambition, while those who are shocked at hypocrisy and ambition are shocked at the Bonapartes, and at the Percevals and Wellesleys too; lastly, the timid and short-sighted turn away from his character as something which they are afraid to contemplate; and thus, between his gross admirers and his gross abusers, the people of this country remain in gaping ignorance of one of the very first things they ought to understand. It is in calm domestic circles only, where taste and virtue are the chief objects of study, and where the present times are regarded as nothing but a portion of future history, that the talents and vices of this man are properly appreciated.

But it is absolutely necessary, if ever we would come to any understanding of or *with* our formidable enemy, that we should get rid of certain prejudices respecting him, equally hurtful to sense and good policy. By this I do not mean that we should cease to decry his vices, under the notion that such proceedings may retard a peace or be visited upon, when it comes, by the Attorney-General; it becomes us, at all times, to shew our sense of what is wrong, but then it is equally becoming to shew an undeviating respect for what is right, and not to confound all the actions and qualities of an individual, because he is our enemy. When people talk of Bonaparte as an "usurper" and "upstart," they forget that a time may come when the courtiers will abuse such a cry as much as they now raise it, and when they will recommend perhaps the weak but well-meaning persons, who persist in it, to the notice of his Majesty's courts of law. Such a charge indeed, as I have just said, would be no argument against the truth or the propriety of any just rebuke of the French Emperor's proceedings; but it would serve very much to shew what mere words these accusations are, even in the mouths of those who repeat them most furiously; and in short, the accusations themselves are unworthy of any thinking person, for the one is, in point of application, untrue, and the other, on the same principle, ridiculous. If by the word "usurper," it is meant that Bonaparte has violated his promises to Holland, has undone the independence of Switzerland, and has seized Spain in a most iniquitous manner, the accusation is perfectly just; he is, in these respects, as gross an usurper, and still grosser, if you please, than ever the English were in India,

or the Bourbons in Spain before him; but applied as the term
is to his possession of the *French* throne, it is in point of fact,
untrue: he is no more the usurper of that throne than the
Princes of Brunswick have been the usurpers of the throne
of Great Britain; and what will be still more shocking perhaps
to the delicate ears of the courtiers is, that the House of
Napoleon had better original right to the Crown than half the
"legitimate" Houses on the Continent. Bonaparte's election
to the throne was by the most indisputable authority that a
Prince can shew for his royalty,— that of the people; it was
by means too of the most open kind of declaration they could
give, that of a subscription of names. It is in vain that our
weak politicians talk, on such an occasion, of popular unwillingness and forced submission; the Jacobites, who were
quite as silly, talked in the same manner at our Glorious
Revolution; and this argument is an edge tool which it would
always be better to let alone. We must look to circumstances
and to national character to judge of these events, and in so
looking we shall find that it was quite as natural for the fickle
and vain-glorious French to desire such an Emperor as it was
for the English to be pleased at the restoration of the Stuarts
after Cromwell, or to thrust out these very Stuarts in favour
of the Guelfs afterwards. It was undoubtedly a much nobler
action in the English people to place the House of Brunswick
on the throne, than it was in the French to establish that of
Napoleon; for the one was the result of a love of freedom,
and the other of a love of conquest and slavish glitter; but
that is the concern of the French themselves. They have been
vain-glorious; but their vain-glory, instead of making Bonaparte an usurper, has made him a *legitimate* Emperor.

The application of the word "upstart" to a man who has
fought his way into worldly greatness by toil and by talent,
is still more weak and absurd than the former. An upstart,
properly speaking, is one who has no superior quality to show
for his sudden elevation: vice does not make a man an upstart,
but want of talent, want of those qualities which tend to lift a
man above his fellows. Mr. Perceval, for instance, considered

as Prime-Minister, is an upstart; the proud and ignorant favourites of weak Princes are upstarts, such as the favourites of James the First in England, of King John in France, and of the late King Charles in Spain: John of Leyden,[2] the fanatical king of the Anabaptists, was an upstart; so were Perkin Warbeck[3] and similar impostors, and Didius Julianus,[4] who purchased a few hours' enjoyment of empire at Rome. But Napoleon, who has beaten down opposition and established a great military name, is no upstart: the famous Sforza[5] of Milan, who had been a peasant, was no upstart, for the same reason; neither was Hyder Aly,[6] who had been a common soldier and who was also an usurper; nor Catherine the First of Russia, who had been a maid-servant; nor Pope Sixtus the Fifth, who had kept hogs. Apply the language of these persons, who are shocked at seeing men of no birth upon thrones, to poetry or philosophy, and see how ridiculous it becomes. Who calls Pope an upstart in poetry because he was the son of a linen-draper, — or Horace, who was the son of a tax-gatherer, — or Shakespeare, who was born of a wool-stapler? There were persons, it is true, in France, who wondered that Molière, an actor, could be thought a great man; but the *old leaven* in this respect will go down no longer, and it becomes us to get rid altogether of a degrading jargon, which in the ignorant is one of the surest proofs of their ignorance, and in better informed minds is nothing but pride and *passion*. One of the first who began to shoot these little pellets of reproach at Bonaparte, was Mr. Pitt, whose father, like Bonaparte, had been a subaltern officer in the army; but I believe, we are all agreed, that Mr. Pitt would have done much better in putting Bonaparte down than in helping him up to a throne and then abusing him for taking it. — Ay — but, says Count Zenobio,[7] Bonaparte is the "son of a *petty* lawyer at Ajaccio." Well — it was unfortunate for the father then that he had so little business, or, in other words perhaps, it was fortunate for the Corsicans. The worthy Count is member of a body who, I believe, are the oldest nobility in Europe; but this very ancient and noble body, not one of whom, for aught we know, was guilty of being a lawyer's son, could not save Venice from subjugation, and from subjugation too, right or wrong, by this very limb of the law. The Count himself is obliged to confess, that the Venetian Government might have been wiser and stronger by throwing open its honours and offices to every deserving citizen, that is to say, in fact, to men of no birth as well as the rest, and of course to the sons of petty lawyers among the number. Would the Count have had any objection to see his country rescued and his estates preserved by one of these sons of lawyers? I think not; at any rate, if his aristocratical pride had prevailed for a moment over his generosity, and made him a little sullen and awkward on the occasion, he would have hardly used the words "son of a lawyer" as a term of reproach. All that need be said of the lawyers at present, is, that they and their connexions are very lucky at what is called getting on in the world, and that Europe bids fair to be governed by them. Bonaparte is the son of a lawyer; his brother Joseph was himself a lawyer; the Crown Prince of Sweden is the son of a lawyer; and the illustrious and ever-to-be-lamented existing Premier of England is a lawyer, nay, a very petty lawyer; but nobody would think of saying any thing about it, if he were any thing *besides*.

CHANCELLORSHIP OF THE UNIVERSITY
OF CAMBRIDGE

March 24, 1811

The connection between politics and literature[1] may well be doubted by those who are accustomed to regard the former in their common-place light of news and party-struggles, and who for more than thirty years have witnessed the utter neglect with which English Ministers have treated the latter. But no doubt was ever entertained on the subject by men of enlarged minds; and no such neglect was ever exhibited by intelligent rulers, whatever may have been their designs or opinions with regard to government in general. Augustus and Alfred, two men whom in point of principle it is almost a profanation of the latter to name together, equally understood the advantages of cultivating learning, the one patronizing it for ambition's sake, the other to render his people wise. Nothing can hinder a proper feeling in this matter but the "necessity" of some vile subserviency to the times, as in the case of Cromwell; or sheer bigotry and ignorance, as in that of the late Spanish Government; or a half-witted idea of politics in general, as we see every day in the conduct of our Ministers. But even these departures from what is wise and liberal betray an unconscious knowledge of the importance of what they avoid, — a sort of instinct which leads them to turn away from what is foreign to their natures and inimical to their designs. Thus power, however bigoted, has always been fond of meddling with the concerns of literature; for where its fears of self-detection have induced it to evince a contempt for learning, its jealousy of others has still been strong enough to make it interfere with it in some way, and endeavour to pollute the republic of letters by introducing into it the influence of courts. It is on this account, that the Newspaper Press, which is constantly before the eyes of

Ministers, and forms an obstacle which they can neither overlook nor despise, attracts the honour of their attention in preference to the more delicate and retired exercises of authorship. It is on this account, that the court has always claimed a jurisdiction over the theatres; that favour is always ready for those who will write, no matter how wretchedly, on the ministerial side of things; and that a particular earnestness is shewn, as in the late contest at Oxford, to maintain an influence in such offices and appointments, as in any degree whatever help to give a tone to the learning of the times, and to facilitate or hinder the pollution above-mentioned.

Our Imperial enemy, who as a leader gives us so many good lessons for adoption, and as a despot so many equally good ones for avoidance, is a complete instance of the use and abuse of patronage in matters of learning. The princely encouragement he shews to chemical and scientific enquiries, to the fine arts, and to ornamental literature, is worthy of the imitation of all governments; but nothing can more plainly shew the fears as well as the natural corruption of arbitrary power, than the slavery to which he has reduced the press in general,[2] and the aversion with which he regards free discussion of every kind, that is not within the limits of his own interest, and calculated to diffuse what he calls his glory. The wretch who is prepared to write in defence of all that he does, — of his tyranny at home and usurpation abroad, — is sure of his countenance; but no Frenchman dares to express a disagreement with the existing state of things, or to hint at the smallest amelioration in the condition of his subjects, that is displeasing to him. Such has been the case, as far as it is possible in a free country, whenever the rulers have been conscious of violating the people's rights, or of acting in any other manner so as to render them impatient of inquiry. What displayed, at once, the whole system of Bonaparte with regard to letters, was his famous Decree of 1798 for the organization of an Imperial University, or rather for the incorporation of all the Colleges and public teachers in the empire into one general body, immediately dependent on the Emperor. By these means, at one stroke of this mighty magician's sceptre, education and slavery were engrafted together all over his empire; and wherever the former springs up, the latter clings round it, to check its growth and poison its productions.

Such a proceeding appears monstrous in the eyes of Englishmen; and long may it be deemed so! But as power, of whatever kind, has a perpetual tendency to encroachment, — as the corruption of our institutions appears to many persons to lead towards despotism, — and as we have daily proof in the neighbour country that the enslavement of men's persons can only be attained and secured by the subjection of their understandings, — there is no jealousy more incumbent upon us all than that which regards the introduction of court influence into the places of education. In most places of the kind there is quite enough already, in consequence of their charters, governors, and public patrons; or where these do not exist, from the natural love of pedagogues for arbitrary power, and the great body of expectant clergy, who have the chief hand in tuition. This is particularly the case with our two Universities, where though there are numbers of liberal men in every class, yet court-influence is predominant to a degree utterly incompatible with the native freedom of literature, setting aside even the frivolous distinctions of worldly rank, the gold tassels, honorary degrees, and all the other petty absurdities so *unconstitutional* in the *republic of letters*. If this influence was used only to encourage a proper spirit of enquiry; — if it rewarded only the meritorious in learning, and set its face against none but the dull and the disorderly, it could well excuse itself, however we might be alarmed at its progress; but it is not the nature of such influence to promote freedom of any kind: it lives upon subserviency; and subserviency therefore is what it desires in preference to every other species of recommendation. Thus the same feeling, which originally forbade the reading of Locke's Works at College, has occupied itself of late years in discountenancing Anti-Pittites and Reformists. Both the Universities are represented in Parliament by men in office; and the influence of one or two great families is notorious: indeed it is never mentioned without indignation by such of its members as have a proper respect either for rational freedom or real learning, and wish to see the highest offices and preferments beyond the reach of bowing courtiers, and dignitaries who are great in nothing but gout.

The Chancellorship, (I shall not stop to enquire how reasonably) is an office confined to men of rank; and is generally bestowed upon such as are of political consequence in the state. There is seldom much choice therefore between two persons who start for its attainment, unless one of them *happens* to be a learned man, or a patron of the liberal arts; and then the hesitation cannot be great in the minds of those who are not immediately under court influence. In the late contest at Oxford, the candidates, though of different parties, were both of what are called *high* state principles, that is to say, staunch aristocrats, and defenders of influence; so that court-feeling, in the abstract, had nothing to lose by the success of either: yet the election of Lord Grenville[3] was thought a singular and almost unaccountable triumph, inasmuch as he was in opposition and a friend to Catholic emancipation. The death of the Duke of Grafton * has occasioned a vacancy in the Chancellorship of the other University; and two candidates have started, who though very different from

* This nobleman, [Augustus Henry Fitzroy, third Duke of Grafton (1735-1811)] who made such a figure in the early part of the present reign as a placeman and man of pleasure, passed the latter part of his life unnoticed; and his death has scarcely called up an observation from the Newspapers. Sic transit gloria mundi! So pass away men of the world! — Unluckily for his Grace, however, he is still to be found in the pages of Junius. — It was curious, though certainly it could not be reasonably censured by the most orthodox churchman, to see the Chancellor of the University of Cambridge going on Sunday to the *Unitarian* Chapel in Essex-street. The regular clergymen might have wished that his Grace had been a little less scrupulous in his arithmetic; but his choice of the sect was at any rate a proof [of] his conscientiousness; and every good Christian must have contemplated with pleasure so great a change in his Grace's life. — The Duke, I believe, did nothing remarkable in his collegiate office, in spite of the poetical anticipations of Gray, who in the Ode on his Grace's installation, seems to have descended a little from that elevation of mind which he affected respecting kings and nobles.

the two just mentioned both in habit and influence, have yet a similar agreement with regard to the general qualifications for the office; that is, they are both highly connected, one of them prepared to think every thing ministerial excellent, and the other, though not thinking so, very far from a connection with what are called the dangerous innovators of the day. The contest therefore is expected to be a sharp one, *solely* because one of them is ministerial, and the other is not: whereas those who think that intelligence and public spirit have any thing to do with the matter, treat the distinction with contempt; and hesitate not a moment in making their choice. The ministerial claimant is the Duke of Rutland;[4] and the grounds on which he anticipates success, are too curious to be abridged from his own words. The following letter from his Grace to the Vice-Chancellor was read in the Senate-House at Cambridge on the 15th instant: —

Belvoir Castle, 6th March.

SIR. — Having heard that the Duke of Grafton is in such a dangerous state of health as to preclude any hope of his recovery, it becomes, therefore, my duty, and I trust that I shall stand excused in your sight for the presumption of my expectations, to notify to you my intention of becoming a candidate for the dignified and distinguished office in your University, which will be vacated by the lamented event of his Grace's death.

I will not, because I cannot, look for foundation to my pretentions in any individual merits of my own; but I ask permission to state, as a circumstance of no trivial importance and gratification to me, my belief that *his Majesty* has been graciously pleased to express himself favourably to my cause; and I have the additional pleasure of receiving the warmest assurances of support from the *Chancellor of the Exchequer, Mr. Perceval.*

I will no further intrude upon you at this present moment, than to request that you will make *such use* of this letter, and of the facts alluded to in it, as may appear adviseable to you, — I have the honour to be, with the greatest respect, Sir, your most obedient and humble servant,

RUTLAND.

The very Rev. the Vice Chancellor.

This curious epistle, of which, it is to lamented, the folly is not so great as the indecency, produced one of same subject from the other candidate, the Duke of Gloucester,[5] who writes as follows: —

March 15th, 1811.

SIR — As my wishes in respect to the Chancellorship of the University have been long and generally known, I should have thought it unneccessary, and perhaps indelicate, to have expressed them formally to you, as Vice Chancellor, before the expected vacancy had taken place. Having learned, however, that another person has officially declared himself a candidate, and even assigned reasons which induce him to hope that the University will support him, and many members of the Senate having solicited me to make a public declaration of my sentiments, I am apprehensive that my silence, if longer continued, might be construed into disrespect.

I will now, therefore, express the very high gratification I should feel at seeing myself chosen to fill the office of Chancellor; if the Senate should think proper to confer upon me a charge that must be so truly flattering to one who was educated at Cambridge, and who feels so warmly attached to the University.

I ground not my pretensions upon the influence of any man, however exalted his rank or character. I ground my pretensions upon my exclusive and unalterable attachment to the place of my education; being the only one of the Royal Family who has studied in an English University.

I should take peculiar pride in promoting the interests of that Body to which I have the honour to belong; and I trust that the unvaried deference to your laws and discipline, which I paid during my residence at Cambridge, will be an earnest of my endeavours to maintain your privileges, if entrusted to me as your Chancellor, — I am, with the highest esteem, and great personal regard, Sir, very sincerely yours,

WILLIAM FREDERICK.

To the Right Worshipful the Vice Chancellor
   of the University of Cambridge.

From these two letters alone, a rational and liberal mind could easily make its choice between the candidates: and indeed there is no light in which they can be viewed together that does not strike forcibly on the superior pretensions of the latter. The first questions an elector puts to himself on such occasions are, Who are these two men? How, and by what, do I know them? For what are they known in general? — To answer these very simple questions with regard to the Duke of Rutland, would be no easy matter even for persons well acquainted with men and things in general. It is true, the Cambridge people know his Grace better than we in London, who are absorbed in politics; but for what do they know him? For his having distinguished himself at his college? or for his notice of others who distinguished themselves? or for his patronage of learning and taste in general? Not a jot of it. They know him as a Duke, as a "ministerial man," as a relation of the Archbishop of Canterbury, as the Recorder of Cambridge, as having great interest in the county, and, I dare say, as possessing real talents for a pursuit in which he is most ambitious of shining, the pursuit of hares and pheasants. So peculiar a feature does this form in his character, that when enquiring persons look into lists of our nobility to see what valuable leaders they possess in these perilous times, they find his Grace immortalized in the Biographical Peerage under these terms, "He takes no active part in politics; but is fond of the sports of the field ." To prove however that though he takes no active part in politics, he takes as laudable a one as he can, his Grace assures us that he has the good word of his Majesty, and has even a warm corner in the heart of Mr. Perceval: and these merits, in the absence of all others, he thinks quite sufficient in the eyes of scholars and divines to make him the head of an English University! His Grace may be in the right; but to persons, who look on without having any interest in the contest, such ideas of the grounds of qualification appear the grossest of all insults, and an aspersion on the character of the University, which nothing but their rejection of him can wipe away.

On the other hand, the Duke of Gloucester is universally known, I believe, out of the immediate sphere of the placemen, universally mentioned with respect. He is known and respected, as a Prince without the usual follies of our living Princes: his excellent conduct when at the University is acknowledged by every body there: — though of the Blood Royal, his politics are independent: if we hear nothing particular of his acquirements as a scholar, he has the next best merit that should recommend him to the honours of learning, an attachment to the arts in general, and particularly to the Fine Arts, of which he is an active encourager; and lastly, his name will be handed down to the respect of posterity, as a member of that noble Institution, and an assistant of those illustrious individuals, by whose exertions Africa has been pronounced free, and an era been marked out for humanity and liberty in an age of bloodshed and subjugation. His Highness might have referred to circumstances like this with much more propriety than his opponent has referred to the favourable opinions of a disordered understanding and an interested Minister: but he chose to act with a spirit becoming his dignity and his pretensions; and to those who are not aware of the influence which is possessed by property in the country, backed by servility to the Minister, it is not easy to conceive how a person, so insignificant in every other respect as the Duke of Rutland, can stand for a moment against the exemplary conduct and enlarged spirit of the Duke of Gloucester.

To his Highness indeed no objection appears to be started, even by those who are friendly to his opponent; and perhaps none can be found, except that they differ with him in politics. The Duke of Rutland, on the contrary, is objectionable in every view of his pretensions, out of the county and in it; — out of it, because he has no character but that of a sportsman; and in it, because he and his family have already great influence there, an influence which it is on no good account desirable to increase. The University of Cambridge has been accustomed to claim a superior spirit of liberality over that of Oxford, perhaps with truth; but if it elect the Duke of Rutland on this occasion, the superiority will hardly be boasted any longer, since Oxford has had the merit of preferring a scholar out of place to a maudlin politician in. His Grace, however, by his great bustle on the occasion, and the visit which he paid to Cambridge the other day, is evidently, alarmed for the event; and it is trusted, that the various manifestations which he has made of his anxiety, in ways certainly very far from what is dignified or delicate, will have their proper effect on the Members of the University, — an effect, not intended by himself, but naturally resulting from his own conduct, and equally to be expected from the learning, the liberality, the respectability and the *self-respect* of that celebrated body.

BONAPARTE, – HIS PRESENT ASPECT AND CHARACTER

September 1, 1811

An occasional glance at the existing circumstances of this extraordinary person[1] always produces just matter of curiosity: and it is a curiosity, which, under proper direction, will always afford us an instructive lesson. In spite of the moral indignation with which countries, suffering under a state of warfare, cry out against ambition and lust of conquest, there is a secret admiration which most men entertain for rank however obtained, and authority however exercised. It arises from a false estimate of *power*, abstractedly considered. The majority of mankind, in their ignorance and weakness, are struck with a consciousness of their own inferiority in proportion as the superiority of a fellow-creature is manifested to their senses, or in proportion as the idea of him is palpable to their grosser fancies, and presents a certain hugeness of image which their coarse vision cannot possibly miss. This is the secret of all common admiration and worldly glory, from the rope-ring of the boxer, who fells his man, to the boundless sphere of the conqueror, who overthrows nations. It is not utility, or wisdom, or the practical wisdom of virtue, that obtains the praise; these are qualities above the estimation of common minds: – it is power, – it is, in fact, sheer physical strength, however decorated or disguised, – the sheer power of bending the necks and scaring the wits of mankind. It is this infatuation which pollutes and keeps miserable all human systems, – which perpetuates the love of war, which has set conquerors and kings by the side of the poet and the philosopher, not only in books and monuments, but in the general feelings; and in fine, which has made religion a thing of earthly mould, and subjected us to the awful reproach of making God in our own image. For one man who appreciates an Alfred, there are

millions who worship an Alexander: — for one man who esti-
mates the power of a calm and peaceable wisdom, which
works on the immortal part of mankind and silently effects
the mighty changes of opinion, there are millions who with
slavish spirits adore the visible strength of arms and grow
enamoured of the pride and glitter of the serpents that destroy
them: — and as man is worshipped, so is the divinity worshipped, — *more* for his power than for any other attribute that
he possesses, as the devotional exercises of all nations most
abundantly and most disgustingly testify.

It is of great use therefore to take every opportunity of
looking into the familiar lives and probable feelings of the
great disturbers of mankind, in order that we may see how far
they merit our real praise, and how far they are recompensed
by their own hearts for the pains they take to astonish us.
Those writers among us, who undertake in common to despise
Bonaparte, and to inveigh against his ambition and contempt
of blood-shed, are unfortunately not the persons to persuade
us, either by the dignity of their tone or the consistency of
their principles. The denouncers of low birth, &c. forget that
they are insulting a great and perhaps meritorious portion of
their readers, and at the same time doing no credit to the high
birth and the greatness it has displaced; — and the defenders
of Indian ambition[2] and Irish despotism must impose upon
sorry minds indeed, if they are regarded in any other light
than as hating the *enemy* instead of his *vices*.

The seizure of the Spanish crown, an act as impolitic as it
was wicked, and accompanied with circumstances of such
despicable perfidy, was followed by events which seem to
have wrought a double change in the general idea of Bonaparte; it has given him the air of a baffled conqueror, and
what is more singular, of an indolent one, — of one that will
try every means of repairing his losses, before he ventures,
as he used to do, upon the experiment in person. General
Sarrazin,[3] in attempting to account for this new appearance
in his character, accuses him of uxoriousness; and though the
authority is no very respectable one, the charge is not im-

probable. The new Empress, young, blooming, and of an origin flattering to his ambition, may have all the charms of a Cleopatra in his eyes, after the matronly mediocrity of her predecessor; the birth of a son has diminished his anxiety respecting the stability of his throne; and with his domestic ties he may have acquired a love of enjoyment, the more dangerous from its contrast with his former toils. What adds to the probability of these suppositions is, that he has settled into a plumpness little less than corpulent, though mere inaction may produce such an effect upon persons inclined to that habit of body. With his flesh, however, he has certainly not increased in the usual good humour attributed to persons of his size, since it is agreed by all who have known any thing of his private manners, whether enemies or friends, that his temper is still impatient and liable to the most undignified starts of anger. It is curious, indeed, as a contradiction to what is said of fat people in general, that the great tyrants of old, the Tiberiuses, Neros, and Domitians, have had bulky and gluttonous appearances. But truth lies as usual in the middle. Health, which produces, or at least ought to produce, even spirits, supposes a proper degree of roundness in flesh; but sheer fat, about which we often see people strangely solicitous, is generally sheer disease, the effect of indolence or repletion, or a constitutional tendency hitherto unexplained. There was a wild story a little time back, which attributed the disgrace of Fouché,[4] the French Minister of Police, to his having told Bonaparte that the Parisians accused him of growing like Nero in face and person. It originated, no doubt, with those inventive Antigallicans among us, who forget that they alternately represent the French as not daring to say a word and daring to say every thing. But it seems to be well ascertained, that Bonaparte's aspect has by no means improved of late, as far as the qualities of his mind may be supposed to have affected it. I saw a head of him the other day, sketched from memory by a French artist who was visiting this country, and who has long been familiar with his face. The artist thought it a good likeness himself, and as he was not deficient in

veneration for the original, it may be supposed that he did
not make it worse than it really is. Nevertheless, there is altogether a revolting character about it, which would not be
expected after seeing the prints of him in London, and which
certainly reminds one of the old tyrants above-mentioned, as
they are seen to this day in gems and busts. The forehead is
good, but by no means of the highest character of thought;
the eye is sunken; the nose more inclined over his lip than has
been represented; the mouth puffy and proud; the jaw and
the neck bulky; the head compact and sturdy; the hair, which
is said to be falling off at top and thickening about the sides
and back, agreeable to that representation, spare and strag-
gling above his forehead, short and mossy, for the remainder.
Upon the whole, the character of the head is stubborn resolution, and not the resolution of good conscience or of considerate wisdom: it has no fine human expression, such as
would take the admiration of high minds: – it seems like the
bull's, made to go sturdily through all opposition: its superiority, such as it is, is made up of an artificial disdain that defies
the opinion of the wise and good, not of a wisdom or goodness
that is above the opinion of the disdainful.

Without recurring, however, to his face for evidence against
him, nothing can be wanting to shew that his enjoyments,
be what they may, have not softened his disposition, and
therefore not added to his heartfelt happiness, after we have
witnessed the additional features of barbarity lately given to
the war in Spain. A luxurious life, so far from begetting benevolence, notoriously renders people selfish, and a new or
unexpected interruption of its enjoyments, is too apt to produce resentment instead of reflection. Bonaparte is informed,
on all sides, that his subjugation of Spain proceeds with
terrible difficulty: his brother makes a hazardous journey,
apparently for the purpose of impressing on him the obnoxious
truth: and what is the consequence? Does the valour of the
Spanish commonalty strike him with a single good impulse?
Does their patriotism the least fall in with his notions of the
great and dignified? Does he, in the bosom of his family, and

in the midst of his new sensations as a father, feel the glimpse
of an emotion in behalf of the families he is rendering miserable, and the domestic ties he has cut asunder? Not he: – his
passion rises; his pride is rendered doubly malignant by
mortification; and from the bosom of his family, this fond
husband and father wages a new war of extermination with
women and with children! It would be self-mockery in anyone of decent principles to ask his heart whether such a man
can be happy. He may be flattered from morning till night;
– he may be "covered with glory," as his people term it; –
he may sophisticate to himself as much as possible respecting
the motives and efforts of his actions; he may be served, like
a magician, with hands starting from every corner, and slavish
spirits trembling at every call; – in short, he may repeat to
himself a thousand times a day, "what a tremendous person
am I thought!" – for such is the amount of this military glory;
– but his enjoyments, let him attempt to gloss them over
never so much to himself, or wear never so lofty a countenance
to the world, are no more to be compared with those of wise,
peaceable, and conscientious men, than the laughter of delir-
ium is with the complacency of health and reason. One year
of the reign of an Alfred, – one year of the Administration of
a L'Hospital,[5] – nay, the very dying hour of a Locke or a
Newton, is worth whole careers of these brilliant madmen,
who live only to destroy life, and are wise only to the per-
petuation of error.

That there are still remaining any reflecting men, who can
think well of Napoleon's intentions, may well surprise all those
who do not consider the obstinacy of pre-conceived opinion,
and the fatality with which ardent men are led into likings
and dislikings by certain narrow views of contrast. It may be
fairly assumed, however, that among these lingering advocates
of a bad cause are to be found neither our most philosophic
thinkers, nor our highest geniuses, nor certainly our men of
loftiest principle. The latter, who in this country, thank God,
have generally included the two former classes, may be truly
said to look down upon the man, notwithstanding his eleva-

tion; nay, I have no doubt there are many persons of much inferior pretension, who, when they consider all the real fame and happiness he has forfeited, and the miseries for which he is responsible, do literally regard him with *pity*. – See to what these mighty conquerors reduce themselves among those who are the only true bestowers of glory! See from what a a class of suffrages, – from what a description of panegyrists, the ambition of such a man as Bonaparte is at once cut off! He imposes upon the vulgar part of mankind, high as well as low, but he does not impose upon these: he gathers round him all the vain-glory, that arms can procure him, that slaves can bestow, and that the prostituted arts can adorn; but upon these he makes no such impression, from these he obtains no such applause; he cannot enter their sphere; his glory durst not venture within that hallowed circle; and if he is the first of all bad men now existing, he must be conscious that there are a set of men and of minds, whom he is as far beneath as noise is beneath music, or earth beneath heaven. That England presents among her poets, her philosophers, and her statesmen, spirits of this stamp, who baffle the rivalry of a worse ambition, is a real glory on her side, that can be no secret to the warrior and his slaves; and the blessings, which in spite of her corrupted institutes she has conferred and is now conferring upon mankind, will command the admiration and gratitude of posterity, when all his wretched splendour is put out, –

> When all
> For which the tyrant of these abject times
> Hath given his honourable name on earth,
> His nights of innocent sleep, his hopes of heav'n;
> When all his triumphs and his deeds of blood,
> The fretful changes of his fev'rish pride,
> His midnight murders and perfidious plots,
> Are but a tale of years so long gone by,
> That they who read distrust the hideous truth,
> Willing to let a charitable doubt
> Abate their horror.

SOUTHEY.

THE LATE MR. HORNE TOOKE

April 5, 1812

After some little consideration of what I intended to write on this extraordinary person,[1] I find it impossible to bring any detailed account of him within reasonable *hebdomedal* bounds, — at least, with that proper accompaniment of remark, which would be due to a right estimation of the times and circumstances in which he has lived. What I have to say, therefore, will rather be the result of an enquiry into his character, than the enquiry itself; and as this kind of summary involves a good deal of assertion on the part of the writer, the *Examiner* will be more particularly open to such of its Correspondents as may think fit to make their remarks on the subject.

It is a perpetual and striking lesson respecting the bad choice which present times almost always make of their leading characters, to observe with what indifference they regard the decease of men who are destined to be the talk of posterity, while the every day proceedings, much more the last moments of any common-place politician, whom they have suffered to be of importance in the State, afford matter of gaping interest to the whole nation, and flatter the poor creatures of the day into a ridiculous expectation of future celebrity. When Milton died, nobody took notice of the circumstance, because the eyes of the people were occupied in watching the politics of a despicable set of beings, who now exist only in the annals of courtiers and demireps. Columbus, whose glory is present to all eyes, with one foot on the Eastern and one on the Western hemisphere, died at a silent distance from the miserable court which had wronged him, and which would have almost ceased to be mentioned but for his connexion with it. Nay, the very names of the persecutors of Socrates, who were in possession, no doubt, of all the talk of their day, are now to be found but in his story. I have no intention of comparing the object of the present paper with these illustrious men, who are some of the very greatest of names for genius and virtue; but in proportion to his merits, he has enjoyed the honour of the usual want of attention in the article of death, and while column after column is wasted away in the public Journals upon the Dukes of Grafton[2] and Portland,[3] a solitary notice from each is reckoned sufficient for one of the acutest politicians of his age, and perhaps the first philologist of his nation.

A man of Mr. Horne Tooke's intellectual rank in society will present himself to future biographers in three points of view, — as a politician, a man of letters, and a private example. It is in the first light that his character assumes most interest at present; and an appreciation of it perhaps is not very difficult to those who wish to be, and can be, impartial. To act up then to the judicial brevity above-mentioned, and state my conclusions at once, — his political character seems to be that of a wrong spirit on a right side of thinking. I say a right side of thinking, not so much upon Swift's canon of criticism, — that every body who thought as he did must be in the right, — but because I assume as a general maxim, that all those who thoroughly value and understand the English Constitution, however they may differ upon present contingencies, are agreed that the true way to preserve it is to prevent as much as possible its departure from first principles; — and I say a wrong spirit, not because I doubt his sincerity upon the great cause which he professed to advocate, but because I do doubt his sincerity or strait-forward conduct upon subordinate points affecting his means of assisting it, and cannot but rank him among those polluted intellects, who, when they think themselves most wise in using a crooked policy for the furtherance of a good object, not only hazard the success of their cause by rendering a detection of their management injurious to its reputation, but disgust the single-minded who are of their side of the question, and in losing sight of the wisdom and attraction of a high conscientiousness, render their very talents a folly and a curse. I shall have occasion, in the course of this

Article, to notice a feature of Mr. Tooke's private history, which might even go near to contradict his sincerity in every ostensible measure of his life; but not to be so uncharitable, or indeed so ill-informed upon human nature, as to make any peculiar frailty responsible for a conduct with which it is not immediately connected, I shall proceed to state briefly the grounds which appear to me to be conclusive both as to his general sincerity and his particular want of it.

With regard to the first, the single fact seems to be sufficient, that notwithstanding the ambitious and other worldly views laid to his charge, he inflexibly adhered to the same political opinions with which he set out in life, unterrified by the many dangers to which he exposed himself in their cause, and unseduced by the wealth and honours which were unquestionably in the reach of a man so gifted and active. The celebrated Junius, under a fit of impatience that he had separated from Wilkes,[4] and a mistaken impression that he had gone over to the Court, set him down at once for a Bishop; and though there might have been more of sarcasm than of intended prophecy in the conclusion, yet he evidently regarded him as a man who might always make his own terms with a Ministry. What he was in those times, he continued to his dying day, — a strenuous and undaunted advocate for Parliamentary Reform, for a check to the increase of power in the Crown, for the individual and minutest rights of the subject, — in a word, for the reduction of the Constitution to its first and simplest principles, as the only method of purifying the system of government and giving a new lease to the existence of the nation. If in the course of his exertions to this end, he once adopted a line of action that rendered his loyalty to the Executive Power a matter of doubt, yet granting even that the suspicion was well founded, and that he would have overturned the government as it then stood, it does not follow, however paradoxical the assertion may appear to weak minds, that he did not continue sincere in his constitutional professions. The wish to alter an existing government argues nothing against a man, of itself: — its propriety or impropriety, its patriotism or traitorousness, depend, like virtue and vice, upon the principles on which it proceeds and the effects it is calculated to produce; and the Englishman, if there be such an Englishman, who would maintain otherwise, would advocate the cause of tyranny in general, and be disloyal to the Brunswick Succession in particular. It may have appeared to Mr. Horne Tooke that the encroachments on the part of the Crown and its advisers had brought about the period when, according to a phrase in his answers to Junius, the conduct of the Executive "justified rebellion"; and he might have thought the Constitution recoverable by no other means. If he did not think so, the *Examiner,* for one, thinks he was egregiously and alarmingly in the wrong, and that he confounded the bad effects of aristocratical carelessness and corruption with the faults of the ruling powers. To restore the Constitution to its fit state of health, the people must unite, not against any one individual or set of individuals, but against the jealousies and corruptions that split their own powers asunder, and render the State liable to be abused by individuals. In former times the personal influence of Kings was dangerous from particular circumstances of civil and religious opinion; but under the present Family, the Aristocracy and Democracy of the country ought to despise themselves to the heart's core, if they cannot resist encroachment on the part of the Executive. It is with them alone to regulate the lesser body by the greater: it is for them alone to touch calmly but powerfully the loud note of reformation; for them alone to restore harmony in the State by clearing their own spheres from obstruction, and striking again into the majestic music of a willing union.

Of Mr. Horne Tooke's insincerity in particular, that is to say, of his condescension to appearances which he privately contradicted, and of the lax and shuffling policy which he occasionally pursued, the proof seems as clear as that of his sincerity in the main. It is to be recollected, that when he set out in public life, he was a Clergyman and held a living; and of course, the least that was to be expected of him, was an ostensible conduct consistent with what his situation professed; yet having sided with the just indignation of the people against the reign of favouritism and persecution that was then commencing, he began his career by fondly associating with Wilkes, a man whose utter want of principle made him dangerous in a good cause, and has since handed over his name, without obstruction, from popularity to infamy. It is true, he forsook Wilkes upon a closer acquaintance with the profligacy of his *politics,* but he must have already been intimate enough with his profligacy in every other respect; and what can be his feelings with regard to the means of action, who scruples not to violate the commonest decencies in their behalf? It was no doubt a conscious inconvenience on this point, added to private as well as public reasons of his own, that induced Mr. Horne Tooke to throw off the clerical character, — a proceeding which has been stigmatized as "indecent" and "impious"; but the indecency and impiety appear rather to have consisted in professing it at all, than in renouncing what he felt no wish to maintain. Unluckily, after rejecting the spiritual pretensions of the Divine, he did not put on the moral dignity of the philosopher. His manners were lax, his society unguarded and indiscriminate, and the general tone of his proceedings contemptuous of opinion. Such a man had no claim to tenderness of criticism; and the consequence was, that when he retired to private life, after his failure in attempting to sit in Parliament, he took with him, and retained ever afterwards, the character of a factious politician, who, though he had a right to the claim of consistency in the general scope of his politics, was in every thing else a mere man of the world, respectable for little but talent, and better to be out of the bustle than in it. It was a great pity, surrounded as he was in his retreat with his books and his friends, and seeing the purer part of his conduct (at least, I hope and trust the purer part), imitated by his favourite companion, that he again interfered personally with politics; but his private attachments conspired with his public opinions to make him impatient of the proceedings of Mr.

Paull,[5] one of the Candidates in a Westminster election; and engaging with that unfortunate adventurer in a paper quarrel, he stumbled upon a piece of meanness, that gave the latter a complete advantage over him, and at the same time converted the doubtful opinion, that still lingered in the minds of a number of persons, into a conviction of his unworthiness. In his pamphlet against this person, he accused him of intruding himself upon the parties at Wimbledon, — of coming there uninvited and undesired, and continuing his visits to a pitch of annoyance. Mr. Tooke even declares that he had a dislike to the man from the very sight of him, and always felt something within him that shuddered at being under the same roof with him — "sub isdem trabibus." What answer does Paull make to these humiliating accusations? He produces, in a counter pamphlet, letters written by Mr. Tooke himself, beginning with "Dear Sir," and containing a general, a friendly, and even earnest invitation to consider himself as possessing a knife and fork at his Sunday table. Mr. Tooke's character has no means of escaping from the effects of this last conviction. One way or other, he had told a direct falsehood to the public, mean, palpable, and malignant. Such did the public pronounce it, and such, and so pitiable, was the close of his public life.

It is fortunate for Mr. Tooke that he had merits of a distinct kind from those of public and political life, which will carry his name down with honour to posterity, and render him celebrated among thousands who will have little or no impression of him in any other shape: — I mean that profound skill in philology, which produced the celebrated grammatical work called the *Diversions of Purley*. The illustrious and infamous Bacon, (with whom however I have no intention of comparing Mr. Tooke either in lustre or bad repute) has a pathetic hope at the close of one of his glorious treatises, that his literary and philosophical renown will retrieve and perhaps do away his political character with posterity; and though it has not succeeded to this extent, yet Bacon is infinitely more known as a writer than a public man, as a miracle of knowledge, rather than as a creature of the Court and a monster of ingratitude. Milton, who in his own age was so little known to the world except as a politician, that Bayle, in concluding his article upon him,[6] merely hints at his being reckoned a great poet by his countrymen, is now scarcely any thing but the great poet, even in England; and inferior examples of literary reputation overcoming that of a different species, are innumerable. Mr. Tooke's will no doubt be as complete of its kind, though not so extensive, as that of poets and philosophers. — I have not room, — nor indeed a sufficient hold of the subject, — to discuss the merits of his performance in this place; but in justice to one of whom I have been speaking so severely in one respect, I cannot help risking the charge of impertinence by declaring myself one of its warmest, though not blindest, admirers, — one of the very many who, at first sight of it, bade adieu to the leaden *Hermes* of Mr. Harris,[7] to admire the more vivacious, engaging, and informing spirit of the *Epea Pieroenta*.[8]

The private life of Mr. Tooke appears to have been what might be guessed from his public one: bustling and somewhat loose in the former part of his career, — and with the exception of that unfortunate ebullition about Paull, peaceable and philosophic towards the close of it. He has left, I believe, two natural daughters; but it remains to be ascertained, whether they were born to him during his clerical situation: — if they were, his contempt for what he was professing is heavily encreased in the guilt of worldliness and hypocrisy. His society, which had never been select, continued to be very much the reverse to the day of his death; and whether it was owing to this circumstance, to the taint of early example, or to an affectation of speaking what he might call his mind, his conversation, though full of a wit and knowledge that should have taught it better, partook of the coarseness of sheer vulgarity. For the rest which I have heard of him, and in which I beg to be corrected if misinformed, he was accounted a good-tempered and social man, hospitable, unassuming, overflowing with information, careless of the morals as well as manners of those about him, and as old Cardan might have said in conclusion, — slovenly in his person and very temperate. The feelings, with which he professed to contemplate the approach of his last moments, are well known to the public, and were not belied by the event. He died like a philosopher, retaining his natural facetiousness to the last, repeating his gratitude for the blessings he had enjoyed in his existence, and expressing his confidence in the final happiness which the Deity must have intended for all his creatures.

To take leave of our subject in charity, let us hope and trust that a death so worthy of men of more perfect lives, and ideas of the Supreme Being so becoming a superior intellect, were accompanied by secret recollections of good, which infinitely surpassed the ill that we know of him. To die well or ill argues nothing in proof of right or wrong opinion, since there are happy and unhappy deaths among sects and systems of every denomination; but the former at least argues a conscious something, whether well or ill founded, superior to the conscious error that may accompany it; and it is not the worst thing to say of Mr. Horne Tooke, that the best feature in his eventful life was the close of it.

THE MANUFACTURERS

May 10, 1812

The lovers of war in this country have always been anxious to make us believe, that it has not tended to diminish our general comfort or internal prosperity.[1] The abhorrence of war, in the abstract, they have ridiculed as a childish folly, or at best agreed with it in a tone of indifference and then begun talking of necessity and natural enemies; but when you came to particulars, and doubted whether the continuance of so long and so losing a struggle would not materially affect our domestic interest, they fairly laughed in your face. What! said they; — have we not the commerce of the world in our hands, and can our manufactures ever want a market? — By degrees, this exclamation began to fail them, as port after port was shut against us;[2] and then came the doctrine of patriotic privations, — a very good one certainly, under proper circumstances, but far from being gracious or seductive when inculcated by six-bottle Ministers and plenitudinous Aldermen. In a short time, however, not a port was left us, and then we were requested to look at our own harbours, and see the shipping we possessed: — if you stated the number of families that were reduced, and the quantity of dependents thrown upon government influence, you were desired to notice the growth of the metropolis; and if you objected to the enormous increase of Bankrupts and to the multitude of persons getting into jail, you were begged, with a smile of pity, to look at the fine roads they had to walk in. At last, as the evils thicken upon us in proportion to the growth and continuance of their causes, comes positive want itself; and notwithstanding our wide-spreading metropolis, notwithstanding our fine roads, our canals, and our granaries, notwithstanding even the profusion of government contracts, and the sleek, persuasive condition in which the maintainers, brothers, and creatures of Ministers are delighted to find themselves, an important class of our countrymen are crying out for bread and employment, and an agonized insurrection is in the heart of our cities.[3]

The House of Commons is now making some inquiry into the necessities of these unfortunate people; and it is agreed on every side, that till something be resolved for their relief, it is at least incumbent upon all to shew a serious interest in their welfare, and not to say or do any thing that shall excite them to proceed to extremities. In pursuance therefore of our duty, as advocates of the same cause and same feelings in general with Sir Francis Burdett,[4] we cannot but deprecate and lament the very unwarrantable, useless, and pernicious violence with which he has spoken of the soldiers that have been called out on this melancholy occasion. We agree with Sir Francis, that weak and guilty rulers, who have reason to dread the bursts of popular feeling, are much too apt to make use of the military and to affect an anti-revolutionary parade with their cannon and drawn swords; we agree with him also, that the law has in general set its face against such appearances in a free state; and that whenever they do appear, they are much greater proofs of a bad government than of any thing else; — but there are times and occasions, in which, whatever may be the *first* cause of the misfortune, and however unattributable to the people, a *recourse* to military interference is absolutely and indispensably necessary for the commonest security of property and life; and the present occasion is one of them. There is no alternative: — either force must be threatened by force, or insurrection must do as it pleases; either a small and disciplined multitude must overawe a larger, or the latter must be left to all the caprices of an *unreasoning* resentment, and terrify, plunder, and destroy to no purpose but to make the case worse. The class, whose sufferings drive them to such extremities, are undoubtedly much to be pitied and much to be forgiven, — just as much as the prime authors of their afflictions ought to be execrated and called to account; but if it can once be proved, as it certainly is in this instance, that their violent proceedings are really as injurious to their own necessities as to the peace of their neighbours, it is but humanity to repress them by violence. Let us continue to speak then, as Englishmen ought, of servile Ministers and profligate Princes, since the spirit of resisting servility and vice is absolutely necessary to our existence as a nation, and these are matters at issue between the Court and the country at large, which must be canvassed for the general good in *spite* of small inconveniences; — but let us not go upon unwarrantable grounds and inflame an unreasoning resentment against measures of absolute necessity. We are very far from thinking, with some people, that Sir Francis Burdett is indebted to Mr. Horne Tooke for all that he has to think and to say; — he speaks, in general, too well and too readily for any such idle suspicion; — but certainly his late ebullition was no favourable specimen of his powers unadvised; and we cannot help suspecting that it would not have taken place, had he still been possessed of the society and experience of that older head.

There is another, however, and still more important view of this subject, which the objectors to Sir Francis' speech, in their anxiety to turn reproach off their own grounds, seem to have entirely overlooked; — and this is, the much greater perniciousness of *wrong doings* compared with *wrong words*. It was very well and profitable for the Chancellor of the Exchequer[5] to get up, and exclaim against the Baronet with horror in his hands and eyeballs, and very allowable in the persons about him to fall into an extatic outcry at finding so much danger to shudder at in a Reformist; but to say the least of it, it was very weak in Mr. Barham and others to make the wrong speeches of Sir Francis Burdett an excuse for going over to the wrong measures of Mr. Perceval:[6] and what is more, it is very impudent in the Corruptionists to lay claim to the feelings of better men and make such an uproar about what was *said* by another, at the very moment when they are *doing* all they can to waste the resources of the State, and to insult the wretchedness of their indigent countrymen by refusing

to retrench the grossest expenditures. — Amidst all the nonsense which these creatures utter about disaffection and mis-
representations, none of them will be ridiculous enough to
assert that the pressure of the times, the absolute want of
employment and bread, — can be owing to speeches: — no;
it originates with the authors and maintainers of a luckless,
an obstinate, and a deadening war; and therefore if any one
set of persons, more than another, ought to feel for the present
distresses, and abstain in action as well as word from adding
bitterness to the popular feeling, those persons are the dis-
ciples of Mr. Pitt, the aiders and abettors of his unfortunate
coalitions, the continuers and even depravers of his system,
the wasters of public credit and confidence, the destroyers
of commerce. Yet the Minister, who gets up to be horrified at
inflammatory speeches, the very Minister, so careful of the
public feeling, — this man, so disdainful of wrong excitements,
so moved in the very nobleness of his nature against all that
even sounds like a want of lofty propriety, bestows an idle
place on his brother of £30,000 a year, is a placeman himself
thrice over, is notoriously the greatest reversionist in the
kingdom, and defends sinecures and reversions, — the most
provoking perhaps of all corruptions, — with all his might, —
whenever there is an attempt to abolish them! What say the
abhorrers to this? Will they venture to tell us that the words
of an individual have more effect than the actions of a government? Not they, unless indeed, as they are used to barefaced
contradictions, they mean to tell us at the same time, that the
revolutions and falls of governments have been owing to idle
speeches instead of bad measures and long misbehaviour.
But if they will still talk of words above things, let them look
to their own side of the question, and hear what George Rose [7]
has to say about people drowning in buckets. We have no wish
to repeat the words in their gravity any more than those of
Sir Francis, for we really do consider them as extremely irritating to the public mind, and uselessly so; but the reader
recollects them, no doubt; — the Birmingham Deputies were
expressing themselves forcibly as to the hardships incurrable

from a dispute between this country and America, and the snug old soul, wishing to make them as resigned as himself to the perplexities of the nation, but at the same time having really nothing to say, worked himself up into a figure of speech, and began talking incontinently about a sinking match on the water.

> Our friend old GEORGY told, you know,
> A tale extremely apropos,
> Name the two states, — and like the c'rowners,
> He had a story of two drowners.

Really, as my Lord Ellenborough said the other day of an unfortunate witness, to the great amusement of the barristers, and indeed almost the convulsion of some of them, — "Such a man as this should not venture upon metaphor." — Oh! cries Mr. Perceval, — what my *Right Honourable Friend* says is quite another matter; I was present at that conversation and do not recollect his having used any such words; but "*even if they had been used,* I am certain they proceeded from no feelings of insensibility, *though it is easy for persons to avail themselves of them so as to make a mischievous impression.*" — Such is the candour, consistency, disinterestedness, and Heaven knows what else, of this transparent-souled Premier! And the reader, we think will want no more said on the subject. — For our parts, we give up the speeches of Mr. Rose and Sir Francis together; and as we do not care an atom what the former has to say in future, convinced as we are that he would rather have the Treasury padlock on his lips than utter any thing more of the kind, — so we earnestly hope that the latter will never again let his resentments get the better of his reason, but always act like a conscientious as well as intrepid Reformist, — be bold at the proper times, and discriminating at all times.

TO THE RIGHT HONOURABLE LORD ELLEN-BOROUGH, CHIEF JUSTICE OF THE COURT OF KING'S BENCH. ONE OF HIS MAJESTY'S PRIVY COUNCIL, &c. &c.

December 6, 1812

My Lord,[1] — I am sorry to disturb you at breakfast, but they who have representations to make to persons in office, naturally chuse a point of time, at which the faculties both of mind and body, according to the respective tastes of the possessors, are supposed to be most at their ease and best satisfied with the world about them; and if I am mistaken in the present instance, common report, and some little testimony on your Lordship's own part, of a nature which goes a good way with observers, must be my apology. At any rate, your Lordship will do justice to my generosity in wishing to find your natural temper as fortified as possible against the annoyance of a little unwelcome truth; and as a further proof of it, my language shall be as easy to you as I can make it, — no roughness, — no inversions, — no intricacies. Your Lordship, as we all know by your Charges, is fond of *a style*; and though I cannot promise to suit your taste altogether, not having practised, since I was a boy, those stilts of sentiment and plays upon a word, for which your Lordship has so natural an affection, yet at least I shall not offend your critical nicety, in other respects, nor move you to that uncomfortable though generous disdain of the illiterate, which renders you now and then so amiably ironical upon the witness-box. If what I am about to serve up to your Lordship be somewhat hard of digestion or provocative of fever, it shall at least be smooth to the tongue and spirited to the sense; and your Lordship knows very well, how much a true Epicurean should endure of after-uneasiness for so much of present enjoyment.

Your Lordship, I trust, will not suffer this good beginning between us to be unpleasantly interrupted, when I tell you that I am going to say a few words on the subject of Wednesday's Trial. — Pray, *my Lord,* be patient and sit still; — your dignity, to say nothing of the urn and the buttered toast, is endangered by these sudden impulses. — I am not going to threaten the Judge, or to prepossess the Jurors; still less is it my intention to enter into the merits of the case: all that we could say on that head will be much better said by our Advocate; and while we are in possession of his assistance and of our own minds, we have nothing to fear from the Bench, and no want of preparation for any thing that may come from the Jury. I merely wish to caution your Lordship against regarding your opinion on this subject, whatever it may be, as calculated to have the least weight with ourselves, — against considering yourself, in the smallest manner, as a person who either has, or ought to have, any judicial authority with us, or with others, particularly in a case like the present. In short, though the proceeding, I am aware, would not have been to our interest, yet for the sake of example, and in order to shew what are and should be the ideas of Englishmen on the real dignity of justice, we should most certainly, if time and situation had been convenient for us to look into the subject a little beforehand, have entered a direct Protest in Court against your Lordship's presidency on this occasion; and in default of our so doing, we put it upon record in this place.

My lord, we have more than once expressed ourselves on this subject; but we now shall do so at large, and enter into a thorough explanation, for your Lordship's benefit. I shall indeed be exceedingly explicit on the occasion, sufficiently so perhaps to enliven your Lordship's perusal of me into a curiosity somewhat professional. Let it be so, my Lord: examine me in your turn; and for this purpose, regard, if you please, the paper before you, as a comment in spirit, if not in letter, upon the approaching Trial, — as another Vindication of the great Censorial Right of the English Press, — another assert-ment of its authority over those moral particulars of Public Character, which lie out of the cognizance of the laws.

My Lord, it is upon two distinct grounds that we object to your fitness for the discharge of the judicial office; we object to it, firstly, inasmuch as you hold a situation under his Majesty incompatible with the nicer feelings of independence required in a Judge, — and secondly, inasmuch as you are in the habit of evincing that species of temper, which is familiarly termed passionate, and which is incompatible with the very nature of judgment.

With regard to the first of these points, — your Lordship's Seat in the Privy Council, — it is not at all necessary to enter upon it as a matter of dispute, of precedent, or of party. The very least that can be said of it is, that it was a most unusual appointment, and calculated to give very needless offence; but I have nothing to do with that part of the question; I may even waive observation on its unconstitutional spirit, which is the same indeed as its unphilosophical, and what I am going to mention: — it is sufficient for me, and ought to have been so for your Lordship, that by courting an honour of this kind, you shewed an eccentric and indecent ambition, without regard to the sphere in which you moved and the singleness that became it, and that by accepting such an honour, you went directly into the way of temptations, the very exposure to which, in a man of your Lordship's situation, is indecency itself. — I am aware of the indignant and sweeping reply which your impatience will repeat to itself at this passage; it will say, of course, that you know yourself too well, — that you understand the duties of a Judge, — that you are an honest man and a gentleman, — in short, that you are not to be tempted. Alas, my Lord, — without meaning to doubt your own good opinion, or even the justice of it to an ordinary extent, — how many well-intentioned persons, who have respectably commenced their career, have said all this to themselves, while they were gradually diverging from the right path, and giving themselves up to the attractions of a Court! Your Lordship is a scholar, and I need not quote to you stale

Latin sentences respecting the insensible growth of corruption; but their commonness is their truth; they describe the true features of human nature; all history, — the history of your own profession, my Lord, — abounds with portraits in illustration; and of all pieces of colouring, their gradation is the most wonderful and instructive. Not to dwell however on what your Lordship, in common with every sensible person, will be so willing to acknowledge in the abstract, — I shall be told another common-place truth in my turn, and be reminded that every rule has its exceptions. It has so; — the rules of self-love in particular consist of nothing but exceptions; but if your Lordship claim an exemption from the frailties of ordinary men, you are bound, even in modesty, to bring us some little proofs of your extraordinary philosophy, or in default of having yet been under the necessity of exerting it, the very least you can do is to convince us there are no proofs to the contrary. Now by what arguments, positive or negative, will your Lordship undertake to persuade us that you have wisely committed yourself to temptation? Shall we find them in your habits, public or private? Shall we find them in the tone of your politics? Shall we find them in your Lordship's increasing awefulness of presence, — in a countenance, my Lord, dilating with aristocratical enjoyment, — in a voice reminiscent of mouthful and burly with luxury? Or to drop this congenial style, — this plethoric roundness of period, — and come at once to the *facts*, will your Lordship venture to assure us that there has been no real change of late years in your character and opinions, — no difference between Mr. Law and Lord Ellenborough, — no change from the untitled advocate, who vindicated the general cause of independence and resisted the overbearing temper of his superiors, to the titled Judge, who is for promulgating the most aristocratical and unconstitutional opinions, and becoming proverbial for an overbearing temper of his own? If so, my Lord, (and I know there are many persons who say that there really *is* no difference), then the public will answer you, that they thought better of you than you deserved. When your Lordship first came to the bench, you affected to have a just recollection of the ungenerous treatment which advocates, especially the younger part of them, sometimes experience from the judge, and you promised, I believe, to set a proper example of encouraging and protecting them. Your promise has remained unredeemed; nay, it has been violated perhaps to an extent as great as you ever resisted in Lord Kenyon;[2] and in the earlier period of our application to the Gentlemen at the bar, we found we had to contend with an apprehension of petty interruptions from the Judge, equally injurious to the dignity of one party and the proper spirit of the other. This impatience and aristocracy of temper has accompanied your Lordship to another scene of action; and as a Peer, you give no more encouragement to the freedom of opinion and the vindication of personal right, than as a Judge. In that House, my Lord, the people have seen you setting your face against every species of liberal reformation; in that House, they have seen you impatiently rising to contradict every liberal authority quoted, and every generous effort made, to free the personal liberty of the subject from encroachment; and to give an instance, which will supersede at once the necessity of all others, in that House they have heard you studiously arguing against one of the first maxims of constitutional freedom, and maintaining that in some cases, justice ought to be delayed in order to let a popular ferment subside. Without stopping, my Lord, to apply this opinion to our own case, or to ask you whether there are not courtly ferments as well as popular ones, and whether they do not outlive the others, — these are not the habits and the opinions that are to convince the people of your Lordship's invincibility to temptation, and of the propriety of uniting the office of a Royal Councillor with that of a Judge. In a word, my Lord, it is not in *human nature,* either with a reference to yourself or to them, that people should have a proper confidence in your Lordship's impartiality under such circumstances; it would not have been wise or delicate, in any character, to have expected it of them; and this very consideration alone should have persuaded your

Lordship not to unite two offices in one person, each of which prevents the proper discharge of the other and the just reputation of both.

You see, my Lord, that this point of your public character is of itself sufficient to do you a serious injury with persons, who nevertheless will not hesitate to say, that they regard you in the abstract both as an able lawyer and a well-intentioned man; but if this point were wanting, the other is equally sufficient for the same purpose, and on a still wider ground; and if they had no objections to you in particular cases as a courtly Judge, they would find you utterly objectionable in all possible cases as a passionate one. This is too clear a matter even for a shadow of dispute; and as the fact is not to be denied or defended, your Lordship will probably reserve your ground of resistance, and plead that common frailty of your nature in one instance, from which you have declared yourself exempt in another. Not to argue however that an extreme violence of temper is by no means among the commonest or most excusable of frailties, your Lordship should be told, that a Judge ought decidedly to be *above* the rest of his species in matters of ordinary humanity; frailties are the very things that bring other people under his judgment, and though he must partake of them as a man, he must not grossly partake of them as an equal; or where is his right to do justice over others? Where is his dignity to do it well? Nay, where is his very power to do it at all? How is he to overawe it with a turbulence and an impotence of his own? In short, how is he to hold the balance with diverted eyes, and a hand that is trembling with passion?

My Lord, these objections from beginning to end are founded upon truths so common and undeniable, that I should be getting into mere declamation to reason upon them. For the sake of justice in general, and the dignity of our own cause in particular, which we cannot suffer to be thought at all cognizable by a Judge of your Lordship's temperament, we have plainly told you our opinions; and we here apprise your Lordship, and all Judges afflicted with similar visitations of error, that no affection of dignity on the part of the Bench, and no grave pretences of confounding good advice with libel, and liberty with licentiousness, will supply it with a character and a public confidence which its own habits have taken away. It will not do. A Courtier might as well talk of his free-will, or an Epicure, over his third plate of turtle, of his philosophy. How to advise your Lordship respecting the two offices, we know not, unless it be to abstain from one of them, since it is unquestionably better to do one thing well, than two things improperly; and in this case, we should recommend to you to give up the Bench, for the trouble of a Court, to say the least of it, will be likely to keep your Lordship's resolutions (if you should make them) in a continual torture of provocation, whereas it is not probable that they would break out much at the Council table. At any rate, we trust that your Lordship will seriously reflect a little on the subject of this unfortunate habit, even if it be for nobody's sake but your own; for we cannot but think that to a person of any pride, and one who deals in good comely sentences and portly veracities, it must be an awkward thing to be liable to so much misconception of feeling, and to have perhaps his warmth in an argument traced to a heating diet, to a superfluity in the humours, or to a sort of gouty tenderness in the apprehension. In a word, my Lord, lower your appetites, both public and private; lower your aspirations after rank and your high sense of the luxurious; and you will find, in due course of time, that the loftiest honour you can attain is that of the public confidence, the best dish you can enjoy is that of a temperate conscientiousness. These are things that give us neither angry days nor uneasy nights; and with my best wishes for peace and pleasant dreams to your Lordship, I am, my Lord, &c., &c.

THE EXAMINER.

FRENCH FASHIONS

Who would not rather get him gone
Beyond th'intolerablest zone,
Or steer his passage through those seas,
That burn in flames, or those that freeze,
Than see one nation go to school,
And learn of another, like a fool,
To study all its tricks and fashions
With epidemic affectations,
And dare to wear no mode or dress,
But what they in their wisdom please,
As monkies are, by being taught
To put on gloves and stockings, caught? —

* * *

To admire whate'er they find abroad,
But nothing here, though e'er so good;
Be natives wheresoe'er they come,
And only foreigners at home;
To which they seem so far estrang'd,
As if they'd been i' th' cradle chang'd,
Or from beyond the seas convey'd
By witches, — not born here, but laid.[1]

Butler.

September 4, 1814

If there be any aristocratical interlopers in the republic of
letters, who should think it frivolous in us politicians and
settlers of destinies to bestow a glance on subjects like the
present,[2] we would remind them of three things: — first, that
our illustrious predecessors, the *Tatler* and *Spectator*, gave
them a considerable part of their attention, and in undertaking
to form the manners and character of the nation, thought it
of no little importance to settle the freaks of tuckers and
petticoats; — second, that personages of mighty political importance in the world, and authorized to speak in the first
person plural as *we* do, are allowed to unbend themselves

(when business or their stays will let them) in matters of similar taste, the only difference perhaps being, that we do it for the beautifying of others, and they for the more effectual glorifying of themselves; — and third, that the said personages, in common with potentates in general, and all who have to look after their fellow-creatures, are actually and of necessity in the habit, as a part of their office, of attending to the smallest and most ordinary concerns of society, at one moment issuing solemn decrees respecting the regulation of old ropes, and at another providing against the hostile incursions of lace and brandy.

Indeed, if the fair sex were the most prominent idea that presented itself to our minds in this discussion, we should think it a most unnecessary thing even to suppose an insinuation against the dignity of the subject; but one of our chief reasons for taking it up, is that these French fashions that have come among us, make an alarming reverse on this point, and threaten to render the wearers of less consequence than the things worn, — a monstrosity which, however it may suit French ladies, was certainly never intended for English.

We must here premise, that we have no objection to fashions and their changes in general. On the contrary, we think that the outcry against them is equally wanting in taste and good sense. We look upon them, in some measure, to be in the artificial world what flowers and their seasons are in the natural; — they are also useful to trade and manufactures, and to the maintenance of good-will between nations (the only point of view in which they are tolerable at present): — in fine, they serve to fill up the time and vary the ideas of a number of persons, who without some such resource would be left to a monotonous and drab-coloured existence, too cruel to think of. It is not every body who could divert tediousness by a round of sleepings, eatings, and drinkings, — still less by writing verses or treatises, or even by that "glorious title to idleness," called sewing.*

---

* It is not of a variety of useful and necessary things we are here speaking, such as cannot be made, or afforded to be made, out-of-doors; though we

We protest then most vehemently against the French dresses that are now in vogue, and which, we understand, are to be seen every day in the streets, to the great gaze and astonishment of the unwary passenger. It may seem odd, we allow, how we, who are in prison, should undertake to say so much of these out-of-door enormities, or should even be acquainted with their existence; but not to mention the occasional glimpses of them which our fair visitors afford us (though we suspect, not in their greatest extent) there are magazines and caricatures to assist us; some of our fair friends are as zealous on the subject as we are, and undertake (as far as the laughableness of the thing will allow them to proceed) to furnish us with descriptions of what they have witnessed; and lastly, a friend just arrived from Paris, has favoured us with a sight of a whole book of the newest fashions. And what a book it is! – Of all the awkward, gaudy, and slatternly visitations, that have ever crossed us, under pretence of being ladies well dressed, these, we think, are the most ridiculous; – and yet they are the very things, it seems, that our countrywomen have chosen to adopt! The colours are like the wreck of a ribbon shop, – the draperies all flounces and furbelows, – the head-dresses so many fantastic exaggerations of pokes, hoods, and chimnies, – the wearers themselves (and here, we trust, the English imitators *must* fail) a set of lax-looking, traipsey, finiking idlers, who seem mincing and tottering home after a sixpenny dance. (We confess, that we feel the humiliation of a description like this; but we must describe such things by their proper terms.) – At one page, – and such, we understand, is the case in our own streets, – a figure comes glaring towards you like the Hooded Serpent, in a kind of bulged-out calash, that seems running away from the cheeks that can wear it; – at another, you are

---

suspect that a short-sighted niggardliness, under pretence of industry, often saves itself money on these occasions, that might be a great deal better bestowed elsewhere; – but of that inveterate habit of stitching, which some well-meaning females are always at, to the exclusion of every thing which informs their minds and renders them agreeable companions. Not to mention the perniciousness of this kind of niggling and sedentary dreaming, with regard to the health.

assaulted by elongations of the forehead, of various descriptions, some jerked up, others down, others poking at you at
once like a unicorn, but all of the most ridiculous length, and
making a little woman look like the bird called a Toucan,
whose beak is the largest part about it; — then, at a third,
comes the grand deformity, and a lamp on two legs seems
tumbling towards you under a hat like a muff-box, with a
huge nosegay stuck on one side, as if she had been robbing a
lord mayor's footman, and a short Dutch petticoat, fringed,
flounced, and sticking out on all sides like a large bell, of
which the two shuffling feet underneath look like the double
clapper. The colours are in proportion to all the rest; — nose-
gays as above, — great sweeps of black contrasted with white
bodies or made heavier with scarlet, — bunches of ribbons
swelling and streaming to the wind; and as to *shape*, a night-
mare has as much. Under the poke and the muff-box, the face
sometimes entirely disappears; the poet would in vain look
for the waist, which he so well described, and that used to be
so common among us,

> Fine by degrees, and beautifully less; —[3]

it is tied up under the arms, — perfectly hung in drapery; and
the man who would repose his griefs, as formerly, on the
bosom that was dearest to him, must first ask permission of
the chin.

The astonishment of the lower orders in London at these
apparitions, is, we understand, of the most unsophisticated
description. Some give a broad grin into the calash as it goes
by; others make way, with expressions of alarm, for the
advancing poke, but at the sight of the muff-box and bell-
petticoat the laugh is loud and general, and we fear, not
always unmixed with a disposition to pelt. By the gentlemen,
we believe, it is reckoned a hardy thing, and an unequivocal
proof of a gallant spirit, to meet and address their fair friends
under these disguises, — some persons we are informed, of a
more bashful disposition, having been known to exclaim "Oh,
there is Mrs. F. or Miss G. coming," and instantly dart round

a corner. To *stop* and talk, however, is accounted too bold a measure for any body in a spot at all crowded, as a mob is apt to collect; but in a quiet sort of street, like those about Portland Place, we understand you may occasionally see a gentleman undergoing the calash or the poke, or discussing something with a hat and flounced petticoat, the former of which now and then nods and bends down as if it made a reply.

Now we can easily imagine why the French ladies have adopted these dresses. We do not mean to be invidious, or to say that our fair neighbours have no good qualities; — far from it: — they are no doubt, a very chatty, pleasant, piquante set of people, and always the same, let whatever will occur. But with submission, they may be occasionally a little more *retiring*, without injuring their attractiveness, and may considerably *add* to their native charms, without diminishing their effect. Dresses, therefore, that tend to conceal the faces now and then, and to substitute the attractions of colour and drapery for those of figure and flesh, may act, in the one instance, as agreeable moderators of their vivacity, and in the other, as suppliers either of their natural deficiencies, or of what they lose much sooner than English women. But what has an English face done, or an English figure wanted, that either should retreat into invisibility? — that the one should withdraw itself, when its natural modesty gives it retirement enough, or the other add to or alter itself, when it is already all that grace and a lovely sufficiency can make it?

The Grecian dresses, lately prevalent, and we hope, still to continue so, are all that such women require, and afford quite enough alteration for the inventiveness of those who make them. By these, as nothing need be covered too little, no grace is shadowed too much; — modesty has at once her reasonable provisions, and nature her proper play. An English woman, in such an attire, with her natural looks, her fine, unsophisticated complexion, her truly feminine manners, the rise and fall of her shape at liberty, and the domestic, affectionate heart beneath it all, is the loveliest object upon earth, and no more wants addition than the lily or the light.

It is not to be supposed that by these observations we hope to do away the present fashions. We know better what it is to attack the absurdities of the superficial. Those who are merely vain and foolish, are of necessity destined to carry them to excess; and many others, we dare say, give into them, in particular circles, from the dread of being regarded as singular, making themselves frights, as Ovid would say, from the fear of being thought frightful. All that we attempt, is to warn the better and lovelier part of our fashionable fair ones against the absurdity, as far as they can avoid it; and to shew our countrywomen in general, that those who chuse not to put up with it at all, will appear with much more ease to themselves in the streets, and find great numbers to agree with and admire them.

We do therefore hereby signify and announce, in our national and censorial office of *Examiner*, that every lady, who chuses to dispense with these outlandish habiliments altogether, and to appear as if she still wished to be thought an Englishwoman, shall have full and free license to do so, — quoting our authority, if necessary, for the appearance, or referring at once to the English character as a summary reason. And we do likewise further announce and ordain, that every such Englishwoman as is guilty of *excess* of a contrary description, shall be considered as forfeiting the said character in proportion to the offence, — losing, for instance, if she exaggerates in the article of the calash and petticoat, her claim to the national modesty, — if in that of the poke or muff-box, her pretensions to the national beauty of face, — if in that of the bolstered-up waist, her credit for partaking of the national figure. The nosegay, if mounted to any extraordinary height or bigness, shall be considered as a defiance to all opinion relative to the whole of these points; and paint, if not laid on with the nicest imitation of the national colour, or if perceptible at once to eyes in general, shall be a direct avowal, that the wearer wishes to be considered a Frenchwoman, and she shall be so considered accordingly.

CHRISTMAS AND OTHER OLD NATIONAL MERRY-MAKINGS CONSIDERED

With reference to the Nature of the Age, and to the Desirableness of their Revival.

— Frame your mind to mirth and merriment,
Which bars a thousand harms, and lengthens life.

SHAKSPEARE.

Why, Gentlemen, doe you know what you doe, ha? Would you ha' kept me out? Christmas, old Christmas?

BEN JONSON.

Read then, and when your faces shine
With buxom meat and capering wine,
Remember us in cups full crown'd;
Until the fired chestnuts leap
For joy.
Then as ye sit about your embers,
Call not to mind those fled Decembers,
But think on these that are to appear,
As daughters to the instant year;
And thus throughout, with Christmas plays,
Frolick the full twelve holidays.

December 21, 1817

The commonness or uncommonness of an old saying will often give us more knowledge of the actual state of things in which we live, than a hundred political treatises.[1] There may be disputes among us, whether our more visible evils are temporary or not; particular circumstances may either blind or enlighten us on the subject; and there is this greater danger in all arguments carried on with the particular or party spirit, — namely, that for the sake of carrying the point in discussion, people will abandon, first willfully and then habitually, their own better convictions, and talk of wealth and poverty, vice and virtue, misery and prosperity, without having any more real meaning in their terms, than if they disputed upon the merits of the syllables fum and hum.

But a saying that is in popular use, or has gone out of it, with regard to the character of a people, speaks to us with the force of time and certainty, not with the weakness of self-love. A nation, it is true, does not allow any one but itself to speak the truth of its own character, in matters of panegyric; but we allude to sayings that imply a habit rather than a merit, however desirable the habit may be. We turn therefore with melancholy recollections, to the old and long-lost phrase of "Merry Old England." We have "Old England" still, but she is a grand-daughter or great-grand-daughter; and does not at all take after her ancestor. She is not a whit merrier than "the Old Lady in Threadneedle Street." She is very bustling, very talkative, and, as the phrase is, very successful in the world; but somehow or other, she is not happy. Nor has she been so, from her birth; though, to hear her talk, one would suppose that all her griefs began with the French Revolution. She was very rich and melancholy long before that. People had never given her, like her ancestor, the title of Merry. Merry Old England died in the country a great while ago; and the sports, the pastimes, the holidays, the Christmas greens and gambols, the archeries, the May-mornings, the May-poles, the country-dances, the masks, the harvest-homes, the new-year's-gifts, the gallantries, the golden means, the poetries, the pleasures, the leisures, the real treasures, — were all buried with her.

Heaven send the race be revived! We do not despair of it, after what the world has lately seen; neither have our efforts been wanting, nor shall they be. But let other individuals recollect, (and luckily we know those who do) that they must act themselves, as well as wish the rest of the world to act. Is enthusiasm to be only on the side of the bad passions, or the threatening, or the surpassing, or the gloomy, or the sarcastic? Stir up your firesides, and your smiles, and your walks abroad; and consent to enjoy the happiness, which you have long been instinctively aware is not to be enjoyed by gain, or gloominess, or mere bustling, or shallow and grave egotisms, or worldliness of any sort, or, (as the secret of *most* people's religion may be called) *other* — worldliness. Every new pleasure added to your Christmas which you did not enjoy before, — every new and kind sociality, — every innocent enjoyment (and innocence has a much wider range of enjoyment, than ignorance would think, or malevolence would give it), — every additional dance, or song, or piece of music, — every fresh thing done to give a joy to a fellow-creature, — every festivity set a going among friends, or servants, or the village, — every fresh grappling with the hale pleasures of winter-time, — every meeting of the country-breezes out of doors, — every rub of one's own hands, and shake of another's, in-doors, — will be so much gain to the spirit and real happiness of the age. Is there a reader that has had any gratification from the writings of the present author, and would willingly give him a personal one in return? A single branch of evergreen put up somewhere, which would not have been put before, will be an ample one. Is there a man who would shew himself manly in the eyes of his fair friend, — or a woman that would shew herself womanly in the eyes of her manly one? The generosities and graces of Christmas time will afford them ample opportunity. Are there admirers of Nature, of simplicity, of cheerfulness, of benevolence, of justice, of poetry or the arts, — of health, spirit, and intelligence, — of the manliest and greatest times of the English character? They may shew it with plucked holly-leaves, the unshamed and unaffected truth, the being pleased, the pleasing, the sympathy with all, the song and dance of old customs, the glowing cheeks, the liberal board, the scorn of sickly gossiping, the wit, the healthy impulses, the social wisdom. — We do not wish to be writing fine periods here. — We feel, and we put down; and if we have any graces by the way, thanks to the nature that gives this recommendation to our sincerity.

Christmas is a dreary business, compared with what it used to be in old times; and scarcely one of the other national holidays is alive. We shall give some accounts of them in the progress of our remarks; when the reader will be struck with the contrast as we were. The nation hardly appears to be the same. There is scarcely a vestige of the rural and out-of-door part of the festivities. In London particularly, nothing of that sort remains but the dancing of the chimney-sweepers on May-day, as if in mockery; and even at Christmas, every thing is withdrawn in doors, and done there with as little mirth as may be. Not even a bough appears in the windows, instead of the universal leafiness that used to take place, from the palace to the stall, as if a rural city had started up in the midst of winter. An air of constraint, and business, is thrown over every thing; and the holiday is rather transacted than enjoyed. There is a difference in different houses; but we are speaking generally. Personal character here and there prevails over custom; but the common amount of the merry-making consists of drawling through the morning either at church, or at home, or in some gaping *bit* of a walk, — having a dinner of roast-beef and plum-pudding, or mince-pies, — and sitting down in the evening to cards, which, in favour of the young people, are for once and a way made something like pleasure instead of profit, and allowed to be a round game. But even this pretended kind of holiday-keeping is by no means general. Some, whose ordinary days are as good and better than other people's Christmas, have their music and enjoyments as usual; but without any distinction of the season, and are not a fiftieth part as merry as they might be. Others, who are in the habit of paying their religion extraordinary compliment, think it profane to be merry at all. And others hardly think about the matter, except just enough perhaps to keep up the beef and mince-pies; for it must be owned, that good eating (with those who can afford it for themselves) is the latest survivor of all festivities in this country, and shews as little inclination to retire, as one of Homer's lions from a carcase.[2]

The causes of this habitual indisposition to enjoyment, which has lost us the amiable title of Merry Old England, we conceive to be, first, the commercial and jobbing spirit, which has infected Government as well as the middle classes, and almost destroyed the middle gentry; — second, the growth of a superstition, which is inflicted with the melancholy disease of taking merriment for vice; — and third, — a very different cause, — the growth of the very opposite of superstition, — that habit of trying every thing by the test of common sense and utility, which is but too apt to stop half way in its ascent to philosophy, and to keep the mind in a state of ludicrous suspense between austerity and pastime, the former of which it avoids as old womanish, and the latter declines joining in with as puerile. This it is that avarice and bigotry are sure to justify all the curses bestowed on them, when they can have their way; and that pleasure gets so abused in all sorts of ways, that it is the very last thing which even reformers know how to set about.

— Bitter shame hath spoiled the sweet world's taste.[3]

SHAKSPEARE.

We should despair (if despair were a word in our dictionary) of seeing causes like these done away, had we no other hope than that of persuading people by dint of argument. And yet not so; for what change has ever been effected in opinion, but by small and individual beginnings? But luckily, society has been accustomed to arguments on various sides long enough to hinder it from becoming an entire dupe. It has undergone also great convulsions, which have thrown it back upon its own thoughts, and shaken up its sensibilities and imagination. The most intellectual part of mankind, those who are most calculated to lead the others, are rather waiting to see what new faiths of opinion and new measures for the general good they shall adopt, than committed with any system, much less with any austere one. The general good itself is perhaps, for the first real time, felt to be not only a public right, but a present one, which must not be sacrificed to any contingencies: — we mean, that men will no longer hold it as a loyal or pious thing, instead of a pernicious thing, to agree that the world which others are so ready to enjoy is a vile one, and that because the next is better, this is to be

suffered to be worth nothing. They see no end to arguments
like this, however beautiful the world may be into which they
get. In short, society cannot go on as it did, and is not now
going on. It has been roused to a sense of its elements, moral
and physical. Its convulsions, after first dividing and then
shaking mankind together more than they have been for
centuries, have rendered it necessary for the most commercial
nations to look to their own *soil*; and however slow may be
the changes which must result, those changes, in Europe at
least, will infallibly be connected *with* the soil, — with sub-
sistence, with internal government, with the cultivation of
home tastes, and consequently with manners and customs,
and the choice of good.

Now then is the time for individuals to exert themselves:
— now is the time for those who would see their native country
blossoming with plenty and joy again, to begin to sow. It is a
noble work, and can do harm to none but the superstitious,
— if harm it is to be called, which would teach even themselves
to do justice to the face both of the earth and of the human
race, and not dishonour the maker of it by rendering it so
dismal. The politicians, whatever may be their opinions, need
not fear it; unless they place their good in the lasting un-
easiness of the majority; which none of them, we believe,
would allow. There is nothing desirable in such a dispensation
but to the selfish and melancholy persons just mentioned, the
Superstitious, who take a strange sick delight in making themselves miserable in this world, and painting their opponents
as so in the next. But if political matters are to remain as they
are (which we are far from thinking), the happier the community are, the better at all events; — if they are to change,
the kinder the temper in which it is done, the safer will it be
both for those who are governed and those who govern no
longer. Our first political reformers subjected themselves to
the ill repute of doing things in bad temper and taste, and
contradicting pleasures because they found them. We have
no such work to perform as they had, and no such melancholy
temptations to encounter, though the foolish criers up of

divine rights would willingly give us the former. Let us shew that had we lived in the days of Charles, we would have kept his taste in enjoyment though not in government; and that if we vindicate real freedom of every sort, it is not in order to be miserable after our own way, but to be happy with every body's.

Up then, up, lovers of old English pleasures as well as freedom, — lovers of what the Shakspeares and Sydneys loved, and what helped to make them the great men they were, — lovers of manly and rural sports, lovers of the free sward and the snow-ball, lovers of song and dance, lovers of mutual happiness in-doors and out of doors, lovers of Nature, and of the Author of the flowers of summer-time and the evergreens of winter. Up, and do what you can, and what you ought. You, who are able, do as the old gentry did, and set your village neighbours in motion with cakes and ale; you, who are able, go out and fetch home your boughs, your laurels, your mistletoe, your glad holly with its shining winter cheeks,

Till Birnam wood do come to Dunsinane; —

and you, who are not, (very few of you, ye rogues) rouse as much mirth as possible nevertheless in-doors; study your books or your good old grandmothers, and revive as many sports, and make them last as many days, as you can. Do not, for Heaven's sake, be always plodding and getting; you see what others have *got* by it, — no ideas, no enjoyments, and the bile. Get enough to live by, but not to die by; and above all, do honour to the memory of Merry Old England this week, till you hear more about her the next.

December 28, 1817

Christmas Day has now passed; but there is New Year's Day to come yet, and Twelfth Day; and our readers, we trust, are aware, that not only these days, but all the rest inclusive are, or ought to be, Christmas, and kept as such. "Frolick the full twelve holidays," says a writer quoted in our last (Robert Herrick), who was the very Robin Goodfellow of poets. This was the custom of our ancestors at the greatest as well as most chearful period of English history; and as we have now ceased to take an infinite number of dullnesses and commonplaces on trust, and are beginning to look at home again a little, let us try if we cannot discover, among other good things, that moderation in gain and mirth in enjoyment are very wise as well as very pleasant ones. The Editor has been delighted to hear, that his first article on this subject made a sensation among his readers. He has no notion, of course, that his single opinion can work any mighty change; but opinions may increase, especially as habits of thinking in other respects are shaken and make room for them; and among the readers of this paper, are to be found, he believes, many, whose example in matters of a chearful and genial taste would go a great way. Something at any rate has been done in some quarters. Some addition has been made to the green leaves and the mirth; and let us see if we cannot prolong the old music that has been struck up, and set more hearts a dancing.

Every day among our ancestors from Christmas Eve to Twelfth Day, and often till Candlemas, was more or less a repetition of the same enjoyments. At Court, and in the houses of the principal noblemen, a temporary merry officer was created, who was jocosely called the Lord of Misrule, and whose business it was to invent and manage the entertainment, and see that they were in proper spirit. In these upper circles, the inmates and visitors all repaired of a morning into the great hall to breakfast; various sports and gambols took place among high and low between that meal and dinner; the dinner was in the highest style of hospitality, with music and other household pomps; and so was the supper, before and after which there were revels, dances, or masks interspersed with singing, almost every decent person in those days being something of a singer and able to take his part in a catch or glee.

The same spirit of festivity took place among the country

Gentlemen and their tenants, the particular enjoyments being of course varied according to the degree and accomplishments of the parties. Mr. Drake, to whose interesting composition on Shakspeare and his Times we are indebted for our immediate information on these heads, has the following extracts from a tract, entitled "Round about our Coal-fire, or Christmas Entertainments." * — "An English Gentleman at the opening of the great day, i.e. on Christmas Day in the morning, had all of his tenants and neighbours to enter his Hall by daybreak. A strong beer was broached, and the black jacks went plentifully about with toast, sugar, nutmeg, and good Cheshire cheese. The Hackin (the great sausage) must be boiled by daybreak, or else two young men must take the maiden (i.e. the cook) by the arms and run her round the market place till she is ashamed of her laziness. — In Christmas Holidays, the tables were all spread from the first to the last; the sirloins of beef, the minced pies, the plumb-porridge, the capons, turkeys, geese, and plumb-puddings, were all brought upon the board: every one eat heartily, and was welcome, which gave rise to the proverb, 'Tis merry in the hall, when beards wag all.'" [4] — Even the smallest farmers and husbandmen vied with each other in making the season spin round plentifully and merrily. All the rustic games that could be played in wintertime, were in requisition; and Dr. Drake thus sums up, from Tasser's Poem on Husbandry, the country bill of fare, general and particular; — "good drinks, a blazing fire in the hall, brawne, pudding and souse, and mustard *with all*, beef, mutton, and pork, shred or minced pies of the best, pig, veal, goose, capon, and turkey, cheese, apples, and nuts, with *jolie carols*." [5] If some of all this plenty appears a little alarming to the weaker digestions of our times, it is to be recollected that the eaters of it were great exercisers; and that the leaping and vaulting and other sports of the country people, the hawking and hunting of the gentry, and the perpetual dancings of the

* See also his books of reference, — Brand's Popular Antiquities, Strutt's Sports and Pastimes of the People of England, and the poets and other writers of the time of Elizabeth.

Ladies, to say nothing of the archeries and the Mayings, &c. &c. completely kept off the night-mares of our sickly, in-door, and counting-house times. It was then *la nation bouquetiere,* not *boutiquiere;* — the bloom-keeping, not shop-keeping nation.

Of the customs most peculiar to Christmas, and now obsolete, may be specified the adorning the inside and outside of the houses with evergreens, the bringing-in and burning the first great log of wood with vocal and instrumental music, the carols, the telling stories round the fire-side before going to bed, the wassel-bowl, and the New Year's gifts among friends or to patrons. The wassel-bowl is easily realized; and our readers must make a point of having one to drink the revival of Merry Old England in. It was a bowl, — let us say, it is a bowl of wine or ale, or mead, or metbeglin, mixed with spices, sugar, toast, and eggs, and crowned with crab or other apples roasted and tossed into it hissing hot. The reader will remember the repeated allusions in poetry to the "roasted crab," and to the "spicy nut-brown ale." This venerable piece of jollity, which came into England with the Saxons, when the fair Rowena knelt before King Vortigern with a cup of wine, and said "Washeil" or "Health be to you,"[6] has long been superseded by less interesting cups, especially by the bowl of raisins fired with spirits, called *snap* or *flap-dragon,* which is of a much less accommodating as well as innocent description. But even the dragon, we believe, has hardly ventured to be merry of late years. There is every reason for reviving the wassel-bowl, and under that particular name. The composition of it can be varied according to the ability or taste of the maker, always provided there be spices in it, and a toast or roasted apple; — the word is the first Saxon or English word known to have been spoken; the custom is the oldest custom; and if we drink it in the spirit of our ancestors, we shall be reviving sociality indeed in its finest shape, for in the wassel-bowl, as a writer glowing with pleasure has informed us, "was drowned every former animosity," — an example worthy modern imitation. But we will quote the passage. "The ingenious remarker on this representation (an engraving of one of them) observes, that it is the figure of the old Wassel-Bowl, so much the delight of our hardy ancestors, who on the vigil of the New Year, never failed to assemble round the glowing hearth with their chearful neighbours, and then in the spicy Wassel-Bowl (which testified the goodness of their hearts) drowned every former animosity, an example worthy modern imitation. Wassel was the word; Wassel every guest returned, as he took the circling goblet from his friend, whilst song and civil mirth brought in the infant year." Brand's Observations by Ellis, vol. 1, p. 3, quoted by Dr. Drake, vol 1, p. 129. Now here is an opportunity for such of our readers as reverence antiquity, enjoy mirth, and love their friends. If they have no quarrels, so much the better; and if they have, they can make them up, and shew themselves worthy of having none.

We cannot also but recommend the other social custom of New Year's Gifts, not to patrons or strangers, but among intimate friends. The gift need not have one of the usual requisites of a present, — rarity, — which, by the way, is often as equivocal a piece of indispensability as not. It may be very cheap or otherwise according to the giver's ability, and to that of his friend to return it; but it should be in as good taste and as suitable as possible. All these things tend to disseminate kindness, to hinder mistakes, and to keep people from degenerating into that kind of reserve and individuality, which brutalize them before they are aware. And setting all this aside, the occasion is a most pleasant one for its own sake. Of Twelfth Day, the ceremonies of which have lasted longest among us, and are well known, we shall say something next week.

Such was the Christmas of our ancestors, till Puritanism spoiled one half of it, and Money-getting the other. Precious personages have they been to us, — Money-getting with his stupid and overbusy-worldliness, and Puritanism and his successor Methodism with his more stupid and melancholy other-worldliness; — for in that one compound word (which we hereby recommend to the reader's use) is contained the whole

secret of *such* religion. Puritanism, with his atrabilious temperament, was the first to baulk the joy of the community,
and to make them doubt whether they served a benevolent
God or a tyrant: — he used other people's words; but the fact
was, he raised Hell to Heaven, and made the very sun look
with a threatening and sulphureous aspect. It was nothing to
him who reigned in Heaven, provided he got a good place
there, or he would not have attributed such monstrous qualities
to his Deity; and if he frightened some better spirits into his
system by dint of their constitutional weakness, the majority
of his sect were made up of the most disagreeable and hard-
hearted beings in existence. Money-getting was not always
of his faction, though he was pretty sure to be of money-
getting's. Money-getting is a less melancholy person, and here
and there shews himself tolerably merry, after a fashion. But
to see the world, which these two vulgar usurpers would have
made for us, and have made for a considerable time past, one
would think that there were no beauties and pleasures in
God's creation. The former indeed is always blasphemously
crying out against "the vile world," and it must be confessed
takes great pains to prove his accusation; for the world is a
vile world, as far as his jaundiced eyes and melancholy im-
pressions upon others can make it. The latter does not talk
much about the vile world; he thinks little concerning the
matter, physically or morally: — the word *world* with him
means his own occupation; he "gets on in the world," — that is
to say, he walks a mile or so to and fro every day between
brick houses, working up so much mud and money; and spoils
all the leisure and enjoyment of himself and his fellow-creatures
by heaping up superfluous possession and rendering it necessary for others to do so, — at least as far as custom and opinion
are concerned. He is "defeated by the means of the ends."
A tenth part of the one would give him all the other, but he
must have nine parts more, and loses both time and relish for
his own object. Where are all the beauties and pleasures of
the world in the mean time, — the unsmoky sunshine, the
glorious prospects, the song of the birds, the song of human

beings, the health, the genuine wealth? Oh he has not *time* for these! "Business must be attended to," — that is to say, not for two or three or four or five hours, as real necessity may require, but ever and for aye. As other-worldliness undertakes to pay GOD the extraordinary compliment of abusing his creation, representing it as full of snares, and identifying it and its loveliest ornaments with the devil, so worldliness instinctively shakes its sorry skull at the very name of pleasure, making its own abuses the measure of all utility, and shocked to think that every body else will not think with it, and enjoy as little. Doubtless those who do not act as worldliness does, will not succeed *in the same manner*; that is to say, they will get a tenth part, and enjoy nine, — not get ten parts, and enjoy none of them; but it is high time to put an end to the shallow fopperies and assumptions, that first give rise to the wretchedest abuses and even vices, and then presume to measure the uses and virtues by them; — that would make a want of ideas and pleasures the standard by which others must think and act; — and that represent a dogged, an unintellectual, and an unhappy industry, as the only rational, knowing, and healthy activity. Industry, properly so called, is no more their sort of industry, than the ceaseless beating of a pendulum's leaden head is; — it is no more their sort of industry than poking all day long at the trunk of an apple-tree is, compared with climbing it, picking some apples, and eating them. Neither is wisdom their wisdom, nor virtue their virtue; otherwise it would be wise to be full of care, and virtuous to be full of selfishness. Their very activity is but the abuse of activity, — plodding, muddle-headed, and unhealthy. Industry, wisdom, and virtue, are things, by which, with as little trouble as Nature not Custom imposes, we procure our own and other's good. By the first, we get the real necessaries of life; by the second, we enjoy its cheap pleasures with health and elegance; by the third, we share the pleasures with others, and help them to bear their pains.

But according to these infatuated people, — the puritanical and the money-getting, — nine parts of all this beautiful world,

nay, ninety-nine parts, are of no use but to torment our for-
bearance or to fill our pockets with bits of metal or paper;
and man is a sheep in a slaughter-house, or at best a mill-
horse. Hear however what an old Christmas and May-day poet
says, who felt the departing warmth of the sunny times of
England, and deplored their loss. He is warning a country
friend against devoting too much of his time to gain; yet
observe, he does not decry a reasonable industry, with which
enjoyment "sees fair May:" —

> Is this a life? To break thy sleep?
> To rise as soon as day doth peep
> And tire thy patient ox or ass
> By noon, and let thy good days pass?
> No; 'tis a life to have thine oil
> Without extortion from thy soil;
> Thy faithful fields to yield thee grain,
> Although with *some*, yet *little* pain;
> To have thy mind, and nuptial bed
> With fears and cares uncumbered;
> This is to live, and to endear
> Those minutes time has lent us here.
> Then while fates suffer, live thou free
> As is the air that circles thee; —
> Then live we mirthful while we should,
> And turn the iron age to gold;
> Let's feast, and frolick, sing and play,
> And thus *less last* than *live* our day.
> Whose life with care is overcast,
> That man's not said to *live* but *last*;
> Nor is't life seventy years to tell,
> But to live half the seventy well.[7]

Herrick.

It was after this fashion that our ancestors lived. They were
industrious as well as we, but they were wiser and more virtuous, and therefore while they got enough for themselves,
they enjoyed and shared their pleasures with others. *They* did
not confound industry with a half-dreaming plodding, nor
call the world a vile world except now and then in a love-song,
nor find it such. They really knew and saw the world, external

and internal, country and town, the fields and the heart of
man. Their ideas were not circumscribed; and this made them
geniuses. Their activity was divided between business and
sport, and accordingly it was manly and healthy; their wisdom
was various, imaginative, sprightly and profound; their virtue
was sprightly also, being of the same growth and hue as their
wisdom, — and it was social, unaffected, elementary, full of
the kind impulses of a healthy body and of the charity of an
all-observing mind. We, of the present day, call ourselves an
enlightened age; first, because great numbers of us are alive
to the absurdities of superstition; and, secondly, because having
degenerated from our ancestors into a very bad and sophisticated way of living, we find out certain luxuries connected
with it, which they did not possess. But there is reason to
believe that the most liberal of our opinions on the former
matters do not exceed those of Shakspeare's time, certainly
not his own opinions, and those of numbers of great men then
living. With the worst and most melancholy diseases of superstition, the more unenlightened part of the community were
not even affected to any thing like the extent of the present, indulging themselves in the young, healthier, and more poetical
dreams of fairy-land, than in any other very visible species
of credulity. And as to luxuries, they had poetry, dance, and
song, — the fields, the rural sports, holidays, masks, and merry-
makings in plenty; and no more wanted *our* luxuries, than
they thought of wishing for our unhappy extremes of dull
riches and shocking poverty, — for our Methodism or our gin-
drinkings, for our crowded smoke, our care-worn faces, our
palsied and green-eyed manufacturers, our jobbing and con-
tracting absurdities, and all they have brought upon us, — our
inquisitorial taxes, — or our common-place rulers, whom the
Sydneys and Grevilles, the Raleighs and Burleighs, would
have taken for dull mockers in their master's absence. — We
are no more to expect that great age in real luxury, than we
are in wit. Nor do we say so because the age is a past one;
for we hold the present to be superior to some past ages (the
latter, among others); and what is more, we think it able to

catch a turn in the tide now, if it pleases, and be a great deal superior to what it is. We are speaking of those particular times, — of *merry* Old England; and we say, that she would no more want our luxuries, than the trees in the forest want flannel-waistcoats, or the birds want cages and indigestion. To read of the two ages, is just indeed as if all the singing birds in the world had been caught and caged up; — the one is so hale, so full of song, and so merry, — the other so dull and so drooping.

But let us not lament; let us reform. The reformation is of a very pleasant nature; and to say the truth, for our own parts, we have fallen into the complaining style unawares, it not being at all our wish to have any other than pleasant reflections on this subject, much less to excite them.

> Then as you sit about the embers,
> Call not to mind those fled Decembers.

Be happy, and make so. This is the sum and substance of all wisdom and virtue.

January 4, 1818

Dost thou think, because thou art virtuous, there shall be no more cakes and ale? — *Twelfth Night.*

The comedy, from which this quotation is made, — (a passage, involving as Shakspeare's pleasantries are apt to do, so much kind-hearted and tolerant wisdom) is supposed, with some reason, to be the last play that he wrote. If so, it is a delightful specimen of the master-spirit of those holiday-times, and of the happy-making disposition he kept up to the last, — and this too, in spite of early ardour, which is so apt to go to another extreme, — of a profession which peculiarly exposed him to the attacks of jealousy and envy, and of other troubles, of various sorts, which too often make men bitter with their nature. It was this sweet greatness of mind which led him to reconcile his deepest tragedies with such exquisite tastes and humanities, that our tears all turn to balm, and we depart with nothing but kind and equal feelings towards our fellow-creatures, instead of peevish or disdainful. His native chear-fulness is even observable, we think, in the titles of his plays. Those of his tragedies are in general mere names of persons; — his comedies are the *Merry Wives of Windsor, As You Like It, Much Ado about Nothing, The Two Gentlemen of Verona, All's Well That Ends Well, Twelfth Night, or What you Will,* &c. What a companion must Shakspeare have been for *Twelfth Night!*

But to return to that subject, — Twelfth Day, which closes the Christmas holidays, is the greatest and has been most preserved of them all, — the crown of the feast. It "has been observed in this kingdom," says Dr. Drake, "ever since the reign of Alfred; in whose days," he adds, quoting from Collier's Ecclesiastical History, "a law was made with relation to Holidays, by virtue of which the twelve days after the Nativity of our Saviour were made festivals." (Drake, Vol. 1, p. 127.) — Thus we see this truly great monarch, (the other greatest name in England with Shakspeare) studying the enjoyment of the subjects whom he so nobly fought for, and regarding the extension of their holidays as a fit task for a paternal legislator.

The reference of Twelfth Day to the Wise Men of the East mentioned in the Bible, who have been mistaken for Kings, is well known. It has been sometimes called the Feast of the Three Kings, as it is still in some other countries; and hence most likely the custom of drawing for King and Queen. We say most likely, for though all our festivals have perhaps a religious origin of some kind or other, and are reasonably mixed up with a religous feeling, (provided it be a chearful one and such as does real honour to the Great Spirit of Nature), yet it is by no means certain that any one of them originates in the Christian Religion exclusively. It has been usual for most nations to make merry at certain marked periods of the year; and several of the customs on such occasions are traceable to the Gothic and Celtic religions, or, as in the case with many of the ceremonies of the Catholic Church, to the worship

of Greece and Rome. It is not necessary therefore to occupy
our attention with points that may have any thing like an
exclusive tendency. Exclusiveness is the bane of humanity
at all times, much more so at times of professed mirth and
benevolence; and holidays that are kept in the true spirit,
that is to say, with hearty sociality, and a feeling for whatever
can contribute to it in external nature, will easily accommodate
the idea of their customs to all descriptions of faith. Christmas,
or the Saturnalia, — May Day, or the Floralia, Holidays, Games,
Fasts, Belteins,[8] Bairams, — a great and good Being will have
been pleased with them all under whatever denomination, if
there has been kindness and happiness among his creatures.

Twelfth Day, as it was kept by our ancestors, was much
the same, in its specific character, as it is now. A king and
queen were created at hazard by means of a bean and a pea,
or other lots, stuck in a cake, which the company broke up;
and a Court being formed by their Majesties, the characters
were kept up till midnight; only with their usual superiority
to us in merry-making, there was a more poetical air given
to the mirth in high life, more carousing and music among
the gentry, more country-sport among the peasantry, and a
greater exhibition every where of sensitiveness to the beauties
and cheap luxuries of nature. Yet what may we not recover
with the help of good-will? The Wassel-bowl,* of which we

---

* Dr. Drake, in mentioning that he has a large silver Wassail-bowl in his
possession, which was given to a member of his family about a hundred and
fifty years ago, and which "is divided by four pegs," quotes a pleasant piece
of information on that subject from Brady's Clavis Calendaria. "Some of these
Peg or Pin Cups or Bowls, and Pin or Peg Tankards, are yet to be found in
the cabinets of antiquaries; and we are to trace from their use some common
terms yet current among us. When a person is much elated, we say he is 'In
a merry Merry Pin,' which no doubt originally meant, he had reached that
mark which had deprived him of his usual sedateness and sobriety; we talk
of taking a man 'a peg lower,' when we imply we shall check him in any for-
wardness: a saying which originated from a regulation that deprived all those
of their turn of drinking, *or of their peg,* who had become troublesome in their
liquor: from the like rule of society came also the expression of 'He is a peg
too low,' i.e. has been restrained too far, when we say that a person is not in
equal spirits with his company; while we also remark of an individual, that
he is getting on 'peg by peg,' or in other words, he is taking greater freedoms

spoke in our last, was in its greatest glory on Twelfth Night; and of the revival of this in some places in town we have had the pleasure to hear in the course of the week, as well as of its existence still in some parts of the country. Those who pique themselves therefore on having a true Old English Shakspearean, Alfredian cup, must do their best next Tuesday; on which day also, of course, the rest of the mirth will be at its climax; — the best wit of old, middle-aged, and young must be in requisition; — the games at cards, if any, by all means *round*, so as to admit players of all ages and sizes; — the king behave himself with true greatness, not making insidious partitions of his neighbour's fish; — the queen be served with infinite gallantry; — and the rest of the characters have their proper effect of shewing how good humouredly we should take such varieties in real life. One dance at least there should be, wherever it can be contrived, for health as well as vivacity's sake; and a little music and song also, to modulate the uproariousness, and remind the Animal Spirits of the presence of the Graces. Here's a sprightly Twelfth Night song by Robert Herrick, which carries its music along with it: —

> Now, now the mirth comes,
> With the cake full of plums,
> Where Bean's the king of the sport here;
> Beside, we must know,
> The Pea also
> Must revel, as queen in the court here.
>
> Begin then to chuse,
> This night as ye use,
> Who shall (for the present delight here)
> Be a king by the lot,
> And who shall not
> Be twelfth-day Queen for the night here.

---

than he ought to do, which formerly meant, he was either drinking out of his turn, or, contrary to express regulation, did not confine himself to his proper portion, or peg, but drank into the next, thereby taking a double quantity." [N. Drake, *Shakspeare and His Times*, I, 131, fn.]

Which known, let us make
Joy-sops with the cake;
And let not a man be seen here,
Who, unurg'd, will not drink,
To the base from the brink,
A health to the king and the queen here.

Next, crown the bowl full
With gentle lambs-wool;*
Add sugar, nutmeg, and ginger,
With store of ale too;†
And thus ye must do
To make the wassail a swinger.

Give then to the king
And queen wassailing;
And though with ale ye be wet here,
Yet part ye from hence
As free from offence,
As when ye innocent met here.

Pray admire the end of this hey-day song of merriment. Could any dance fall into a prettier, modester courtesy? Could any sermon end better? How much more efficacious, in behalf of real virtue, to inspire hilarity, and then appeal to the *kindly* passions excited, — than to threaten, and frighten, and make gloomy, and then expect peace and charity to ensue! The title of one of Ben Jonson's Masques, which was presented at Court on Twelfth Night, is "Pleasure reconciled to Virtue." This has long been a very desirable reconciliation indeed, and only because Pleasure and Virtue have both been so little understood. They have no more right to be kept asunder, than inclination; but the world has made so many artificial Pleasures and Virtues, and taken such extraordinary pains to separate the two ideas (in spite of some professions and recommendations to the contrary), that, by selfish pretenders or foolish mistakers, real Pleasure is almost always lost as much sight of as the Golden Age itself; while real Virtue is too often defied by those, who just see far enough to detect

* Roasted apples.   † Or wine.

the false. The reason is, that Virtue is too much made to consist of compromises with really vicious and foolish and overworked states of society, which of necessity *cannot* attain to pleasure; and so Innocence or Hurtlessness comes to mean things, both in abstinence and practice, which it would not otherwise do; and Happiness is despaired of in this beautiful world,— nay, often made a *merit* of being despaired of! So invincible almost is the tendency to get pleasurable sensation of some sort; and yet such modes does human folly discover at the very same time, of cutting off its own power of returning to them! — We hope the days will yet come when the world will be wiser; and when it will think it as barbarous to make these intellectual and moral sacrifices of human beings to the Molochs of Gain and Superstition, as it now holds it to have been barbarous to sacrifice their bodies. At all events, things may be better and more chearful than they are now; they have been so; and as these are the two great steps towards improvement, — first, not to despair, — and second, not to delay, —here's to their speedy reformation, and to the reader's health, in a Wassel-cup made by "a Wife, a Mother, and an English-woman." [9]

We conclude these articles for the present; though we must own we do so with an unwillingness, which will be pardoned by such of our brother-politicians as do not confine their notions of politics to a question of the day, or their enthusiasm for the good and beautiful to the faces of the Allied Sovereigns. We shall continue them however from time to time, as the seasons of the old holidays come round, — particularly on May Day; for besides the pleasure of writing upon such subjects, and of hoping that they may be of some little service, we have now the additional and delightful excitement of knowing that they have already been so. We have had accounts from various quarters of the revival of old festivities, — some brought us by friends, some that have come round to us by chance, to the great surprise of those who witnessed them, — and some sent us by correspondents on the subject, among whom we have particularly to thank those who appear in our present paper, with a fair and true woman at their head. We should formerly have left out the complimentary parts of their letters, perhaps because we were more proud, or less understood what was due to others, or less felt the value of sympathy; but we now leave them in, and feel ourselves much more than overpaid by the accounts and reflections which they accompany. The letter of our fair stranger in particular happened to come upon us in the midst of some very wintery reflections indeed, and roused us up again like a beam of sunshine. — This has been one of the pleasantest periods of our public life.

DISTRESSED SEAMEN, AND DISTRESS
OF THE POOR IN GENERAL

January 11, 1818

Ever since the late war, thousands of sailors have been in a very distressed condition.[1] Many persons must have seen them crossing the country in rags and disease, and begging their way to their respective parishes; and in London the sights have been a great deal worse. A Meeting was held in consequence last Monday in the City, "for the purpose of taking into consideration the best means of affording relief to unemployed and distressed Seamen, and for aiding in the enforcement of the laws against impostors assuming the appearance of Seamen for the purpose of begging." This latter resolution is an excellent one, when coupled with the former. To detect impostors is to do great service to those who are none; but then it should be made manifest, that the object in detecting impostors *is* to do service to the really suffering. All that has ever been complained of on this head is, — first, that persons are quick to cry out against or detect impostors, and to go no farther; and second, that impostors in the abstract, that is to say, impostors as far as some particular pretension is concerned, are sometimes in great want of charity upon other grounds, and sometimes driven upon that very species of imposture by real want. When the husband in the *Tatler* fell down by the side of his second wife during one of her pretended fits at being denied a coach or some such thing, and whispered in her ear, "This will never do, my dear," he acted like a man, and a really kind one; but if the same husband had shewn himself insensible to faded cheeks or a wasted figure, and had not at least inquired into the causes of it and ascertained whether it was owing to circumstances which he could relieve or not, he would not have done his duty even towards a person who had endeavoured to impose upon him in other respects. Nothing is more common, when a crowd collects about an object, than for some of the byestanders to say, — "Ah, — drunk: — an impostor! — an old offender no doubt" — and a great many other phrases which would make any of themselves as mad as fury, if they had cut their little finger; — but while it is acknowledged that there are many impostors, how many of these byestanders are impostors themselves? That is to say, how many of them are there, who in pretended zeal for sincerity and the really afflicted, are quick to make themselves these excuses for doing nothing, whether the object be afflicted or not? It is enough, we should think, for people to find out occasionally, in their rubs through this life, that they have hurt the feelings of fellow-creatures out of the pale of their own particular habits and associations, and thereby subjected themselves, with greater or less degrees of justice, to charges of self-love or of selfishness; but to turn wilfully away from the sight of persons suffering under mis-fortunes, which our common nature may easily lead us to apprehend, — under cold, hunger, pain, and the failing spirit of disease, — and to go from all this into warm and curtained rooms, where the fire welcomes our feet, and plenty is to be served up at a ring of the bell, — this indeed shews a want of feeling rendered callous by bad habits, or a want of imagination whose best excuse is stupidity. Those, who have been merely irritated into a neglect of such scenes by imposture, would, we are sure, hasten to prove the cause to their own consciences, by not neglecting them very long.

At the Meeting in the City, a Captain in the Navy (Capt. Gordon[2]) drew a picture of the state of the seamen in the metropolis, that should stand in stead of a thousand arguments. "One evening, he went to one of those miserable places in St. Botolph, Aldgate, where these creatures spent the night. In four small rooms, 14 feet by 16, he found fourscore wretches, *in a state, to describe which was truly impossible.* He could discern among them few men, for they were really skeletons, *Seamen's* skeletons as he could well perceive. He questioned them about what exertions they had made to procure a ship, when one and all expressed with eagerness their wish to serve, but that from their naked appearance no one would employ them. Willing to work, they were alone prevented from doing so by their miserable appearance. Nothing he was confident could have induced them to resort to that place, that noxious place, but their being reduced to the last shift. — He might well call it a noxious place, for the smell was intolerable, and the air most baneful. That it could not be otherwise might easily be seen from what he had stated respecting the size of the miserable holes they were placed in, as those who could pay three-pence a night were allowed a bed, that is, allowed to lie on an old torn mattress on the floor, without a covering, and those who could pay only two-pence, were allowed to come in but not to lie down; while those who could not afford that miserable pittance, were debarred from entering. On his return from this miserable place, he found *five in the streets, who had not been fortunate enough to raise this two-pence.* They were standing in the streets in a cold frosty night, shivering in the cold, while their uncovered limbs were exposed to all the severities of the weather. *One of them was lying with his tongue out, in a very great fever. Numerous* were the instances which had occurred of these brave defenders of their country, these men who were worthy of a better fate, perishing *from actual starvation.* One was about three weeks ago *found* dead; another carried to St. George's Hospital, *where he died;* while a third *yielded up a miserable existence on Greenwich beach.* When such things were thought of, when such things were known to be facts, it became every man to be active and do his duty."

It does indeed. We are surprised, we confess, that no one would employ them on account of an appearance which was one of the greatest proofs of their want of employment; and we recommend to the consideration of those who are so ready to pass on with the word impostor in their mouths, the account of the five houseless ones, who had not been "fortunate" enough to raise two-pence apiece for a night's-lodging. But what surprises us most, or rather what *would* surprise us,

if the Constitution were preserved as it ought to be, is, that
Government seem to act, and even to talk, as if they could do
nothing on these occasions. We are told in the course of the
speeches at this Meeting, that an *application* had been made
to the Lords of the Admiralty, — not, observe, that the Admiralty had of their own accord taken any steps to relieve
these dreadful cases; — then we are informed, that in consequence of the application, "their Lordships would concur
with the wishes of the Committee as far as they could *with
propriety;*" — and that this propriety consisted in offering a
ship or two for the use of the Committee, but without officers,
"their Lordships' reason for not giving officers to the vessel
being, that they could not enforce orders on board of such a
vessel, the men not being entered as usual!" Now really, unless
some explanation be given on the subject (and explanation is
the least which their Lordships can give), this excuse must
be considered as the very paltriest on record. They could not
enforce orders! And what can the Committee do? Can they
enforce orders? Or do they think orders *necessary* to be en-
forced? Or would their Lordships, the Lords of the Admiralty,
have us believe, that a direction, — a request, — an implied
wish, from Government, — especially on an occasion like this,
would not have its full effect on hundreds of officers, from
whom they might select the small number requisite? It is
well known what pains the late Lord Mayor[3] took on this
very matter a year or two back. He and some of his fellow-
magistrates were roused to its consideration, in common with
others of his fellow-creatures (their Lordships of the Admiralty
excepted) by the shocking sights of distress throughout the
metropolis. They waited on their very unshocked and placid
Lordships accordingly; and were received, saith Sir James
Shaw[4] ("as it is but justice to say") "with the utmost politeness
and attention." Oh, doubtless; — politeness and attention on
such occasions cost nothing but what is very pleasant and
repaying; — and besides, it would be very shocking if a Lord
of the Admiralty were not very polite, — not to say condescend-
ing, — to a Lord Mayor. Doubtless had his Lordship made a

little mistake, and called upon their Lordships while drinking their Burgundy and cracking their walnuts, they would not have contented themselves with begging him to partake of some empty *hulls*; — they would doubtless have begged him to take some of the kernels, and even invited him to save his teeth with crackers, albeit they could not *enforce* the use of the said crackers. Well; — the Lord Mayor proposed to have a vessel stationed in the river, and to use it for the purpose of clearing the streets of the distressed sailors; and their Lordships very graciously *consenting*, the plan was carried into execution, and the naked clothed (which was something) from the government stores. Yet this vessel had since been removed, though *how* it had been removed the above-mentioned Sir James could not say, "neither" (which is very awful) "would he attempt to say;" yet the Worthy Alderman "had no difficulty in asserting, from the kind attention thus shewn by his Majesty's Ministers, that it would now succeed were an *application* made to Government, and that similar good would follow." But, we repeat, why does it become necessary that Government, — that the Admiralty, — should be eternally *applied* to? Ought not the distress of the seamen, of "the gallant tars," — of those whose exploits are so exultingly as well as justly cried up, when there is need of them, — to be considered as under the Admiralty's peculiar jurisdiction? Where are the funds out of which the creature Croker was to have his war salary in time of peace? Where, also, as Lord Cochrane[5] asked, are those "funds which are the exclusive property of seamen?" Where are the Droits of Admiralty? "And why was no meeting heard of for the relief of soldiers perishing in the streets? Why, in the name of God," cried his Lordship, agitated, "is this *German* difference made?"

We shall conclude this article next week; and if any ministerialist, as will most likely be the case, shall take up our paper from motives foreign to any proper species of sympathy, we will try if he has not a little decent humanity left in him nevertheless. The other subject we have put at the head of our paper for the present, chiefly to shew that we do not overlook it. We shall have too many opportunities, we fear, of returning to that.

January 18, 1818

We write in behalf of this gallant and suffering body of men, while the fierce winds, which they have so often battled with, are roaring about our ears. Those winds, which in their muttering intervals seem to be scorning human weakness, and then in their wilder contempt to come rushing over our petty affectations of pride and power, — what do *they* say to our rulers respecting the darers of storms and waves? They seem to say, — We sweep the ocean now as we will; the gallantest spirits among you are wanted no longer to contend with us, and you neglect them; they who dared us at our height, and who ran the race of the elements with us over the tops of the waters, you now suffer to be shrunk up with poverty and nakedness, and to be forced to hide from us under bulks and penthouses! Do *you* pretend to be the master-spirits of the world! We roll over your heartless nonsense with disdain.

The conduct of Government indeed on occasions of this kind is most extraordinary. Whenever sailors are wanted during a war, we hear of nothing but their gallantry and infinite services; — "the gallant tars," the "hearts of oak," the lions in battle and lambs afterwards, the conquerors but to save, the heroes of "our wooden walls," the invincible maintainers of the British flag, the sweepers of the seas, England's impregnable bulwarks, — what should we do without them? — Yes, *that* is the question: — What should we do without them? — and accordingly when we cannot do without them, we praise and flatter them to the skies; their virtues are every thing that is generous and fine-hearted; their defects are stuffed out into virtues; they are the representatives and epitomes of all that is truly English; they sail off among shouts and hurras, they meet the enemy, plunge into all the chaos of battle, get lopped, maimed, splintered, burnt, bruised, battered, blown up, drenched in water and in blood; return with thinned numbers, with tattered flags, and with wounds; and there is an illumination. The Boroughmongers have dinners together; some Officers get promoted, if they have interest; others commence a life of half-pay and tattered memorials; the Government papers talk of glory, safety, magnanimity, invincibility, proud day, and eternal gratitude; such of the "gallant tars," as have "had the luck to have their legs shot off," have a chance of getting into Greenwich Hospital; the rest, who have the merit only of courage and poverty, must congratulate themselves on having their legs to live upon; and a creature of the name of Croker begins speculating how he shall keep a war-salary in time of peace.

Such has been the case, more or less, during our naval wars and the intervals. Whenever the necessity for battle comes again, then the trumpets and flatteries are revived, and we are to have eternal glory, and to shew eternal gratitude. When the necessity is over, the trumpets and flatteries are dumb, and we hear a vast deal about impostors. At last, the seas are absolutely swept clean of all our enemies; we say so, and boast of it; and shortly after, we hear that multitudes of Seamen are perishing in our streets. *Twice,* since the close of the war, has their condition been brought before Government; *twice* have others done what the Government ought to have done; and *twice* have the Government rather acquiesced in the proposal made for relieving them, than blushed for their previous neglect, and taken up the subject warmly. It was that active and meritorious person, the late Lord Mayor, who first urged it to them, — who first urged them to cast a gracious eye towards hundreds of their own saviours. A ship, with some coyness, was granted for their accommodation, — one perhaps in which many of these saviours had fought and bled, and had their limbs torn asunder, that we might all enjoy ourselves safe and sound at home. What is better, they were relieved of their nakedness out of the naval stores; and for a time, people thought that the preservers of our homes had something like a bit of a home as well as ourselves. But somehow or other, this ship has disappeared; nobody can tell

what has become of it; a grave and prudent Government
Alderman says he cannot even venture to guess; and in the
mean time, multitudes of shivering and starving sailors having
again made their appearance, something must be done again
by persons out of the pale of Government, and again the
Government is applied to. It answers, it will do what it can
"with propriety," a ship or two is granted as before, and
hundreds of Seamen have already been relieved by persons,
who have neither the means, nor the influence, nor the
imperious duty upon them to interfere in such cases, which
Government has.

Now, that these persons have so interfered, and that hundreds of the Seamen have been relieved in consequence, is a
most excellent thing; but the public have a right to demand
a most serious explanation from Government. Did the Admiralty and others mean then to do nothing at all, had others
done nothing? It seems so. And how are they to account for
their neglect, as it is? For our parts, we cannot, with all the
ingenuity we can muster up, and really with all the sincerity
we can add to it, present to our imagination one single excuse
they can have to make. That they were not aware of the
circumstances, they cannot possibly say; that it is not a case
under their jurisdiction, the Sailors not being in actual service,
they cannot with any decency say either, when we consider
how they interfere with their press-warrants, and how they
take cognizance of all things connected with the service that
are at all to their advantage, though, now we think of it, we
suspect that this will be their attempt at an excuse. That the
country does not owe at least sufficient gratitude to Seamen
to keep them from starving, the hardiest of them (we mean
the hardiest-faced) will not venture to assert; and if the country
owes thus much, which is the most decent medium through
which it shall be paid? That they have no funds, is another
thing impossible to allege; for where, as Lord Cochrane asked,
are the Droits of Admiralty,[6] and to whom do those misused
funds belong, if not to the Seamen who won them? That they
have no money to *spare*, can still less, if possible, be alleged;

for they have several rank sinecures among their lordly offices. the existence of which is a scandal at any time, much more in times like the present. And granting that even that were not the case, there is not a Lord or Secretary of the Admiralty who ought not to forego at least the most unnecessary part of his luxuries, when such objects as these were brought before his attention. But *this*! Oh, *this* would be reckoned prodigiously romantic, that is to say, silly! We cannot but fancy Mr. Croker chuckling over the idea! And yet these men and their masters are among the persons who call upon *us*, upon the rest of the world, for generosities and sacrifices of all sorts! They have succeeded, till lately, upon the strength of the world's being more generous and trusting than themselves; but cunning is not wisdom, though it may ape it for a time; and the world are so thoroughly disgusted and undeceived at last, that these generosities and sacrifices will not be found forthcoming much longer. And this is the time which the servants of the Boroughmongers select for disgusting the community with their conduct to one of the bravest part of it! the time which they select for reminding us of their former flatteries and uproarious congratulations, by looking cold upon their friends and saviours, and talking of doing what they can "with *propriety*!" Oh, if these gentlemen had *been fought* for, only as far as "*propriety*" went! If their respective natures and intentions had all been inquired into to see which of them could or could not have been kept safe and sound, and suffered to grow rich, with "*propriety*!" If their words, actions, possessions, or claims had all been made to undergo the test of "*propriety*!" Propriety means right of possession, what is proper or belonging to any one, *own*-ness; and by moral metaphor, it comes to mean decency, justice, what is becoming under such and such circumstances, what is due to this or that person, or set of persons, and may in moral as well as civil justice be called their own, whether all or in part. Now we should like to hear the inheritor of Lord Melville's fortune and titles, or Mr. Croker who wanted to have so many salaries of widows in addition to his own, discuss to us the particular use of the word on the present occasion. We know not the talents of his Lordship this way, nor how far he could make the meaning and application of the term fall in with the Droits and the Sinecures; but with Mr. Croker, who has read Shakspeare, propriety is doubtless — as it were — a sort of — as one should say — propriety; that is, if one is very hard pushed, and obliged to face the matter out, propriety is letting hundreds of human beings, who have been the saviours of us, huddle together under pent-houses, cold, hungry, and sick, — and adding to one's own salary, already underserved, in order that we may be able to give dinners to our great friends the Boroughmongers.

January 25, 1818

The causes of this tendency to a neglect so disgraceful are various. In the first place, Seamen are more out of sight than any other class of the community; and an old proverb tells us, "out of sight, out of mind." We think of them when they are of immediate use to us, and praise and seem to promise them enough, as we have shewn; but when the illuminations for victory are done with, and the conquerors have gone to sea again, the idea of them seldom presents itself to those who ought to cherish it; it is encountered by none of the latter's ordinary habits or mental associations. This excuse however, bad as it is in such a case, will not serve a part of the Government, like the Admiralty.

In the second place, Seamen contribute nothing to the finery or self-love of a court. They are seldom or never there; and if any one goes, his nature, if it is of the true sailor description, is not likely to render him very welcome. They are not dressers or courtiers. They are not parade-men.

Thirdly, Seamen are not only not courtiers; but partly from the nature of their profession, and partly from the treatment they experience, their political leanings are apt to be averse from the court's opinions.

And last but not least, there has been a tendency in the

German succession to give particular effect to these causes by its special landsman ideas at one time, its love of military finery at another, and its continental predilections at all times. One cannot well fancy two more dissimilar animals than a British seaman, and a German soldier of the old school, — the one with his hearty thoughtlessness, his lax and billowy gait, his weather-beaten humanity, and his fine mixture of necessary submission and an independence conscious of its utility, — and the other, pettily careful, stiff, trimmed up and buckramed, without an idea in his head, but of barracks, rations, and sentry-boxes, and a mere tool in the hands of men who were themselves little better than automatons. We do not confound the modern Germans with these machines, since the modern writers and the French revolution made them discover themselves to be a people; but the mechanical rogues are still to be found here and there at a court or so; and pains are taken to revive the breed in some places, particularly at Hanover. The young French republicans broke them in pieces, like so many plaister-of-Paris images. The British sailor never met with his match, but in the American, who is of the same race with himself, and flourishes under a government, which pays him especial attention, and to which the unaccountable European governments seem to insist upon turning our eyes.

The savage posthumous treatment of the illustrious Blake, the Nelson of former times, is alone a remarkable specimen of the length to which courts will go against difference of opinion in the naval defenders of their country. Blake said, that it was not his business to meddle with politics, but to fight for his country; and so he fought for the Commonwealth in such manner as to clear the seas for them of very formidable enemies, and to make their name as respected for naval greatness, as Cromwell did for military and political. He died universally respected for his integrity as well as courage and skill; and yet at the Restoration, nothing, not even Charles the Second's own predilection for nautical matters, could prevail upon that blessed personage and his courtiers to hinder the body of this famous Commander from being dug up out of its resting place, and treated like a dog's. A less important, but pleasanter anecdote connected with the memory of the patriot seaman, will shew the eternity of these anti-pathies in certain quarters. A youth, the son of a Noble Lord who is now living, and who has been concerned in naval administration, hearing the name of Blake mentioned at a dinner, asked out loud, with a delightful simplicity, who he was; upon which his Lordship, with a saving grace equally delicious, exclaimed, "What, — Mr. So-and-so, — are you so *loyal a man*, that you do not even *know* then who Blake was?"

Even Nelson was not always regarded with a very favour-able eye for some of his political opinions, though his hatred of the French, and his fierce despotic tendencies and sub-serviences in some matters, (witness the blot on his scutcheon at Naples) rendered his great naval talents doubly acceptable as instruments in the late "legitimate" war. Still, he earnea his honours hardly; he fought his way up into them; and a man of a higher cast of mind than he, Sir Sydney Smith, has not been able to do even that, to the great astonishment of his countrymen. He was the first Englishman that gave a personal check to Bonaparte, and his chivalrous exploits are known all over the world; yet his very knighthood is of a foreign order. On the other hand, the devout and trusting Admiral Gambier,[8] who confines his achievements to bom-barding neutral cities, and takes for his motto, — *Fide non Armis,* By faith and not fighting, — is made a Lord.

But these inconsistencies are far from being the worst. We have already mentioned the scandalous attempt to keep up Mr. Croker's salary in time of peace, at a time when hundreds of unequivocally deserving officers, with every species of real claim upon any addition, were thrown out of employment upon a pittance, and the widows of others were begging for a pittance more. But the reader has no notion how the Borough-mongers (the eternal preventers of a proper understanding between prince and people) have been in the habit of lording it at the Admiralty. We ourselves are intimate with a most gallant officer and excellent man, who after serving in all

parts of the world, after being weather-beaten like an old
boatswain, after being gazetted and recommended by his
commanders for his lion-like valour, and after meeting with
wounds in various parts of his body, which will sometimes
put him to torments upon a mere change of the weather, had
to go backwards and forwards from sea to the Admiralty, and
from the Admiralty to sea, soliciting promotion in vain; till
at last, the very persons promoted over his head blushed for
their own success; and he himself was moved to exclaim one
day in the Admiralty Office, even to the blushing of the
official retainers, that he saw *that* was not the place for merit
without interest. Is it possible that even a remote family connection with *us* should have helped to produce this unworthy
treatment? We might have thought so, from a date which he
once put by chance to one of his memorials; but it is possible
also, that it might have had a very different effect, had it
been thought of; and personal politics, even if existing, cannot
have been the cause of similar treatment experienced by so
many others, whose memorials and constitutions waste away
together.

Not even all this, however, can account for the sights which
have lately been witnessed in the metropolis of this island, —
the multitudes of squalid and starving Seamen, whom Government took not a single step of its own accord to relieve. We
hope, and indeed we are sure, when we consider what old
English individuals still survive, that a most serious explanation
will be demanded of it in Parliament. Several Seamen had
died already; crowds of them were hungry and wasting; and
if some humane private individuals had not interfered, God
knows what might have ensued; for these gallant sufferers
are as little ostentatious of their sufferings as their merits, and
thousands may hide and die in a city like this. Those who
know what misery and death were quietly taking place in the
Spital-fields district a little time back, may easily imagine it.
The sufferer is not always likely even to know how ill he is.
He pines away on an occasional morsel, and endeavours to
save himself from absolute public beggary, and grows pale

and weak, and gets into a kind of waking melancholy doze, and may have more than an hour's notice, before death puts out his gallant struggling spirit. A friend of ours, who has been at sea himself, and knows what humanity is in all its senses, perceived a Sailor the other day lying silently under a little penthouse of some kind by a shop. He stopped, and with a Sailor's phrase of companionship, asked him to bring his face forth into the light, and let him see him. The man did so most unaffectedly, even smilingly; and exhibited a face in which starvation was beginning its pallid work. He could get no employment or food; and yet was lying there without a word, serious, but yet stout-hearted, and ready even to put on a cheerful look. Yet with what feelings could this man have listened to the winds!

Hundreds of human beings like this, and in worse condition, have been relieved, we are happy to say, by the subscription now going forward, both with food and clothing, and many have succeeded in getting employment; but hundreds still remain; the wants of all are numerous, though modest; and our readers will particularly keep in mind, that the duty in matters like these is not to give much, but that *as many as possible* should give *something*. There is a fear very often among individuals, that they shall not be thought to give enough; and some, not naturally unkind, will too often be apt to conclude, that enough will be done by others. But the business is, not what may be thought by the world in these matters, but what our conscience thinks of them, and above all, what sheer, equal-dealing justice and a consideration of the common wants of humanity think; and as to others doing enough, we should rather suspect, if we consult our own experience, that others will be likely to say the same thing, and leave the matter to *others*. It is no unamusing, still less unprofitable task, to a mind that can afford it, though some times bought by sorrow or humiliation, to watch the tricks it is apt to play with itself on occasions that concern one's indolence or other self-indulgence.

We conclude with an excellent old song, which by the

way, has as excellent a tune to it, and which was wrung from
the feelings of some indignant Englishman at sights like those
we have been describing. It is another illustration also of the
political part of our subject; and to ourselves it happens to be
particularly affecting, from associations of various sorts with
a faded voice that used to attempt to sing parts of it. *Salve,
mater patiens.*

> I sing the British seaman's praise,
>   A theme renowned in story;
> It well deserves more polished lays;
>   Oh, tis your boast and glory!
> When mad-brained war spreads death around,
>   By them you are protected;
> But when in peace the nation's found,
>   These bulwarks are neglected.
>   Then, oh, protect the hardy Tar,
>   Be mindful of his merit;
>   And when again you're plunged in war,
>   He'll shew his daring spirit.
>
> Why should the man who knows no fear,
>   In peace be then neglected?
> Behold him move along the pier,
>   Pale, meagre, and dejected!
> Behold him begging for employ!
>   Behold him disregarded!
> Then view the anguish in his eye,
>   And say, — Are Tars rewarded?
>   Then, oh, protect, &c.
>
> To them your dearest rights you owe;
>   In peace then would you starve them?
> What say ye, Britain's sons? — Oh no,
>   Protect them and preserve them.
> Shield them from poverty and pain,
>   Tis policy to do it;
> Or when grim War shall come again,
>   Oh, Britons, ye may rue it.
>   Then, oh! protect the hardy Tar,
>   Be mindful of his merit;
>   And when again you're plunged in War,
>   He'll shew his daring spirit.[9]

ON THE INTELLECTUAL INFERIORITY OF PARLIAMENT TO THE DEMANDS OF THE AGE

February 8, 1818

The Parliament has met again; and again have people been struck with a conviction which has been rapidly growing upon the community of late; we mean, the great inferiority of that Assembly to what should be expected of it in point of intellect as well as integrity.[1] It satisfies none of the best qualities of the observers. By far the greater part of the House of Commons are known to be corruptly chosen; and the minds neither of them, nor of the Peers who return them, are at all such as to make up for this outrage upon decency. Their reflections and speeches are dull; their arguments neither good nor new; their information confined in small and partial spheres, and additionally cramped by the falsest notions of self-interest. When they first assemble, it is curious to see how completely their observations have been anticipated by the newspapers, and made in a better manner; and they go on in the same dogged way from beginning to end, blinking the real question if they are on the defensive side, and often avoiding it even on the other from a common sense of interest. It is a mere waste of time to confute them. It might have been otherwise once; but it is no longer necessary. The community see through their bad arguments in knowing their actual condition; for they know they cannot palter with it; it is *Do so, or go out.* There may be a few independent individuals, and there may be a few more individuals working their way up into independence, or into ambitious or even patriotic action; but the majority — the great majority, are clearly a very dull, interested, and contented set, who content nobody else; and the public are as sick of them, as of an old prosing and pretending gentleman in a coffee-room.

That there are clever men in Parliament nobody will deny. The names of Lord Holland alone in the upper House, and of Brougham, Burdett, Folkstone,[2] Tierney,[3] and Canning, in the lower, are sufficient to shew it. Lord Wellesley and Lord Grey are intelligent men; and so seems Lord Bathurst,[4] in spite of his want of proper taste and magnanimity in joking about the captive Napoleon. In Lord Grenville, we must own, we never could discover any thing but a heavy and formal aristocracy, gifted with much diplomacy of talking. Lord Stanhope, a shrewd and original head, is unfortunately gone, and has left a successor, who seems in haste to shew himself his direct opposite, in eccentricity, opinion, wit, knowledge, and every thing else. Curran,[5] another shrewd and clever man, has gone too; but Ireland, scandalously treated Ireland, still furnishes more than her due share of talent in this as in other respects, while Grattan and Plunkett[6] survive.

But some of the best speakers in the House are not those which speak oftenest; and the cause of this is the same which prevents the herd of common-place men from speaking at all. It is the unnatural ascendancy of common-place itself. A few men, who are the representatives of the oligarchy of Borough-mongers, and who at once govern and serve them, carry every measure they please, that is not calculated to disturb the usurpers themselves; and as the clever men in the House cannot, for very shame and indignation, but come forward now and then to express their feelings, so the multitude of minds who are akin to the ruling powers have neither the ability nor the necessity to say any thing but Aye and No. The rulers themselves would say as little, if their very office did not compel them to talk.

We have heard it said, that there are many clever men in the House among those who never speak; and when we inquire further on the subject, we find that such and such a gentleman is very pleasant at table; that another is the author of some anonymous pamphlet; that a third is a elegant scholar, and was in high reputation at Eton or St. John's; that a fourth is shrewdly suspected of being the writer of some verses in the

Anti-Jacobin, or the Odes for the Laureatship; that a fifth enjoys the admiration of Higgins or Tomkins, both of them very eminent with each other; and that a sixth is so very clever — Good God! how very clever he is!

Now we are not disposed to deny the merits of these gentlemen in their way. We are admirers of elegant scholarship, and still more of pleasant companionship; and it would be hard if corruption had so corrupted even the yea and nay retainers of Ministers, as to do away all the effects of education, and of that really wiser time of life when some little degree of sentiment or enthusiasm was mingled with their speculations. But it is easy for people to be all which these well educated persons are understood to be, with the help of a little early acquired taste. They are still far from what the times and the public intellect require; and can muster up so little original talent as well as independence among them, that a single sturdy English writer (Cobbett), in spite of the nonsense he talks about the learned languages, from knowing nothing about them, is enabled to talk it with the more effect on account of the really poor figure which these elegant gentlemen cut.

This is one class of the retainers of corruption; and it may be observed of them generally, that they are just informed and learned enough to be worldly wise, and ornament a little the dullness of their masters; — in other words, they are just accomplished enough to be livery servants to a more cunning or peremptory ignorance, and just clever enough to bully their own minds into a notion that they are successful and happy, when they feel and carry in their very faces that they are otherwise. Their scholarship, whatever words it may understand, is ignorant of the best meaning of them; it has no sentiment, no perception of the soul of beauty, no elevation. The very best which it has done for them is to polish a joke; and even this talent, besides being confined to but one or two, seems to have been spent together with the animal spirits of youth. It is curious to observe, either what an inferior man Canning is to his Antijacobin days, or how impossible he finds it to be free and jocose under the dispensation of his dull and powerful friends.

In truth, the schools from which these more elegant retainers of stupidity issue forth, are very bad ones both for patriotism and genius. We allude to such as Eton and Westminster, where a system is carried on, with the countenance of the masters, calculated, under pretence of fitting the future men for the world, to render them nothing but alternate slaves and tyrants. Fit them for one sort of world it does, but only such a world as is most unfit for a generous youth to enter; a world, which sordid and violent minds have first made what it is, and then must spoil the better wisdom of youth in order to maintain.

February 15, 1818

We have spoken of the more scholarly part of the retainers of corruption, whose books would have taught them better, had their teachers given them better habits. We wish to observe however, that in the remark we made on this subject we meant to confine it, as we actually did, to the earlier places of education, and not to the universities. There are many political objections, it is true, to the system pursued at the latter; * but it is not liable to the same great and elementary objections as the former, especially when we consider how many university-men are not brought up in the schools alluded to. Many young men, who know nothing of their alternate slavery and tyranny, are sent to Cambridge and Oxford from more private schools, or from foundations of a truly manlier character; many come from educations entirely private; and some from little or no education, out of a voluntary impulse towards knowledge. We have had a variety of great men from the Universities, but very few of them came from the more fashionable schools; and of those who have come, we suspect that a remarkable circumstance will almost invariably be

---

* See a chapter on this subject in Goldsmith's Treatise on the State of Polite Learning in Europe. [See ch. 12, "Of Universities."]

found true; and that is, that their character and opinions have
been materially modified by an antipathy against what they
had experienced, rather than a love for it.

A less informed part of the ministerial majorities is composed of money-getters, whether they are called the trading
interest, or fund-holders, or what not. The ministerial system
could no more go on without these persons than without the
Boroughmongers; and one day or other, not far distant, they
will most likely be the death of it, not without terrible scars
on their own side; — but this is not the subject of our present
paper. These gentlemen, with very few exceptions indeed,
are as profoundly ignorant as they well can be. They know
nothing out of the pale of their own sordid desires. They put
on guineas for spectacles, and can see nothing else. They live
in a murky and yellow atmosphere, which makes the petty
objects about them appear great; and see nothing beyond it,
however grand, or vital, or even alarming. A wide policy, a
distant but certain danger, an extended view of any thing, is
to them as shut out from sight, as the hills of Surrey from
Lombard-street. They seldom speak in the House even on
their own subjects, so little knowledge have they of the smallest
accomplishments, or so little necessity to say any thing which
the Minister is not well assured of beforehand. This is the
consequence of that fatal ascendancy of mere riches, between
which and ignorance a perpetual reaction takes place. One
produces the other, and is reproduced by it in turn. The true
mercantile spirit, — that which made the Lorenzo de Medicis
of old, the gallant discoverers of a subsequent period, and a
few independent men of wealth in later times, whose connection with remote and unfamiliar countries gave a tinge
of something romantic to their speculations, — can exist only
at intervals of that nature, — at periods when it grows young
again. When mere plodding begins, it is gone; and then comes
an alarming time for a nation which has begun to be corrupted
by a bribing Government, — we mean the time when the most
powerful facilities are laid open to every coarse hand; and
any body can obtain influence and a silent share in that

Government by one single unintellectual talent, — that of physical application. It is the same with this class of persons as with the former; — the truly generous spirits who get in it by chance are quick in despising its habits, and grow fond of theories which seem to threaten their own interest. They may say as the Jailer does in *Cymbeline:* — "I speak against my present profit; but my wish hath a preferment in it." However, there are few such in Parliament. The money-getters go there as they go elsewhere, purely to get money or the influence connected with money; and a most wretched figure they cut, — seldom daring to utter a word, blundering when they do, and contemptible always.

The mere clerks in office are another class of the corrupt majority, including however some of each of those just mentioned. Most of them are adventurers, of the true description; that is to say, persons, whose sole object is to get on, as the phrase is, in the world, — ready to work for their hire's sake, and to speak as well as act just as they are ordered. They are getters of any thing, as contrasted with the mere money-getters; and their diversity of object is favourable to them in one respect, inasmuch as they have a few more ideas in their head, and are obliged to be a little readier with their wits. The late Mr. Rose, and the living Croker, are good specimens of the two chief varieties of this species, the dull and the pert, — each occasionally making incursions into the other's territory. Rose (whom we mention as well as the other, because everybody knows him) was the ultimatum of a plodder, — the very Deity of Tare and Tret. He was prudent, indefatigable, cold blooded from a half experience, with a conscience as elastic as his purse, carrying off matters nevertheless to other people, and doubtless in great measure to himself, by a certain air of plainness and good intention, — and finally, extremely fond of the sense of power for its own sake, — an appetite foolishly attributed to genius exclusively, but in fact not belonging to the very highest, nor ever so strongly possessed as by instinctive imbecility. Weakness loves a sense of power, as bad nerves love drams. Rose contented himself with getting

on, and saying Aye and No, while his old masters were alive;
but when Mr. Pitt's young clerks got into office, and took the
lead of him by dint of not being quite such plodders as himself, he mustered up a little courage and began to have some
opinions, always falling in however with the powers that were.
His old age too relaxed his dullness a little; and he "vowed
to God" with so much vivacity, that the persons whom he
undertook to speak for trembled both for him and themselves.
On the other hand, Croker does not wait for old age to render
him confident. He would be as busy or at least as humming
as a bee, if his employers or something else would let him;
and perks himself forward as much as he can in the *Courier*
and the *Quarterly*, if not in the House. He began with voluntarily turning spy on Mrs. Clarke, *after* she had quarrelled
with the Duke of York; and has ended, for the present, with
having grave letters addressed to him from the most manly
and above-board set of men in the world, — the British naval
officers. He also urged his wish to keep his war-salary in time
of peace, at a time when numbers of those officers were
thrown out of employment, and the widows of others were
lifting up their feeble hands for a little more help. Such are
the freaks, tastes, and pretensions of this class of government
retainers. Mr. Canning would be numbered among them, and
indeed richly deserves it for some things, especially for his
strange taste in taunting people with the origin of their
ancestors; but it must be acknowledged, that he has talents
which give him some just pretensions to publicity, though not
sufficient to render him impatient of serving his present dull
masters. Croker to Canning is what a shrewd footman is to a
shrewder butler, who surpasses all the rest of the mansion.

By the way, since noticing in our last the apparent neutral-
ization of Mr. Canning's wit by the prevailing dullness of his
more powerful friends, he has issued forth again, and made
one of the best displays of himself we ever remember. (For
the report at length, the reader must consult the *Courier*.)
Look at the *reasoning* part of it however; and see to what
sorry sophistications he is reduced. The stratagem, upon which

his speech manoeuvred, is curious and worth the public attention. Mr. Fazakerly[7] (a gentleman, we believe, of taste and
spirit, whom we are glad to see coming forward out of the
better class of the silent) made a motion, the object of which
was to instruct the Committee of Secrecy to inquire into the
conduct of Oliver[8] and the other spies. Now the Committee
of Secrecy had been justly ridiculed and denounced by the
Opposition, as a set of self-nominated persons interested in
quashing or misrepresenting the very inquiries they pretended
to institute; and this, which is a truth notorious to the whole
country, Mr. Canning took occasion to thrust in the teeth of
the mover as a piece of reaction against his proposal; asking
with what face the gentlemen of the other side could propose
to submit so vital a matter to a Committee of so deadly a
nature. The question seems but just, and the result was — as
it would have been under any circumstances; the Ministers
got their majority. But the fact is, that although Mr. Canning
pretended, and enabled the majority to pretend, that the
tables were turned upon the mover solely because the Opposition had convicted themselves of an accusation which
they did not feel to be just, or rather of a mere inconsistency,
he and the others knew very well, that the motion was in
reality absurd, *not* because the Secret Committee had been
so characterized by the Opposition, but because they had
been *rightly* characterized. It was the very consciousness of
the hollowness of the Committee which enabled its own
friends to pretend, that the Opposition had been discomfited
for falsely accusing it! — Such are the strange freaks of a state
of things so sophisticated.

Mr. Fazakerly was overmatched in *cunning.* He was complimented too — (we were going to say *however,* but we
changed the word instinctively) — he was complimented, in
the midst of a quantity of *sarcasm,* on his talent and independence, and on his ingenuousness. Ingenuousness is a noble
thing, and the mark of something much wiser than cunning;
and we hope to see that Mr. Fazakerly has not been dashed
back into silence by the sarcasms, or bowed, and smiled, and

frightened back by the compliment, — by the *good* opinion.

But see the upper hand which corruption first gets, which folly gravely upholds, and *face* carries through. The Opposition denounce the Committee seriously, — and then it is a very shocking accusation, and the Ministers hum and haw and look big: — but a Member not accustomed to make motions, suddenly takes the advocates of the Committee at their word, and proposes to lay some grave matters before it; and then up starts the gayest of its friends, and says "What, bring honest and grave matters before so shocking a Committee!" and all the dull rogues laugh, and the resistance is effected either way.

This comes of the flattering Yea-and-Nay habits to which a bad state of things has habituated all classes in the House. It is high time for the really honest part of its Members to forego the habits of their respective parties, and speak out; for let Mr. Canning talk as he will about Robespierre and such stuff, and endeavour to revive the Anti-Jacobin enthusiasm as well as joking, the time is gone by; and the Country is not much longer to be trifled with, whatever the House may be.

Febuary 22, 1818.

There is a body of men in the House of Commons, who are sometimes spoken of with great gravity and respect as the solidest part of the representation, and often alluded to with levity as no very profound persons, for whose especial benefit Latin quotations are to be translated. We mean the Members known by the appellation of *country-gentlemen.* The class however is of a very miscellaneous description, and generally speaking has very doubtful pretensions to this title, — at least in its old acceptation. That they are not remarkable for wisdom, however, is certain; and it is equally true, that the majority of them are alternately corrupted and frightened by the Boroughmongers, according as the questions they are to vote upon are supposed to be matters of personal indifference or alarm. If they see no immediate danger to their interests, they are heartily willing to say Aye, out of mere ignorance of the subject; and if they fancy they do, they are terrified into compliance by alarms about revolution, out of a credulity equally short-sighted.

Let us not confound however the mongrel breed with the true. The great majority of the real country-gentlemen will be found, upon inspection, not to be on the very worst and most trusting side of corruption; though at the same time this great and real majority will dwindle to a very small number, — exceedingly small certainly to what it ought to be in a House of Representatives.

It is no news to tell the reader that the race of *middle* country gentlemen, who used to form so useful and indeed noble a link between the upper class and the peasantry, has long been extinct in this country. This was the consequence of the ascendancy of mere money-getting, the union it formed with mere power, and the precious game those two have been playing ever since with their jobs and their wars. As the money-getters rose, and the taxes pressed, the middle gentry disappeared; — they were gradually withered where they grew, or transplanted to the metropolis where they were compelled to change their nature. There was a talk then, as there still is in some obstinate quarters which think to browbeat us with their egotism when their argument or their principle is no longer held worth a rush, of a certain amiable and silvery return of these taxes in "fertilizing showers." They have certainly not fertilized the domains of the gentry in question, nor indeed any others in this country; — no, not a jot more than the clouds which go over our heads to drop fatness among the Germans. The smoke which reeks out of our chimnies returns to us just as much; and a considerable addition to the town smoke is just what the country has gained by the extinction of this once illustrious body of Englishmen. For every half dozen flimsy houses which the pedestrian passes in the suburbs, he may reckon upon the loss of a solid family house in the country, or at least upon its being occupied by a lawyer, an apothecary, a distiller, a Methodist parson, or some other such fattener upon the distresses of the community.

Of this class therefore we are to look for none in the House of Commons, though we may find some of their grandsons and great-grandsons there in other shapes. An investigation into the other class would make a curious treatise, and be worth a good deal as an illustration of the changes of manners and fortunes. It may be divided perhaps into landholders who have merged into the peerage, landholders who remain as they were, and adventurers in trade or office who have been enabled to succeed to the property of those whom their system has ruined. The first are of course in the House of Lords, and form part of the Boroughmongers there who kindly take the trouble of representation out of the hands of the people. Of this class is Lord Lonsdale[9] (Lowther of Lowther), the greatest Boroughmonger in England. Of the second is Mr. Coke[10] of Norfolk, the Heathcote and Shelley families, and a few others, who are chiefly on the side of the Whigs. Of the third are the Dutch family of the Vansittarts,[11] who give us Ministers; and the late George Rose, who acquired a large property in Hampshire by having places and sinecures in London. There are a great number of these spurious country gentlemen in Parliament, many of whom have usurped the places of the others without succeeding to their interest in the soil; that is to say, who make a great show with mansions and a little park or so, but have the chief of their property in the funds and foreign adventures. There is Sir William Curtis,[12] who, if he could have carried on his biscuit-baking a little more surreptitiously, and not manifested himself to us so gloriously as an Alderman, might have passed for as honest and blunt a country gentleman as any of them, especially as he knows so little of Latin, or English either.

On the other hand, there is a celebrated Member of Parliament, whom the Ministerial jobbers and the degraders of the cause of Reform have delighted, from a conscious knowledge of the reverse, to represent as a mere lawyer and adventurer; but whose talent in reality lies in statistics, and who is of one of those ancient English families, which, like the Hampdens, Congreves, and Miltons, share their names with their native places, — Brougham of Brougham. This Gentleman, with a spirit worthy of his descent as well as abilities, is at this very moment contesting the representation of his native county, Westmoreland, of which Brougham is a town, with the dictatorship of the Lowthers, who have so long ruled it with a rod of Treasury gold, and made such a dull as well as corrupt business of the matter in Parliament. They have in fact long ceased to be representatives of the Commons part of the county. They are Peers and Peerlings, very rich and very borough-mongering, with an influence which reduces the whole business at last to a mere personal feeling of the aristocratic and all-ruling, and which would degrade the inhabitants of this one free, happy, and plentiful soil to the condition of subjects of a Venetian oligarchy, to which indeed the State has long had a considerable resemblance.

How far Mr. Brougham will succeed, we know not; that is to say, we know not whether sufficient English spirit has been left in the county of Westmoreland to inspire the inhabitants with energy to resist dictation as well as impatience to feel it. The times must surely have done much to enlighten them; and Mr. Brougham, we trust, will do his part to keep their eyes open. But this we know, and this we must say to all the gentry of England, that unless they really rouse themselves as he has done, and keep up to the mark as we hope he will do, — above all, if they do not get some feelings out of the pale of this and that party, and cultivate some real enthusiasm on its own account for the country and the people, an inevitable convulsion will infallibly reach them as well as every one else, small landholders as well as great fundholders, and tear every species of property out of their hands, like weapons of which they are unworthy.

CAUSE OF THE INFERIORITY OF
PARLIAMENT TO THE DEMANDS
OF THE PRESENT AGE

March 1, 1818

What renders the Parliament[1] so inferior to the growing intellect out of doors, is what has been hurting the national character and happiness, ever since we deserved the title of a nation of shopkeepers; — we mean a want of enthusiasm. We have had none of the right sort ever since the Brunswick Succession. Our literature, till the French revolution excited it, was cold and common place. Our national music is so still. A painter, who should try to rouse a real feeling for his art, was and is still thought to be a kind of rebel against academies; and Sir Joshua Reynolds was frightened, and subsided in a courtier. Our war with France, as to any thing generous, was a pretence and an affectation. We had just fought America, because she struggled for real liberty; and now, out of the same fear, a junto of courtiers and money-getters fought the French. The people acquiesced, because the passion for war is always cultivated as much as possible among them by the interested, and because they were always to be roused against the French, as little boys are against one another at school — "What! Won't you fight Jenkings?" But the truth is, they neither loved the legitimate, nor were in any pain for liberties to which they were growing unaccustomed. They had no enthusiasm, bad or good, except for money-getting. Any turn-coat made tools of them, provided he was on the jobbing side; and Pitt and Burke made them fight and even advance money, in the hope of its being repaid with interest. But they fought to no purpose except to get jobs from Government, and drain the blood and resources of the middle gentry and the lower orders; nor would they have fought to more purpose at last, had it not been for the rashness of Bonaparte himself, whom they first encouraged to resemble their masters and then taught to despite both. The battle of Waterloo, setting aside other causes which are yet to be explained on the French side, was gained partly by passive force, and partly by some remainder of that better national spirit which our ancestors obtained for us, and which we had been losing every day. So precious are the very dregs of freedom.

This victory however contained within it some seeds of a wholesome reaction. It was obtained by popular strength, — the same weapon which has rendered the German people so sensible of their own consequence, whether against foreign or home despots. A new generation too, in the mean while was growing up; and the immediate events of the world, a new and a better school of letters, and particularly the outrageous faithlessness of the Allies to their promises, fell in as excitements to that spirit of enthusiasm, which is in some degree natural to youth. See how the youth of Germany have been venting their feelings. A similar intelligence is rapidly increasing among the younger part of the people of England. They have been taught in a less dull school than their Anti-Gallican predecessors, and in a less extreme one than the Jacobin; and are therefore neither witless nor hopeless. They need not the love of money to put an idea in their heads; nor retreat into the most selfish prejudices for comfort. Above all, they have seen what poor figures their predecessors cut as sordid traffickers, tools, and empty heads; and as is generally the case with the intelligent children of the foolish or gross, they are inclined to the very opposite tastes and opinions of their fathers.

Now the House of Commons is behind hand in this respect. Some of the leaders of it are as old or older than Mr. Pitt himself would have been; and most of them, who are middle aged, were young men, spoiled by him when he was in the height of his hopes and power. The rest, generally speaking, are pretty nearly of the same age and bad habits, old hangers-on of the club-rooms, place-men and expecters of places, persons implicated with every part of a corrupt system; men with a great many wants and bad tastes, and not the spirits or strength of mind to lessen them; servants of the aristocracy and the other House; yea and nay voters with war-makers, who are ignorant of the next island in the Channel; making full Houses when the Peers and other Boroughmongers are to be maintained, more than half empty ones when the best interests of the people of England are to be brought before them, and fairly running away from the very mention of Ireland; — in short, wretched talkers when they do speak, dumb voters away of property and liberties in general, sharers of the artificial and poverty-making wealth of the paper system, and maintaining that all is well, in spite of starvation and secret imprisonment, as long as they have their horses and boots of a morning, their white waistcoat and bottle of an evening, and as few ideas in their heads as can give them trouble.

There are exceptions of course; but this description is only the sum and substance of what the persons excepted have told them over and over again to their faces, when despairing of seeing the most decent or urgent measure carried. A correspondent wonders that the men of ability and integrity in the House do not fairly get up and walk out in a body, when common sense and decency is about to be contradicted as it so often is by the votes of the majority. The idea has a good appearance; and in truth has often been before us; but there must be a much greater number of really independent men in the House, before a body of them could be either numerous or spirited enough to act in this manner, and to give it any effect. It is the people that must do the work themselves; — it is the people that must refuse to hear the daily dictatorial shallowness of the Ministers, and the hopeless and feeble opposition of a few men; — it is the people that must again render the House constitutional, intelligent, and free.

Let them perpetually then keep these memorandums before their thoughts: —

First, That it is hopeless to expect a Reform from *within* the House, as now constituted: —

Second, That it is their great duty as well as interest to avert if possible that alternative of which a celebrated statesman forewarned them — A Reform "*with a vengeance from without*": —

Third, That the upper classes of the democracy and their traffickers are, for the most and elder part, men whose minds have been long stagnant from sordid and unenquiring habits; that they have no enthusiasm for any thing great, good, and unselfish; — none for natural and rural habits as in Elizabeth's time; none for popular liberty as in that of the Charleses; none for elegant taste and sociality as in Queen Anne's; nothing to remind them of real pleasure for themselves, or justice towards others.

Fourth and last, — That the younger as well as other more intelligent parts of the community have felt and seen better; that circumstances have given them minds and hopes superior to those of their predecessors; that corruption and worldliness are never so corrupt, and worldy, and foolish, as when they are old; that they never atone for their sins to this world, even if they become aware of them, but only endeavour to make the best for themselves in the next; that they are too old to be taught, and too human and owing to previous circumstances to be treated vindictively; — in short, that the hopes of Reform and of all our influence upon mankind are in the hands of the younger part of the community; that you will do well to encourage them as much as you can, to get as many as possible into Parliament; and in a word, assist by every means in your power, the new growth of taste, liberality, popular feeling, and a love of nature and justice, as at once the only weapons, and the very best rewards, of your approaching victories over the dull and the sordid.

DEATH AND CHARACTER OF THE QUEEN

November 22, 1818

As we are in general more elaborate than most papers in our notices of deceased persons that have been before the public, it will be expected perhaps that we should make our first article out of the present subject.[1] We do so.

Our brother journalists have relieved us from the necessity of entering into any historical details of her Majesty's life. All that can be collected on the subject from the daily papers will be found in our subsequent columns. To the writer of the *Times*[2] in particular we are indebted for what is called "breaking the ice" respecting her Majesty's character and reputation with the public; — an example the more refreshing, inasmuch as the ministerial and opposition papers seem resolved to say as little as possible about the matter. The *Courier*, which does not think itself bound to be courtly except to its masters the Ministers, and its masters' masters the Borough-mongers, contents itself with a paragraph or so of vague panegyric. The *Chronicle* says nothing. As for ourselves, the subject is a personage whom we seldom thought of; — we do not conceive that all the influence of Royalty is likely to give it any undue gilding with the public; — and — — we shall hasten to say all that seems necessary.

We may as well begin with quoting the whole passage in the *Courier*. It is a sort of epitome of the cant common on these occasions, being studiously general instead of particular, commonplace to the last degree in its sententiousness, extravagant as if in despair of being true, exceedingly "brief and tedious," — in short, very insufficient and very sufficing.

"It has been our melancholy task this day," says our Official Mourner, "to collect and arrange every particular, within our reach, which might tend to illustrate the eminently virtuous character of our departed Queen. It is by posterity alone that the conduct of Princes can be impartially estimated. They who are but coldly praised while living, become objects of unmingled affection and applause after death. The meed of justice is too often tardily bestowed. It is proud consolation, however, to the British nation to reflect, that only one opinion exists throughout all ranks of society, as to the unblemished and irreproachable character of a Queen, whose virtues on the throne have contributed, in a high degree, to improve the moral character of the people. — In all those points that constitute female excellence, she was pre-eminently distinguished, and when this sentence is pronounced, what higher eulogy can be bestowed? That her late Majesty partook of the common infirmities of human nature, it would be foolish adulation to deny; but her portion of them was never such as marked her out, even in her elevated station, with all eyes drawn upon her, for the censure of the most severe moralist. This tribute to her memory is but an act of common justice; and, with pleasure we add, it is a tribute which we pay in common with all our contemporaries."

Now all this etiquette sort of eulogy, when translated into the language of truth and common sense, really means nothing more than that her Majesty was what is called decorous. "Eminently virtuous" means that she was not notoriously vicious; — "unblemished and irreproachable" mean that she was chaste; "all those points that constitute female excellence" — (what talking, to be sure!) amount to about the same thing; — and the praise, that she was not liable to "the censure of the most severe moralist," is only another variation of it. This is the usual way of comprising all the compliments that are thought payable to the sex, regal or otherwise; and a worse mode of paying them, or a more confined notion of what is praise-worthy, could not be invented.

That the late Queen had the virtues of appearance in some respects, and may have had virtues in reality, we do not deny. But we must plainly say, that when we come to be told of her obvious, great, and undeniable virtues, we must be then allowed the privilege of differing in opinion, or at least of enquiring what sort of virtues they were. If we are told to act upon our usual professions of charity, and give her Majesty credit for what we did *not* know, on account of what we did, we must as plainly say, that we knew little or nothing; and that we want some popular kind of reputation for virtue, such as a queen might easily obtain to form a ground upon which to attribute the rest. When we saw the Princess Charlotte give way as she did to her feelings of sympathy for her Mother, we augured favourably of her nature in other things. When we remembered that Sheridan had sympathised to the last with his old friendships, though *a friend*[3] at the last forsook him, we attributed his errors to circumstances rather than to vice. When we found that Sir Samuel Romilly[4] killed himself out of an impatient sympathy with his old habits and affections, we said, here is a man who fell a victim to the diseased excess of a good thing and not of a bad one. All these persons, though in different ways, and in different degrees of disinterestedness, evidently lived for others as well as themselves; and therefore, in *spite* of the violations of decorum in one, and of custom in another, we attributed, and were bound to attribute to them, an additional and gratuitous measure of virtue. But we know of nothing ever done or exhibited by the Queen, which might not have been done by a merely prudent person, whether virtuous or not. She was chaste; but so are many vicious as well as virtuous persons. She was decorous; but so may the greatest hypocrite be. She was prudent, but so may be the greatest miser and the most cunning intriguer upon earth. We do not say that her Majesty was vicious or hypocritical, nor would we undervalue prudence, except when old *Philpot* in the *Citizen*[5] talks of it; but we say, that what merely proves the absence of certain vices, does not prove the possession of any virtue.

On the other hand, though the non-exhibition of any thing which the world agrees to call vice is of so little avail in proving actual virtue, the non-exhibition of certain virtues, in so eminent and maternal a station, goes a good way to prove, that they, at least, hardly existed. It was a pretty

general opinion, for instance, that the late Queen wanted
charity, in more senses than one; and notwithstanding the
Courier's attempt to confine virtue to the most ordinary and
conventional notions of it, we hold this to be a little "blemish"
and "reproach" in a person's reputation. Her Majesty was
understood to be rich; — indeed she must have been so, from the
property that belonged to her, and that came into her management, by law; — the calls, which it has been alleged *might*
have been made upon her, there is no reason to suppose ever
were, at least to any purpose; for we know where, and how
often, they were made in other quarters; and in short, whether
she was marvellously rich, or more marvellously poor, a generous woman in her condition of life would always have had it
in her power to make the whole nation *ring* with her noble
qualities.

In the great Christian virtue then of charity, or generosity
in money-matters (and her Majesty piqued herself upon her
Christianity), appearances and popular opinion are certainly
against her. In the other equally indispensable Christian
charity, of benignity of sentiment, and mutual forgiveness of
error, the case, we are afraid, is the same. It appears from
the autobiography of a late Prelate, that even a Bishop could
not differ in opinion with her Majesty, but she would contrive
to show him a sour face. But a remarkable and well-known
instance occurred but a short time since, even to the avowed
surprise of Members of the Senate; and it was in resolute
existence to her last moment. We allude to her Majesty's
obstinate refusal to admit the Duchess of Cumberland to
Court, on the ground, says a Daily Paper, of "a taint" in her
reputation. This taint (for the apparent virtues of her Royal
Highness in other matters will warrant us in dispensing with
the trouble of mystery on a subject mysterious to no one) was
alleged to be a former reputation for want of chastity. We say
former; for her Royal Highness's manner of life in England
precluded all notion of any such thing here. But, "Go, and
sin no more," was not the doctrine, it seems, to be practiced
in this instance; though a belief in its propriety was indispen-

sable. It was, "Go at all events, and come not near me." If her Majesty, in spite of all her Christianity, would have said this to the woman taken in adultery, what, in Christ's name, would she have said to a woman like Mary Magdalen, who is understood to have sinned more than once or twice; and yet Christ, we see, preferred her, after all, to the over-careful Martha. He also rebuked his Apostles, who misunderstood him,* when, with a sweet appreciation of sentiment, she lavished the rich ointment on his feet. The reason was, that he knew very well that the ordinary conventional virtues of society might even be superseded by greater ones; but that none of them could produce disinterestedness and happiness when the greater ones were all absent. But to resume. As chastity is at best a virtue as little questioned or understood as it is rigorously and partially exacted, so the loss of it may either be the consequence of some of the coarsest or some of the finest feelings of human nature. It may either be mere impudence and defiance, — or it may be the result of the most conscious virtue and trusting simplicity; and we know not which is the greater fool, — the seducer, for his wickedness in violating such confidence, or not repairing it, — or the callous bigot, for his stupidity in thinking it an unpardonable sin. We know not what was the natural moral character of the Princess in question. Her alleged faults, if they existed, may have been the result of neither vice nor confidence, but of the manners of the court in which she lived; and what particularly astonished people was, that at the very time when the Queen set her face in this manner against her daughter-in-law, she had herself taken a sudden vagary for being gay and festive in her old age, at a new court not very famous for its scruples,

---

* We suspect that *this was the case* many a time; and that it would be a new and useful thing to keep an eye to the fact, *throughout their biographies of that Divine Person.* If nobody takes this hint, and does it before us, we hope, before we die, to write a treatise on this principle, which may help to rescue the exquisite philosophical beauty of his doctrines from the inconsistent dogmas and threats with which they are mingled, and those pernicious sine-qua-nons of faith, which have turned them into dispute, selfishness, and bloodshed.

and at a time when her Husband was prevented in the most unhappy manner from expressing his known dislike of such habits.* Other ladies who had admission were at least tainted in their reputation, if unjustly; if the seduced might not be there, nobody, we are sure, will deny the absence of seducers.

And this brings us to speak of a passage in her Majesty's life, which does not appear to us to have abounded even in decorum, nor even when decorum would have looked most like a virtue. The above is one instance; and another is her having had supper parties in Windsor Castle, while her Husband was in his present unhappy condition there. We should have been the more loth to call this to mind, had not the *Courier* the other day, in one of his strange forgetful fits, thought proper to tax the public at large with inattention to the King's situation! — the public! who wait in silent delicacy and sympathy to hear news of their old Sovereign, and who wonder (as we told the ministerialists *some time ago*) at not hearing of him more frequently, or rather particularly!

We noticed the suppers we allude to at the time; and we are not at all sure that our notice may not have been useful; for to come to another point in her Majesty's reputation, it may afford no uncurious specimen of her alleged attention to every thing that passed in the political world, to mention, that she was a subscriber for many years, perhaps all her life, to the *Examiner;* and was in the habit of having two numbers of it. The pretence of some of her eulogists, that she did not interfere in politics and intrigue, is refuted not only by all probability, but by what politicians themselves have shewn. Her attachment, after the fashion of the old German school, to divinity, and the love of power which manifested itself in her love of riches, led her, it is understood, to cherish a particular influence with respect to all graver matters and personages,—in the nomination of zealous Bishops, and decorous Ministers of State. — Her Majesty is said to have written out, with her own hand, a manuscript Life of James the Second,

* We should not wonder if these sudden trespasses upon her usual manner of life, at so advanced an age, were the original cause of her death.

sufficiently Tory; and furthermore, to have translated from
the German the sermons of Zollikoffer,[6] — a name provocative
of a rhyme.

Her ministerialist eulogist, who is too modest to be long,
is of opinion that "posterity alone can estimate the conduct
of princes," and that "they who are but coldly praised while
living, become objects of unmingled affection and applause
after death." The observations, no doubt, are extremely original, and perfectly inapplicable: — "exceeding good sense"-
less. Princes must at least have done something in their own
times in order to be judged or applauded by posterity. The
late Queen did nothing; and if posterity is not informed on the
subject, especially by something else than the *Gazette*, we
venture to assert, that their mis-information, if they thought
about the matter at all, would be as great as their total indifference is certain. We lay the passage out of it before our
readers as something which will really astonish them. It would
make a most illustrative figure in Mr. Bentham's late famous
work on the *insincerity* that is taught the nation by its creeds
and systems.

Whitehall, Nov. 17, 1818.

This day, at one o'clock, the Queen departed this life, to the
inexpressible grief of ALL the Royal Family, after a tedious illness,
which her Majesty bore with the most pious fortitude and resignation.— *The many great and exemplary virtues which so eminently
distinguished her Majesty throughout her long life, were the object
of universal esteem and ADMIRATION amongst ALL classes of
his Majesty's subjects, and render the death of this illustrious and
most excellent Princess AN UNSPEAKABLE LOSS to the WHOLE
Nation.*

We recover our breath merely to add, by way of summary,
that the late Queen was not at all popular; nor does she appear
to have been a favourite with the family, if we may judge
from the singular and apparently studious absence of the
greater part of her children and connexions. She seems to have
been a negative character, with little sympathy of any sort,
but with a good deal of royal wilfulness, and an abundance of

that sort of prudence, which has a steady half-shut eye to its own personal comfort both in this world and the next. — Her Majesty was of a small stature, and is said to have had a pleasing figure when young. Her face, it is agreed, was never handsome. We think there was a remarkable likeness in it to the prints of *Joanna Southcott*.[7]

CROWDING OF CONVICTS IN PRISON-SHIPS

January 31, 1819

The reader will find in our parliamentary abridgment a dialogue respecting the transportation of convicts.[1] Mr. Bennet,[2] who is as unceasing in running his warm round of humanity as is the blood from his heart, went down the other day to enquire into the state of a prison-ship which was about to carry Dr. O'Halloran[3] to Botany Bay. He found him crowded with twenty other human beings in a cabin twelve feet square, and *in cribs six feet and a half broad by five feet and a half long, into each of which were stuffed six of them!* The space thus allotted to each convict was one foot one inch by six feet, which is five inches less than the room afforded to a negro in an African slave-ship. The vessel contained altogether between two and three hundred human beings, all stowed in about fifty cribs. The places of stowage were so dark, that although it was only three o'clock in the day, it was necessary to use candles; and "never" Mr. Bennet said, "should he forget the loathsome scene which the vessel exhibited." The vessel, a short time before, had got on a bank in a gale of wind, and been nearly lost; the agitation of the storm had occasioned a violent sea-sickness, and those who were lowest down were almost suffocated with the consequences. In this state when sick, in a worse if possible when passing the line, and in a torturing, angry-making, and demoralizing one always, are these wretched men *shut down* for *fifteen hours out of the twenty-four!*

How is this answered, when Mr. Bennet makes the representation? Why, nobody present knows any thing about the matter: — none of our humane, enquiring, intelligent, and all-suffcent Representatives can tell. All that Mr. Bathurst[4] could say was, that the ship was "fitted up in the way ships of that kind usually were fitted up." — "It was impossible for him to state what the dimensions really were." — "It was not for want of attention that he had not noticed this subject, but because he had not the means of knowing what the circumstances were." (Not the means!) "He could not assert positively that this ship was fitted out as others were; but he had no reason to think otherwise: — it was commanded by an officer in his Majesty's service: — *that* was all the general knowledge he had: — he should endeavour to inform himself on the subject." A very good though rather dilatory resolution, for it would seem that the ship has sailed. While he is about it, the Right Honourable would do well also to inform himself on a few other subjects, lest he should again be taken unawares. Mr. Clive[5] added, that the average of *deaths* in prison-ships is only two in six-hundred; and the only other Member who appeared in the shape of an advocate for Government on this occasion, and who declared himself acquainted with the Inspector of Convicts, said he happened to know that the Surgeons in these ships were paid if they landed the convicts alive" — which creating a laugh of indignation, he added, "paid in proportion to the number of convicts landed in good health."

Nor on this occasion had the *Courier* any thing to say to the particular case, notwithstanding all his demi-official knowledge of humanity, obtained from the demi-gods admitted to the board of Jupiter Dapsilis.

Regalis inter mensas laticemque Lyaeum.[6]

He said he should leave the question to be discussed by the Government, who intend, it seems, to take up the subject; that is to say, take up in the sense of arrest; for such is the usual result of their pretended adoption of such subjects. For the present, he contented himself with shewing what his masters would do, by begging the question at once, and calling all those whimperers and whiners who do not agree with him! Thus my Lord Eldon, who thinks every thing right that is done by Government, and weeps out of an excess of satisfaction at Pitt dinners, is a proper specimen of your manly nature, as Canning and Castlereagh are of your humane; but

Capt. Bennet, who takes the trouble while others are feasting and lounging and being maudlin, of visiting prisons and prison-ships, and interests himself most actively in behalf of every kind of suffering humanity, is "a whimperer and whiner," and has a "puling sensibility!"

Next night however Sir Thomas Martin,[7] the head of the Transport Board, comes forward with some information; and then the *Courier* is glad enough to forget his general abuse and his patient impatience, and repeat the details afforded him. We will give the information in his own account of it. "What are the *facts*," he cries, "disclosed by Sir Thomas Byam Martin? First, that out of 6,409 convicts, sent to Botany Bay since the 1st of January, 1816, only 53 had died on the passage, being in the proportion of 1 to 112; secondly, that instead of *six* persons being crammed into a space of $6\frac{1}{2}$ feet by $5\frac{1}{2}$, the number of persons was only *four*; and thirdly, 'that the space allowed to a convict was as great as that allowed to a British soldier, and greater than that allowed to a British sailor.' Is it not disgusting, in the very teeth of these *facts*, to read the maudlin details of hardships to which felons, forsooth, are exposed? They are provided with *greater* accommodations than our brave seamen, and are placed upon an *equal footing* with our brave soldiers: but the inevitable privations to which those men are subjected, who go forth to fight the battles of their country, are intolerable when endured by men, who are banished for their crimes, from that country which they had disgraced and injured. We leave it to every reflecting individual in the kingdom to draw his own conclusions from the comparison."

Well; these *reflecting* individuals (not the persons whom the *Courier* means, when he flatters them with that title) will draw their own conclusions, but they will be very different ones from his. In the first place, it is observable that Sir Thomas gives a different account of the deaths from the one which Mr. Clive ventured upon the night preceding. Mr. Clive reckoned the deaths as one in 300; Sir Thomas Martin says they are one in 112. But more on the subject of deaths presently. In the second place, Sir Thomas asserts that four persons, and not six, *are* put into the space mentioned by Captain Bennet; and thirdly, he says that the room of a convict *is* as great as that of a soldier, and greater than that of a sailor. But what does he mean by both these assertions? That such is *actually* the case? No, but that such is the *provision author-ized.* Therefore, with the usual gratuitousness of office, he insinuates that because such is the law, it is of course acted upon; and the *Courier*, in the same spirit exaggerated, follows him, and triumphantly confounds *a provision* with *a fact!*

But what does Mr. Bennet say? He does not deny that such is the provision; he says that the fact, as far as he came to the knowledge of it, is otherwise; and therefore, whether provided against or not, ought to be enquired into. If the Government, he argues, have not provided against it, they ought, in common humanity: — if they have, it is incumbent upon them, for the same reason, to see their provision acted upon.

According to the *Courier*, when a charge is brought against the Government for misconduct, one of the ministers or ministerialists has nothing to do but to get up, and say, that the law is not so, and therefore the conduct could not have been so. Upon this reasoning, we are all in a blissful state: there is no such thing as illegality and corruption; the Habeas Corpus is never suspended, because Magna Charta is against it; Lord Castlereagh did not sell a seat in Parliament to Quintin Dick,[8] because it was a crime against the Constitution; nor does the *Courier* almost every day defend immorality, sedition, and ruin, under pretence of crying out against all three. Sir Thomas Martin says, that such and such a space is allotted to only four men; Mr. Bennet says, that on enquiry he found it occupied by six. What is the question for "reflect-ing" men? The argument about the soldier and sailor falls to nothing as easily. They are not stowed so thickly together; and they can also relieve each other, and go on deck. If they could not, enquiry would be equally necessary for them. The statement respecting the deaths is as little to the purpose, granting of course that it is true, which remains however to be proved on enquiry. A man may be in a state of anguish for months, aye, and for years, without dying; and he may recover his health when the torture is removed. But how does this vindicate the torture? Mr. Bennet does not complain that the men were killed, but that they were agonized; and he is answered by a reference to the deaths. The tortures of the Inquisition might be defended on the same principle; for the Inquisitors have surgeons to stand by and see that the agony does all but kill. As to the unlawful, foolish, and vindictive notion, that criminals are to suffer punishment, not contemplated by the law or by a due consideration of all that made them criminals, we disdain to answer it further at present. Perhaps we shall one day have to refute it in favour of the very slaves who now bring it forward, — those greater criminals, who, as the *Chronicle* well observed, "first pillage and then insult their country."

The plain truth, no doubt, is, that in some vessels at least, owing to gradual carelessness on the part of the authorities, more human being are crowded together than the provision contemplates. The consequent duty of the authorities is obvious, notwithstanding the yelping of their curs, who howl indiscriminately at the approach of bad and good.

There can hardly indeed be a more odious sight than a servile and interested adherent starting forward to advocate the petty and particular conduct of his employers, let the question be of never so much consequence to humanity. He persuades himself, as a celebrated writer said of a dissipated prince, that every thing goes on perfectly well, because he has had a good dinner. He does more. The least notion of being put to trouble for humanity at large, — the remotest suspicion that a single luxury may be missed from his table, — fills him with malignant indignation against the greatest claims of his fellow-creatures; and he would rather let them be suffocated by dozens, with heat, sickness, and horror, than get up out of the easy chair of his egotism and selfishness. The Governor at Calcutta was not to be waked when our stifled countrymen were expiring in the Black Hole, and shrieking out "Water! For God's sake!"

The excellent person, who brought forward this matter in Parliament, did not draw a picture a twentieth part strong enough. Imagine a multitude of human beings, of all ages, descriptions, and varieties of criminality, crowded together in dark, irritating, and noisome narrowness. They contemplate their long voyage and exile with different feelings, but all of them, most likely, with more or less bitterness. Some are hardened offenders, who help to spoil the rest. Some are old and infirm, some young and stout, some young and delicate, some impudent, some comparatively modest, some only foolish. Some speculate with desperation on the country they are going to, some with induced callousness, some perhaps with ardour, some with the most wretched recollections of home. By degrees the hardened grow more angry, and the comparatively virtuous more vicious; the melancholy are made ashamed with taunts and bravadoes; but let all of them pretend mirth as they may, wretchedness is at the bottom of it. They are squeezed and shut down in their cribs; and here commences a Pandemonium of heat, and darkness, and irritability, and oaths, and obscenities, and loathsomeness, and ghastly laughter, and misery. The first gale of wind and pitching of the vessel sickens them, and produces a scene from which the imagination is quick to escape; — but they would do so in vain. Conceive the loathing ideas produced of each other by infirmities which cannot be then treated with levity, — which levity itself only assists to give a degrading idea of human nature, and which nothing but the most delicate and affectionate spirit can afford, as it were, to surmount. They come into the tropical regions, and here the heat and loathsomeness are doubled, and the spirit of the most defying made weary. Fancy a crowd of human beings put down in darkness, by sixes and sixes, in cribs of six feet and a half by five and a half, and panting upwards, under the hot boards, for fifteen hours out of the four and twenty. Fancy the loathsomeness, the gasping suffocation, the oaths, the execrations, the rage of the strong, the despair of the weak, the yearning impatience not only for home, but for a little breath of fresh air, — the half-maddened wonder of the thinking, — the confirmed disdain, hatred, and abandonment of the profligate. Punishment of crimes! *Such* punishments tend to make the worst crimes in the world, by begetting that contempt of one's fellow-creatures, which equally renders callous the felon and the statesman; — and the callous statesman is infinitely the worse of the two, for it is he that has the greatest hand in making the other.

MR. COBBETT, AND WHAT IS WANTED
IN PARLIAMENT

March 12, 1820

They say that Mr. Cobbett will really get into Parliament.[1] We were afraid at first that it was a piece of electioneering cant; but we find it believed, as well as reported, by very intelligent persons. The friends of a candidate always talk so sanguinely on these occasions, that the more they insist, the less we are generally inclined to believe them. It is counted a part of electioneering tactics. The voters make a point of being out of their wits with certainty. To hear them talk, one would suppose that the voters on the other side must be in the last stage of despondency; but go among them, and you find that they are in the same state of rapture. The candidate may groan over his hopes in secret; but he takes care to issue forth with a delighted countenance. He rages only behind the door. He keeps his "Damnations!" for his particular friends. His prospect may be the dreariest in the world, and we may think it so; but he will point out the beauties of it with transport, calling his thistles roses, a slough a velvet mead, and a dead wall a boundless extent of country. He marches up to the cannon's mouth, calling out to all the spectators to witness what a pop-gun it is; and is blown to pieces in a rapture of success. These tactics go upon a good principle; but then they should have other good principles with them, or they only end in making hope ridiculous. But there is generally so much shuffling going on in the mean time; so much paltering with this and that principle; so much shyness on this point, and over-wrought pretence upon that; so much enthusiasm got up for the moment, which we know is not likely to last; so much complimenting, and excessive personal attention; so much interest taken in the looks of Mr. Jones, and the opinions of Mr. Jenkins, and the cough of

Mrs. Tomkins; and above all, the whole facts, connected with the election, past, present, and to come, are generally so well known by all the parties interested, that whether the candidate meets with success or not, the sanguine anticipation of it only takes its rank with the numerous other manifest insincerities got up for the occasion. What, in fact, do the nation care in general, whether the anticipators succeed or not? They are tired of cant on all sides. They do not want individuals to have hopes; they want hopes themselves, and the way to supply them is to renounce every species of cant, and speak a language as different as possible from what is common to the insincere. Cant came back with the victory at Waterloo; and though she has an enemy in the mere existence of the press, which she had at no such former period of the world, yet those who have common cause with the press, should take care how they condescend to use even her most specious language. Cunning has been tried long enough; and only does good after all to the upper orders of the foolish. Why should wiser men try only to be as wise as they? They can be much better. Do we suppose that Castlereagh and such men, whom an intelligent mind would not give twopence to converse an hour with, could ever be at the top of affairs, but for some egregious mistakes and compromises on the part of their betters? And do we suppose that the same mistakes are likely to pull them down? To succeed, once and away, in opposing them is nothing. It is worse than nothing. It is only the exception which proves the rule of folly. If we were election candidates, we would have no recourse to anticipations, which have been used and abused by every body, and in which, after all, there is the hazard of diminishing exertion as well as increasing it. If a man cannot get into Parliament but by dint of insincerity, we would not trust him when there. Over the whole of civilized Europe at present, there is a strong feeling that power is a canting and a rotten thing, as opposed to the progress of opinion. A wise man should make the distinction logically, which all Europe thus makes instinctively. He should put on the side of this power all that is canting and rotten, and keep on the side of this progressive opinion all that is cordial and sincere. To copy the language and usages of the former, is to do for despotism, and for the perpetual reign of nonsense, what the courts of Europe did for France, when they all agreed to copy her language and fashions. We know of few things more disgusting than the electioneering advertisements which now appear in the newspapers, especially the ministerial advertisements. Their appeals to the feelings of the constituents, to their *knowledge* of the parties, &c. their regrets at not being able to *wait* upon them in person, or their delight at the prospect of *being* able; their gravities, loyal and religious; their vivacities, old and customary; their anticipations of success founded on the goodness of the cause, and their own individual merits; — all this, when they know very well that not one jot of it has really to do with their return to the House, is perfectly nauseous. We would not make use of a syllable of it. To anticipate success, it is true, is natural to sanguine men. We would anticipate it, if we felt what we said; but we would do so briefly, and in the course of action; and not constantly harp upon a subject, the repetition of which would indicate, that success, merely as such, was what we aimed at. The way is, not to doat upon our future triumph, but to secure it by weakening the enemy, and by strengthening the principles that fight for us. For we cannot too often repeat, that the success of this or that individual is nothing. It has been tried over and over again, and found wanting. Trust has been put in names; and petty things, as it is supposed, sacrificed for securing a great object. But the sacrifice of these petty things has generally ended in securing nothing but the individual's return. What was got for him with insincerity, he has repaid in the same coin. Plain, unaffected, honest language, and a contradiction of the pretensions of the stupid "legitimate," — these are what society want; and if these are not the only things that secure success, they are the only things by which we can secure a success of any use to us. When Mr. Hobhouse[2] anticipates the surgery of posterity, and cuts up the corrupt body of Ministers, we feel that he is then shewing the true strength, skill, and value of his hand. When Mr. Brougham, extricating himself from the courtesies which are as pernicious on some occasions as they are pleasant and humane on most, not only fights the war of the people of Westmoreland against the dictation of a strong-pursed and weak-headed family, but denounces "the cant of this most canting age," he carries his likelihood of victory beyond that mere contest with existing power: — he fights for the age to come.

To return to our first subject. There are things in Mr. Cobbett which are not to our "fastidious" taste; but we should like much to see him in Parliament. His interests, small as well as great, are those of the age; and he has sense enough to perceive it. Then he has a considerable knowledge of statistics; he speaks as he writes, a good clear idiomatic style; he is quick at detecting such absurdities as ministerial men commit; he is healthy, active, and zealous; he has had experience of several conditions of life; and lastly, he has risen, not merely from the people, but from their very poorest ranks, and is therefore a striking specimen of that intellectual power, and that ascendancy of opinion and acquirement, which has come up in these latter times to confront and pull down the otherwise victorious assumptions of brute authority.

There has been a great talk of grenades, and of the confusion which their explosion would have made among the Members of Government. But of all implements to be pitched among a set of Ministers, and to confuse and scatter their faculties, commend us to the Cobbett. Neither grenade from Cato-street,[3] nor shell from Copenhagen, no, nor even Infernal Machine from Paris, could carry such inevitable worry and horror among the Treasury benches, as the appearance of this blowing-up figure. How genteelly would the slender mightiness of my Lord Castlereagh recoil! What would be the petty perturbutions of Mr. Vansittart! What the queer consciousness of Mr. Croker! What the affected indifference of the counter orb of Mr. Canning! Think also of the sidelong glances of Mr. Tierney; of the solemn expectations of the country gentlemen; of the careless pride and perplexity of the young politicians; of the proud but scrambling resort of the young members in general to their university common-places; and last but not least, of the disjointed and whiffling confidence of that old babe of grace, Mr. Wilberforce.

But here some creature of parliamentary habit may exclaim, "Cobbett! What can *he* do? He, who has no parliamentary influence, no connexions, no money, no tactics? He may speak occasionally; but who will listen?"

The People.

The country is in great want of such a Member of Parliament as Cobbett; of one who has none of the usual drawbacks arising from place, or pension, or titled connexions, or the indolent possession of wealth, or the interchange of endearments in St. James's-street, or a hundred other "delicacies," which do and must "awe a man from the career of his humour."[4] When he shall think of any plan that may benefit his country, he will have no need to consider what Tomkins will say to it. He need not waive inquiring into this or that matter, out of deference to Blenkinsop. There will not be infinite things to be concealed and dallied with between him and the consciences of office. If ever he should be in the humour to coalesce with the corrupt, he is not a man to be coalesced with. Power and privilege will do every thing they can, rather than let in among them the plebeian faculty, — the mere untitled, and unprivileged, and unpolite, and uninheriting possession of intellect. It has been said that all classes of mental, as well as pecuniary property, find their representatives in the House of Commons. It is a saying as false as an allied monarch. Its object is to smooth down the popular intellect, and to pretend that its rights are not only recognized, but taken care of; whereas the popular intellect, taking such a man as Cobbett for its representative has never yet made its way into that House. Neither the popular, nor, if we are to believe the strange warning of a Noble and accomplished Member of the other House, the unpopular intellect, has yet found its representative in Parliament; for as there has never yet been a Member to lay the same zealous and sympathetic stress on the claims and knowledge of the poorer orders, while there are hundreds to take infinite care of all the rest, so there was not a man in Parliament the other day, who in this denounced age of infidelity, ventured a syllable in behalf of an honest want of religious faith. We once heard an eminent Counsel say before the Lord Chancellor, and without any one's thinking of contradicting him, though he had opponents enough, — that Deism, or the belief in a God separated from any other faith, was notoriously the religion of almost all the literati of Europe. Has the literary religion of Europe then a representative in the House of Commons? Yes; many in secret; but what is a secret representative? What would secret representatives of Protestantism have done for the growth of religious liberty, if they had contented themselves with keeping their testimonies to their own book-cases, and continued to vote with Popery? So much for the "unpopular" intellect. The popular, we fear, has not even this kind of coy image, afraid of beholding too much sincerity in its looking-glass. Doubtless, besides Whigs and Tories, there are members who are neither Whig nor Tory; at least, who go all lengths with neither, and who sometimes say and do very useful and very popular things. We admire those sayings and those deeds accordingly; especially when we consider all the habits and other temptations which might have prevented them. These are men also extremely useful and respectable, even as a class by themselves. Neither do we mean to assert here, that a proper quantum of Toryism may not have its representative, with advantage to existing institutions. It has plenty at all events; — a great deal too many. But what the country wants in Parliament, is men who can come forward and state plainly, without any reserve whatsoever, the very same arguments and feelings which occupy the enlightened part of the poorer orders; men, who have been of that class themselves; who have acquired knowledge enough of their own to see beyond the superficial assumption of others, and to denounce them; who will not be content with saving the reputation of their better wits by hinting a joke at Lord Castlereagh, but will get up and say plainly, that he is a very shallow person, and prove him so in good round terms and logic; — who will discuss an income tax without mere reference to the purses present; — who will handle a corn bill, not with tenderness to the value of the sheaves, but to the wants of the people's pockets and stomachs; — who will take a leading part in questions of finance, and not suffer them to be lorded over by placemen and ex-placemen; who will regard the heavy assumptions of Grenvilles, and the genteeler fopperies of Castlereaghs, and the Tory-propping opposition of mere Whigs, and the shambling independence of Saints, as a heap of impertinence which it becomes the age to leave behind it: — in short, who will not merely declaim once and away on the subject of Reform, but talk of it, and urge it without ceasing; who will tell us all plainly what he means by it, and what we have a right to possess; and who will expose all the contented and contenting sophistry, the nonsense, solomn or smiling, the round-about stuff, bad grammar, and mincing parliamentary cant of those, whose corruptions are "as notorious as the sun at noon-day."

If Mr. Brougham, a Whig by connexion, a lawyer by education, and a patrician by birth, is nevertheless a most liberal representative of law and jurisprudence, especially in those noble toils of his for the schools; — if Sir Francis Burdett, considering his wealth, rank, and propensity to enjoyment, deserves the praise and gratitude of his country for being so good a representative of the independent English gentlemen; and if Mr. Hobhouse would make a good, indignant representative of the more intelligent and independent part of the younger men of the same class, disgusted at seeing the affairs of the world lorded over by their inferiors; still there wants somebody to speak the sense and feelings of the largest and most important class of the community, who are the pith of the body politic, and without a perfect understanding of whose rights and feelings, it may still turn to a mass of corruption.

Now, we know of no man, whose experience, whose interest, and whose acquirements, point him out as a fitter person to be such a representative than Mr. Cobbett; and therefore we cordially wish to see him in his place. We are the more anxious to see him there, because, whatever the House may in the first instance affect to think him, we are persuaded that no man will supply a more desirable share of the Parliamentary Reports; and our anxiety is increased by a supposition which seems prevalent, that the general returns to Parliament will be favourable to Ministers. And why will they be so? Because corruption, after provoking violence, is enabled to take advantage of its misdeeds by the hypocritical fears of the *expedient* and *accommodating*. These alleged conspirators in Cato-street would no doubt have done something for the corruptions which provoked them, out of the mere blindness and stupidity of those who cannot see the provocation; but the timidity, which leads people to blink the real question, and to answer to the menacing and impudent call of the corrupt upon all "loyal and honest men" for their denouncement of assassination, will do infinitely more. Fear and insincerity are always thus hindering the progress of knowledge and justice: and therefore, for our parts, nothing upon earth shall induce us to truckle to either.

THE LATE QUEEN OF ENGLAND,
HER FUNERAL, &c.

August 19, 1821

We return to a subject,[1] which an accident prevented us from treating at the proper length last week. It is a custom with this paper to pay more than ordinary attention to the memories of those who have interested the community; and it is certainly not on the present occasion that we shall make an exception to our rule.

Caroline Amelia Elizabeth, Queen-Consort of England, was a Princess of the reigning House of Brunswick, and was born there May 17, 1768. Her father and brother, Dukes of that House, perished in the late wars against the French; to whom they were such bitter enemies, that the inheritance of their strength of spirit without its national antipathies was one of the many singular charges, which Christians have not hesitated to bring against their kinswoman. She is said to have been the gayest of the gay at her father's court; and was probably indulged a good deal in that mixture of princely self-will with personal good-nature, which is by no means a combination of qualities always observable in princes, and which has helped in consequence to bring her to her grave.

On the 8th of April, 1795, her Serene Highness was married to her cousin the Prince of Wales, who being overwhelmed with debts, and told that nothing but a wife's hand should help him out of them, did not scruple to avail himself of one accordingly.[2] It does not enter into the range of prince's ideas to take to his renunciations and water-bottles on these occasions; neither would judicious and loyal subjects permit it. They insist upon his being extremely splendid and costly; and he gratifies them enough, God knows.

Of this "Happy Union," which was destined to be broken almost as soon as the biscuits which recorded it, the only issue was the late Princess Charlotte. The Prince, being set at ease with the very delicate persons about him, speedily dismissed his wife, upon the plea that her manners were not sufficiently worthy of that epithet. A letter was drawn up in which he said that "our inclinations are not in our power"; a gracious piece of information, for which the lady and her sex might have had more reason to thank the Royal Casuist, had they not since been told, that this ready-made sentiment was only to be construed in favour of the stronger side. His Royal Highness continued to live as usual; but the sprightly disposition of his discarded wife was made a ground for "the most criminal charges"; that is to say, according to the interpretation of his Royal Highness's singular and libellous friends, — charges of leading the same kind of life as himself. The charges were so strongly disproved, under the auspices of the present Ministers, who were then in opposition to her husband, and servants to her friend the late King, that some of the principal and "most respectable" of the witnesses against her were pronounced to have perjured themselves; and the "Delicate Investigation" ended in a caution to her how she gave way to an unprincely vivacity and good-nature. Her Royal Highness then went abroad by the advice of some of these Ministers, and against the earnest entreaties of the late lamented Mr. Whitbread, who saw too well the advantages that might be taken of her abode in a sprightly climate.

In the mean time, the Prince of Wales succeeded to the throne; and the result was what we have all seen. The vivacity, which they *knew* was indestructible in her, was watched; the manners to which they *knew* she must in some measure accommodate herself, and which suited her natural affability, were turned against her; the appearances, to which they *knew* she would be liable, and against which she might be the less cautious in very scorn of her persecutors, as well as confidence in her protectors, were made the grounds, the sole grounds, for threatening her with Divorce and Degradation, in case she did not submit quietly to have every court in Europe shut against her. She took her resolution. She landed in England, to the consternation of all the servile and corrupt, attended only by one honest man, Mr. Alderman Wood, who has secured a place in history as the friend of a Queen and her sex. The Lords contradicted themselves in their perplexity; the Commons were prevailed upon to go down on their knees; but she would not submit to be treated unjustly; and the people's hearts thronged about her for her determination. The trial then took place in the Upper House. Eighty-three days did that trial go on, presenting to the disgusted eyes of the world the spectacle of a grave and powerful assembly of men, who in spite of the privileges of conduct which they allow themselves, consented to be at once the accusers and judges of a woman, to enquire into all sorts of particulars made nauseous by the enquiry, and to listen to a set of imported foreigners who contradicted themselves in the grossest man- ner, and to some of whom that woman had been a kind mistress. Eighty-three days did that trial go on; and for eighty-three days did the untitled population of England, male and female, pour before her with address upon address, struck to the heart with the new and great questions of justice which had come before them, and beholding in her the undaunted representative of the natural rights of Fair Play, Freedom, and Womanhood. At length she is pronounced "Guilty" by a majority of nine, the exact amount of the Ministers; she, whom no fact whatsoever proved to be guilty, and whom, whether guilty or not before guilty eyes, the whole justice and enthusiasm of society immediately pronounced innocent. The Bill against her was instinctively thrown out; and London was in a blaze of illumination for three nights. Compare with that blaze the lighting up for the Coronation! What were the consequences of the trial? Additional injury to royalty; odium to the church; a goading of the public feeling to the borders of revolution; and an awakened sense of those first, kindest, and justest elements of morality, before which no selfishness can ultimately prevail.

This triumph, however, now turns out to have been more on the side of the people than of the Queen. Positive as it

was to her in some respects, it was negative in others; and
it appears that her Majesty felt the negation much more
than the success. Her enemies had misrepresented her in
nothing more than in the ability to live and flourish in a
circle of her own without the attentions to which royalty is
accustomed. They did not believe themselves while they
reproached her; or else they thought she could not hold up, in
the long run, under mortifications which would have crushed
hundreds of themselves at once; for they assailed her in
every possible way. They denied her every thing they could
deny; then embittered every thing which they were obliged to
grant; they calumniated her systematically; they caricatured
her, and the caricaturists, though the most stupid in the
world, were welcomed at court; they endeavoured to frighten
every body that visited her; and they did undoubtedly keep
away great numbers; for nothing alarms the weakness of
ordinary individuals so much as being left out of the aggregate
strength of their bundle of sticks. Her enemies were in the
right. It is only minds of an original cast, habituated to
privations of every sort, and accustomed to go for refuge to
nature, who can dispense with the attentions of those that
are emphatically called the world. The Queen's was an ardent
and a generous mind, but it was not a great one; and royalty,
while it rendered it less yielding, had not helped to strengthen
it. See the unfortunate lot of this unnatural condition of life,
which is fitted to bear neither prosperity nor adversity! Her
Majesty was in vain referred to public opinion, that is to say,
to the opinion of the democracy, as a refuge from despair.
In wanting "the privileges, the power, the dignities of a Queen
of England," she thought she wanted every thing that made
life desirable. "No, no," said she, "I am a mere private person
— I am not Queen of England." To be a private person beloved
by ninety-nine people out of every hundred was not enough.
So surely does royalty make slavish the best as well as worst
dispositions, and render the very self-will that destroys them
a necessary of life. Her Majesty undoubtedly became somewhat too personal in her resistance; and thought to oppose

the main force of sovereign power with a similar exertion of stubbornness. But this of necessity became a drawn fight between great physical force and none. Her strength was in a sentiment, not in a personal display of resistance; and though she acted in many instances with equal spirit and judgment, she did not know, in others, when to add to her strength by appearing to waive it. We differ with some friends respecting her coronation endeavours in particular. Mere remonstrances were sufficient to do away the idea of allowing a precedent to be made of her treatment. To go to the Westminster Hall door,[3] and subject herself to be turned back, was only to bring the comparative insignificance above-mentioned to the test of all eyes and understandings; and we should not wonder, if a new and humiliating sense of the mock-heroic effect of this mistake was the main thing that mortally preyed upon her.

But all this is calculated, if possible, to render the sense of the monstrous injustice she experienced still more powerful. The possessors of all which she did not possess, only felt the necessity of that possession for their own comfort to heap her with denial and privation. The notorious practisers of all which she was merely charged with practising, only visited her alleged "offences" the more, because public justice dared to say they had no more right to commit them than she had. There is one person among her enemies, who for reasons more honourable to others than to himself, and on the score too of his very infirmities, we wish to abstain from treating with a ridicule that is always tempting us; but we must say, that we never could sufficiently express our grave sense of the injustice with which this unfortunate woman has been treated. Faults might have been found in her manners. A person of great delicacy and justice might with reason perhaps have objected to her something masculine on this or that occasion, and something too careless on many others. But how many excuses would not the same sort of person find for her, and how many much worse violations of delicacy would he not denounce in her enemies! The people call to mind without ceasing the circumstances under which she was married. The people unceasingly call to mind the unwarrantable demand of all delicacy and perfection made upon her, when every real delicacy had been of necessity violated towards herself. The people unceasingly call to mind the letter, or letters, of license; the persecution upon grounds of misconduct, as if no such license existed, or as if the other party had not taken every species of license; the spies set about a gay-hearted woman of avowedly foreign manners; their pursuit of her[4] to a country where the most allowable manners, in unison with her own, were to be hypocritically brought to the test of those of England; the repeated Commissions; the horrible spectacles of perjury exhibited at the bar of the House of Lords; and fifty other enormities, which we need not repeat, and which with the united aid of multitudes whom we blush to name, and who would have worshipped her had she been a Queen reigning, terminated in breaking the heart of a *woman*! — Go, ye well-dressed mob, and learn the vulgarity of your own!

The Queen was *charged* with having committed adultery. She was "accused" of it; she was "suspected" of it; it was "alleged," and alleged only; for heaven and earth were moved to establish the proofs, and they failed. What must the public think, when in the same identical newspapers, which announce the fatal result of these accusations upon a woman's life, they read of the King's sitting upon the deck of a vessel, amidst the life-sustaining breezes of the sea, and surrounded by all that can contribute to his comfort and pay homage to his rank, earnestly conversing with a convicted adulterer! We are sorry to use these terms, and nobody will suspect us of cant in using them; for the Editor's opinions respecting the necessity of a liberal reform in the relations between the sexes are well known, and resemble those of Helvetius, Wieland, and other philosophers. But we use the terms that are opprobriously used by the Queen's enemies; and we ask them, not with what face they can allude to the charges against the Queen, and at the same time record the King's intimacy with Lords Anglesea and Headfort (for this would be to ask figures of brass, how they came to be brazen), but we ask them, with what feelings do they think the public at large can regard so gross, so unjust, so outrageous an inconsistency?

We have said the Queen died of a broken heart. We conclude so, because every thing announced it, and because it was in the nature of things that a woman like her should so do. "Oh no!" cry her conscious enemies: — "she died of a common disease:" — and then they talk, like a pack of nauseous gossips, or as Lord Lauderdale did about his own complaints in the House of Lords, of physic and magnesia. All that they say however may be true, and the phrase of the broken heart a just one nevertheless. Broken hearts are but too common now-a-days with very different classes of people, and mean in fact nothing more than broken stomachs, or the destruction of the digestive powers by thought and suffering. Her Majesty may not have been able to keep up her patience longer; she probably was not aware of, or could not practice, the only remedies for such disorders, — changes of air, new sights, and the best though slowest of all, a return to the simplest modes of living. The natural eagerness of misery to vary its sensations probably tempted her upon this or that food, which was unfit for her; her impatience for a remedy may have made her heap dose of physic upon dose; fevers and inflammations take place; and her life breaks down, not because the same things would have broken it down under other circumstances, but because her constitution was prepared for the catastrophe by a debilitating sorrow.

Setting aside this regret of royalty, which may however be well pardoned to one of its most generous victims, the Queen's death was worthy of her best and most social qualities. She pardoned her enemies, and comforted her friends. Nor was the courage with which she met it hurried and artificial. She welcomed it, but the welcome was quiet and leisurely. She lay down quietly to die, communing with her own thoughts, and anticipating a kinder treatment in the bosom of the next world, than she had met with from beings equally culpable and uninformed. It is easy to believe the

general report, that such a death has converted hundreds
of sceptics — hundreds of persons who thought that there
must be something criminal in what was so roundly asserted,
and who did not expect a termination of life so unmarked
with violence and alarm. It has been objected, we understand, to her Will, that while she left money to Lord and
Lady Hood, she left nothing but her picture to her constant
attendant and friend Lady Ann Hamilton. But instead of
a want of delicacy, this appears to us a striking instance of it.
Lady Ann Hamilton was emphatically her friend, and it is
to be presumed *wanted* no such legacy on any score. Had she
done so, the bequest would no doubt have been proportion-
ately otherwise. On the other hand, Lord and Lady Hood,
however cordially they conducted themselves in their office,
were later and more official acquaintances; and it may be
presumed, even with regard to them, that in one respect
money may not have been unacceptable. Why nothing is
said of some other friends, it is not so easy to conjecture.

But even if her Majesty's death had not made the great
additional impression which it has, — if it had strengthened
doubt instead of decreasing it, and could possibly have
tended in any way to exonerate some of the proceedings of
her enemies, — nothing could have turned its effect to what
it now is, more than the impolitic and unfeeling mode in
which it was attempted to convey her corpse out of the
country. Nothing was right in it. Nothing was judicious,
delicate, or even agreeable to decent common sense. It was
the climax of all the folly and mockery, which marked the
proceedings towards her whilst living. In the first place, and
in the teeth of her executers, there was the cant of pretending
to consult her own wishes, after every thing had been done
to thwart them when she had life to feel with, and in the
only instance in which her wishes happened to accord with
those of her enemies. In the second place, there was the
mockery of military attendance; *another* respect paid to her
when she could no longer feel it, and when it happened to
be convenient to their own notions and fears. Lastly, there

was the attempt to smuggle her dead body out of the country by a bye-road, — a plain proof that they would shew no sort of respect to her which they considered inconvenient to themselves, and a gross insult offered to the common understanding, feeling, and courage of the nation: for they must have either known that something riotous would happen[5] and bloodshed be hazarded, or they must have reckoned upon a tame acquiescence to the most disputable and most irritating shew of authority. Why did they not confine themselves to the decent preservation of order by the civil power, and let the funeral be conducted through the city at once? They must have known that nothing but a quiet sensation *could* have been created on such an occasion, for the people would never have broken into a tumult, while the funeral was going on: and if the *after*-thoughts of the people were dreaded, how have they lessened the dread by the mingled audacity and pusillanimity of the measure they ordered? The advisers of his Majesty have undoubtedly brought us to an awful crisis; and he himself may possibly think so, when he hears what has been taking place in the metropolis of the nation, during the imaginary and festive security of the holiday at Dublin. It appears by Lord Liverpool's answer to the very excellent, off-hand, and ingenuous letter of Lady Hood, that the orders transmitted to him were peremptory; and much sorrow and wonder are expressed by her Ladyship, and we understand by some others, at his Lordship's being the instrument of such proceedings. We know nothing, for our parts, of the virtues of the Noble Earl. We can give him credit for all the morality that is attributed to him; and we know also that in numberless instances, especially in times like the present, nothing more may be necessary for loading a man with the reputation of virtues of all sorts, than his exercise of a reasonable quantity of negative ones, and his offering no annoyance to the self-love of mediocrity. But we must say on this occasion, as we have said a hundred times before, that we de not understand the morality of a Government which patronizes gambling while it hangs the desperate,

and which lends itself to the ruin of a woman charged with
adultery, while it pays homage to a Sovereign, who has led
a pretty free life, cheek by jowl *with* adultery. But we have
already alluded, in the present paper, to the fantastic melancholy of these incoherent spectacles. Our repetition of the
allusion will only serve to shew, how impossible it is for the
public to get them out of their head. Impossible! Aye, and
how *wrong* it would be, were it possible; for melancholy
indeed would be the state to which a nation once free had
arrived, could they witness, without perpetually recalling it
to mind, the spectacle of one code of morals assumed and
countenanced for the convenience of authority, and another
acted upon against those whom it dislikes. Whether the
moral question itself requires revision, is another matter. We,
for one, think it does; though to be approached with all due
calmness and conscientiousness. But a different conclusion is
assumed by those who nevertheless violate it; and it is this
strange pretension, among other deplorable contrasts between
the few and the many, which serves to render the present
crisis more awful. We use an epithet unfortunately not too
strong. The awfulness is not to be denied. Orders for a violent
and unwise measure come over from Dublin, we can easily
guess by whose advice. Its right is disputed by the Queen's
friends, legal as well as familiar. The people consider it an
insult to her memory, and to the metropolis. They blockade
the passes into the bye-road by a regular military movement.
Some of the military, provoked at finding their efforts to
force a passage fruitless, fire upon the people, and cause the
destruction of a couple of lives, and the deliberate aimer of
one of them is a young officer, no other, it is reported, than
the son of the Marquis of Anglesea! In spite of these mortal
doings, the people obtain their object. One band of the
soldiers does not even exhibit an agreement of opinion with
the other; for which the people know no bounds to their
gratitude. The procession is turned into the path it wished
to avoid; and the undeniable tears of thousands of persons, in
the most important city of the kingdom, welcome the funeral

of an injured and broken-hearted woman, whom her enemies would have deprived even of that last honour of the wretched. "I had the gratification," says a Correspondent of the *Traveller,* "of seeing, under the protection of a band of English soldiers, and preceding the hearse of a Queen of England, these glorious, emphatic, and memorable words, 'The Power of Public Opinion.'"

In leaving the reader to the important and obvious reflections which cannot but arise out of this event, we shall only add a word or two upon one or two sad pieces of cant and absurdity, with which her Majesty's deadly persecutors are at present attempting to blind us to their enormities. One journal says that now she is dead, it hopes people will "bury all animosities." We dare say, it does. It is a very convenient doctrine, when you have helped to kill a person, to hope that no further notice will be taken of the killing. As if forsooth, a great question of justice and injustice were settled by the death of an individual sufferer! No: all the people more or less, and not all the people, but *all their posterity,* are concerned in having these questions thoroughly sifted and understood. The Prince of Wales's discarded wife may have been the only thing in the question considered by her enemies. They themselves now confess as much. But truly as the public sympathized with her, and strongly as they have stood by her to the last, it was because, in addition to the interest excited by her forlorn situation as a woman, they saw the interests of all other women, and of society at large, connected with her treatment. — Again, we are told in other quarters, that it was Lady Hood's letter, which in requesting the Government not to hazard bloodshed, produced what it affected to deprecate. And thirdly, we are informed in the same pleasant places, that force must be used in breaking down opposition to "lawful authority." Yes: authority is to hazard any thing; and then if you advise it not to do so, it is you who cause the hazard! Authority does a foolish thing which provokes opposition; and then force is to be used at all events to maintain its folly! We need not put cases to shew the absurdity of his reasoning, or what we should all have been, if it had been successful in England up to the present period. "What the lawful authority is in this case," says the *Traveller*, — "whether the Ministers or the Executors, is not clear: — but for what *purpose* is any lawful authority constituted? Not to set itself on immaterial points, in opposition to the will of the people, even though it should be able to subdue that will by the sword. Even popular resistance has not a greater tendency to destroy' lawful authority,' than the capricious and wanton use of it by its holders." A greater! No: not a fiftieth part as great; for the patience of a people, — their natural dislike to originate movements that may compromise individual comfort and security, is notorious all over the world. The bloodiest revolution which the world ever saw, and which will no doubt prevent the recurrence and the necessity of another as bloody, was the result of the longest and basest ill-treatment, which at last wore out the patience of the people, and made them drunk with frenzy and revenge. We conclude with a remark of the above excellent journal: —

The same dull, cold malignity, which has characterized the unparalleled enmity ever since the failure of the grand attack is consistently maintained to the last; — an enmity a thousand times more hateful than that which boils in the blood of a savage, and equally destitute of the sentiment which, in better natures, ever tinges hostility with courtesy, and imposes restraint upon the worst properties of our common nature. And this, from the chivalric side too, to support Royalty! — But so it is; the records of all history, ancient and modern, prove that it has been precisely this sort of loyalty which, in all ages and countries, has formed a railway to revolution.

ON THE KEEPING OF TWELFTH-NIGHT

TO THE EDITOR OF THE NEW MONTHLY MAGAZINE.

January 1829

Sir. — If the following remarks should be thought not
unworthy of your publication during the present good-
humoured season, when it is agreed by all parties to be more
merry than wise, they will be glad of a Christmas corner in it,

Your humble servant,

Perennis.

Twelfth-night is perhaps the most agreeable of all the
domestic holidays.[1] It has not the novelty of Christmas day,
which is the great breaking up of the dreariness of winter;
but it is at once quieter and more social; select friends are
invited, which is not always the case with the family Christmas party; every body becomes of importance, young as well
as old, for every one on Twelfth-night has a "character;"
and then there is the Cake, an eatable sacred to that night
only; the Wassail-Bowl also emphatically belongs to it, above
all other nights in the season; the company assume the dignity
as well as vivacity of a set of *dramatis personæ*; games and
forfeits derive a new piquancy from the additional stock of
wit generated by that circumstance; and as the mistletoe is
still flourishing, the evening includes all the general merriment of Christmas with its own particular seasoning.[2]

So much has been said of late years, in a variety of publications, respecting the origin of Twelfth-night, and the way
in which it is kept in different parts of the world, that it is
needless to repeat them here. Suffice it to say, that all these
great holidays originate with nature itself and the operations
of her seasons; and that our European Twelfth-night (for all
civilized nations partake of it) is a Christian version of one
of the old nights of the Saturnalia, when the ancients drew

lots for imaginary kingdoms. The royalty of the Twelfth-cake derives itself from the Wise Men of the East, who are said to have been kings; and those also who would keep the night in perfection, should sustain the royal character the whole evening, and run their satire, not on persons and things in general, but on the fopperies of courtiers, their intrigues, adulations, &c. To be more wise than nice, however, belongs neither to cake nor wisdom; and they who prefer the general custom, should continue to prefer it. Animal spirits are the great thing, in this as in all other holidays, especially in winter time, when the want of sunshine is to be supplied by the fire-side, and the blood to be spun round by a little extra festivity. Besides, all the follies may be invited to court, and the monarch not be the less royal.

There are four things necessary to a due keeping of Twelfth-night: — the cake, the wassail-bowl, the installation of king and queen, and the sustaining of divers characters, illustrative of the follies of society. The satire, for the most part, runs on the fashions and affectations of the day, and the different excesses of gormandizing and grudging. Fops and mincing ladies are always brought in. The prude who thinks herself most qualified to object to others, is sacrificed, in order to show how much the season, for all its satire, sets its face against envy and ill-humour. The miser, if introduced, is sure to have no quarter; while on the other hand, the gourmand is allowed to cut a figure more ridiculous than unsocial, to let us see on which side excess is the more pardonable, especially at Christmas.

Misers, however, are seldom thought of, for they can hardly be present. Indeed, if they were, the subject would almost be too tender, especially if the caricature which introduced it (for these things are generally casual, and arise from the pictures bought at the shops) attached to the master or mistress of the house. A miser giving a Twelfth-cake seems hardly possible. It is true, he may make a show once and away, and buy the privilege of being asked out to a hundred good dinners by giving one. We dined once with a rich old lady, who used to have an anniversary of this sort, in a great room without a carpet. Never did she catch us there again. It makes us long to chuck the butter-boat over one's host instead of the pudding. But miserly people cannot give a proper Twelfth-night. Something will be wanting — the cake will be large and bad; or good and too small; or there will be a niggardliness in the Wassail-Bowl; or the worst fruit will have been bought for the dessert; or the company will detect one of the subtleties too commonly practised upon children, and be malignantly pressed to eat heartily at tea. Now it would not do to satirize such persons. They would be too sore. The gourmand cares little for the character of Sir Tunbelly Clumsy. He thinks it in character with the season, and has it in common with too many. Besides, he may be as generous to other people's bodies as he is to his own. The fop and the fine lady can bear as much, for similar reasons; and they have a reserve of self-love which is proof against bitterness; as it ought to be, if they are good-humoured. As to the prude, it might be supposed that the best way to satirize her would be to take her under a mistletoe, and give her a kiss. Fancy it not. Of all persons in the room she longs for one most; — and with reason; for she and the scold are the only women to whom it is difficult to give one.

A Twelfth-cake should be as large as possible for all to share alike (for there should be no respect of ages in cake), and it should be as good as possible, consistent with a due regard to health. It is easy to see what is spared for health's sake, and what for the pocket's. The plainer the cake, the greater should be the expense in some other matter. Large then, and good should be the cake, tall, wide, stout, well citroned, crowned with figures in painted sugar (things always longed for by the little boys, and never to be eaten), and presenting, when cut open, the look of a fine pit of tawny coloured earth, surmounted with snow. May the ragged urchin, who has stood half an hour gazing on it in the confectioner's window, with cold feet, and his nose flattened against the glass, get a piece of the like somewhere! If you saw him, and it was a little vagabond whom you knew, — the potboy's cousin perhaps, or one who has filial claims on the ostler, — send him a piece out by the footman.

For the Wassail-Bowl, which, as it has only been restored in the metropolis for the last few years, is still a mystery in the manufacture to some, take the following receipt from a good hand. It implies a good handsome bowl, and a reasonable number of people, not professed wine-drinkers, — say from twelve persons to sixteen. Those who prefer wine, can have it alone.

"Imprimis," quoth our fair informant,[3] "direct a small quantity of spices to be simmered gently in a tea-cupful of water, for fifteen or twenty minutes; to wit, cardamoms, clove, nutmeg, mace, ginger, cinnamon, and coriander. Put the spices, when done, to four bottles of white wine, not sweet, and a pound and a half of loaf sugar; and set them on the fire, altogether, in a large saucepan. Meanwhile, let the bowl have been prepared, and the yolks of twelve and the whites of six eggs well beaten up in it. Then, when the spiced and sugared wine is a little warm, take a tea-cupful of it and mix it in the bowl with the eggs; when a little warmer, another tea-cupful; and so on, for three or four; after which, when it boils, add the whole of the remainder, pouring it in gradually, and stirring it briskly all the time, so as to froth it. The moment it froths, toss in a dozen well-roasted apples, and send it up as hot as it can be.

"N.B. Should the wine be British, dry raisin is to be preferred; and three quarters of a pint of brandy should be added. It makes, perhaps, as good a Wassail as the best."

The Twelfth-night characters purchased at the shops are best for companies in ordinary; and they are always pleasant to the children. Parties that dispense with them in their own persons, should still have them for the little boys and girls. It is hazardous, also, to invent characters to suit. Care should be taken that they trench as little as possible on actual infirmities, and that the drawers should be very good-humoured. The best way, provided there is enough wit in the room, is

to see if the picture-characters will do; and if not, to strike
up some invention on the sudden. Merriment is always best
when least premeditated. But a great help on these occasions
will be found in the idea of a Court; which is undoubtedly
also the properest mode of supporting the King and Queen.
Courtiers, chamberlains, maids of honour, &c. are easily
thought of, and suggest a great deal of mock-heroic dignity.
We have known evenings passed in this manner, when, in
addition to the other dramatic piquances, the principal character spoke in blank verse;[4] a much easier matter than might
be supposed, and such as few lovers of books would fail in,
if they took courage. The verse itself, be it observed, is to be
caricatured, and may be as bad as possible, all advantages
being taken of inversions and the artificial style. There is no
finer ground for satire than a Court; the more imperial and
despotic the better; and, on this account, the most loyal need
not fear to represent it, especially in liberal times like these.
A King who can do liberal things, and the abstract idea of a
king, are two different matters. The caricature must of necessity tend to as great a degree of remoteness as possible from
a limited monarchy. A Sultan would do well for it; the present
Sultan,[5] for instance, — and a naval ambassador might be
brought in, after the battle of Navarino,[6] to throw his court
into consternation. Or the King of Persia would do, with his
unlimited will, and his hundred children. A fine opportunity
here for Sultanas and compliments. But there is no necessity
for these foreign versions. The abstract idea of royalty and
its self-will is the great point; and a piquancy is given to its
Oriental extravagance by retaining our every-day dress, or a
caricature of it, as we may see in the farce of "Tom Thumb."[7]

CHRISTMAS DAY

December 25, 1830

The antiquities of Christmas, its origin, old customs, rustic usages and mention by the poets, have been so abundantly treated in various publications of late years, that we should have nothing to say on the subject, if the season itself, and the fire-side, did not set us talking.[1] We hope our readers will all enjoy themselves heartily to-day; but to that end, we have first a word or two to say of a graver tendency. We are not going to tell them that they must have no mirth, because there are many who have a great deal of sorrow. It would be a great pity, were there no sunshine in one place, because there is rain in another. There are many things in the present state of the world, and of our own country in particular, calculated to disturb even a momentary spirit of enjoyment, if our very humanity did not help to re-assure us. We firmly believe, that the end of all the present tribulations of Europe will be a glorious advance in the well-being of society. This reflection alone may enable the lovers of their species to endure many evils, and to persevere with renewed cheerfulness, in the struggles that yet remain for them to go through. We believe also, with equal assuredness, that the end of the present dreadful calamities of the poor in England, will be a proportionate advance in the whole condition of the English community; and therefore uneasy and cheerful thoughts chase one another in our contemplations, as images of the present or future predominate; but when we propose to ourselves a special day of enjoyment, or relief, or whatever else it may be called, in proportion to the cares of the individual, it appears to us that we ought not to take it, without doing what we can towards diminishing some portion of it in others, even should our circumstances allow us to do no more than give them an apple or a crust. What we mean, in short, is, that in all neighbourhoods, there are fellow-creatures to whom Christmas is little or no Christmas, except in reminding them that they cannot keep it; and we would have everybody do something, however small, to shew them that we would fain have it otherwise. The rich can do something in this way, to gladden the hearts of many families; others may be able to do but little for three or four; others for a less number; and some for none at all, to any serious degree, except that the least attention to the poor is welcomed as a serious blessing. But we would say to every one who can spare a slice from his pudding, or an apple from his little children's dessert, "If you can send nothing else, send that." If you know of no actual distress, still the slice of meat or pudding may be welcome; the servant will, probably, know somebody who would be glad of it. There is the washerwoman, or the errand-boy, or the poor man who sweeps the cold street at the corner,—send out your charity somewhere, and it will find a call for its tenderness. We give this advice, not because your heart may be wanting in natural kindness, or you may not be even actively beneficent, when affliction is brought before your eyes; but because the best hearted joy may sometimes forget others, in its vivacity, or not have been sufficiently taught to share what it can; but having thus earned a right to be sympathized with by those about you, we say *then*, "*Do forget, if you can, all others.*" Shut out the world and its sorrows, as you do the darkness of the evening with your curtains, and realize the happiness which you would bestow on all. It is a part of your duty to enjoy what pleasures you can, not inconsistent with others' welfare or your own.

The true keeping of Christmas is to be found among those who are neither rich nor poor. The rich have too much Christmas all the year round. They invite their friends indeed, eat mince-pies, relax from Parliament, and, if they are above the vulgar sort, or lofty enough in another way to dispense with mere fashion, and its face-making, contrive to imitate the middle classes as much as they can, in their diversions. But there is no genuine Christmas, at present, except among those

to whom a season of festivity is altogether rare; who cannot
keep open house in general. We take the perfection of a
Christmas-day, for instance, (and if we were as rich as my
Lord Grosvenor, we should confine ourselves to the fare, on
that day), to consist in things held peculiar to the season, —
we do not mean in niceties of dace and tench, or anything that
Mr. Gunter[2] could do for us, but in plain honest beef and
pudding, mince-pies, roasted chesnuts, and a wassail bowl.
Mince-pies are peculiar to the season; and roast-beef and
plum-pudding necessary to it. The pies may be dispensed
with, but the roast-beef and plum-pudding are essential. A
man might as well set up at once for a fellow of infinite no-
jest, and most un-excellent fancy, who should order boiled
beef on a Christmas-day, when he might have it roasted, or
insult the proper place at table with any other pudding than
plum. Even turkey and sausages, though common to the day,
are neither peculiar to it, or necessary, nor is wine either,
though, as there must be something to drink, it should either
be the wassail-bowl, however composed, or the great country
wine that we see growing in such pretty clumps in the hedges,
in the shape of the elder-tree; a production which, according
to Evelyn, possesses all the virtues under the sun.[3] We have
a friendship for port wine, and love champagne as we do wit;
but not to mention that reformers and authors must often
make up their minds to be content without either, we could
make out a very good case for our Christmas evening, by the
help of Mr. Evelyn's Nepenthe, always provided that our beef
be roast, and our eyes be gladdened by the goodly orb of the
plum-pudding. The elder, too, should be genuine, neither sour,
nor too much spiced; the former condition being totally opposite to its healing character, and the latter converting it into
a caustic, resembling the quintessence of the scrapings of tea-
kettles. For genuine elder we have a degree of respect that
Mr. Evelyn himself would have approved. Mr. Lamb, in his
eulogy on tobacco, calls it,

"Brother of Bacchus, later born."

Elder should be styled

         Brother of Bacchus, *elder* born.

We have a notion that the Bearded Bacchus was its prototype. In short, elder is emphatically the Christmas wine; the proper cake to it, is a piece of toast. The dessert is a roasted pear, apple, or chesnut. Some foreigner, insolent with his happy climate, said that there was no ripe fruit in England but the roasted apples. We could have told him that we have eaten finer peaches in England than in Italy; but at all events, he might have added the roasted chesnut, — a plebeian elegance, better than the raw beans which we have seen the young ladies take out of their reticules, and munch, in that charming country. Chesnuts furnish a sport by the fire-side, such as may be enjoyed by rich and poor, provided they are either young enough to be wise, or wise enough to be young. Milton, in one of his Latin poems,[5] has recorded his fondness, when a youth, for roasting chesnuts and pears, and seeing them crackle and hiss upon the bars, so that we hope nobody will be ashamed of sharing with merry children, this cheap and illustrious pastime.

And this brings us to another indispensable requisite for Christmas enjoyment, — the fire itself. If at dinner we must all sit round a great pudding, it is no less necessary that we pass the evening round a great fire, staring our eyes out at the coals, and nibbling cake and fruit, twice as much as we ought to do. In this condition, we play at forfeits and other games; and ingenuous youth err out of too much gallantry, in not taking a lady for a candlestick. And then there is the mistletoe hung at the ceiling, "shedding sweet influence." This, till within a short period, used to be confined to the kitchen, because, among the great, people never kiss. But we remember some years ago, a young German diplomatist who astonished his female acquaintances, by coming into rooms, and with a sudden flourish of this mysterious plant over their heads, telling them that they must submit to the "compliments of the season;" since which time, we have noticed it, in divers ingenuous houses.

But the holly is more indispensable than the mistletoe. Perhaps the holly is as necessary to the shew of Christmas, as beef and pudding to the substance of it. Everything green that can be found, belongs to Christmas; but the holly more particularly. Its beautiful scarlet berries render it the most cheerful thing the summer has left us; and so we bring the cheerfulness of nature out of doors to mingle with the joy within. Swift said, that a Lord Mayor was a man sitting on a great horse, eating custard [6] (which were the city modes in those times); and that a judge was made up of certain combinations of wig and ermine, a bishop of wig and lawn, &c.[7] Christmas, in like manner, may be defined to be a season composed of roast-beef, plum-pudding, a great fire, holly, and a wassail-bowl. The wassail-bowl has been so often described, that we need not say any more about it. We hold the countryman's panacea, elder, equally to belong to the season, as we have already shewn; but this, if the reader pleases, may come under the head of wassail; because wassail means the drinking of healths, and those may be drank in anything, even in imagination; in which cheapest and richest of all cups we have the pleasure of wishing him a merry Christmas and a happy New-year.

THE WISHING CAP

No. III

Undue inequalities in society, not an eternal or necessary consequence of inequality of understanding. Genius has had little to do with founding or maintaining the privileged orders. An answer to the best argument for the existence of those orders. Reform and privileged breeding how far compatible. Necessity of Lord Brougham to the Whig Ministry. His reputation with posterity. A Wish for Ireland. Reason why the Ministers have chosen to govern Ireland in a spirit of fear, and not of love. A question respecting Napoleon.

May, 1833

We have already observed that the moment we put on our Wishing Cap,[1] we can enjoy whatever we have a mind to, as far as it depends upon ourself; but that it does not confer upon us the same unlimited power, in matters that concern others. We have also confessed that, agreeably to a known principle of human nature, the more we can indulge our wishes, the more wishes we are apt to have; and that when they touch upon these obstacles, we sometimes get very impatient. For instance, we are accustomed to wish that all mankind were happy; and find ourselves perplexing our head about the situation of things in Asia and Africa. We reconcile the fondness of this desire to our good sense, by an opinion which grows upon us the more we reflect upon it; to wit, that the human species, generally speaking, never will be happy, till all are agreed upon doing the best for one another — till knowledge enlarges from man to man, and nation to nation; and there is an end to grudges, and monopolies, and all sorts of prosperous inequality. As to inequalities of faculty, which, it is assumed, will always exist in their present degrees of relation, and therefore prevent equalization in every other respect, we hold them to be of no weight whatsoever in the question: for there is really nothing to shew for it in the actual condition of the world. Does not the figment vanish at the very interrogation? Do we fancy, for one moment, after we have asked the question, that the wisest men in France are at the top of France? or in Russia, of Russia? or in the Austrian dominions, of Austria? It is a sheer piece of egotism in the aristocratical and educated classes, to suppose that intellectual superiority has put them in their present state of privilege. Education would do just as much for others as it has done for them — a good deal, if it proceed properly. Genius has not made them lords and squires. It raises a man here and there; and in the first foundations of the present system of society, it may have laid a few of the stones; but accident, and subserviency, and brute force, laid by far the greater number. What may have been got by genius in the first instance, has certainly not been kept by it. Acquiescence and lying have been the great selfish conservatives. Great geniuses seldom appear in the world but to give it a lift in spite of itself, and die of ill-treatment in the operation. Others remain in the class in which they were found; and are content with those simple pleasures, the sufficiency of which is an eternal argument against those who think that a man of superior faculties can never be easy, without subjecting his fellow-creatures to him in a worldly point of view. It is his very superiority that enables him to be more content. A political genius, we grant, has a wish to be stirring, especially in times that need him; but genius, considered merely in itself, and as a thing full of resources, wants nothing but itself for its honour and dignity. Praise it may need, because it is full of sympathy; and praise it gets or looks for. To common wants it is superior. Do we think that Sophocles, or Virgil, or Newton, or Locke, or Raphael, cared for any thing in the world, provided they could indulge their intellectual impulses, and obtain admiration? Did Schiller or Wieland care? Does Mr. Wordsworth?

We do not say that individual breeding does not sometimes make a difference, or that men of genius care nothing for the welfare of their species; but we mean that, as a body, and as far as regards their salaries, they are indifferent to every other superiority over their fellowmen, than such as the consciousness of genius can supply. If all the world had been in a condition of rational equality, *they* would not have been the men to want ten thousand beef-steaks a-day, or parks ten miles round in the neighbourhood of starving weavers.

Great geniuses have helped to change the world, because the first movements towards change can only proceed from original thinkers, or men in advance of their times; but they have not been in the habit of ruling the world, because political government has been an easy thing, especially upon the commonplace principle, or rather want of principle, that has regulated it. Look back upon history, and consider the innumerable series of kings that have governed it; and then observe how few of their names are regarded with any respect, or have a right to it. Divest even those of the adventitious ornaments of rank and title, and the brute honours of war, and take from them the aid of social habit, and the natural tendencies of custom, and the love of order, and then calculate how much merit would remain, even to some of the most celebrated. So little real talent is required to make a statesman in office, that a conclusion has been drawn from it, to the disadvantage of the common faculties of mankind; which it is thought must be very small, to put up with such small ascendency. And it may be so; but this does not make it the less desirable, that the world should be taught better, and that we should have statesmen superior to its commonplaces, and able to advance it. If mankind have been silly enough to put up too long with the dregs of arbitrary systems, and to be content to see themselves divided into the few who have too much, and the many who have too little, — (which is found to be none of the best of dispensations for either of the parties, nor such as prevents the rich from lamenting the common lot of evil, and talking of this "vale of tears,") — there are but two

conclusions to come to with those who see thoroughly into
their mistake, — first, that it is an ambition, "frivolous and
vexatious," to be desirous of perpetuating such half-witted
domination; and, second, that such an insight having been
obtained into the mistake, the domination cannot be maintained much longer, if men of sense choose to put an end to it.
The only difficulty in the way, (and it is a formidable one,
though not to the extent supposed,) is, that such of the men
of sense as are sharers in the "too much," have had their
understandings so perplexed, and their wills so prejudiced in
its favour, that with all their wish for the general advancement, they are for taking those very superfluities with them
which are not only its main impediments, but the very evils,
eye-sores and heart-sores, which are the most necessary to
be done away.

We are of opinion, that the Whigs, as a body, mean well to
the people, and that they think they mean the best; but this
best is identified in their minds with a very strange proposi-
tion, to wit, that the good of the majority, and the far superior
good of the few, are the same thing. It is as if a man, in dividing
a loaf among his brethren, were to say, "It is undeniably just
and necessary that you should all have enough; but it is
equally so that I should have too much." Now the justice of
this dogma will be obvious to none but such as are possessed
of the superfluity. The by-stander will never see it. The noble
Earl at the head of the present Government[2] would probably
smile with a polite superiority, if he heard this statement of
the case, and say that we mistook it. He would tell us that it
is not the "too much" that is necessary, but the elegance and
the grace of it, and the balmy effect which it produces on the
manners of those who have less. To say the very best for this
argument, the noble Lord confounds an accompaniment, or
thing co-existing, with cause and effect. He might as well tell
us that despotism is good for good manners, because there is
a great deal of politeness in Persia and China. Polite manners
are the result of an understood necessity, and flourish wherever
they are required. They also flourish in the proportion required;

and the necessity is sometimes more artificial than it should be, and the amenity in proportion to the secret barbarism or want of merit — a side of the question which the Premier, perhaps, has not very zealously looked into. At the time when swords were worn, manners were politer than they are now, because there was a greater fear of giving offence. The excessive politeness of what is called "the old school," is a remnant of the breeding of those days. Men kept their toes from one another, and took off their hats with an ostentation of lift, and a remoteness of deference, unknown to the courtiers of the present day, because they carried their resentments at their sides in the shape of cold iron; and an offender, in the twinkling of an eye, might have a remonstrance through him under his fifth rib. Here was "secret barbarism." The instinct and artifice of "want of merit," tends to maintain a similar shew of considerateness; for if we are not to be polite to one another in the absence of virtue, patriotism, and justice, what are we to be? If we are not to impute merit by our smiles and our shews of respect, to whom is respect to be shewn? From whom is it not to be withheld? And what guarantees will Lords A., B., and C. have, that we do not tweak them by the noses, and call them blackguards? "Oh, but," his Lordship might say, with another of his smiles, "politeness of manners would be good under any circumstances, as a general rule; and it is one of the utilities of my 'order,' notwithstanding the exceptions you speak of, and which I heartily give up." Good: but this is plain sense and philosophy, not aristocracy. It is a perception of the understanding, not an argument for a lie. Politeness may have come up with a lie by the side of it, because of the various barbarisms through which knowledge and right feeling have helped it to grow; but it does not follow that it is connected with that lie, or that it might not get rid of it when the lie is found out. Even the imputation of merit may be a good thing, as long as it leads the imagination to the side of grace and benevolence, and in so doing tends to no violation of first principles, or a merciless forgetfulness of first wants; but it ceases to be good when folly and wickedness stare our better knowledge in the face, and we are required to impute merit to a parcel of selfish impostors, who not only impute nothing to us in return, but pick our pockets, and eat and drink while we labour.

It is possible that the naturally good faculties of the Premier have forced him to think, now and then, of these perplexities. It is probable that others of the Ministry have reflected upon them with less unwillingness, and reconciled them, as ingeniously as they could, to their better reason, and their enormous estates. And there is at least one person in the administration, whom we cannot but consider as a philosopher deeply interesting himself in the advancement of his species, however he may have been prevailed upon by immediate circumstances, or his own prejudices of education, to identify, or to appear to identify, himself with a declining system.

In Lord Grey's mind, moral order, and the privileged order — his "order," as he has emphatically called it, are manifestly pretty much on a par. We may expect all the advancement from him which is consistent with driving those two strange yoke-fellows in the same chariot, but no farther. Let one of them be ever so much a jade, he is prepared to die with it in the "last ditch," rather than drive on with the other.

Lord John Russell[3] is a man of elegant literature, probably with all the graces of mind and private conduct becoming it. All that we know of him in that way is to his credit, and the general character of his public conduct highly so. But he is son of a ducal family enriched by preposterous gifts of abbey lands; and, though the family is a very liberal one for its station, and perhaps was never so much so as now, who is to expect it to be perfectly impartial in matters of public justice? The famous Lord Russell[4] himself, who appears so entire a martyr till we look closely into his history, and the tears of whose widow (his best glory) have helped to embalm his name with posterity, died perhaps quite as much for the abbey lands as for liberty. Liberty and property were the cry in his day, especially religious liberty; and that meant security from the Popish designs of James II who had a sharp eye upon those same abbey lands, and was for restoring them to their Catholic owners.

Lord Brougham,[5] in accepting a coronet, helped to save the coronets of these his friends; and, in so doing, helped to save the coronets of the Tories. We certainly believe that the fury of the Tories was very ungratefully wasted on their old opponents, who, at that moment, were the best friends they had in the world, and prevented a frightful concussion with the people; and we feel almost as certain that the House of Lords could not have done without Lord Brougham on the woolsack.[6] Who else could have sat there, as he did, to answer all objections, parry all attacks, expose all absurdities, and make the forlorn hopes and flashmen of Toryism give up their idle siege? This is a strong answer for him to those who ask why he accepted a peerage at all; and why he was not content with a name which he had rendered superior to titles. It is true, he disclaims the apology; he professes to think of the "order" as Lord Grey does, at least with regard to its utility; and if, for our parts, we are hardly sure he does not speak on this point as a lawyer, or whether he has not a secret regard for that ornament, which is at present found in titles and emblazonment, and which we are poetical enough ourselves to wish to see compatible with freer, unhereditary systems, (for nature loves ornament — all creation is full of it,) he will probably think the doubt as little unbecoming a good statesman as a grateful observer. But weak or strong as may be this side of him, he is unquestionably a man for mankind, and not merely for a party. His ambition is as superior to common partisanship as his genius is. He has not merely a House of Lords for his audience; he has a world. His views upon other ages are not confined to the narrow track of an ennobled family; he would fain live in a thousand radiating lines, diffusing light as a philosopher. Whether he think it politic, or necessary, or good, to become part of a fugitive system, for the purpose of checking too great a haste in alteration, or in order that he may partake of its advantages before it goes, thinking it "as well to do so as not;" or whether he accepted a peerage merely out of what he thought the necessity of the moment, and for fear of seeing himself and the House of Commons left in the lurch together by the Tories; whatever, in short, may be the policy which has allowed him to become what he is, he is a thousand times more a man of talent than he is a lord; that is to say, as his old acquaintance Majocchi would have expressed it, a thousand times more something than nothing, or, "yes than no." Nothing will hinder his being regarded one of the great workers for posterity, any more than worse things have hindered a greater man, (Lord Bacon). He will be looked upon as one of the great movers in God's good work of bringing about human advancement by human means; and therefore, to come to the great *wish* we meant to express in this our paper, we ask him, in God's name, and in the name of his own sense and sensibility, (for he has assuredly a great deal of the latter, you cannot look in his face, and not see it, to say nothing of his actions,) why did he not labour to make the ministers rule Ireland, *in a spirit of love,* and not of fear?[7]

Fear! It is no new experiment with poor Ireland! It is the old system! How long has it not been tried! How invariably has it not failed!!

But *love!* When was anything done out of love for Ireland, out of sympathy with the Irish as fellow-men? One thing has been *conceded* — the Catholic claims; but that was not out of loving-kindness. Concession is not generosity: it is not "the love that meets return." The Catholic claims were conceded because they had been long claimed, and because there was fear of a civil war, had the claim been longer resisted. But when was anything voluntarily done for Ireland? When was she governed by any thing but a system of mingled dread and dislike, and of the injury that causes dislike, and brute force, and exaction, and contempt (rack-renting and absenteeism,) and all the irritable absurdities of conscious tyranny? When did the arbitrary elder brother voluntarily leave off his ill usage, and shew himself grown old enough to be wise and kind? When was the rod spared, *and the dinner shared?* When, in short, was Ireland treated in any other way than a poor

relation, whom we found ill-educated, and kept so; helping
ourselves to its rights of property; and vilifying, striking, and
humiliating it at every turn, *because* it was ill-used; *because*
it piqued our better instinct of propriety, and exasperated our
conscience. A late unfortunate Minister talked of an ignorant
impatience of taxation. He and all his predecessors in Irish
government, acted under an ignorant impatience of their own
inability to govern, and their successors are now imitating
them. We owe Ireland food, encouragement, and respect; and
we give her starvation, hard works, and blows. She despairs
of finding a crumb in her pocket, and we tie her hands behind
her, that we may search for it, and give it to the *clergymen!!*

We verily believe that if the Ministers had shewn nothing
but kindness to Ireland, Ireland would have been at their feet.
See how O'Connell came forward, the instant he heard the
diminution of the bishopricks[8] mentioned, and grasped their
hands (as it were) with all an Irishman's fervour and *credulity.*
His views may be talked of as people please, and they may
be *rendered* perhaps what would be very displeasing; for our
own part, we profess to know nothing of what passes in his
mind, except from what he says and looks; and coupling his
looks and his speeches together, we should say, that he is the
Irish character in its harder and most active condition; that
he is the daring pupil and representative of Irish *circumstance;*
and that as it might not be impossible to drive him into un-
compromising rebellion, by taking all hope out of his country,
so nothing is more probable than that he retains enough of
Irish imagination, and the kindlier part of Irish self-love, to
become feeble and unnerved before generous treatment. It is
the Irish character. Every nation is vain in some way. The
Scotsman is vain of his prudence; the Englishman is vain of
his supposed freedom from vanity; the Irishman is vain of his
generosity, and will doat on you for appealing to it. Remember
how George the Fourth was received in Dublin, notwithstanding his broken promises to the nation. He paid the people
he had ill-treated a visit; and merely on that account, and
because of the compliment it implied to their generosity, they

loved him for it, and thought he was going to be a good boy in his old age. Oh, children of fancy and impulse, and the Milesian fables![9] Yet it is this people, so trusting, so forgiving, so willing to be cheated for a thousandth time by a kind word, that the liberal Whig Ministry, the criers out, for thirty or forty years, against the systems of Camden[10] and Castle-reagh,[11] are for again treating with that system; sweetened by a promise of kindness, if they will suffer themselves to be flogged patiently! They shew them a bit of sugar, and say, "Now take again the old infernal physic which has never done you any good; but do take it, purely because we wish to shew our vigour, and would have you take it."

Greatly do we fear, seeing what we see of the weaknesses of human nature, and knowing well enough that ministerial nature is not free from them, that the real reason for the severe measure against Ireland is no better than the one here intimated. We do not mean to say, that there is a consciousness to that effect. We have no such ill opinion of any one man in the ministry, much less of its ornaments. Neither are we blind to the possibility of there having been some doubt, or division of council, upon the coercion measure, — some un-easiness of conscience to those who have nevertheless thought themselves justified in coming to the conclusion of the major-ity. The probability is, that there has been a private avowal of regret among the ministers at their being "compelled to resort to the measure," and that they justify it to one another by an express determination to be as kind as they are severe. In other words, we really do believe that there is a strong feeling among the better part of them, and an admission of its perplexity among the rest, to the effect that a loving, is better than a scourging government; and that if Ireland is now to be treated with a "father's severity," it is, hereafter, at all "statesman-like opportunities," to be indulged, and won over, by a "father's heart." And yet not the less do we entertain a strong suspicion, that this is but a self-deception practised upon themselves, as men not ungenerous or unwise; and that their artificial and aristocratical condition, as peers and ministers, and lordly rivals of Toryism, has suggested to them the real paramount cause of the measure; to wit, a fear of the Tories, and a fear of what the Tories would *say*, and how they would laugh if their successors were not "vigorous." To tear power out of the hands of their rivals is one thing. They could endure plenty of taunts, and laughter, and incredulity, while they were doing *that;* for they knew that the possession of power would vindicate its own dignity, especially in eyes that respect nothing else. But to be thought not "vigorous," not statesman-like in the old worldly sense, — not superior to sentiment and the "bookmen,"—not good peers and aristocrats, and high-fellows, — not of the "order," the "blood," the "dear, ducal" *game,* that was the misgiving that gave the last casting vote in favour of "strong measures" against poor Ireland.

> Ask you why Wharton broke through every rule?
> 'Twas all for fear the knaves should call him fool.[12]

Ask you why the Whigs, in this instance, have acted like the Tories? It is because they live with Tories; because they meet them in clubs, and ball-rooms, at dinner-tables, and at court; because they are themselves of the Tory *"order;"* because the world of man's habits and daily sphere is more important to him, except with the very greatest, than the world of his species; in short, because many a clever man before them has done a silly thing for fear of being thought silly by his caste, and not knowing how to look Tom and Dick in the face.

We can find no better clue to the secret. The lawyer may sophisticate about respect for the laws; the kind man about the kindness which he mixes with his severity: but where kindness by itself would manifestly be sufficient, considering the character of the Irish; nay, where a policy of that nature would perhaps be even a dangerous policy in men ambitious of smoothing the way to a new mode of arbitrary power, (and we have *at least* as much right to assume this, as the Whigs have to assert that a resort to the old measures under the new circumstances can do good,) something strange and superfluous remains to be accounted for, out of the pale of the ordinary argument, when we see them resuming the measures which they have so often denounced as infamous, and not to be thought of under any possible modification of circumstances. And we can find no other. We admit that all Ministries have talked in one manner when out, and have acted in another when in; and we make allowance for that commonplace inconsistency. But setting aside the new and peculiar pretensions of the present Ministry, so remote as they would have us believe from commonplaces of all sorts, we are of opinion that one of the grounds of that inconsistency itself is not always the necessity which is pleaded for it, but no other than this very weakness and corporate vanity; the ambition of shewing the riders of the high horse, that their successors can ride with as much pride and power as they.

We look, in short, upon the Duke of Wellington and the circles as the real authors of the Irish Disturbance Bill. It is civil power piqued by the military, the new by the old, and giving it to understand that it can "do as strong things," and be as bold and contemptuous.

Oh! weak strength! Oh! boldness arising out of fear, and forgetting that there is a boldness superior both to military insensibility and civil craft! We say nothing about the church, because we verily believe that neither party care for the church; neither for what it thinks, nor what it could do. The church is abided by, not for its own sake, but from dread of letting innovation through its buttresses in too large a flood for the safety of lay-proprietors. Mr. Townsend,[13] one of the Durham prebendaries, in his vigorous pamphlet, has hit that nail on the head; and the sound has gone out into every abbey-land in the kingdom. But, if the Whigs had cared for the church, the policy of love, and of entirely kind dealing with Ireland, would still have been the best, for the reasons already stated on other accounts. The Irish would have been quick, perhaps too quick, to concede in return. *Their* time would have now come for concession, since concession was no longer the point, but generosity. Love would have brought them to the knees of the ministers, of the court, almost of the clergy.

It would have been a struggle on their side, how many rights they could have waived or compounded for; and O'Connell might, with safety and honour, have sunk into a member of the administration, as he most likely would.

When, alas, will the wise men of this world learn to be really wise, and have the courage to put in practice the doctrines which they approve! If the Irish had been ruled with love instead of fear, their history would not have been the mass of blood and corruption which fear has rendered it. Ireland would not have been the starved, indignant, and lawless younger brother of a tyrannical child. If Napoleon, *instead of reviving the Toryism of dynasties, and old courts, and the shooting of exasperated insurgents,* under pretence of their being necessary to good order, — *had followed up his victories over corruption* with a reign of love, *issuing none but edicts of kindness and justice, and meeting the long, secret, enraptured wishes of the human race; who among us that peruses these words, doubts for one instant, that* he would now have been at the top of the world!

THE WISHING CAP

No. VII

Answer to a Singular Argument of the Tories, about Human Happiness and Misery

July, 1833

We have heard of a singular argument lately adduced by the Tory Philosophers, in order to shew that reform is of no use.[1] They say, that let mankind apparently alter their condition as they will, the amount of happiness and misery in the world is the same in all ages; that Providence evidently designs it to remain so; and that, consequently, all men upon an average, are equally happy and miserable, and one person's lot, deeply considered, no better than another's. We do not know, indeed, whether this latter consequence has been stated by the arguers; but it must be assumed as a necessary deduction, otherwise the first one would be of no importance; since, although the average amount of happiness and misery might be the same in all ages, the individual shares might be unequal. Some even might bear the whole amount of the misery, and others have all the happiness; or, at any rate, some might have the far greater portion of the happiness, and others of the misery; nine might walk on, tottering under their burdens, and the tenth have no burden at all, and be carried on their shoulders besides. And such is supposed to be the actual condition of society in general. Such is supposed to be the miserable condition of the persons for whose benefit this argument is put forth, and such the flourishing condition of these modest Tory sages who preach the endurance from the tops of the others' backs.

When Tories resort to philosophy, it is always to recommend some endurance on the part of others. Touch their own toes and they are all for fire and fury, or for genteelly shedding "a little blood or so," *à la Claverhouse*,[2] and having no pity.

Fiat Toryismus, ruat cœlum. They would blow Christianity
itself to the Devil, if it did not mean the Bishops. We have
an intimation how cavalierly they could treat the Divine Being
in the Introduction to Faust, which is all fine and philosophical,
being written by a Minister of State,[3] but would be sheer
blasphemy, and could have no possible good aim, had it come
from the pen of a Radical. It might be advisable even to be
cautious how any Radical eye ventured to discern a good
through the evil of that introduction, a piety through the
impiety. Such strong perceptions are a privilege for those
whose mode of turning them to account, demands to be
treated with still greater respect, and to be considered everything that is Christian while it violates every Christian principle, —

> Proving their doctrine orthodox
> By apostolic blows and knocks.

It was a Christian minister of this sort, who, having a dispute
with another as to the right of reading a funeral service, came
rushing in, when his rival was commencing with the words
"I am the resurrection and the life;" and exclaimed, snatching
the prayer-book out of his hand, "*You* the resurrection and the
life: a pretty piece of impudence, i'faith! *I* am the resurrection
and the life."

It is *possible* that the average amount of happiness and
misery is the same in all ages, and in all conditions of society;
but as there is no *possibility of proving it,* it is an assumption
good only for the last resources of endurance; and unless a
further proof could be adduced in favour of the equal happiness of men at all times, the whole notion comes to nothing
in the eyes of activity and want, and of the desire of improving
one's condition. If we, for one, thought the state of mankind
unalterable, we should be heartily for making the best of it
as it is; nay, and we are for making the best of it at all events:
in theory, by supposing the best necessity for all that has ever
happened in the world; and in practice, both by making the
best of what good we possess, and endeavouring to bring

about all the good we can conceive. We grant, furthermore, that there is a great deal more good in the world than the world turns to account. One of our greatest hopes of its improvement is connected with that belief; and we are of opinion, also, that much of what is considered in a light fit for lamentation, is not at all so; that the blessings we bestow on less civilized foreign nations are not seldom nuisances, only to be reconciled to a sound philanthropy, by the hope of their leading to something better for us all; and finally, we believe that a great deal of the real happiness of mankind arises from the mind's being in a state of activity or movement, apart from any thing specifically happy or miserable, motion being in the nature of all things, and good for its own sake. But a wonderful deal of care remains which the human being struggles to get rid of, and which puts the struggle to a pain beyond that which is good and wholesome; and to suppose that mankind can or ought to be content with the misery of this struggling, out of a notion that they would not be the happier without it, and that they are all equally happy, struggling or not struggling, is to suppose, that endeavour itself is not a part of man's nature, or that you could persuade a Tory, when his horse has thrown him in a ditch, that he might as well live in the ditch all day, as get up and go to dinner.

The remark that the amount of happiness and misery has ever been the same is not new; though there is something new enough in the fancy that it can be brought forward at the present moment to stop the progress of the world. It is just as if you were to tell a hungry man, that hunger and a satisfied appetite are equally pleasant. The poor want bread. They are getting knowledge, and knowledge teaches how to get power: and they will have both bread and power. When a little better share of both these advantages is in their possession, it will be time enough to recommend to their consideration the average quantity of human happiness and misery.

The tragedy runs instinctively into farce, or the chief actors in it themselves could not bear it. It is out of this perplexity between the habitual selfishness, and the natural humanity of the very Tories, that they exhibit, to those who know them thoroughly, so ludicrous, yet so appalling a combination of an endeavour to be in earnest, with jovial escapes of candour, and a frightful effort to represent their wretched transitory system of violence and injustice, as a beautiful and permanent manifestation of God's providence. It is for a similar reason, and partly to attempt a cheat upon their own consciences, that they talk so much about resignation; of making the best of things; and of the certainty that God will dispose of everything as it best pleases him; — meaning, that he so disposes it in the instance of their ascendency, and that whatever enormities they may commit to sustain it, success will establish their justice. Yet the resignation, observe, is never on their own sides. They put no trust in God as long as they can have recourse to bribery and corruption, and a good knock on the head. They are for doing what they like "with their own;" but by no means for letting you, or the Almighty himself, do a bit of it, — supposing resignation to be from Him. One aristocratic philosopher turns round from a table monopolized by a few, and overflowing with "every luxury in season," and has the face to tell the starving fellow-creature who made it, that "the table's full." Another asks them what is the use of making a noise, since the amount of happiness and misery has been the same in all ages, and therefore to have no dinner is as good as turtle.

The arguments about Providence and moral order are soon disposed of. It must be admitted, that if Providence, or the making provision for the good of the world, — and moral order, or the smooth and happy working of the system, — consist in three men's sitting down to table and stuffing themselves, while three thousand are looking on and complaining, — and if it be the will of Heaven, for its inscrutable purposes, (and in this part of our sentence we desire to express ourselves very gravely and religiously,) that a system apparently so unaccountable should continue, it will continue, do or say what we may against it. The Tories need not write in its favour, any more than the Radicals need oppose it. But if there is

something in the nature of man which induces him, on reflection, as well as in his first impulses, not to regard this view
of the designs of Providence as the just one, but more or less
to labour to prove it another, and if, in the course of these
labours, governments are altered, kings are overthrown, political ascendencies swept away, and the arguments of those
who maintain it are otherwise perplexed, then the chance is,
that Providence intends *some further working of its providence*
to be manifested in due season. And if it be replied, that all
this uneasy endeavour and occasional change is only a part
of the action necessary to human kind, (which the far greater
part of the rich, observe, do not share in,) the rejoinder is, that
it is impossible to prove it; that the ascendency of unjust
power, long as it has existed in one sense, has been but of
inconceivably short duration in the amount of time; and that
the same excuse which gives any sort of power all the power
it really possesses, to wit, the sympathy and acquiescence of
mankind, would render the very best and justest power the very
greatest and most durable, because it would unite in its favour
all which reason and prosperity could do for it, as well as the
force of habit.

As to the assumption that all men, somehow or other, have
an equal portion of happiness and misery, there is an easy
and visible proof to the contrary, which stares every one in
the face. It is in the faces of the poor. Go to any assembly of
the rich, and you may see, it is true, marks of many cares and
many follies; and evidences to make you wonder how so
insipid and trifling a generation are allowed to have privileges
of superfluity injurious to millions who are certainly not their
inferiors; but you will see, nevertheless, a great amount of
comfort and health, and this, too, in spite of bad hours and
other abuses of luxury. They are not so happy as might be
supposed. They want employment enough, ideas, and good
faith in one another. They are obliged to think ill of mankind
in order to reconcile the secret sense of the injustice of their
position; intrigue of all sorts will not allow them to think too
well of their own class, and they go through life gaping,

lounging, tattling, drinking, and being satiated, and asking themselves at the close of youth "What it is worth?" This is true, and shews that the rich are in a wrong position as well as the poor. Whatsoever shall render the condition of all classes more equal will do good to all. But still, look at their faces, and you will see that they are not a twentieth part so unhappy as the poor. They are not afflicted with the worst evils of life, such as make the cheeks and the eyes hollow, even in the prime of a man's days, and torment his heart for what shall happen to his family. They are in easy physical condition; they are at least negatively happy compared with the others; they are not beset with the taskmaster and the tax-gatherer; they may indulge the natural affections; they know not the misery of wanting food and clothing; they do not dream of the work-house and the hospital, nor wake to see such dreams realized; in short, again we say, look at them, and look also at their children; look at their sons and daughters, with their handsome smooth faces, and the world of elegant comfort in which they are bred up; and then compare *those few* with *these many*. Go through a manufacturing town; see the masters and their clerks looking as comfortable as in most other places, notwithstanding what is said of bad air and unwholesome occupations, (the worst air is the breath of sorrow); and then look at the operatives, the workmen, and see what *their* faces tell you; see, in contrast with the few people at the head of an establishment, the many who do the hard work for it, and who make it rich; behold their sunken and discoloured cheeks, their eyes staring with wretched and wondering thoughts; and observe, in the faces of their children, the premature, worldly trouble, and (what would be worse, if it were not an effort of nature at relief) the premature worldly vices, the cunning, the bad opinion, the sensuality, the hard and impudent instinct of despair and self-defence. We have seen girls of twelve years of age at Nottingham, with the looks of half-starved abandoned women of forty. The purse-proud aristocrat turns away from them in disgust, and sits down to a dinner of repletion collected out of their labours.

When the poor have faces as healthy and careless as the rich, then, and not till then, let the argument about the average amount of happiness be brought forward; or let the rich give up their good dinners and good looks, and say they are as happy in misery as they were in happiness. These fine gratuitous abstractions, very amusing to gentlemen who crack their walnuts after a good dinner, and push the bottle, only serve to irritate those who are hungering and thirsting, and cursing the tax-gatherers. And this position of the two parties is never to be lost sight of. If the aristocratical, and those who are well off, are not always pushing the bottle, while they are lecturing the poor, they are more or less under the influence of a state of blood and body produced by it, or at least by good living. *Parliament legislates under it. Magistrates commit under it. Bishops preach under it. Generals and Field-marshals are for being "vigorous" under it.* Our government is a bottle-and-beef government, with bowels closed against compassion by the fat of the land. Its least "refreshment,"—its common every-day lunch, — would be a feast to a labouring man, such as he would chalk up the days for, till it arrived. Its dinners would bewilder him to look at; and yet, so small is its imagination, so wonderfully unsympathetic and in bad taste its public habits, that it is ostentatious of its feast days and its luxurious tables. It is always dining out, and in public; and shewing the indignant penny-reader of the newspapers how it revels in "every luxury of the season." Royalty is always dining thus; and thus dineth mayoralty: — thus dine the judges, and the ministers, and the generals, and the *Nulli Secundus* clubs,[5] and the parish officers; and by the side of the columns which record the dining, are recorded the people who starve upon the three-and-twopence a week, who die at the doorways of parish officers, or who, as the only means of avoiding death, steal with the avowed purpose of getting into prison, and go to it rejoicing, that they are to have a fiftieth part of the bit of bread which the gourmand has steeped into his turtle — contrasts disgraceful to an age pretending to be civilized; and yet so common, that the mention of them is received with canting bursts of angry hypocrisy, and pretences that they cannot be helped!

Little is a similar answer thought decent or humane, when angry Revolution comes, and starved madmen thrust their bloody hands into the teeth of madmen stuffed full. May God, and those who help his good work, avert from mankind the necessity of any more such frightful lessons. And averted, we believe, it will be; not because "rich men" have grown wiser, or their money-changers know much more of the right path than they; but because the poor are daily increasing in the calm power of knowledge, which, while it brings patience to endure humanely, brings authority to demand invincibly.

The best answer to a bad argument is a Birmingham meeting.[6]

THE TOWNSMAN

Nos. II, III, IV

A RAMBLE IN MARY-LE-BONE

September 8, 1833

Resolving to have a look at some popular quarter of the town, in the commencement of these our most metropolitan papers,[1] and being perplexed with diversity of choice, who should come up to us, in the most obliging manner, with a book in his hand, written on purpose to free us from the dilemma, but Mr. Thomas Smith, author of a *Topographical and Historical Account of the Parish of Mary-le-bone, comprising a Copious Description of its Public Buildings, Antiquities, Schools, Charitable Endowments, Sources of Public Amusement, &c. &c., with Biographical Notices of Eminent Persons, Illustrated with Six Views and a Map, the whole Compiled and Arranged by* the said Thomas, and *published by John Smith* of Long Acre, together with an indescribable number of Mary-le-bone booksellers? Smith, it delighteth us to take thine arm, and we will have a ramble with thee, but chiefly among thine older, and less fashionable, and less monotonous places. We should care more for all the elegant streets and squares recorded by thee, the inhabitants of which will doubtless have thy volume in every one of their houses, (being in some sort a looking-glass of their merits of rank and wealth,) if we thought that any one of their names, or those of their possessors, would be in existence two hundred years hence, or if the possessors did not in the meanwhile monopolize a comfort which ought to be better distributed, and which, for that reason, hindereth the monopolizers themselves from being as comfortable as they would give out. Furthermore, we have seen the streets of Florence and Genoa, and consider most of these elegant Mary-le-bone streets as being little better than barracks to look at in the comparison, comfortably furnished as they may be, and doubtless are, inside, for the consolation of the superfluous; and if thou hadst seen what we have, thou, who hast such a good eye for a church and steeple, and wouldst assuredly not have all our public buildings alike, wouldst agree with us respecting private buildings, and no longer quarrel with Portman-square for not being quite "uniform." Does it not strike thee, Smith, on the instant, that, generally speaking, it would be better to have all great houses to be so many various pictures and specimens of good architecture, for the better manifestation of the possessor's taste, and delight of the variety-loving eye of man; though we confess we should have no objection to the occasional lumping together of one side of a square or so in some magnificent façade. The variety should be of all sorts, provided it were good; and the afore uniformity itself should not be omitted, as being a part of it. But what right have the dull polite of this generation to laugh at Mr. Owen and his parallelograms,[2] when they have their own parallelograms run to seed, and the frightful continuity, under the illustrious-obscure names of Wigmore, and Welbeck, and Wimpole-streets, all with their eternally repeated door and two windows,—door and two windows,—door and two windows,—like the knop and the flower of the Jewish architect, with the everlasting three-windowed stories above, and the absence of all generous orna-ment, the windows being cut into the walls, without even the humanity of a border, and the whole "set out," looking as if Elwes the miser[3] built it, which in part he actually did! in-cluding "the barracks and stables of the 2d regiment of Life Guards!" He thought, while he was about it, he might as well build barracks for every body. The town-house of Elwes was in Welbeck-street; whence he "was persuaded," says our author, "to *allow* himself to be taken *gratuitously*" into Berkshire, where he died. Reader, whenever you pass up through the delicious dulness of Welbeck or Wimpole-street, remember Elwes the barrack-builder, and observe the savings he has made in the

doors and windows. All the house-builders in this most generous nation have imitated him, till at length they have pared
walls and floors so closely, that it is dangerous to dance in
them; and clauses are inserted in your lease, prohibiting so
ruinous an entertainment!

Nevertheless, we learn from our topographical companion,
that Elwes built part of Portman-square, (we suppose the
worst part,) nay, that Portland-place "rose out of his property."
Whether this means that he or his heirs built it, we cannot say.
Elwes had fits of generosity, and could lend a man a thousand
pounds after haggling with a grazier in Smithfield for a shilling.
But if he was sure of his tenants, it needed no romance to
enable him to erect a suite of dwellings for noblemen and
rich merchants.

Dear reader, never forget that these rich people are not so
much happier than the poor, as not to require change in their
condition and be allowed excuse for their want of sympathy.
They are what that system and their fathers have made them,
and are subject to the distresses and diseases arising from
pride, and discord, and repletion. It seems to be a kindly
severity of nature, that no class of mankind shall be really
happy, till all are so. We hold much to this opinion, and beg
you to reflect upon it. People are too apt to stop short in their
reflections upon human trouble, partly out of dread, partly
out of impatience. They think that mankind are intended to
be unhappy. But if they would look round at the beautiful
world they live in, which is such a splendid contrast to the
unhappiness in it, and consider that it is not likely the Divine
Being would have put them into such a place to turn it to
no account, they may begin to regard their unhappiness as a
thing to be got rid of, and the general unhappiness as an
incitement to all to get rid of it. If all the world were to hurt
their legs to-morrow morning, depend upon it all the world
would begin rubbing them, and looking for plasters, and not
sit down and mourn over the *shins* of mankind. Now, why
should we endure greater wounds when we will not endure
less? But the world has now got some new lights on this

subject, and new means of turning them to account. So let us hope the best of each other's legs, and, above all, not kick them more than we can help; no, not even the gouts of the rich, if they do not absolutely fling their crutches at the spindle-shanks of the poor.

The five things that make a place interesting are — personal feelings connected with it, its beauty, its antiquities, its eminent men, and its future destiny. There are no antiquities extant in Mary-le-bone. It is a new place. Nor was it ever abundant in old things, except fields and meadows; though, like all places near a great metropolis, it is not without its interest, old as well as new. Mary-le-bone extends to Oxford-street on the south; to the Edgware-road, as far as Kilburn, on the west; to Primrose-hill on the north; and nearly to Tottenham-court-road on the east. It includes one side of Paddington, which is a name as old, we believe, as the Conquest, and once had an abbey to it. At Lissongreen (a corruption of Lilestone — we learn all these particulars from Mr. Smith), the priory of St. John of Jerusalem had a manor. Henry VIII built another more eastward, a remnant of which was standing not long since at the top of High-street, nearly opposite the old church; and to this manor was attached a park, on a portion of the site of which (curiously enough) has now sprung the Regent's Park.

In Queen Elizabeth's reign the Russian ambassador and his retinue rode through the city to Mary-le-bone-park, and hunted there; and there Sir Charles Blount, afterwards Earl of Devonshire, fought with the noble-hearted Earl of Essex, the friend of Spenser, because his lordship was jealous of a toy the queen had given him! Such simpletons have royalty and aristocracy made of the wisest.

Elizabeth and Mary occasionally lodged in this house. The gardens at the back afterwards became a place of musical and other entertainment, like the modern Vauxhall, but on a poorer scale. Nevertheless, some of Handel's music came out there, and Arne was for some time director of the orchestra. The neighbourhood objected to the peril of the rockets, and the entertainments were put an end to. The house has now vanished, and the site is occupied by stables. The gardens were on the site occupied by Beaumont-street, Devonshire-street, and part of Devonshire-place. Mr. Smith has a good anecdote of Handel, showing, that if writers of no genius are apt to think they can do nothing badly, genius knows itself better. The anecdote is taken from "one of Mr. Hone's publications," and is part of a letter from a grandson of the Rev. Mr. Fountayne, who occasionally officiated at the old church.

"While Mary-le-bone Gardens were flourishing, the enchanting music of Handel, and probably of Arne was often heard from the orchestra there. One evening, as my grandfather and Handel were walking together and alone, a new piece was struck up by the band. 'Come, Mr. Fountayne,' said Handel, 'let us sit down and listen to this piece, I want to know your opinion of it.' Down they sat, and after some time the old parson, turning to his companion, said, 'It is not worth listening to; it is very poor stuff.' 'You are right, Mr. Fountayne,' said Handel, 'it is very poor stuff; I thought so myself when I had finished it.' The old gentleman, being taken by surprise, was beginning to apologise, but Handel assured him there was no necessity; that the music was really bad, having been composed hastily, and his time for the production limited; and that the opinion given was as correct as it was honest." — p. 34.[4]

"High-street," says Mr. Smith, "formerly comprised the principal part of the *village of Mary-le-bone*; the church, the royal palace, the Rose Tavern and bowling green, the splendid mansion (now no more) built for the purpose of containing the Earl of Oxford's library, the Rose of Normandy, and a few detached gardens with houses, formed the prominent features of its early days. The Rose of Normandy, supposed to have been built about 200 years ago, and the oldest house now existing in the parish, is situated on the east side of the street, and was formerly a detached building, used as a house of entertainment, in connexion with the bowling-green at its back." It "is now one of the best conducted public houses in the parish; the company consisting of the most respectable tradesmen and ancient inhabitants of the neighbourhood; the worthy host, Mr. Bradley, having tenanted the house for more than twenty-six years, and the obliging hostess having been born in the old manor-house."

Come — this is something like a real link of new with old. We thank Mr. Smith for it; and to drink his and Mr. and Mrs. Bradley's health in a pot of imaginary triple X.

The Bowling-green, or greens, here spoken of, the name of which still survives in the streets on the site of it, and which was subsequently incorporated in Mary-le-bone Gardens, is no doubt the place "alluded to by Lady Mary Wortley Montague, in the line

'Some dukes at Marybone bowl time away;'"

and which is meant by Pennant, who, when speaking of the Duke of Buckingham's (Sheffield's) minute description of the house afterwards the Queen's palace, and his manner of living there, says: "He has omitted his constant visits to the noted gaming-house at Marybone; the place of assemblage of all the infamous sharpers at the time; to whom his Grace always gave a dinner at the conclusion of the season, and his parting toast was, 'May as many of us as remain unhanged next spring meet here again.'" — p. 162.[5] Very candid and ducal, and aristocratically superior to vulgar expectations.

The little old church has been several times rebuilt. Wolsey was the first rector of it. It is one of the scenes of Hogarth's *Rake's Progress*, where the rake is marrying the rich old woman; and there is that piece of wit, a spider's web over the poor's-box.

In the time of Henry VIII, the present Portman estate was let at an annual rent under ten pounds.

But far later than this, at the beginning of the last century, Mary-le-bone was so little in town, that Mr. Smith tells us it was the practice of "travellers" to stop for refreshment at the White Hart, at the corner of Welbeck-street, "and examine their fire-arms, previously to crossing the fields to Lisson-green." — p. 205.

Even Oxford-street is described by Pennant, who was born at the same period, as "a deep hollow road, full of sloughs, with here and there a ragged house, the lurking place of cut-throats; insomuch (says he), that I never was taken that way by night, in my hackney-coach, to a worthy uncle's, who gave me lodgings at his house in George-street, but I went in dread the whole way."[6]

The famous Tyburn gallows, at the end of this street, stood "on the identical spot where a toll-house has been since erected by the Uxbridge-road trust." It is even extant in the shape of "stands for beer-butts, in the cellars of a public house in the neighbourhood, viz. the Carpenter's Arms in Adam-street." At least a carpenter bought and converted it to that purpose in 1783, when it was taken down.

Under this gallows Charles the First's haughty queen, Henrietta Maria, once did penance at the command of her confessor. Among others, Felton, who killed the duke of Buckingham, was executed at this spot; Dr. Dodd; Hackman, who shot Miss Ray for "love;" and Ryland the engraver. Ryland was the last that suffered.

Tyburn ought never to be forgotten, if it were only for the song in the *Beggar's Opera,* the moral of which has been getting strength and echo in the public voice ever since. We will repeat it here, and imagine it sung in Mr. Bradley's tap: —

> Since laws were made for every degree,
> To curb vice in others as well as in me,
> I wonder we haven't better company
>
> > Upon Tyburn tree.

> But gold from law can take out the sting,
> And if the great men were like us to swing,
> 'Twould thin the land such numbers to string
>
> > Upon Tyburn tree.[7]

Tyburn was called from a bourne, or brook, which ran from Hampstead to the Thames, and is now a sewer. From this bourne, and a church near it, the parish was called St. Mary *at the Bourne,* subsequently corrupted to *Marybourne, Mary-bone, Mary-la-bonne,* and now, by a most ridiculous misnomer, and to the confusion of all genders and tongues, *St. Mary-le-bone*; that is to say, *St. Mary the good man,* or *St. Mary* with a *masculine French "the,"* and a *"bone"!!* Sir Roger de Cover-ley might have been thrice puzzled at this appellation; for it is he, or some *other* real person, we believe, of whom it is related, that, during the disputes between the papistical Tories and the Whigs, he once asked, when a little boy, his way to "Marybone," of a gentleman who happened to be of the former faction, and who told him to "go along for a little heretic," because he had left out the "Saint:" — upon which, resolving to be right with the next person he met, he asked his way to "Saint Marybone," and was desired to "get away with him, for a papistical little varlet."[8]

We have now gone through the principal *memorabilia* of the parish, and have little to say of the rest, except that Ugo Foscolo lived in it (at one of the Alpha Cottages); that Mrs. Siddons died in her house at the north-east corner of Upper Baker-street; that Mrs. Montague,[9] who is worth mentioning, on account of the annual dinner she gave the chimney-sweepers, lived in the large house at the corner of Portman-square; that Stephen Storace,[10] a composer who deserves grateful recollection for his sweet songs in *"No Song No Supper,"* and other dramas, lies in the little old church; Dr. Geddes and Curran[11] (and Mrs. Siddons) in the burying ground of Paddington Church; Baretti,[12] and Ferguson[13] the astronomer, in the cemetery in Paddington-street; and Mr. Holcroft[14] lived in Clipstone-street, Elliston and Cosway[15] in Stratford-place, Tyrwhitt[16] in Welbeck-street, Barry[17] the cynical painter, in Castle-street, where his dirty and broken-windowed house was long a spectacle; — Cumberland[18] in Queen Anne-street, and Gibbon in Bentinck-street. Mr. Smith can add some of these names to his next edition. Chatterton also may be mentioned, as having produced one of the bur-lettas at Mary-le-bone Gardens. The Miss Davies,[19] mentioned at pp. 168 and 9, as singing there nearly seventy years ago, is the once celebrated Miss Davies, surnamed by the Italians *Inglesina*, the little Englishwoman, having been a highly admired singer abroad as well as at home. *She is now living, a respectable and interesting old lady, in all but the last stage of poverty: the boasted English nobility being the richest and most ungenerous specimen of their "order" in Europe.*

We have little to say of new buildings and improvements which every body is acquainted with; but no charge of egotism or sub-urbanity shall hinder us from expressing our gratitude to filial and village recollections converted into Paddington, or to the dear old fields that once occupied the site of the Regent's Park, where we made verses, and saw visions of mythological beauty, from morning till night. We knew an old lady,[20] who was proprietor of some houses in the Edge-ware-road between Paddington and Oxford-street, one of which had an almond tree in the garden, which still flourishes, and which has a blessing from us whenever we pass it; for to that house, and its eternally merry inmate, the gayest old charmer we ever met with, did we delightedly trudge when a little boy, holding by the hand of a beloved mother, and rejoicing at our first glimpse of the green rails, as if they were the gates of Elysium. No green ever appeared to us so green as that. We are accustomed to think of it, when we would have a test of green; and Titian never loved better the brightest bit on his palette. In those fields we speak of was Willan's Farm, where we have eaten "creams and other country messes." There it was that the path ran from the New-road all the way to Hampstead through beautiful meadows, some of which, with the termination of the path, are still to be found near that delightful village, as beautiful as ever. There did Edwin Landseer,[21] then a smiling boy, whom we used to meet and talk with, make his first studies in that knowledge of animals and the country, which will immortalise him; and therein, one gentle morn, whom should we see, to the discomfiture of our young and crude criticism, sitting on a stile, meditating, and giving a polite sanction to these sub-urbanities, but the sweetest-natured of men, Lumley St. George Skeffington, now

Sir Lumley, who thinks the human being capable of all good and graceful things, and even worthy to be dressed in the best manner: and we think it an honour to ourselves to agree with him.

Nor must we close without a parting word of gratitude to Mr. Smith, not only for his book in general, but for his special mention of us at p. 124, and of the beloved radical paper we formerly edited; a mention which we take with great kindness of him, because it is bold and honest, and hardly to have been looked for in the historian of so aristocratical neighbourhood.

Thomas, thou hast touched our heart, and we trust we shall have done no harm to thy pocket.

September 15, 1833

We feel that we have more to say about Marylebone, and of a more modern interest than we thought at first. Architectural books and daily pedestrians call out upon us for our further opinion on the streets and buildings; our old friends the shops and bookstalls reproach us for passing them by; and other personal recollections tax our silence with ingratitude.

To speak, then, in the lump, of architectural Marylebone, we repeat that its streets compared with those of some foreign capitals, are in bad, monotonous, brickbuilding taste — a series of polite barracks — and that its churches, for the most part, are worthy of them. Let us hear no more against Mr. Owen's parallelograms. Almost all the streets at the west end of the town are parallelograms run to seed; at least they may be called so in the same spirit of objection; and they have not the recommendations of his love of justice, nor of his trees and gardens. Wimpole-street, Welbeck-street, Harley-street, *et hoc genus omne,* including the whole of the new buildings about Dorset and Bryanstone squares, are all of the barrack-building description; and the squares are no better. The fronts of the houses have no architecture, no variety, no taste; not even a handsome proportion between the doors and windows. They are all built in the same bald, insipid style of sordid utility, and as if the eyes and enjoyments of the spectators were worth nothing.

The churches are a disgrace, partly to the parish authorities, partly to the builders. They consist either of mere stone or brick boxes, made to suit the "barracks," and to do as cheap honour to God as may be; or they present us with a Greek portico, or a bit of one, surmounted with other stolen or compiled bits of pepper-boxes, and outhouses, about which, we may rest assured, the builder had as few settled ideas in his head as he has given the spectator; and the rest of the church shifts for itself as well as it can, in the most approved style of the architectural tailor's pattern-book. The parish grudges its money, and the "architect" will do nothing for honour. Mr. Nash,[22] who has a laudable ambition to vary from his brethren, and whose diversities in Regent-street would be better if they were less flimsy, must needs set up a spire,[23] as sharp as a "needle," in the midst of all the hardness, the squareness, and the sharpness of the buildings about Langham-place. Stone nor pavement could not satisfy him, but he must fairly make a weapon out of them, tip it with metal, to render it "the more acute" (as Mr. Smith says), and run it into the eyes of the groaning spectators. A spire should ascend out of a tufted village, and not surmount a heap of square, mathematical buildings, with the reverse of something to relieve them. We like, however, to praise where we can, especially where we have been forced to dispraise. Mr. Nash is a better layer out of grounds than architect, and the public have reason to thank him for what he has done for the Regent's Park. Our gratitude on that point induces us to say as little as we can of the houses there, with their toppling statues, and other ornamented efforts to escape from the barrack style. One or two rows of the buildings are really not without handsome proportion; those with the statues among them; and so thankful are we for any diversity in this land of insipid building, where it does not absolutely mortify the taste, that we accept even the pumpkins of Sussex-place as a refreshment. We don't know what they mean, nor why they are there; but there is something Eastern in their look, and they remind us, among other things, by a fantastic but not unpleasing link in our memory, of the time *when we have sat up in a tree in this very neighbourhood, reading the Arabian Nights!* The grove, still remaining at the end of the street called Lisson Grove, was then a prominent object in the fields; and St. John's Wood Farm was an isolated, rustic spot, with a cottage near it, lying in the midst of beautiful meadows. At present, houses, as well as holiday folks, are invading poor Primrose Hill; and Hampstead is threatened with hostilities east and west. There is said to be an old prophecy, that Hampstead is to be in the middle of London! Steam-carriage will save us from that! Meanwhile, we have reason to be thankful that the Regent's Park has saved us from worse places in the same quarter; for it is at all events a park, and has trees and grass, and is a breathing-place between town and country. It has prevented Harley and Wimpole-streets from going further; has checked, in that quarter at least, the monstrous brick cancer that was extending its arms in every direction.

This reminds us that we have to thank also the builder of the Alpha Cottages, whoever he was, and however badly they are built. They are sorry things in themselves; jumbles of closets and inconvenience; but they are separate from one another — have gardens and trees — add to the breathing room of the metropolis — and diminish the number of streets; and for all this we are thankful. We mentioned in our last that in one of these cottages lived Ugo Foscolo, the Italian poet and critic, author of the Essays on Petrarch, and some charming articles on his country's literature, which were translated into the Edinburgh and Quarterly Reviews. He was a wayward and vehement sort of personage, taking upon himself to be somewhat more excessive in a variety of ways than the occasion warranted; but a man of genius, and in a false position. He once did us the honour of a visit, and with his cavernous whiskers, furcollared greatcoat, and thin prominent face, looked like an antelope thrusting his face through a hedge.

We learn from Mr. Smith's book, that in the cemetery in

Paddington-street is a stone, erected in 1777, to the memory of George Canning, Esq., father of the late minister, with the following pretty inscription: —

> Thy virtue and my love no words can tell,
> Therefore, a little while, my George, farewell;
> For faith and love like ours, heaven has in store
> Its last best gift — to meet and part no more.

"This stone and its inscription," says Mr. Smith, "are fast mouldering to dust. A trifling sum would restore it to its pristine beauty; and when one considers the character, worth, and wealth of many individuals connected with the name of Canning, one is more than surprised, that this tribute to the memory of the father of one of the most eminent orators and statesmen that ever graced the annals of this, or of any other country, should be suffered to sink into oblivion." — *History of Marylebone*, p. 130.

As to gracing the annals of "this, or any other country," it is a pleasing mode of speaking, Mr. Smith. *Passe pour cela*. Mr. Canning's mother, we believe, had the illegitimate misfortune of being a woman of talents, and turning them to account for her livelihood. She was an actress. Hence, perhaps, the mouldering stone. *Hinc illae lachrymae non depromendae*. But the lines, which Mr. Smith says are now scarcely legible, deserve to be restored for their own sakes. The first couplet, in particular, with its loving familiarity, is very sweetly turned, and gives us a sense of a real affection: —

> *Thy* virtue, and *my* love —
> Therefore, little while, *my* George, farewell.

A modern fashionable woman would not dare to speak in this manner on the tomb of her husband.

In the same burial-ground is the following curious record: — Henry Stuart, S.S., B. 28th. Sept. 1793, D. 9th July 1794. Also Charles Henry Stuart, S.S., B. 17th March, D. 1st Oct. 1802. Sons of J. Ferdinand Smyth Stuart, *Great Grandson of King Charles II.*, rest here. 'Most beautiful smiling innocents. Alas! How fallen! How changed!' And Spencer Perceval Stuart, S.S., B. June 14th, D. Aug. 4, 1807.

A "great grandson of Charles II" would claim to be cousin to the last known legitimate male descendant of the House of Stuart, the Cardinal of York; who died at Rome not long since, and was styled on his tomb, "Henry the 9th, King of Great Britain." Two of the children here mentioned appear to have been named after him. The legitimate heir to the English throne, according to that divine right for which the holy allies fought, and Tories ought still to contend, is the present King of Sardinia. He is nearer to the Stuart blood than the House of Hanover.

We must indulge ourselves in one more article on this subject, being obliged to bring the present abruptly to a close.

September 22, 1833

To return a moment to the neglected inscription on the tombstone of Mr. Canning's father. It must be acknowledged that our beloved countrymen are not famous for paying attention to their deceased friends and relations. "Business! business!" as the King of the Sandwich Islands said — business must be attended to. One has no time to attend to a dead father. In France, and other parts of the Continent, they strew roses on the graves of their kindred. In China, memorials are put up to the deceased in the houses of their children; and a retrospective piety towards their progenitors is diligently cultivated. Life is so short, and affection so strong, that in these countries people think they cannot do too much for one another towards extending the very idea of existence, and keeping themselves together as long as possible. In England, commerce, and wealth, and poverty, have driven all our thoughts so inward upon ourselves, making us look so exclusively to "number one" (to use a charming phrase of ours), that we are in a constant drive and whirlwind either of business, or fashion, or horrible necessity. In Wales, which is out of the high road of trade and riches, and where the people can better endure a poverty which is more left to itself, to work out its case with God and nature, the traveller is pleasingly surprised with the view of graves dressed with flowers, and with mourners who have leisure to indulge the best affections of the heart.

Oh! — but an Englishman thinks of the departed, though he does not visit their graves, or do any thing to honour them. He feels, though he does not talk. There is no outside show about him, &c. &c. These are the flattering unctions we lay to our souls, in order to soothe and blind ourselves to the points in which we are inferior to other nations, and maintain all the while our assumption of being superior. We are disagreeable, only because we are the more agreeable; unsociable, because we are the reverse; forgetful, only to prove our extreme recollection — our absorption in tender memories. By the same process of self-evidence we are unsociable, (in stage-coaches, for instance,) not because we are sulky or do not care for one another, but because we are modest. We are inhospitable to strangers for a like reason, and not because we are deficient in address and good humour. And we insisted upon going to war with republican France, not because we were fond of dictation, and jealous of her doing any thing towards surpassing, or even equalling us in our old boast of liberty, but out of regard for liberty itself, which the throne and the stock-exchange could not bear to see violated!

Adversity, the press, and a better acquaintance with other countries, have made the sensible among us begin to reform these errors. They see that it is as silly a thing in a nation to stick to its faults purely because they are its own, as it would be to cherish cholera or the rickets; and that the true commerce of the world has begun the interchange of self-knowledge and moral advancement. If the French have discovered that it will do them no harm to lay down a little of their levity, and acquire more of our characteristic firmness of purpose, we begin to discern that their old claim to the *savoir vivre* is true, and that a greater share of their good humour and kindness to one another is a profitable importation. It was from our old republican times, and the example of our brethren in science, that they learnt to throw off the slavery with which we used to taunt them. We borrow from them in turn consideration for the very beasts whom we bring from abroad, and whom we now give houses and scenes of their own to live in, instead of stifling them in a box of dens. All this is doing ourselves honour as well as them, and showing that both nations have arrived to true years of manhood. We have just taken from them the idea of a cemetery; and probably our cemetery will not exist another year, before some of us begin to strew its graves with flowers, and thus render death itself at once more pathetic and less gloomy. The close of life is surely too painful already for all parties, even the dullest, and yet too full of the capabilities of sweet thoughts, to need being made blacker or more repulsive than it is. We ought to struggle kindly with heaven for it, and enable it to set in roses.

Mr. Smith tells us, that the vaults of the chapel of St. John's Wood, in this parish, are remarkable for the slow decay of the bodies, a proof of the purity of the air in that quarter. Among these lies poor nonsensical Joanna Southcott,[24] who showed the natural connexion between a destitution of all common pretensions and the most frightful assumption. She died in Manchester-street, and was carried to her grave under a feigned name, for fear of interruption. Did the reader ever happen to notice the resemblance in her portraits to those of Queen Charlotte, the wife of George the Third? In the New-road is an excellent institution, an inscription upon which purports that it is "Queen Charlotte's Lying-In Hospital." When we first saw this inscription, we hailed it as the only evidence that had ever come to our knowledge of a quality which in that royal personage was not supposed to be very abundant. Upon looking down lower, we saw added, "Supported by voluntary contributions." The royal endowment, therefore, consisted in a name.

There are several excellent charities in this parish, particularly for poor women and children. That for the "Orphans of the Clergy" is among them. But what a shame, that in a country like this, with prelates rolling in wealth, there should be children of poor clergy that go to the parish! How little would this be the case, if clergymen were found only where they are wanted, and their congregation supported them.

Marylebone is not a very interesting district to walk in. The streets are monotonous and ill-built, and the memorials of celebrated men few, and not of the first eminence. The best parts are Oxford-street, where you are entertained with the succession of shops; and the Regent's Park, where you may go to the Zoological Gardens,[25] and find the bear and the zebu at home. These foreign visitors of ours are well fed and well guarded; otherwise a morbid imagination, going home at twelve o'clock at night, might be startled to think that, in turning a corner, it might encounter, not a policeman, but a lion! Or fancy an easy gentleman, lazily returning from a party, twirling his glove, and suddenly breasted by a rhinoceros; or clasped in the arms, not of some ultra-vivacious fair one, but of bruin on his hind legs.

What strange vicissitudes happen in a short time! Who that sat, as we did, not a great while since, on the grass in this place, would have supposed it possible that in the course of a few years, perhaps on the very spot of ground, ladies would be amusing themselves with coquetting with monkeys, or giving oranges to a bear in a pit! Or, that in a house in the neighbourhood (in the Crescent in Portland-place) should be living Joseph Napoleon, King of Spain and the Indies! Who would have fancied, too, that a King of Spain, so living, would have nobody to visit him; while a daughter of the Viscount Eugene Beauharnois, who was a prince only by grace of Joseph's brother, should go to court as her Imperial Majesty the Duchess of Braganza, carrying with her a little Queen, whom she has secured for the Viscount's son, from the fatherly designs of a schoolmaster of the house of Orleans, now occupying the throne of Bonaparte and the Bourbons!

Paoli, the Corsican general, lived in the Edgeware-road. He knew Bonaparte when a child. What a wild imagination would have been his, had he thought that, in the same parish, would live a brother of his little friend, the dethroned royal brother of a dethroned emperor, with *Bishop* Talleyrand living near him as the forsaker of both, and the ambassador from a teacher of mathematics!

We must conclude this article on Marylebone with an anecdote we read the other day of the American traitor, Arnold, who lived in the parish, we will not say in what street, lest any inhabitant should be disgusted. We are sorry we forget where we read the anecdote because we cannot refer to the book for the name of the nobleman concerned in it. But the story, and a good one it is, ran thus: — Arnold, as is well known, after having betrayed his country, had a pension from the British government, and was honoured, to their mutual glory, with the countenance of George the Third. The king one day introduced him to the nobleman alluded to (our readers would greatly oblige us if they could tell us his name). The nobleman (truly deserving that much-abused appellation) drew himself back with dignity, and exclaimed, "What, Sir, the *traitor* Arnold?" Arnold challenged him. They met, and the traitor had the first fire. His antagonist having received it, turned round without firing, and looking over his shoulder, said, "I leave you, Sir, to the executioner!"

THE TOWNSMAN

No. V

September 29, 1833

The reader, no doubt, on some occasion during the course of his life, has happened to put away something in so very safe a place that he could not find it.[1] He has also, perhaps, been to some party or meeting, or friend's house, resolving to do or say something of peculiar importance to him at the moment, and come away without recollecting it. He does not think of it till he is half-way between his friend's house and his own: the streets are all silent; the people are all gone to bed: he cannot return, and it will be too late to do it to-morrow. He stops short a moment, having almost been running hitherto in the gaiety of his animal spirits and the perfection of his evening; and for the remainder of his way he lags like a criminal, moving the slower because it seems as if he ought to go back, though he knows it is of no use. Furthermore, it may have chanced, that he has made a knot in his pocket handkerchief, on purpose that he might put forgetfulness out of the question.

Few recollections, after this fashion, have been more secure-ly reckoned upon, or more thoroughly brought to nothing, than a memorandum we had made in a corner of our hearts, touching a certain street in Marylebone, and a certain house in that street, to which, with a love overcoming all shame (for we have the advantage in that matter of our friend above mentioned), we now return, in order to pay respect to some of the most precious memories of our childhood. It is to a house we allude, which stand just opposite to the opening of Castle Street, — the residence of the late Mr. West,[2] President of the Royal Academy, now desecrated by the presumptions of Mr. Irving.[3] Good God! to think of the changes of this life, and how much one thing is misunderstood for another, — the worse for the better, contumely for piety, intolerance and nonsense for a perfected Christianity! In those gentle rooms, where nothing was to be seen but elegance and reason, and nothing heard but the bland accents of a kind old man, happily employed upon an art which is one of the most pleasing gifts of the Author of all kindness, there must now be a contention betwixt vanity, bigotry, and disease, which shall incite the other to do the more injury to the reputation of heaven, and the poor nerves and imaginations of one another! The robust, who can afford, or thought they could afford, to play with these firebrands, frighten the weak, and ultimately themselves; the weak mislead the robust; those who have some imagination, mistake it for the perfection of that faculty, which is the ornament of the perfection of reason. The mechanical minded, or those who have no imagination, know not where to stop from that very circumstance: false, threatening notions of the Divine Being confuse and fever them all, and the place resounds with the impieties of presumptuous folly. We are sorry for Mr. Irving, whom we believe to be an honest man, spoiled (for such is the anti-climax of these things!) between his inability to comprehend Mr. Coleridge,[4] and the vanity arising from a fine person; and we are sorry for his congregations, who are doubtless more honest than wise. But it is too much to see people's wits sported with in this manner; and when we think it is done in one of the very nests of our childhood, an absolute Paradise of quiet, and good sense, and benevolence, and refinement, we cannot help feeling a movement of indignation. We should be ready to tear the hair off our heads to think of it, if the very education it helped us to receive did not save us from the extremes of Mr. Irving's convulsionaries. When we first heard of it, we almost felt like Mr. Cobbett, when he saw the broom-girl in the way that broom-girls wish to be who love their Englishmen; that sight of which he said, "you might have knocked me down with a feather."

Dear 1833, (for the good and advancement in you surpasses after all the bad, and reconciles us to vicissitude,) fall back awhile, and be as if thou had'st never been! Roll back, even thou dearer 1830, with thy golden Three Days, and all thou struggling interval, during which we have fought the good fight through scars innumerable, and bring back the time when we never suspected that such fights would be necessary; when we thought only of war itself as the trumpet of Homer, or the red-coated elegancies of a parade. 'Tis of a period between the year '91 and 1800 that we speak — our schooldays, when as yet half of Marylebone was not, and the whole of London was new to us, even though we were bred in the heart of the City. But our "cloister" (Christ's Hospital) truly deserved its appellation in those days; it was a place (so to speak) truly "shut up," monachal, scholastic, (at least with us of the Grammar-school,) not abounding in generalities, and long holidays, and sleepings out of doors, (*monstra refanda!*) as in these more universal times: so that a walk from the City to Newman-street was like going from one kind of retirement to another, through a never-ceasing novelty of bustle and astonishment by the way.

Newman-street, at that time, was the head-quarters of art, as the neighbourhood of Leicester-fields was before it, and that of the Regent's-park will be, perhaps, in future; artists, like poets, as the critics have noticed in Milton's days, affecting abodes on the outskirts of the town, where they can have what used to be called "garden-houses." Newman-street contains, we believe, some artists now, particularly the venerable Mr. Stothard,[5] a host in himself, who, indeed, may be said to make it the head-quarters of art still; for nobody living equals him as a miscellaneous painter, especially in the feeling of beauty, and a certain Raphaelesque innocence and sincerity. We will take this opportunity of telling an anecdote of him, nothing very epigrammatic, or striking in an ordinary way, but characteristic and "superior." We had occasion once to call upon him, and found some of his servants quarrelling and making a great noise on the staircase. We went upstairs through the tumult, and knocking hard at his study-door (for he is deaf), were desired, in gentle tones, to come in. We entered, and found the painter, with his silver locks and placid countenance, occupied with one of his most beautiful scenes out of Boccaccio, a garden full of trees, fountains, and love. In this he was as much immersed as if he was a thousand miles off; for he had not heard a syllable of the noise.

We have mentioned whereabouts the house of Mr. West is situate: we have noticed the place before in other publications;[6] but in this our "Townsman," as is fitting, we mean to indulge ourselves with a larger and more particular account. The premises at the back are not as they were then: they were altered after his death for the better exhibition of his paintings. Somebody took them afterwards for a manufactory, and, we suppose, altered them farther. And now! — but we will have done, once for all, with these profanations. Mr. West was not so great a painter as he was thought; but he had the true love of the art in him in certain respects, and he had built himself a truly elegant place for the cultivation of it. It is of this, and certain associations of ideas connected with it, we propose to speak, and not so much of himself.

The following, then, used to be our thoughts, as we paced up Holborn and Oxford-street, occasionally staring at the shops, and stared at (for our dress)[7] by the passengers: — It will not be long before we are there, and then we shall see the long, quiet gallery, with its paintings all along it, and the statues at the turnings of the corners; and we shall see Mr. West, with his kind even face, and *hear* the very quiet of his rooms. And Mrs. West, (our kinswoman, reader,) will be occupied as usual with her book, and will ask us how we do, in her quiet voice, and with her sly smile; and there will be the dog, and the squirrel, and the window looking into the garden; Rubens' Lion-Hunt; and the awful mystery of Raphael's "God the Father," sitting on that strange arch on the top of the Fathers of the Church, hardly (we thought) lawful to be looked at. And there, above all, will be our beloved Angelica and Medoro, the most delightful of fire-screens,[8] making us in love with Ariosto before we knew him — aye, and with love itself, of whom we knew as little. But we had a soul ready made for the *belle passion,* and for all the strange tricks and surprises it was prepared to play us; and there sat we, oppressed, we knew not why, with all this beauty and happiness; and every now and then heaving great sighs, which it pleased our shrewd kinswoman to jest withal, offering us her half-crown if we could sit half an hour "without doing it:" and we lost.

Mr. West had bought this house, built all the premises at the back, and fairly lined the whole of the walls with pictures, passage and all. On passing the hall and the parlour doors, you came to what would have been the back of the house, in another tenement, and looked through a glass door into the first gallery. This was a long, slender covered way, with a skylight (like all the rest), walled with sketches, and terminating its vista in a large window, which looked into an elegant little garden in the Italian fashion, with a grass-plat and an arcade round it, set with busts on pedestals. But the gallery itself did not terminate. It turned to the left through a shorter one, in the further corner of which, to the left also, was a study-door, with a statue on each side (the Apollo of the Vatican and the Venus de Medicis); while to the right it extended into a longer gallery than the first, hung also with sketches and paintings, and terminating in a door. This door led into a noble lofty room, containing some of the artist's larger pictures, several of them enormous (as we then fancied), and looking as large as the Sinai mountains, and other awful subjects with they represented. Opposite this door was another; and this final door led into another room equally noble, in which the artist was at work. He wore a flannel gown, and a dress neat and gentlemanly throughout, with powdered hair, and was sure to be found with palette and brush in hand, advancing and receding before one of his pictures, as if existence and painting were one and the same thing to him, — and they were. He had not an idea out of his painting room, except that he was historical painter to the king; that he was

very fond and proud, nevertheless, of his native country,
America; and that Bonaparte was a great man. We believe
that, in the king's regard for him, there was a little mixture
of spite towards America; as much as to say, — "You see your
men of genius are on my side — at least your painters; and
that I patronise them, and they grace my throne." Mr. West,
however, was as staunch a republican as a man could be who
contrived to be a royal painter and an admirer of Buonaparte.
He went over to Paris during the peace (God knows what they
thought of it at court; but they did not pay him well, and so
he had a hold over them in that quarter); and Buonaparte
complimented him, and he said that the First Consul had the
handsomest smile and leg that he had ever beheld.

Mr. West had a tall porter, well made, and of a striking yet
placid countenance, who used to stand for his apostles, particularly St. Peter, and is very like that saint in his pictures.
There was also a little elderly, powder-headed butler, who
imitated his master's absurdities,[9] and was the vainest little
fellow we remember, wearing a miniature of himself in a
shirt-pin. The porter we never could truly identify with his
condition of servant. He was an old family servant, with the
usual becoming familiarity allowed to such friends; and when
he spoke to us, we thought of friend, servant, and St. Peter all
in one: and the effect was very Christian.

The writer's mother generally accompanied him in these
delightful visits. She was fond of pointing out to him such of
the pictures as contained religious or historical subjects, particularly those inculcating charity and patriotism, such as,
"Christ healing the Sick," "Agrippina returning to Rome with
the Ashes of Germanicus," and "Sir Philip Sydney giving up
his draught of water to the dying Soldier." May her memory
be blest, both for the pleasures and the pains those lessons
have produced to us, — for the good of them has outweighed
the suffering; and the children who come after us will be the
better enabled to excuse what our defects may have left undone for them, in consideration of the love we bore her. We
looked with never-ending reverence on these pictures, and,

indeed, on the whole gallery; though a more cheerful delight was mixed with our admiration of the Graces and Cupids, and the occasional little landscapes, in which the artist indulged himself, some of them very pleasing. Nor did our love of romance and chivalry fail to make us deeply interested in those gorgeous, azure-garmented paintings, sown with lions and fleurs-de-lis, of "Battles of Cressy and Poitiers," and "Installations of Knights of the Garter," with their draperied steeds, crested and crowned helmet, bronze-visaged warriors, and kings all over heraldry; all which, in spite of our Americanisms and our patriotism, fostered in us a secret reverence for courts, which time and the tax-gatherer have most thoroughly undone.

Among the visitors at Mr. West's, we recollect Sir Francis Bourgeois,[10] who gave the pictures to the Dulwich Gallery, and who was a pleasant-looking man, with a dashing exterior; Sir Thomas (then Mr.) Lawrence,[11] smiling with white teeth, who had the dandy, artificial manner, betwixt ease and affectation, which he put in his portraits; Mary Lloyd, a female R.A., and celebrated painter of flowers, who was said to have been in love with Fuseli; and Mr. Beckford,[12] of Fonthill, who came there about some picture he had ordered, and talked well about Grecian art, and contemptuously of the English climate, saying, in answer to somebody who spoke of its being a fine day, that he had "never seen the sun in England." He repeated, also, if we remember, the joke of the Neapolitan ambassador, who said, that the only ripe fruit in England were the roasted apples.

But our great delight was to be *en famille* in the back-parlour (the principal one) with our dear Angelica and Medoro, and the look into the garden (into which a door descended), and Mrs. West and her book, with conversations now and then between the kinswomen about America, and Raphael's mystery over the sideboard, and the rich Lion-Hunt of Rubens (a large coloured engraving), and the lap-dog, who barked with an absurd inefficiency, and our little friend the squirrel, who went round and round in his cage, and helped us to doubt the propriety of putting animals into cages. His nibble, and his lively eye, looked as if he ought to be whisking among the trees.

All this beloved scene is now gone: — the mild painter is gone; the shrewd aunt; the beloved brother; the pictures, the garden, (at least it is blocked up or hidden somehow, and we dare not inquire for it); and even the Angelica and Medoro are not to be found. It was such a blow to us, when we heard the pictures were to be sold, and "by auction," under the cruel thumps of a hammer, that we never thought of attending or applying to see if we could bear off a relic. B. W. or Raphael W.[13] (as humane as his name) would surely have given us the Lovers had we asked for them; for, after all, they were but engravings on screens, the designs of pretty Angelica Kauffman; but grief never suffered the idea to come into our heads.

Nevertheless, the Angelica and Medoro we have in our breasts, (heaven, and the good-natured soul of that poet, be thanked!) and the other pictures are in our memory, and the house too, and the garden; and in heaven itself, as well as in our heart (like the moon reflected in water) is that sweet and patient mother, if ever mother was there, together with all whom she loved; and love itself survives and is ever young, though we are growing old; and nature is never old, nor hope in those that know her; and thank God, we do not see a bit of difference in ourselves, — no, not an atom — as far as the love of all which is loveable is concerned, — from what we were at twelve and fourteen years of age; which, to be able to say it at the age of forty-nine, is something upon which a poor battered cosmopolite may have leave to congratulate himself, without much grudging on the part of the rich and the wealthy.

THE TOWNSMAN

No. XI (ET SEQ.)

A WALK TO CHELSEA

November 10, 1833

A Townsman is not the less a townsman, because he sometimes goes *out* of town.[1] On the contrary, it refreshes him for
his *townosophy*, and makes him see more in the very shops
than he would otherwise. He knows what the bulbs mean in
a seedsman's windows; and is not to be mystified at the sight
of the plaster-cast figure of the cow, in those that exhibit no
other tokens of milk. He even walks the better in the streets,
for his last Sunday's walk in the country, or his pull up the
river. It takes a week to get the sense of vigour and Richmond
Hill out of him. If he gets, for a fortnight or so, as far as
Brighton, he thinks he is sunburnt for the rest of the year, —
quite brown and healthy, and that he may eat, drink, write,
cipher, stay in doors, or go too much to the theatres, with
impunity. He may be mistaken in some of these items, but
upon the whole he has a larger and more liberal sense both
of town and country for it, and would be mistaken in a worse
manner if he did nothing but stop at home. His surfeits would
be without redemption; and he would have no right to admire
Rosina, or Love in a Village.[2] He would not understand the
pink and green of Madame Vestris's[3] play bills.

It is true, if he were a school-boy without holidays, or a
monk after the fashion of those in old Austin Friars or the
Black Friars (who have bequeathed their names to those
places), his very imprisonment in the town might give him
a more intense idea of the forbidden beauties of the country.
He could read his Horace and Virgil, or the lives of St. Francis
and St. Teresa, and doat upon a bit of church-yard tree, or
the face of a maid-servant, far beyond the more informed
conceptions of the most accomplished modern cit. But it falls

to the lot of few, perhaps of none now-a-days, to have their poetical ignorance pampered in this manner. The old bye-roads, and secluded no-thoroughfares, are shut up, or inhabited. We can get nothing by those passages. We must realise all our good through the road of knowledge; and happier for all is the prospect, if we become knowing indeed, and see what to allow, and when to begin to teach. We may lay such habits in childhood as shall give us all the benefits and none of the disadvantages of the old ignorance; and what is trivial or palling now, shall then be full of endless curiosity and delight.

But we are diverging from our path. We have begun the present article in the above manner, because the word "Chelsea," in book-loving ears, has still something of a country sound, and because, furthermore, we intend to take a Sunday trip with the reader to some place up the river in that direction. Chelsea, however, now belongs still more to town than to country, having become, in fact, one of the immediate suburbs of the metropolis, – a demi-green border, half house and half garden. A very few years back there were still some fields between it and London, known by the name of the Five-Fields, which are now swallowed up by the streets between Brompton and Pimlico, and the new buildings on the estate of Lord Grosvenor. We cannot say we admire those streets, or even the fine new squares thereabouts. We cannot help thinking the place is flat and unhealthy, and that the solidest and hugest of the houses have a sort of flimsy look, as if, like ill-set plants, they grew more big than stout. But we have not examined them with an eye to criticism, and this may be prejudice. One redeeming thing, however, we know of this quarter; and that is, that Mozart lived there when he was in England. We cannot say in what part of it. But the circumstance, (which we learnt from Mr. Novello's[4] "Life of Purcell," prefixed to that gentleman's edition of the works of the great English composer,) reconciled the whole quarter to us directly. Instead of thinking of brick and plaster, and the superfluous wealth of a great aristocrat, good neither for himself nor the country, it enabled us, in future, wherever we should happen to be, thus to think of the divine German musician, who has done good to all the world. Hail, therefore, still, ye Five Fields! though ye are no longer extant, ye shall still be "green in song!" And hail Ebury-street, and Eaton-street, and Pimlico, and even thou, Belgrave-square, and dreadful ci-devant "Bloody Bridge," now called "Grosvenor," though thy master be worth millions, and thy name not worth a straw. A great and generous name has been among you, and left sweetness on your walls, like the sunbeams that drew music out of the Egyptian stone; even his, whose soul was all movement and grace, and whose wife said he was a still finer dancer than a musician, (delightful conjugal extravagance!) and who one day, because he had no money in his pocket (which is apt to be the case with richer men), drew upon his genius for an alms to a poor man (which is not apt to be the case with them), and sent him with an extempore piece of music to a music-buyer, who gave him five gold pieces for it (we forget of what value), which is as much as some rich men would fain give for the money's worth, and haggle for it into the bargain.

Well; God bless musicians, and painters, and poets, and all the rest of them, and just enable them to get their bread (for they cannot expect to have the advantage of Marquisses in every thing); and meanwhile a time is coming about, when the names of streets shall have some meaning, and people will find out whereabouts Mozart lived in the realms of Eaton and Grosvenor, and the street shall be called Mozart-street, and men shall bless it; as sure as the press is the press; and primogeniture will go to the devil.

When Mozart was in England, he was a child of eight years of age, but a man in talent, modulating and playing fugues on given subjects, in the most extraordinary manner, and already evincing the greatest genius. The young Apollo had already his beams about him. His father, who brought him here, probably chose his residence in this quarter, in order to be near the Queen, who patronised him.

But in order to connect Chelsea in its most obvious and pleasantly approachable manner with the town, we will here make our choice of the various entrances to it from the east, take the same direction of roads as the carriages and the omnibuses, and so come round at the conclusion by the oldest part of the village and the river side. The King's road is now a fashionable drive from the neighbourhood of Belgrave Square; and the omnibuses go down Sloane-street and Little Chelsea. Our best way will be to dispatch Little Chelsea first, and then to come back and enter Great Chelsea by Sloane-street, and so up to the King's-road. Our guide to the localities, and to many of the literary reminiscences, also, will be the very pains-taking and praiseworthy *Historical and Topographical Description of Chelsea and its Environs,* written by Mr. Thomas Faulkner, a bookseller in that place.

Little Chelsea, so called from its rising into a hamlet long after the existence of the old village, lies in the road that goes from Brompton to Fulham, — the one that turns off to the left at the parting of the two roads in Knightsbridge, the other going to Kensington. It has little to detain us. The old house, now the workhouse of St. George's, Hanover-square, was once the residence of the celebrated Earl of Shaftesbury, author of the "Characteristics." His friend Locke is said, with great probability, to have written part of his essay in it, and Addison to have composed "several of the Spectators." What Addison did in the house of the infidel earl, we cannot say. Locke had been his tutor. The house was afterwards the residence of Serjeant Wynne,[5] author of "Eunomus."

Robert Boyle, the great chemical philosopher, lived in this part of Chelsea; here was born his nephew Charles, fourth Earl of Orrery, the witty disputant with Bentley[6] about the "Epistles of Phalaris," in which the wit had the worst of it.

In the front of the public-house, called the Green Elm, is a curiosity in the humble shape of a tall white post, not long since painted, and patched in the side with a plate of metal. It appears to issue out of the flat surface of an old trunk of a tree, levelled with the ground, and in fact does so, being no less than the only remains of the tree itself; which was the celebrated one known by the name of the Queen's Elm, from a tradition that Queen Elizabeth, on her way to a house which Lord Burleigh had in this neighbourhood, was overtaken, in company with his lordship, by a shower of rain, and retreated for shelter under this elm, which she desired in future might be called hers. It is a pity to see the elm gone, considering that Elizabeth was not a mere queen, but the queen of Shakspeare and Spenser, and the Raleighs and Sydneys: but the post is better than nothing. One gives it a grip and a friendly pat, on coming up with it, as if one had the advantage of her Majesty's sacred person, and made friends with her tall and somewhat angular sides.

Posthoc meminisse juvabit

The sign of the "Goat and Boots" in this road is said to have been painted by Morland,[7] when reduced to one of his usual shifts to pay his alehouse bill.

Park-walk, leading to Old Chelsea, ran by the side of a large piece of ground, of forty acres, formerly called Chelsea-park, and still containing a house and grounds, not long since occupied by Mr. Stephens,[8] a well-known contributor to the *Monthly Magazine*. Chelsea-park was a portion of the property in this neighbourhood belonging to Sir Thomas More, and afterwards came into possession of Lionel Cranfield, Earl of Middlesex, whose daughter married the Earl of Dorset, father of the witty earl of that name, and used to boast (according to Pope) of her gallantries with Sir John Suckling.

But more of her ladyship when we come to Great Chelsea, to which place we invite the reader's company next week, not without some confidence that if he is a lover of books and old times, he may find some entertainment in it, as it is unquestionably, next to the Borough, the most classic ground in the neighbourhood of London. So little have the lasting memories of wit and genius to do with the ephemeral splendours of fashion.

November 17, 1833

We spoke, in our last, of a time to come, when the street in which Mozart lived at Chelsea would be called after the name of that delightful musician. We are serious upon this point, and think that the world will have taken another advance in good sense and the art of living, when the example already set by the chief masters in that art, the French, shall take effect in this new christening of streets. Consider the vexatious or frivolous thoughts in which people are for the most part occupied when they are passing along, and how glad they are of any agreeable surprise, or whatsoever enlivens the current of their reflections. A man, for instance, is thinking of his domestic troubles, or a bill, or the window-tax, or his head ache, or what a fool Smith is, or what Johnson has been saying to vex him, or how cold it is, or how wet, or what a noise the dustman is making, or of the funds, or the gutter, or a tight boot, or an indigestion, or how wonderfully happy he deserves to be and is not, or how happy he does not deserve to be, or how ugly the women look to-day, or how sweet and unlike his wife; — in short not to fill up our paper with these postulates (upon which we must have an article by itself), he is thinking of something very dull or disagreeable, and he looks up and sees the words Eaton-street, or Ebury-street, or Jebotherick-street, and he says to himself, "What's Eaton-street or Ebury-street to me? Who, or what is Eaton? Some bricklayer, I suppose, or builder, who took himself for an architect, and thinks to immortalise himself by telling the world that there was once living a silly fellow of that name, of whom nobody knows any thing. What a dull street, and what a stupid name!" But suppose, instead of Eaton-street, he sees the words Mozart-street, and that they are inscribed in such a manner as to shew that the celebrated man of that name lived there; this (unless he is a man insensible to all harp and dulcimer, and "fit for treason, stratagems, and spoils,"[9]) puts an idea into his head, and a very pleasant one; and he says to himself, "Aha; there has been a famous man

here. I wonder in which house he lived. It is not a very lively
street; but famous men do not always live in lively streets;
and lively must the house have been in which he lived and
played his music. What a charming composer he is! What a
march that is in *Figaro!* What a minuet in *Don Giovanni!*
What a duet, *Crudel perche!* And what a capital page Madame
Vestris makes in that little rogue, *Cherubino!* Though, for that
matter, my sweet little friend, Miss Talbot, sings Mozart as
well as any body. She is very handsome, and she loves poetry
and painting, too. And how fond she is of flowers! To see her
among her roses and myrtles really seems like poetry itself
made true. Whenever I think of her, I think of the summer-
time, and of the pretty place in which I first saw her. I wish
I could sing. However, I am very fond of singing. Yes, I
certainly have a very good taste. She looked at me, I remember, when somebody said so, as if it pleased her to be of the
same opinion; and her eyes are prodigiously fine — wonderfully sincere. Jones says so, and he is a wonderfully clever
fellow, is Jones, though ugly. I'll not ask him to settle that
account just now. It will be inconvenient to him, poor dog.
It shall stand over. I like to mix generosity with prudence.
Yes, I certainly am a very generous man. I must make Miss
Talbot a present of some piece of music, and we'll have a
party, and I'll ask Jones to meet her. He sings — not very
well, it is true — hoarsely, somehow — but in tune; and better
than that smooth-faced puppy, Collins, who thinks of nothing
but himself. *He* understand Mozart! A fellow in love with the
creeking of his own boots! Mozart is to be understood by
none but such as Miss Talbot and myself — people of hearts,
my boy, and modesty, and taste, and discernment, and a perception of the beauties of all things."

Our friend, you see, dear reader, may not have a perfect
self knowledge, or an entire freedom from the infirmities of
human nature; but, take his soliloquy altogether, and you
will observe that a delightful name has put him into a train
of pleasant thoughts of music, and poetry, and love, and the
summer flowers. From such dull thraldoms as Eaton-street and

Ebury-street he is utterly delivered. He remembers nothing
about them. He does not see even the dull houses on each
side of him, — nor the dull weather, — nor the potato-shop, —
nor the butcher's, nor the fine insipid houses, — all with areas,
and verandas, and heavy knockers, and monotonous brick-
work, and now and then a footman at the door, in powder and
velvet breeches. Not an atom does he see of all these. His soul
is far away, with music, and Miss Talbot, and the roses. He
has thought of them all the way from Mozart-street to St.
James's Park; and, as he lifts up his eyes, and finds himself
among grass and trees, instead of brick-work, he almost fancies
he has —

> Waked, and found the vision true.

Such magic is there in a name.

Why, then, should not all our streets, which have been
inhabited, or made otherwise famous, by eminent men, be put
in possession of their magic rights, and thus furnish a series
of pleasant thoughts or encouraging examples? Why should
not Gerard-street, Soho, be called *Dryden*-street; and Lombard-
street *Pope*-street; and St. Martin's-street, (Leicester-square,)
Newton-street; and so on? Who cares any thing for the names
Gerard, or Lombard, or St. Martin's; or of what use are they
to us, when we lift up our eyes on a dull day, their lids,
perhaps, heavy with care, and receive nothing upon them but
the rain-drops?

Mr. Wordsworth, in a passage unworthy of his great genius,
and written with his will upon him instead of his understanding, and in his ill-will instead of his good, flings against the
French people the extraordinary accusation of their having

> Equally a want of books and men.

The countrymen of Montaigne, and Pascal, and Molière, and
Corneille, and Voltaire, and Rousseau, and Claude, and Poussin
(for their pictures are books), and the Chancellor Hospital,
and the Chevalier Bayard, and Eustace St. Pierre, and St.
Francis de Sales, and Henry IV, and Sully, and all the generous

portion of the victims who fell in the Revolution, whether on
the royal side or the republican, and the heroes of the Three
Days, and the numerous other adorners of the annals of noble
peril, in tempest and in war, surely form a multitude, grand
enough and awful enough, and with reproach in the pale visages
of their memory, to answer with dumb disproof to this spleen of
their unenjoying neighbour. But we should like to know in
which of the two countries Mr. Wordsworth himself could have
stood the chance of having his genius sooner acknowledged,
and a street or a district named after him? One of the most frequented streets in Paris is called *Jean Jacques Rousseau-Street*
— not simply Rousseau, which might confound the name with
ordinary ones, but Christian names and all, that there may
be no chance of mistake. There is also a *Quay Voltaire*, another frequented place; and neither of these names did the
Bourbons venture to touch; no, not with the help of all the
thrones and superstitions which those great men ventured to
shake. Have we done anything like this in England for *our*
great men — men among the very greatest of the earth, and
without whose first utterances of freedom and philosophy
those later voices might not have been heard? Where have
we a Francis Bacon Street? or a John Milton Street? or an
Isaac Newton Street? or Wickliffe, Shakspeare, Geoffrey Chaucer, or Edmund Spenser Street? or Samuel Johnson or John
Howard Street? though we erect a monument occasionally to
such men, in cold cathedrals, where poor tax-paying people
are afraid of going in, because of the verger and his impious
paw. The lawyers in Gray's Inn have got a Verulam-building;
but this is hiding their light as much as they can under a
bushel; for Verulam was but one of Bacon's titles, and the
true name to know him by is his own — Francis Bacon. People,
out of an instinct to this effect, misnomer his title, and call
him Lord Bacon (which he was not) rather than merge his
illustrious appellation in the honours of a court. Francis Bacon
is the thing. He begins one of his works with saying: "Francis
Bacon thought thus." He did not say the Lord Verulam, or
the Viscount St. Albans. He knew that the Lord and the

Viscount thought nothing about the matter. It was Francis Bacon that thought. The Lord and the Viscount were inferior people, aye, even in his own illustrious person, and he lived bitterly to know it.

Begging the reader's pardon for this digression, we resume our walk to Chelsea, beginning now to proceed to Great Chelsea, or Chelsea, simply so called, and taking our way to it down the well-known thoroughfare of Sloane-street, and so up the now fashionable drive, the King's-road. Sloane-street is not liable to so much objection on the score we have just been speaking of, as most others. The name has a record in it, and not an unworthy one, being that of the once celebrated Sir Hans Sloane,[10] the physician and collector of curiosities, who, though not so great a man as his collection and his riches helped him to be taken for by his neighbours in this quarter, where he was lord of the manor, was an intelligent and estimable person, and lived to a fine old age. We shall have occasion to say more of him as we go along. The names of him and his connexions, the Cadogans, are frequent in the streets hereabouts; but the truest honours of the spot consist in its having two of our most popular writers for inhabitants – Mr. Allan Cunningham, who lives near Sloane-street, and Miss Landon,[11] who, with an instinct common to poets that live in cities, and congenial with the graces of her muse, has contrived to pitch herself into the prettiest and most arboraceous nest in the neighbourhood, – a house in Hans-place, which has the trees of the square in front of it, and (if we are not mistaken) those of the gardens belonging to the house called the Pavilion, at the back. This Pavilion, if we are to believe Mr. Faulkner's book, and the engraving in it, is a true specimen, in the best sense of the phrase, of the *"rus in urbe,"* contriving not only to have a good deal of ground about it, with trees and water, but even deer! Mr. Allan Cunningham, we suppose, does not care to pitch himself so luxuriously, not being able to get any moorland or heathery valley hereabouts. Luckily, he can make them in his study.

The Botanic garden in Sloane-street "is so formed," according to Mr. Faulkner, "that persons may walk nearly two miles without entering the same path twice." This seems extraordinary, to look at the place. It is said to contain the greatest collection of orange trees near London. A garden thus publicly presenting itself like that of a square, is an object for which one cannot but feel grateful; and the regret is proportionate, if thinking that a spot so near town cannot be favourable to many of its plants. There is a great want of such walks, however, in and near the metropolis — and partial unfitness is well recompensed (at least to the walker) by general beauty and convenience. In the course of time, an ornamented public walk, near every populous district, will be regarded as a necessary of life. The public mind will have grown up to it, and the rational demands of health and cheerfulness be attended to.

At the end of Sloane-street you turn to the right and left into the King's-road, the high old Chelsea thoroughfare betwixt town and country, leading to Parson's-green and Fulham. A person not in the habit of frequenting this neighbourhood would be astonished, as we were last summer, in witnessing the throng of carriages and riders that pour up the King's-road when the town is full, and the weather in reasonable condition. Thus do fashions come round. The road, at the time of the Restoration, was a mere passage between the grounds belonging to farmers and gardeners. It was widened, we are told, for the convenience of Charles II, in his journey to Hampton Court; and hence the name of King's-road, which some have fancied to be no older than the reign of George III. But Charles had other conveniences in view than those of Hampton. Lady Castlemain, at one time, lived out this way, and the Duchess of Mazarin, and, it is said, Nell Gwynn, — probably half the fashion of the court; for it was then the custom to travel by water as well as land; and the Chelsea bank of the Thames was studded, as we shall see, with courtly abodes. The back gardens of some of these formerly abutted on the road; but, as they looked towards the river, it will be proper to notice them when we return that way. As this, however, leaves our immediate path without any interest till we come as far as a public house called the World's End, we shall speed to that alarming confine at once.

Alas, that the world should come to such an end as this! and, above all, the fashionable world! the great world! *the* world! as it is called, by way of eminence, and to distinguish it from the little vulgar world, known by the name of the terra-queous globe. The Chelsea World's End was formerly the end of that village, and of the objects which the fashionable world had in coming to visit it. Here ended the nearest cluster of houses to the metropolis, and hereabouts lay the most fashionable country houses at no farther distance from town. When people had arrived at the house and grounds of my Lady Stanley and his Grace the Duke of Buckingham, they had got to the World's End. Nothing could "touch them farther;" unless, indeed, they went to Hampton Court, and that was "going to heaven."

But very much the reverse of mortal or solemn were the doings at the World's End. It was a tavern "of a certain reputation." In Mr. Faulkner's History of Chelsea (vol. I. p. 34) is a print of it in its former condition. It was a wooden building of very moderate dimensions, exactly resembling some of the middle-sized public-houses that still exist in the neighbourhood of the metropolis. The present humble brickbuilding is not so picturesque, but is probably nearly as large; though our authority tells us that the former had extensive grounds attached to it, which is not the case with the present. Neither fashion nor gallantry, however, stands upon ceremony; and wit can make classical ground of what has no other title to consecration. It is this house which Congreve alludes to in a famous passage of his comedy of "Love for Love;" which, in justice to Mr. Faulkner's pages, and as we should not have recollected the name of the place without them, we shall quote from our brother historian accordingly: —

Mrs. Foresight. — I suppose you would not go alone to the World's End?

Mrs. Frail. — The World's End! What, do you mean to banter me?

Mrs. Foresight. — Poor innocent! you don't know that there is a place called the World's End. I'll swear you can keep countenance: surely you'll make an admirable player.

Mrs. Frail. — I'll swear you have a great deal of impudence, and, in my mind, too much for the stage.

Mrs. Foresight. — Very well; that will appear who has most. You never were at the World's End?

Mrs. Frail. — No.

Mrs. Foresight. — You deny it positively to my face?

Mrs. Frail. — Your face! What's your face?

Mrs. Foresight. — No matter for that: it is as good a face as yours.

Mrs. Frail. — Not by a dozen years' wearing. But I do deny it, positively, to your face, then.

Mrs. Foresight. — I'll allow you to find fault with my face; for I'll swear your impudence has put me out of countenance. But look you here now; where did you lose this gold bodkin? Oh, sister! Oh, sister!

Mrs. Frail. — My bodkin?

Mrs. Foresight. — Nay, it is yours — look at it.

Mrs. Frail. — Well, if you go to that, *where did you find this bodkin?* Oh, sister! sister! sister every way!

Mrs. Foresight (aside). — Oh! devil on't, that I could not discover her without betraying myself![12]

November 24, 1833

We omitted to mention in our last, that the French, in their anxiety to do honour to their great men, and turn their memory to the best account, have pointed out the houses in which some of them lived, by inscriptions. This is the case with the house in which Molière was born in Paris, with that in which Corneille died, and with that of Le Sage at Boulogne. The visitor of the place looks up and sees, "Here lived Molière," and his mind becomes a thoroughfare of pleasant thoughts connected with comedy and the stage, and the generosity of that extraordinary man. He sees a bust of Corneille inscribed "The Cid" (the title of his greatest tragedy); and instantly all the best part of the grandeur of the age of Louis the XIVth, pass before him. At Boulogne he is shown the house which Le Sage made so snug and comfortable, and in which he was

accustomed to walk up and down a trellised passage while
composing: and straightway he thinks of "Gil Blas," and the
"Devil upon Two Sticks," and the house in which the secretary
of the Count de Lemos found repose at last. It is Voltaire's
last residence which has given its name to the Quai Voltaire;
and we observe, on referring to a list of the streets in Paris,
that many of them are named after celebrated men. In fact,
we scarcely miss a celebrated name that we look for. There
are Molière, Corneille, Racine, and Voltaire street, Rousseau-
street, (as we noticed last week; it is the most public one in
Paris, the Post-office being in it,) La Fontaine-street, Sully-
street, Buffon-street, Descartes, Helvetius, Merivaux, Masil-
lon, and Crebillon streets, — Gretry-street (after the musician),
and even a street "Du Contrat Social," so named after a book
of Rousseau's. When shall we hear of "Fairy Queen" or "Political Justice"-street? Nay, our goodnatured neighbours, who
are thought to be so jealous of English fame (it is only the
jealous that so think them), have got a "Cafe Byron"! It is
in the Boulevard of the Capuchins! Don Juan got into a
monastery!

The only memories which we of this "thinking nation,"
glorify in the names of our streets, are those of soldiers and
bricklayers! We do not mean to deny the talents of great
generals, though how far they are overrated, in consequence
of the startling nature of their field of operations, is a question
worthy of reflection. We have Waterloo and Wellington-
streets in plenty. The French, in like manner, have their
Rivoli and Ulm-streets, and Places des Victoires. Perhaps, also,
they have streets named after bricklayers. It is impossible to
say. It is certain that we have plenty of them in London. The
belligerent and the brick-building may be said to divide the
honours of the metropolis between them, — no great thing
surely on which to pride ourselves; we, who have produced
the greatest poets and philosophers of the modern world.

Then, with regard to statues. When will the metropolis of
the country of Bacon and Shakspeare, of Locke, Hobbes,
Newton, Marvell, Sidney, Hampden, and a multitude of others,

men of "earth's first blood" (as Wordsworth finely says), be delivered from the opprobrium of not having a single image, standing in public, of any truly great individual, while it slavishly exalts a number of royal nobodies, whom, in the course of a few generations, nobody knows! Who can tell the names of the various stone and gilded statues, that occupy the middle of our squares? And when found out, who respects them, or does not see that they ought to be displaced (as they surely will be) by the likenesses of men and women who have honoured their country? Goldsmith says of somebody, "that he was famous for having a statue in Westminster Abbey." These gentlemen and ladies would be famous for having statues in the squares, if having a statue in a square had not been a thing opposed to all notion of celebrity!

It is true, on second thoughts, we recollect that there are statues of Pitt, and Fox, and Major Cartwright,[13] — all people of history, and that may reasonably be thus recorded; though we doubt whether the statue of the great god of fundholders will last many years. If it does, it will be out of a spirit of public generosity, and as a mark to be pitied. Fox, besides his talents, had a fine nature, deserving the regard of his fellow-men; and Cartwright's statue is the very personification of honest perseverance. All honour to it. But where are the statues of the men above-named? and why must the erection of the best of these monuments look too much like the result of party and present feeling, seeing that we are ungrateful to the memories consecrated by time, and that have made England respected for centuries?

Reserving our right to digress after this fashion whenever we please, like proper free-born pedestrians, we now resume our pleasant because classical way up the King's-road, which, if it does not abound just now in country beauties or court beauties, blossoms with memories of them all, and even with the laurels of Spenser; for our progress has now brought us to Stanley-place and Stanley-house, near the nursery grounds of Mr. Knight; and this Stanley-house was originally built by Sir Arthur Gorges,[14] the intimate friend of the poet, and him-

self a poet, as may be seen by the quotation from him in
Mr. Todd's life of the great minstrel of the Fairy Queen. As
the family of the Gorges were among the chief landholders in
Chelsea, and the poet's friend built this house for his own
special use and recreation, it is hazarding little to suppose
that Spenser must have been among its visitors. The very
probability serves to hallow the place. It gives it a new colour,
superior even to Mr. Knight's dahlias, which make such a
magnificent show in autumn in the high road leading to it,
and almost cast a light on the dead wall on the other side of
the way. The house, from the glimpse we catch of it over its
garden wall, seems a good old house, after the right comfortable fashion of buildings — solid and plentiful; and it has a
butler to show occasionally at the gate, jolly, old, and rubi-
cund, with a red waistcoat to match his cheeks, and a powdered
head, who looks as if he had been in the family now residing
there for these fifty years. But though on the same site, the
present house is not the "old original" one. It was called
Stanley House in consequence of its being bequeathed by the
widow of Sir Arthur Gorges to Lady Elizabeth, wife of Sir
Robert Stanley, her daughter, and was rebuilt at the end of
the seventeenth century. In 1743 Sir Charles Wager, the
admiral, died in it. It afterwards belonged to poor Lady Strathmore,[15] celebrated for her love of botany, and for throwing
herself away in marriage upon the infamous Robinson Bowes,
who, in his mad villainy and self-will, was said to have carried
his barbarous treatment of her so far, as to bore her tongue
with a needle! Her very graces probably exasperated his
conscious unworthiness of them. We remember his being
pointed out to us in our childhood. He was a tall thin man,
with a cocked hat and aquiline nose; not unlike Junius's Duke
of Grafton.

Stanley House, some time afterwards, became the residence
of Dr. Warren, the physician. The last thing Mr. Faulkner
records of it was its occupation by the present Marquis of
Queensbury.

Close to the house and grounds is the bridge over the canal

from the Thames, a rivulet which has been made navigable as far as Kensington. This bridge forms the western limit of Chelsea; but hold — we do not turn back yet —there is a house just on the other side of the bridge, which drew even the grave eye of Mr. Faulkner out of its bounds; and thus he candidly recordeth his supererogation: —

Although not in this parish, yet I cannot quit this spot without noticing the residence of Eleanor Gwynn, now called Sandford Manor House, a mansion of venerable appearance, immediately in front of which are four walnut trees, said to have been planted by royal hands. A medallion in plaster, of the fair Eleanor, was some years ago dug up on the premises. The adjoining lands are now occupied by the works of the Imperial Gas and Coke Company. Mr. Addison also resided on this spot in 1708; two charming letters, written by him to the young Earl of Warwick, and dated by him from Sandy End, have already been printed. (In the Author's "History of Kensington.")

"Mr. Addison" and Nell Gwynn! the two extremes of reserve and open-heartedness! But softly — there is yet a story, if we mistake not, of this same Sandy End, which goes to show that Mr. Addison himself was not unimpressed with recollections of the "fair Eleanor." Of the house a print was published some years back in the old *Monthly Magazine*. It stands to the left, a very little way beyond the bridge, and is easily recognised by the triple, undulating division of its front parapet. Well — let us speak low, and with all due reverence to the Spectator, and still greater reverence to the light which not long hence shall be struck out of the conflicts now occupying the minds of men; but it was in this house, if we mistake not, that the future moralist, who was to have such an effect upon the world towards keeping things as they were, and vice and virtue in their alleged exquisite state of balance, is said to have contributed his quota of "wild oats' 'to the system, in the shape of a certain little human being, of which it was not exactly known whether he or his friend Steele was the father. They both occupied the house together, and therein ministered to their domesticities a maid servant, who appears to have been struck with the wit and agreeableness of both, and who was in a pleasing state of perplexity as to which of the two illustrious lodgers she admired most. The conclusion to which they themselves came (if we recollect rightly) was, that if the little stranger was fair, it should be reckoned to belong to Addison, but, if dark, to Steele. The story is to be found in a late biographical notice, and is related in a very good spirit, with all due considerateness towards the human nature of those benefactors of their species; and in a spirit no less good do we repeat it, albeit we have an eye to the conflicts above noticed, and to the consideration thereof. Poor, delightful, candid, open-hearted Steele! He took more than one sin of his friend upon him. Query, whether the illegitimate daughter which he avowed was the little puzzler in question?[16] Addison avowed neither illegitimate daughter, nor inconvenient writings, though he had a legitimate daughter by a perverse and scornful wife, who taught her to hate him. What became of the maid-servant we are not told. Maid-servants, like a very different class, — old maids, go for nothing under the old system. Moralists sacrifice them, and wonder how you can have the want of candour to express an interest in their welfare, and a doubt of the advantages of the sacrifice. We should like to see that question discussed, instead of begged, between the Sunday papers and the readers of Colquhoun, Haslam, and the author of "England and America." However, we may be sure that, in the present instance, there was no ultra-prudential consideration in behalf of the poor suffering male sex and their distressing necessity to ruin and debauch, — at least not on the side of one of the parties.

Steele did a delicious thing with regard to this natural daughter of his, whoever she was. When he married, he took his wife a jaunt to a country boarding-school, saying, he had a little friend there, whom he wished to introduce to her, and whom it was fit she should know. When they entered, a sprightly girl came running to him in a way which would have let the lady into the secret, if she had not guessed it already. She acted as became the wife of such a man, and said she would be a mother to her, as no doubt she was. A compliment to her heart and understanding, so genuine, could hardly have been lost on any woman at all worthy of being Steele's companion.

December 1, 1833

We are glad to find that the fame of this our Townsman is going forth into all quarters, and its words unto the ends of the suburbs. The *Greenwich Gazette* compliments us; and saith, moreover, that we and the literary historian of the *Athenaeum* are complimenting one another,[17] which we are glad to hear; being of opinion that the more goodwill there is among men of letters, the better; and that if our brethren duly took that matter into consideration, they might govern the world; as indeed they and the *other* working classes seem likely to do. But our brother of the *Greenwich Gazette* justly confideth in his gentlemanly construction of things, when he saith that the reciprocity he alludeth to is all in good faith, and founded in nothing mercenary; for it was from himself we first learnt the honour that had befallen us, an accident having prevented us from seeing the literary history in question.

Having thus looked in at Greenwich in the omnibus of our imagination (as a Persian poet would say) we return to the place where we left off last week; to wit, the western extremity of Chelsea, and propose to come back, city-wards, through the oldest and best known part of it, by the water's side.

And luckily we have another pleasant name to commence with, such as helps to give the neighbourhood not only a celebrated but a good-natured memory, — Hoadly,[18] the author of the *Suspicious Husband.* He was the son of the famous Bishop Hoadly, who also lived for some time in this district; which appears to have pleased the family so much, that the dramatist built a house in it. It is on the west of Chelsea Farm, or the Stadium, as it is now called, and is a good old mansion, looking over handsome grounds to the river in front, and having a prospect of Harrow Hill from the back windows. It is now called Ashburnham House, from having been possessed some time by one of the family of that name. Hoadly died in this house ten years after its erection, and in the life-time of his father. He was a physician, and is remarkable for having united a turn for the exact sciences, with the animal spirits that produced one of the pleasantest comedies in the language. These bishops' sons, by some process or other of contrast, or suppression, or hidden sympathy, are famous for turning out ultra-vivacious. Fletcher was a son of a bishop of London; and Bishop Burnet's son was one of the wildest fellows about town, and a leader of "Mohawks." Hoadly's vivacity, however, was all good-natured and gentlemanly; and those who think ill of some exuberances in his play, mistake one extreme for another, and confound good will with bad. He was an amiable man in private, — the kind son of a kind father.

To the east of Ashburnham, or Hoadly House, (as it used to be, and ought to be called; for what is the word Ashburnham? there is nothing in it;) stands Chelsea Farm, or the Stadium, not long since the Villa of Lord Cremorne, and now a place laid out for the cultivation of gymnastics and shooting, by subscription. The villa was first formed by Theophilus Earl of Huntingdon, brother of the fair Protestant saint, Lady Elizabeth Hastings,[19] who made Congreve sentimental. It afterwards belonged to Shenstone's friend, Sir Thomas Lyttelton, who married the Duchess of Bridgewater, and who is described in the poet's letters as being so remarkable for his good fortune. "He is a man of courage, genius, generosity, and politeness," says Shenstone, "has been fortunate in the world; was made a colonel at about six and twenty; distinguished himself in several campaigns, married the Duchess of Bridgewater, and had the other day about sixteen thousand pounds left him by Colonel Jefferies, a very distant relation. He has a seat, and speaks in the House of Commons: has bought a town and country house, the latter of which he is ornamenting in the modern way; his Duchess is the most unceremonious and even tempered woman that lives." *

* Shenstone's Letters, No. 60.

This was certainly a climax of good fortune — to be brave, rich, generous, and a man of genius, and to marry the best tempered woman living!

The Duchess appears to have retained the villa after his death, and to have died in it. It then came into possession of the Cremorne family, acquaintances of the celebrated Mr. Carter, who was a visitor here.

The north-eastern corner of Chelsea farm, and the public-house called the World's End, are close together. Leaving this angle behind us, and coming away through the palings and other passages that tend eastward, we issue upon the banks of the river, and arrive at Lindsey House, now part of a row of houses, but easily distinguished by the general unity of its appearance. It is a comfort, in the midst of the barrack or workhouse style of modern building, to look upon these good old mansions, with their large and handsome proportions, their windows set in frames, and their generous quantity of material. Lindsey House was erected in the days of Charles the Second, by Robert, third Earl of Lindsey, on the site of a house originally built by Sir Theodore Magerne, physician first to Henry the Fourth of France, and afterwards to James and Charles the First and Charles the Second. Magerne died at this place upwards of eighty years of age, Granger says of drinking bad wine; an odd death for a physician, particularly of one who was a reformer in medicine, and among the introducers of the art chemical into the practice of it.*

Miss Hawkins, in her memoirs, speaks of an old inhabitant of Chelsea, who said that the Duchess of Mazarin[20] was once in possession of Lindsey-house; but diligent inquiries do not appear to have sanctioned the assertion. We shall hear of the duchess in another part of the village.

About eighty years back, the house was occupied, during

---

* He died of the effects of bad wine; a *slow*, which the weakness of age turned into a *quick*, poison. He foretold the time of his death to his friend, with whom he had been drinking moderately at a tavern in the Strand; and it happened according to his prediction. — *Granger's Biographical History of England*, Fifth Edit. Vol. III p. 116.

his residence in England, by the celebrated enthusiast, Count Zinzendorf,[21] and some of his Moravian brethren. This strange but respectable sect (who unite people in marriage without consulting the parties, but are remarkable for their unity and honesty) have still a burial-ground in the neighbourhood.

In one of the houses into which the mansion has since been divided, now called Lindsey-row, lived, during his latter years, Mr. Henry Constantine Jennings,[22] an eccentric virtuoso, who fairly tired out his good fortune by incurring repeated embarrassments for very little reason, and who, in some respects, died a martyr to his love of "curiosities." The truth is, he had more love for them than taste, and more eccentricity than either. A gentleman, who visited him in Lindsey-row about the year 1803, has left the following description of him: —

On the left hand of the drawing-room door was to be seen a very old and decrepid man, generally clothed in a brown suit of coarse cloth, with immense large silver buttons awkwardly fastened to the breast of his coat. He constantly wore a small hat both at home and abroad, and possessed both a white and a black beaver, the former of which was always selected for great occasions. Sitting in an immense arm chair lined with carpet, his body was mechanically placed in a reclining position, approaching nearly to the horizontal. This was effected by invariably reposing his legs and feet on a Roman triclinium, which he valued greatly. This venererable figure, with a sharp and croaking voice, saluted the visitor, whom he recognised by means of a mirror, and to whom he scarcely deigned to turn his head. He appeared to sit in all the majesty of *virtu,* amidst his books, his pictures, and his shells; and never willingly arose, but to gratify himself and his guest by exhibiting some, or all of these objects.*

The poor gentleman died in the rules of the King's Bench.

Lindsey-row is close to Battersea-bridge. Opposite one of the houses, in a little detached garden-plot by the water-side, is a large and beautiful willow-tree, reckoned one of the finest of its kind in England.

We now come to a *locality* highly interesting for the celebrity and variety of the personages that have occupied it; but,

* *Gorton's Biographical Dictionary,* Vol. 2. p. 198.

unfortunately, it has left no visible traces beyond a bit of an old wall or so. To the east of Lindsey-row is Beaufort-row, and on the site of Beaufort-row, according to the convincing evidence of Dr. King,* stood the house that was once occupied by Sir Thomas More, as well as by a variety of eminent persons after him. It stood midway between the Thames and the King's-road, with its front to the river, and is recorded in the annals of the parish as Beaufort-house, from its occupation by one of the dukes of that name. Sir Thomas More built it himself when he was in power. Here he lodged Holbein with him for three years, and was visited by Erasmus. Here he entertained the royal tiger, Henry the Eighth, who walked with him in his garden, with his arm (we beg pardon, *paw,*) round his neck; and hence he was taken, by the tyrant's order, to be imprisoned and put to death.

There is one thing, however, to be said for Henry's treatment of More, and, indeed, in palliation of his mortal modes of proceeding in general, considering the age in which he lived; and that is, however startling — but it is fit to say it — that had More been in his place, it would not have been surprising had he treated Henry in like manner. More, perhaps, is the most remarkable and puzzling instance on record of the anomalies produced in a man's character by education, and by encouraging him to identify his right of action with God's. According to all testimony, he was one of the most amiable of men in his house; and was an angel of consideration and kindness, not only to a beloved daughter and to his son-in-law and his servants, but to a crabbed and homely old wife, who appears to have had no feelings in common with him, and whom he married when she was a widow, and not young; though, by the way, how he came to marry such a woman at all, God only knows. People, to be sure, marry with their imaginations; but they are not apt to keep them for ever up in this extraordinary way. However, be this as it may, angel he was even to this very unangelical person, who furthermore reproached and laughed at him during his imprisonment. He tried hard in her

* See his M.S., quoted in Faulkner's *History of Chelsea*, Vol. 1, p. 119.

old age, to make her play on the lute! and succeeded! an
excess of good nature, and indeed of wisdom, considering how
it would help to tame her and keep her occupied for the time;
but if it were not a piece of super-celestial good humour, it
would look like an irony. The same man wrote a Utopia, or
imaginary form of government, in which, among other curious
liberalities for those times, he advocates religious toleration;
and yet he, even he, this cheerful-hearted, kind-hearted, ultra-
considerate, and seraphical Sir Thomas More, the bewitcher
of tyrants and charmer of crabbed women, the Utopian philosopher, who was all for love and reason, piqued himself upon
being a pursuer of heretics, and absolutely applied the torture
with his own hand to a young woman!! [23] Was it out of the
very extremity of love that he did it, and because he could
not bear that so gentle a creature should differ with him?
It might, by some awful possibility, be so; yet how fearful not
to have seen farther into the horror and iniquity of such a
meeting of extremes! and what a lesson to the proud luck of
inferior natures, in these more generally enlightened times,
not to presume upon their exemption from the errors of intolerance, but to keep perpetual watch, lest they, too, confound
an honest intention, or an impatience of sympathy itself, with
a right to be inhuman!

We shall have more to say of Sir Thomas when we come
to the church. He walked often at Chelsea by the river's side,
kept a barge for his recreation, and was very kind to the poor.
It may be added, in proof of the infirmities to which wise and
good men are subject, in times of *preposterous bringing up
in religious matters,* that Sir Thomas More's answer to Luther,
according to Atterbury, was nothing but a heap of the most
shocking ribaldry, "without a grain of reason to support it."
One is almost inclined to misgive one's better conclusions
about him when one hears such things, and suspect that he
was only as dulcet and reasonable as he was, at other times,
because he was in a state of rule, and had everything his own
way. But then, what is to be said of his wife? unless scorn
itself performed the task of love; and how could that be the

case with a tyrannical nature? Truly, Sir Thomas was not only a great man, but a great puzzle.

After Sir Thomas's death, his house, as if it was destined to be as much in extremes as its builder, was granted to that prince of courtiers, the Marquis of Winchester, who was a favourite under the shifting interests of Henry, Edward, Mary, and Elizabeth, and who being asked how he contrived it, made that famous impudent answer, — "By being a willow, and not an oak."

After going into the Dacre family, the mansion was bequeathed by one of them to the famous Lord Burleigh,[24] from whom, or jointly with whom, it seems to have passed, by some means that do not appear, into a right of possession on the part of Thomas Lord Buckhurst,[25] a connection of the Dacres, author of the fine induction to the *Mirror for Magistrates*, the solemn dawn of the splendours of the Fairy Queen. Burleigh's son, Cecil, Earl of Salisbury, then had the house; some think, rebuilt it; from whom it passed to an Earl of Lincoln, and from him to Sir Arthur Gorges, the friend of Spenser, mentioned in our last, who had married the Earl's daughter, and who sold it to Lionel Cranfield, Earl of Middlesex, father of that Countess of Dorset who boasted of being mistress to Sir John Suckling, and who was mother of the witty Earl of Charles the Second's days. We thought Suckling had mentioned the house in his letters; but on getting a friend to look at them (for we have not the book by us), he can see no such passage. Lord Middlesex sold the house to Charles the First, who granted it to the first Villiers, Duke of Buckingham, from whom, after being in possession of Lisle and Whitslocke during the Commonwealth, it came to the second Villiers, Charles the Second's Buckingham, who sold it to pay his creditors.

Many a sad pull must he have had up the river with his companions, fair and *unfair*, between this and Whitehall. In those times, while coaches were yet rare and lumbering, people who lived near the Thames, visited as much by water as by land. But more of this when we come to speak of the river separately.

From Buckingham's creditors the mansion went to a worthy successor, that clever fool, George Earl of Digby, who, for his eloquence, his tergiversation, and his plots, was the admiration of all, and the respect of nobody. His widow sold it to Henry, first Duke of Beaufort, from whom it was called Beaufort-house, and in whose family it remained till it was purchased by Sir Hans Sloane, four years after which it was pulled down. There is a print of it which has been often republished, and which, in some measure, keeps it eternally existing for us. There was a gate to it, built by Inigo Jones,[26] for Lord Middlesex, which Sir Hans Sloane gave to the Earl of Burlington, whose removal of it to his gardens at Chiswick occasioned the well-known lines of Pope: —

PASSENGER.
O Gate, how cam'st thou here?
GATE.
I was brought from Chelsea last year,
Batter'd with wind and weather.
Inigo Jones put me together;
Sir Hans Sloane
Let me alone,
Burlington brought me hither.[27]

The local historians add some lines written by a lady, on seeing a gate carried by two men, which reminded her of the illustrious brother-moveable: —

O Gate, where art thou going?
But it was not so knowing
As yonder gate
That talk'd of late;
So it went on, without reply:
At least I heard it not, not I.

One reminiscence brings up another. The following Italian couplet was said to have been written on the strange screen of pillars that stood the other day in front of Carlton House: —

Care colonne, che fate qua?
Non sappiamo in verita.

PASSENGER.
Dear colonade, how came you so?
COLONADE.
Indeed, my good Sir, I don't know.

We hope to have done with Chelsea in our next; otherwise we shall never get out of this place. But "there's cheese and pippins to come;" to wit, Swift and the Duchess of Mazarin. Item, Queen Elizabeth's freaks when a girl; and Smollett and Steele, and St. Evremond and the Bun-house, and Ranelagh and Dr. Johnson, and Miss Hawkins knows what besides.

December 8, 1833

Our materials (thanks to Mr. Faulkner's most laudable and most particular history, to which our obligations are endless) now begin to crowd on us in such profusion, that we give up all hope of concluding with this suburb in our present number; and we should have to apologise to the reader on that account, did we not hope that, by dint of taking occasion to notice some additional characteristic touches of the wits and other celebrated Chelsea residents that we meet with, we may render him not unwilling to stay in it a little longer than he expected. What better company can we be in than Swift's, and Arbuthnot's and Steele's; or what better church go to than Old Chelsea church, with Dr. Donne preaching in it, or Sir Thomas More singing (as he actually did) in a white surplice, among the choristers? Or whom, reader, would you fain go and see coming out of church (your own lady-love excepted) of a more heavenly womanhood than Mistress Mary Astell,[28] the friend of all the seraphical doctors of her time? Especially since, by following her to her house in "Paradise-row," you may have the opportunity of contrasting her with an angel of a different sort, oddly, somehow, got into the same heaven, and singing opera songs instead of hymns; to wit, the fair Duchess of Mazarin, whom Charles the Second was in love with when he was a boy, and St. Evremond[29] when he was an old man! People must live and pass their time somewhere. Why not here, in this article of ours, no *articulum mortis*, as well as read something else? or as well as go and see Smith; or ride badly; or look out of window; or wonder what o'clock it is; or promenade in tight boots, or think that every body sees how badly you have put your neckcloth on; or meet the Miss Jeffses, and not know what to say? We have often thought of this in coaches and omnibuses, where people, whether compelled or not, are always for getting as fast as possible to their journey's end; whereas, for the most part, and for any great good they are to get or to give, they might as well live in the omnibus as any where else: nay, better, according to Johnson, who thought that life had few better things than being rolled along a road, and that the idea of getting at the journey's end was its only drawback! But the passengers in these vehicles are generally bound on some moneyed business; and there is no arguing with the monomania of the purse.

Danvers-street, which turns northward from between the bridge and the church, took its name from Sir John Danvers,[30] the Regicide, whose house stood here, afterwards called Wharton house, from its occupation by Thomas Lord Wharton,[31] the Whig viceroy, on whom Swift and Pope have written so severely. He was husband of Ann Wharton, the poetess, who was a relation of Lord Rochester's, and the friend of Waller. *Duke-street* was christened after the Duke of Buckingham. In *Lombard-street,* five doors west of the house called the Rising Sun, resided for many years Mr. W. Lewis, bookbinder, the friend of Smollett, and said to have been the *Strap* of *Roderick Random.* Mr. Faulkner, who resided seven years in the same house with his widow, tells us that he had frequently heard from her "a confirmation of the anecdotes of her husband, as related by the novelist."

Among the householders and lodgers in Church-lane were Swift, Atterbury, Arbuthnot, Shadwell, and Martyn,[32] the botanist, father of Professor Martyn, and author of the interesting edition of Virgil's "Georgics." He was the man who discovered that the hyacinth of the ancient poets was not the hyacinth now so called, but the Martagon or Turk's Cap Lily. He married the daughter of Dr. King, the rector of Chelsea, and all his children by her were born in the house in which she was born and died, and in which her father died before her.

Shadwell, the Whig laureate, who was under-rated by Dryden, and more over-rated by his party, died at his house in Church-lane, in consequence, it is supposed, of taking an over-dose of opium; a drug to which he was unfortunately addicted. He probably came to Chelsea for the benefit of his health; as his son, a physician, afterwards resided in this lane, in a house previously occupied by another physician, the famous Arbuthnot — a name alone sufficient to throw an air of wit and learning over any place. Yet here also resided Atterbury for several years, first in a house facing the river, (which must have been the south-western corner house, for the church is over the way,) and afterwards higher up the lane; and opposite Atterbury, for a short time, resided Swift. It was during his melancholy pursuit of church patronage, when he was absent from Stella, and entangled with Miss Vanhomrigh. He came here for his health, in order that he might sleep in the fresh air, and be compelled to walk to and from town. Some of his memorandums of the place, recorded in his journal to Stella,[33] are too characteristic to be omitted: —

CHELSEA, April 26. — I got here in the stage-coach, with Patrick and my portmanteau, for sixpence,* and pay six shillings a week for one silly room with confounded coarse sheets. We have had such a horrible deal of rain that there is no walking to London, and I must go as I came, until it ends; and besides, the whelp has taken my lodging as far from London as this town could afford, at least half a mile farther than he need; but I must be content. The best is, I lodge just over against Dr. Atterbury's house, *and yet perhaps I shall not like the place the better for that.*

27. — I dined at Mr. Harley's (the minister), came away at six,†

* Thus it is that things come round and cheap improve[ment]s are not so cheap and extraordinary as we suppose. Six[penc]e is the modern omnibus fare to Chelsea from Piccadilly, [yet] Swift came from Suffolk-street, Charing-cross, for no greater [su]m, with his servant and portmanteau, apparently into the [barg]ain.

† Compare these with the modern hours. We have extracted [th]e other passages, not entirely relating to Chelsea in [order] to [sho]w the manners of the times, which are always agreeable [accom]paniments to local history, sometimes necessary ones.

shifted my gown, cassock, and periwig, and [walked hither to Chelsea, as I always design to do when it is fair.]

28. — At night. I say at night, because I finished my twenty-first this morning here, and put it into the post-office myself, like a good boy. . . . I got to town between twelve and one, and put on my new gown and periwig, and dined with Lord Abercorn, where I had not been since the marriage of his son Lord Peasley, who has got ten thousand pounds with a wife. I am now a country gentleman. I walked home as I went, and am a little weary, and am got into bed. I hope in God the air and exercise will do me a little good.

29. — I had a charming walk to and from town to-day: I washed, shaved and all, and changed gown and periwig by half an hour after nine, and went to the Secretary (Lord Bolingbroke), who told me how he had differed with his friends in parliament . . . . (Swift walked, like other clergymen of that time, in his every-day gown and cassock, and changed them for his best when he went to visit. The latter he kept at the house of Miss Vanhomrigh's mother, which made poor Stella jealous.)

30. — Morn. I am here in a pretty pickle: it rains hard; and the cunning natives of Chelsea have outwitted me, and taken up all the three stage coaches. This is the blind side of my lodging out of town; I must expect such inconveniences as these. Faith, I will walk in the rain. At night. I got a gentleman's chaise by chance, and so went to town for a shilling, and lie this night in town. . . I lie at a friend's in the city.

May 1. — I have had just now a compliment from Dean Atterbury's lady, to command the garden and library, and whatever the house affords. The Dean is in town with his convocation; so I have my Dean and prolocutor as well as you, young women (Stella and a friend of hers, to whom he wrote conjointly), though he has not so good wine, nor so much meat.

2. — A fine day, but begins to grow a little warm; and that makes your little fat Presto sweat in the forehead. Pray, are not the fine buns sold here in our town? Was it not Rrrrrrrrrare Rrrrrrrrrare Chelsea Buns?* I bought one to-day in my walk: it cost me a penny; it was stale, and I did not like it, as the man said.

3. — I did not go to town to-day, it was so terrible rainy; nor have I stirred out of my room till eight this evening, when I

---

* Swift's particularity in putting exactly the same number of [r's] into this humorous imitation of the famous Chelsea cry, is [no]t unworthy of observation, as an instance of his fidgetty nicety [.It] was in the same spirit that he made all the proportions of [th]e men, houses, trees, &c., in Gulliver, mathematically correct.

crossed the way to see Mrs. Atterbury, and thank her for her civilities. She would needs send me some veal, and small beer, and ale, to-day at dinner; and I have lived a scurvy, dull, splenetic day for want of M.D. (Stella and her friend.)

5. — I walked here after nine, two miles, and I found a parson drunk, fighting with a seaman. *Smoak* how wide the lines are, but, faith, I do not do it on purpose; but I have changed my side in this new Chelsea bed, and I do not know how, methinks, but it is so unfit, and so awkward; never saw the like.

15. — My walk to town to-day was after ten, and prodigiously hot. My way is this: I leave my best gown and periwig at Mrs. Vanhomrigh's, then walk up the Pall-Mall, through the Park, out at Buckingham-house, and so to Chelsea, a little beyond the church. I set out about sunset, and got here in something less than an hour; it is two good miles, *and just five thousand seven hundred and forty-eight steps*; so there is four miles a day walking, without reckoning what I walk while I stay in town. When I pass the Mall in the evening, it is prodigious to see the number of ladies walking there; and I always cry shame at the ladies of Ireland, who never walk at all, as if their legs were of no use but to — (The Dean here becomes a little too unclerical for our pages. Mr. Beverley would say we have not got university license.)

June 5. — I am cruel thirsty this hot weather. I am just this minute going to swim. I take Patrick down with me, to hold my night-gown, shirt, and slippers, and borrow a napkin of my landlady for a cap. So farewell till I come up; but there is no danger, do not be frighted. — I have been swimming this half hour and more; and when I was coming out, I dived to make my head and all through wet, like a cold bath; but, as I dived, the napkin fell off and is lost, and I have that to pay for. O faith, the great stones are so sharp, I could hardly set my feet on them as I came out. It was pure and warm. I got to bed, and will now go sleep.

July 5. — This day I left Chelsea for good (that is a genteel phrase), and am got into Suffolk-street.

Having thus furnished the Chelsea visitor with illustrious example, in case he wishes to lodge there, or swim, or eat a Chelsea bun, or count his steps through [34] [the] Park to Pimlico, we take leave of Church-lane with [a brief] mention of the very old public house in it, [?] White Horse, built in the Tudor style, and [believed] to be the only specimen of it now remaining [in this par]ish. At all events it is so old, that you evi[dently see] it in the same aspect in which it was beheld [by the] eminent men of whom we have been speaking; [prob]ably every eye in Chelsea has looked upon the [?] doorposts with their quaint imagery, from Sir [Thomas] More to the present day.

December 15, 1833

In our notice of Church-lane we omitted to mention a large, solitary, old house, apparently the largest which ever stood in it, called Church-place, which is still remaining, and which possibly may have been the second abode of Atterbury, during his residence in this village, as his wife spoke with complacency to Swift of the "library and garden," which she would hardly have done, had the latter been small. This house is now let out in lodgings to the poor. It is understood to be but a part of the old structure, which, Mr. Faulkner tells us, "is confidently said to have been the palace of the Earl of Essex."

Before we come to the church, we may as well notice the only other old-fashioned relic in this quarter, — a little prominent object with a great clock in it, in Milman-row, called the Clock-house. It was originally a lodge at the stable-gate of Sir Thomas More's house, and abuts upon a remnant of its garden, in which, we suppose, it raises the herbs from which the distilled waters are made that are now sold in it. Not long since, it belonged to the family of a Quaker-gardener who had been in the service of Sir Hans Sloane, and who rendered it eminent for its figs, flowers, and gingerbread. The venerable Miss Hawkins, who is so severe upon sweet teeth of another sort, and will not let her naughty contemporaries alone, records her love of the innocent suavities of the Quaker.

The clock, which was made by the Quaker's brother, is large and old-fashioned enough to be a curiosity. Adorning a house of but one story high, it is big enough for a church; and besides telling the hour and minute, it saves the neighbours an almanac by exhibiting the day of the month. Upon the whole, this little bit of a house, though not one of the most ancient (for it must have been built by some of the latest possessors of the old mansion), is one of the pleasantest remains of old Chelsea. It stands by itself, its shape is good, its clock fantastic, and it is one the most *village-looking* things in the place — one of the remotest from suburban ideas.

Hail, from river-side or from land-side, old Chelsea church! thou weather-beaten old brick tower and outhouse, with not a bit of beauty in thee, but with plenty of reverend age and illustrious memories! How many human beings have sate in thee, have prayed in thee, have suffered in thee, have received consolation, have looked upon the dear cold stones containing the beloved dust of wives, husbands, and children, — their own place of rest, into which themselves have afterwards been gathered! In thee Sir Thomas More has sung hymns like a child; and Donne has preached, with the tears in his eyes; and Sidney's mother has prayed in thee, still kneeling against thy wall in effigy; and in thee lies Gorges, the friend of Spenser; and a whole throng of the Lawrence family, the family of Milton's friend [35] of that name, — perhaps his friend himself; [*] and Dr. Chamberlayne [36] learnedly addresses us from thine outer wall, in favour of epitaphs which all may behold; and Sir Hans Sloane, somewhat ostentatiously, arresteth attention to his importance at thy London corner; and in the corner behind thee, as if he would find a bit of garden to lie in, reposes gentle Philip Miller, [37] the prince of horticulturists.

Old Chelsea church (we shall speak of the new hereafter) appears to have been so patched and re-edified at different times, that, in all probability, it resembles the first structure as little as the old silk stocking which, from constant darning, became worsted. Its origin is supposed to be coeval with its annals, which commence in the reign of Edward the Second, the time of Chaucer. The date of the first rector mentioned in its books is 1316, which was some years before the poet's birth. The advowson anciently belonged to the Abbot and

---

[*] Compare Mr. Faulkner's account of the Lawrence family (Hist. of Chelsea, vol. 1, p. 223.) with that of ..... [The rest is obliterated. Possibly a reference to Todd's life of Milton.]

Chapter of Westminster, then passed into the hands of the crown, then into several noble families, and was finally annexed to the manor; in consequence of which, it now belongs to the Cadogan family, who inherited the manor from the daughter of Sir Hans Sloane. Sir Thomas More, who was lord of the manor, added a chapel to it, after the fashion of the Catholics; and the Lawrences, also lords of the manor, another.

More's monument, erected by himself, remains, and has been lately refreshed.

In the inscription on this monument is an awful instance of the folly to which dogmatism gives rise, even in men otherwise the wisest. In one part of it is a gap, in which two words have been obliterated. These words were *and heretics*. The passage, as it was written by More himself, and sent by him to Erasmus (who must have shaken his head at it), purported that he was a thorn in the sides of *thieves, murderers, and heretics,* "furibus, homicidis, hæreticisque molestus."

More *succeeded better in love than hate*; a lesson for us all. He was only a poor, perplexed, angry, mistaken human being when he wrote those two words, or when he put his hand to the rack that tortured a woman; [38] but he was almost an angel, when he made his house and his friends love him, when he made his daughter look up to him as a pattern of sweet wisdom, and tell him that she called to mind the example he had set them all, as her best consolation, even under the chance of losing him by a violent death. Why should we be forced to doubt of such a man, whether it was out of fear or love that he would dress himself in the surplice of a chorister, and sing hymns to God in this church like a common chaunter? He did this while he was Chancellor, — an unusual thing even for the devoutest in those days, and calculated to baffle the conventional wits of his brother statesmen. The Duke of Norfolk coming one day to dine with him, found him at church in this condition, and was highly scandalised. "God's body! my Lord Chancellor," said he, as they returned to the house, "what! a parish clerk! a parish clerk! You dishonour the King and his office." "Nay," said Sir Thomas, "you may not think

your master and mine will be offended with me for serving
God, *his* master, or thereby count his office dishonoured."
Alas! Henry shewed him that if God was his master, his own
will and pleasure was more his master; and the Chancellor
found that he was no more to be allowed to serve God his
own way, than he allowed the poor girl to serve him. We
suspect, from all which is to be gathered of the character of
those times, that there was a reserve of coarseness, and even
of brutality, in the pleasures and the breeding of the best men,
that left the hardest part of human nature too much room for
rough play, even in them: how much more in a king and a
born despot. The common, and with it the uncommon, clay
has refined much since then. Our planet is throwing off its
lees; to negative humanity will succeed positive; and God's
hopes of his creatures will be realised.

That we may omit nothing interesting which has been
related of Sir Thomas More, in connexion with Chelsea, we
will here supply an omission in a former paper by repeating
one of Aubrey's anecdotes, which, however, we think we
have seen related of somebody else. We are not sure whether
it was not Dr. Barrow, or one of the physicians of Bedlam
Hospital: —

"His country house," says Aubrey, "was at Chelsey, in
Middlesex, where Sir John Danvers built his house. The
chimney-piece of marble, in Sir John's chamber, was the
chimney-piece of Sir Thomas More's chamber, as Sir John
himself told me. Where the gate is now adorned with two
noble pyramids, there stood originally a gate-house, which
was flat on the top, leaded, from whence is a most pleasant
prospect of the Thames, and the fields beyond: on this place
the Lord Chancellor More was wont to recreate himself and
contemplate. It happened one time that a Tom of Bedlam
came up to him, and had a mind to have thrown him from the
battlements. 'Leap, Tom, leap.' The Chancellor was in his
gown, and besides ancient, and not able to struggle with such
a strong fellow. My Lord had a little dog with him; says he,
'Let us first throw the dog down, and see what sport that will

be;' so the dog was thrown over. 'This is very fine sport,' said my Lord; 'fetch him up, and try once more.' While the madman was going down, my Lord fastened the door, and called for help; but ever after kept the door shut."

To return to the church: — Donne, the famous wit and metaphysical poet of the time of James I, preached the funeral sermon of the wife of this Sir John Danvers, and Walton, who was present, describes him as unable to refrain from tears. Donne was very sickly at that time, and died about four years afterwards. But we do not mean to say that his tenderness was owing to his bad health, though he might have been rendered by it more unable to restrain those proofs of what he felt. He was one of the most thoughtful and kind-hearted of men; and probably called to mind the loss of his own wife, which had greatly afflicted him.

The monument of Sir Arthur Gorges, friend of our great poet of the Fairy Queen, has entirely disappeared; but a tablet remains to his son. The monument of one of the Lawrences, with effigies of him, and his wife and children, is extant; there is a print of it in Faulkner; and so there is of Sir Thomas More's, of Sir Hans Sloane's, of Miller's, and of that of the Duchess of Northumberland, with portraits of herself and her five daughters, the eldest of whom was the mother of Sir Philip Sidney.

Dr. Chamberlayne, who has his monument outside the church, on the wall looking towards the river, and who was one of the first fellows of the Royal Society, and a stirring man in his day, connected with embassies and royal tutorships, left a singular instance behind him of literary weakness, which the friend who erected his monument has recorded in the inscription. He directed that certain books of his writing should be buried with him, to escape the chances of time, and for the benefit of posterity, — as if books that could be totally forgotten meanwhile, in spite of his possession of the public good-will, should be likely to do honour to their resurrection. One of them was "A Dialogue between an Englishman and a Dutchman, on the last Dutch War"! The tomb appears to have been opened in due time, but nothing transpired of the contents.

The Chamberlaynes were a stirring race, not inclined to associate even the tomb with an idea of dullness. Two of the doctor's sons, who appear to have been educated with different views, went into the army, and their example was followed by their sister, — his only daughter; who "long declining wedlock" (the Latin of the epitaph is stronger — it says "*spreto connubio*," despising it) "and aspiring above her sex and age, fought under her brother, with arms and manly attire, in a fire-ship against the French, for six hours, on the 30th of June, 1698,[39] — a maiden heroine! Had life been granted (continues the inscription) she might have borne a race of naval warriors. Returning from a sea engagement, and within some months marrying Sir John Spragg, Knight, with whom she lived very affectionately eighteen months, at last giving birth to a daughter, she died a few days after, on the 30th of October, 1691. Her sorrowful husband raised this monument to a most chaste and much-beloved wife."

Sir John Spragg was the famous Admiral. Being one of the boldest of seamen, he had a right to one of the most intrepid of water-nymphs. For our parts, we would rather have encountered his enemies than his wife. It is alarming to read of a woman, however respectable, who felt such life in giving death to others, and died only when she was giving life.

January 5, 1834

The Editor of the *Greenwich Gazette*, always a gentleman, has made some observations on the subject of our last two articles,[40] very kind towards ourselves, and as little inculpatory as possible towards our critic. We desire nothing better. We are very grateful for it. It is not our wish that any body should be blamed more than can be helped, even those who blame us erroneously. We fear we have said a great deal more than was necessary ourselves, especially in a country where money means delicacy; but the truth is, that on that very account, we were frightened for the popularity (such as it is) of a pen burthened with many interests, and became anxious to show that at least our own conscience was easy on the subject. We now return to pleasanter matter; and as we are in the habit, when writing, of fancying that we are more especially talking to some readers than others, particularly old friends, we shall beg of the editor of the *Gazette*, in our poor acknowledgment of the many kind things which his liberal nature has induced him to say of us, that he will permit us to consider him as one of those friends, and continue his encouraging thoughts of us, even at the hazard of thinking a little too well; which is a mistake allowable to generous understandings. He will be in company (if he knew them all) of which any man might be proud; and will not be sorry to think that they have conceived a regard and respect for him.

———

Resuming our course eastward from Chelsea Church, we turn out of Church-lane into Justice-walk, and thence into Lawrence-street, the former so called from an "illustrious obscure" magistrate who once lived there, but eminent in comparison with the north-eastern range of houses in that street, for having been the scene of Dr. Johnson's dabbling in the making of china. There was a china manufactory here in his time, and the illustrious lexicographer who used to amuse himself with chemistry, had got a fancy in his head that he could improve upon it. He applied accordingly to the directors for permission to make use of their oven, and was allowed to do so.

"He was accustomed," Mr. Faulkner tells us, (on the authority of the late Mr. A. Stephens,[41] who had his information from the foreman) "to go down with his housekeeper about twice a week, and staid the whole day, she carrying a basket of provisions with her. The doctor, who was not allowed to enter the *mixing*-room, had access to every part of the house, and formed his composition in a particular apartment, without being overlooked by any one. He had also free access to the oven, and superintended the whole of the process; but completely failed, both as to composition and baking, for his materials always yielded to the intensity of the heat, while those of the company came out of the furnace perfect and complete. The Doctor retired in disgust, but not in despair, for he afterwards gave a dissertation on this very subject in his works; but the overseer assured Mr. Stephens, in the spring of 1814, that he was still ignorant of the nature of the operation. He seemed to think that the Doctor imagined one single subject was sufficient; while he, on the other hand, asserted that he always used sixteen, and he must have had some practice, as he had nearly lost his eyesight, by firing batches of china, both at Chelsea and Derby, to which the manufacture was afterwards carried." Vol. 1, p. 273.

This manufactory of Chelsea china had for a short time great celebrity, and made the fortune of its projector; but it came to nothing in the hands of his successors. Its prosperity, perhaps, went with its novelty; though it is said to have been really valuable, and to fetch great prices still when met with at sales. But except with exquisite judges, who are content with the beauty and good taste of a piece of art, — nay, even with those, too, to a certain extent, —the prejudice in favour of things made in remote countries is natural, and not unmixed with reason. It gives to their imagination the additional idea of the regions from which they came, and of the testimony borne to their merits by the care and cost of the importation. The poet aggrandises the worth of his perfumes by calling them

> Pecious odours *fetch'd from far away.*[42]

Lawrence-street was so called from the family already mentioned, the kindred of Milton's Lawrences, who were lords of the manor of Chelsea; and built a mansion-house on the spot. In "the great house" in this street, we know not whether the same, or a descendant of it, the Duchess of Monmouth, widow of the son of Charles the Second, resided, "about the year 1714," says the Chelsea historian; which was the year

Gay resigned his office of secretary to her Grace; so that it cannot be known whether the good-natured poet is to be ranked among the Chelsea residents or not.

But the same house, part of which, in a dilapidated state, is still remaining at the north end of the street, afterwards became celebrated as the residence of Smollett, when he had given up practice, or attempts at practice, as a physician, and settled himself to writing as a profession. He here produced his "Count Fathom," his "History of England," and was the busy and turbulent editor of the "Critical Review,"— the first systematic example, we fear, of the degrading and portentous union of genius with personality. Here also he lost his health and his only child; and, finally, here it was that he gave those dinners to his poorer literary brethren, of which he has left so curious an account in the novel of "Humphrey Clinker." He appears to have dined and teased them at the same time; set them squabbling, to see their humours, and gave them "audiences" under some filbert-trees in his garden! *

Smollett,[43] an inferior genius to Fielding,[44] for he could not create his fictions out of truth alone, but a great genius, nevertheless, in the humourous and ridiculous, appears to have been the victim of a temperament over fond of power and a sensation. He was generous, but had bad blood, and the overweening self-opinion of a man who, at too early an age, and in too circumscribed a sphere, had been the lord of his associates. Hence his generosity became the servant of his pride, and even his malice; and he was always getting into unseemly squabbles with his contemporaries, begun by his own irritability and presumption. Believing, however, in good and generous qualities to the last, because he partook them himself, and otherwise cordial in his affections towards those whom he perhaps tormented with his ill-humour, he gives one the idea of an illustrious overgrown schoolboy, who could never forego the malicious pranks of his youth, though they turned to very serious troubles both for himself and others.

*See Limbird's edition of Humphry Clinker. p. 55.

His heroes may be called *ugly ideals* of his own character, and are certainly very disagreeable people, for all their cleverness; especially that intense blackguard, Peregrine Pickle. The only real gentleman he has drawn is Sir Launcelot Greaves, and him he has made a madman. Yet in this book is the most affecting scene of domestic tragedy and degradation that ever a thoughtful heart conceived, — that of the once refined, happy, and amiable married couple, one of whom is fighting another blackguard in a prison yard, while the wife is acting the part of bottle-holder — a scene we never think of without an effort at restraining our tears. The most unrefined of Smollett's novels, however, are to be looked upon, not as deteriorations of something which he might have done better, but as proofs of the good and the entertainment that may be wrought out of unpleasant materials by the saving grace of genius; for as to any harm they can do to young men "entering upon town," it is a mere fancy for that very reason. The young men will know all he can tell them; and you might know it in a worse manner without him, they with a less redemption of generosity.

January 12, 1834

That row of mingled houses and shops, of tall dwellings and low, ancient and modern, which presents the face of Chelsea to the river, and looks so well with its elm-trees, and a certain aspect of rustic urbanity, like a bit of old Tunbridge, or other watering-place, is called Cheyné-walk, and is the summer Chelsea promenade. The river on the opposite side is more woody than might be expected so near London, and the houses have a pleasant view over it towards Wandsworth and the Surrey hills, where Chaucer's Pilgrims are continually threading their way, and fancy's eye sees a house among the trees at Dulwich, lustrous with art.

A stranger coming suddenly upon this place in summer time, when the ladies are abroad, the benches occupied under the trees, and the white sails gliding along the river, is surprised to find how like a country town it looks; and can easily fancy

Steele and the ladies of the last century, in their wigs and hoops, promenading before those good old houses, flanked with little shops of millinery, and pastry, cottage-topped. Over the way, at Battersea, is Lord Bolingbroke; and up the river is Pope, at Twickenham.

Not having the pains of those times to go through, and the times themselves being singularly quiet and domestic, and with but a narrow circle of politics, compared with ours, (however grandly they talked of their Louis the 14th, and their Marlborough,) there is no bit of the past that we sooner put in a small and pleasant frame to picture to one's imagination. The manners of the days of Addison and Steele, of Pope, Parnell, and Gay, all turn upon a ground of domesticity; their learning is what they brought from school and the university (they had no Asiatic Journals and Hindu dramas then); and their sylvan remoteness was in the next field, with the sheep, and a "swain," and "Delia," who was a lady in a hoop, and a cottage bonnet, holding a crook. You may see her in Shenstone's poems, or on the mantel-pieces about Red Lion square. No offence to those venerable dwellings, which we respect for their solid walls and considerate doorways, and love for reminding us of our grandmothers. You may go to grander mantel-pieces westward, and fare worse; it being a notion with many fine rooms in that quarter, that the "high thing" is to have nothing at all in them, save the chairs and tables; not even a picture; which surely is as blank and stupid a notion as can be, and argues much want of furniture in the family brains.

The houses in Cheyné-walk are not old enough to carry the imagination farther back than these times, otherwise here the spectator might fancy Henry the Eighth walking, and Sir Thomas More, and Queen Catherine Parr, and the Seymours, and Anne of Cleves, and Elizabeth, and the Dukes of Shrewsbury and Northumberland, and Whitelock, and Pym, and a hundred fine ladies and gentlemen out of the pictures of Vandyck; for all these names were among the Chelsea residents, most of them on this spot; nor were there wanting a succession of fashionable promenaders from Henry the Seventh's time to that of the Georges.

Cheyné-walk, politely corrupted by some into China-walk (an excusable supposition, saith Miss Hawkins,) is so called from the Cheyne or Cheney family, who were lords of the manor in the seventeenth century, and whose name, of Norman origin, refers to the oak trees (*chêne*) that invested their ancient seat in Buckinghamshire. There is still the village of Cheneys in that county. The famous Earl of Surrey, if our memory is not mistaken, has a sonnet in his poems addressed to one of the family, who was his squire. They were ennobled by Henry the Seventh, for services at Bosworth; but the title has long been extinct. There was a Lord Newhaven of the family; but his title also has gone, and nothing further is known of him or them than what is to be dug up out of parish registers. Their greatest lustre now depends upon a word stuck up at the corner of two or three streets in Chelsea; and people take it for a misnomer, and that it means china-ware, and the neighbourhood of a manufactory! So little difference is there between the fragilities of Cheney and China — a title and a toy!

Cheyné-row, Upper Cheyné-row, and Manor-street are places of no celebrity, except as forming parts of the ground on which these mansions and their gardens stood; but there may be some interest in this to an imaginative inhabitant, as we shall see presently, and the lookout from some of them, over the gardens at the back of Cheyné-walk, present a *coup d'œil* singularly old and village-like for a spot so near London, owing to the age of the houses and the intermixture of cottage and paddock. A man might sit in some of the upper windows and fancy himself in some old country town. The chapel in Cook's Ground, the thoroughfare from these places to the King's-road, has a claim to notice, from its having originally been built for the use of the French Protestants at the revocation of the Edict of Nantes, some of whom settled in this neighbourhood as gardeners.

But we have yet to say much of Cheyné-walk, for it was

chiefly on this spot, and a little to the east and west, that there stood a succession of princely mansions, which formerly procured Chelsea the title of a "Village of Palaces."

We will begin with the one nearest the church, to wit, Shrewsbury-house, which stood facing the river, just at the corner of Cheyné-row, and was for many years the residence of the Talbots, Earls of Shrewsbury. Some used to think it the same with Sir Thomas More's house; but that opinion has been long set aside and disproved. It was an irregular brick building, forming three sides of a quadrangle, and had a room in it a hundred and twenty feet long, wainscotted with carved oak. There is a print of the house in Faulkner's *Chelsea* (vol. i., p. 282). It is now vanished, every atom — all at least that stood above ground; but there is a subterraneous passage remaining, which puzzles the neighbours, and affords them a pleasing doubt over their tea, whether they may not be sitting over the remains of some mysterious murder. Its first direction is towards the King's-road; but it is supposed to turn off to the river. The tradition is, that it communicated with a "cave or dungeon," at a considerable distance from the house. "Cave *or* dungeon." Consider the rich alternative to a lover of the mysterious. Either will do. As it is not every day that one realises any thing like a bit of Radcliffe romance, we will give an extract on the subject from a letter with which Mr. Faulkner has furnished his readers, written by "Miss Gulston to Miss Tate, the proprietor of the estate." There is a little unromantic point or two about paper-staining and common every day theft, unrelieved by any circumstances of horror; but the subject is just of the kind upon which one young lady ought to write to another. One only wishes they had been parties more concerned, and that a cavalier, muffled up in a cloak, had been waiting for the fair writer, to furnish her with additional correspondence. The contrivance, however, for concealing the door, and the great pains taken to secure it, are circumstances really curious, and set us upon reflecting on the history of the noble inmates. The last occupants of the house were paper-stainers, and Miss Gulston met with one of them in his old age, from whom, and some drawings of the place, she got the following description of it: —

"The entrance," she tells us, "was from the room used by the paper-stainers as a drying place. It had no fire-place in it; the dimensions were nearly as follows: — twenty-five feet high, fifty long, thirty-six wide. The ceiling was strong with beams, to sustain the upper floors, but without any plastered ceiling. You descended into it by a wide winding staircase, through a circular top door, strongly fortified with rivets and four large hinges; this door was so contrived that it opened far enough back to hide the approach to the whole, and could there be fastened so as to have the appearance of belonging to the large room, and the circular steps leading to it caused the more deception.

"The side walls are all brick. This man never could proceed with his light more than a distance of thirty yards, when the light invariably went out. The passage is free from any encumbrance of earth, or from any part of the side walls having given way. As far as could be ascertained, its direction was towards the river.

"It is regularly paved with two flag-stones, leaving a border of six inches of earth; width three feet, length five and a half feet.

"This passage was discovered owing to the proprietor having been robbed of a quantity of paper for years. The man now alive volunteered to detect the thief; the paper was found on the staircase descending to the passage."

There is something in this account for the imagination to go upon. The neighbours have warrant, we think, for getting up a good reasonable suspicion, and enhancing the security of present times and manners with an occasional quiver of the memory at the idea of a skeleton or a ghost. The skeleton may have mouldered by this time; but as an ingenious youth said to us, to whom we were relating the story, and whose imagination we were quieting with that reflection, "ghosts keep a long time. They are a sort of preserve."

There are two conjectures which may reasonably be entertained respecting this passage; either that it was a passage to the river, for the facilitation of entrance to the house for goods and servants, or the master himself; or that it was concerned in matters of state and secrecy, and led to a prison. The strong fortification with rivets might have been a security either against rescuers or thieves; and the pains taken to conceal the look of a passage by the architect, might only have been a compliance with a fashion. But it is to be recollected, that dungeons were too much used of old for state purposes, and by violent or crafty chiefs; and such of the Shrewsbury family as resided here, were much in the confidence of sovereigns who dealt in jailery, — George, fourth Earl, in that of Henry VIII; Francis his son in Henry's, Edward's, and Queen Mary's (a suspicious instance of accommodation); and George, the son of Francis, was jailor of the Queen of Scots, under Elizabeth. He might have had a Scotchman or so in keeping here, or a suspected Papist.

One person he certainly had in his house, whom it cost him great trouble to keep in order; if, indeed, he was not saved the trouble, by being kept in order himself. This was his wife, Elizabeth, Countess of Shrewsbury, the widow of three husbands; a charming, quadrigamous personage, whose portrait has been thus bewitchingly drawn by Mr. Lodge: —

She had been already thrice married; to Robert Barley, Esq., of Barley, in the county of Derby; to Sir William Cavendish; and to Sir William St. Lo, Captain of the Guard to Queen Elizabeth. She prevailed on the first of these gentlemen, who died without issue, to settle his estate on her and her heirs, who were abundantly produced from her second marriage. Her third husband, who was very rich, was led by her persuasions to make a similar disposition of his fortune, to the utter prejudice of his daughters by a former wife; and now, unsated with the wealth and caresses of three husbands, she finished her conquests by marrying the Earl of Shrewsbury, the richest and most powerful peer of this time. To sum up her character, she was a woman of masculine understanding and conduct; proud, furious, selfish, and unfeeling. She was a builder, buyer and seller of estates, a money-lender, a farmer, and a merchant of lead, coals, and timber. She lived to a great old age, and died in 1607, immensely rich.*

The idea of such a she-devil as this roaming about the grounds, seeking what husband or estate she might devour, would be enough to desecrate the place in the fancies of the

---

* *Burke's Peerage,* in the article *Shrewsbury.*

inhabitants, if humaner memories were not at hand to relieve them. No objection need be made to the four husbands, had she been a right hearty-souled woman, who had been too happy with one not to have another, or too miserable not to make a better experiment; but the combination of the fury, and the luxuriousness, and the money-getting!! *Forty* ounces of civet, good Mr. Kendall, to get rid of the imagination! And what devils of money-lovers, or angels of good faith and credulity, or pure fools, her husbands must have been, to be able to take such a wife! The woman was clever and handsome; and clever women, bad or good, are apt to have certain talent for pleasing the other sex, setting aside even beauty, which is no mean addition; but then, one would think, their badness must not be a very "masculine" badness, nor incompatible with some show of generosity and sweetness of blood; yet here was a woman, "proud, furious, selfish, and unfeeling," who succeeded in getting four husbands, all men of importance and wealth, and one of them, at least, very clever himself; for the Cavendish here mentioned was Wolsey's Cavendish, his secretary, and "honest chronicler," as Queen Catherine called him. But the truth is, that even the wisest men, who have not been very wisely brought up, are sometimes great fools with their passions; and "Bess of Hardwick," as they called her from her father's estate, was handsome and accomplished; and every man who doubts the abstract good qualities of the woman he is going to marry, flatters his vanity with the notion that they will manifest themselves in his favour, and be confirmed by the love and glory of his encouragement. Poor devils! and so they all married "Bess of Hardwick," and were her slaves to their dying day, having been forced (doubtless) to give up all their fancies and wills one after the other for the sake of a quiet life, even to the dispossessing their natural heirs. The "rascal" (as the Copper Captain justly calls Estifania —women foregoing the appellative privileges of their sex, when they cease to be women,) must have been very rich and withal horribly healthy, and of a fine iron constitution. What a woman to embrace! with ribs like a railway and a soul made of shares

in a coal mine! Imprimis, she was an heiress — Bess of Hardwick — that is to say, heiress of one Hardwick of that ilk. At "fourteen" she married poor unfortunate Robert Barley, who died in about two years, and "left her a very rich widow." *
Then comes poor Sir William Cavendish, who brings her a title; aye, and more money too, for he had a slice of the abbey lands, now held by his descendants, the Dukes of Devonshire. Her third husband is poor Sir William St. Lo, Captain of the Guard to Queen Elizabeth, and doubtless, a proper man and tall, as good Queen Bess's guards were wont to be: —

(The cowslips tall her pensioners be.)[45]

We thought Bess of Hardwick had married the captain of the Guard solely to please her fancy, which would have been a lift to her character; but this third husband also, it seems, was "very rich." Having thus obtained wealth upon wealth, and husband upon husband, she finishes by marrying the Earl of Shrewsbury, "the richest and most powerful peer of the realm."

We are convinced her husbands must all have been asses, at least woman-wards; victims of their own vanity and avarice, and the reputation of getting the "handsome, rich widow." They did it, not so much to please themselves as to out-bid Tom and Harry, and add a schedule to their list of estates. It is astonishing how much rich men think of the items of their riches, and what they will do to add —

The sum of more to that which hath too much.[46]

They feel themselves poor with what they have (from finding its inability to make them happy), and yet think that the next new sum is to realise their expectations. Nothing can rest in tranquillity but justice — nothing else realise it as it goes. Bess of Hardwick built three magnificent seats in Derbyshire — Oldcotes, Hardwick, and Chatsworth — yet was furious to the last. She became joint keeper, with her husband, of Mary Queen of Scots, and plagued them both with her jealousy of

---

* Granger's *Biographical History of England*, Fifth Edit., vol. ii., p. 170.

the poor captive. She well might be jealous, though Mary was then getting old herself, and crippled; for the Queen, whatever guilt may have been mixed up with her fortunes and her unlucky education, never ceased to be a woman, and generous; and "Mad Bess" must have seemed a perfect devil by her side. Such was the fury's constitution, however, that she lived to be eigthy-seven years[47] of age, and died, no doubt, in all the glory of will-making, and jewel counting, and plaguing all those who had expectations of her.

It is curious to observe, in the wills of those times, what a profound sense rich people had of every single jewel and toy, and of this and that gown edged with fur, and "kirtle of blue velvet," with the "fayre wrought sleeves." The lords and ladies, in these instances, all seem like bankers leaving off business and dying milliners.

We have not got a great way this time, towards our departure out of Chelsea; but we have been led to conclude that the reader does not care what we talk about, provided it be not unentertaining, nor void of matter for reflection.

January 19, 1834

For want of some books to refer to this week, we are under the necessity of diverging a little from our proper subject; but we have something to say upon a point connected with our last article, which, with the reader's indulgence, will probably enable us to make out a paper which he may not be altogether unwilling to read. We omitted last week, at the close of our account of strange "Bess of Hardwick," to take care of a matter on which we pique ourselves; namely, the doing justice to devils. Startle not, dear casual reader — beloved "slight acquaintance;" for if thou art a Christian, thou wilt feel that thy charity cannot be too great; and if thou art no Christian, then do we extremely exhort thee to learn what real Christianity is, and thou wilt become one, and wish an end to all false notions of it, including injustice to the devil himself. Doth not the good proverb recommend us to give him "his due?"

and did not dear Burns, who was a better Christian than John Knox, fairly wish him to "take a thought and mend," and get out of his "den?" — Now if poor "Bess of Hardwick" (for we begin to pity her, seeing all that horrible load of obloquy under which we left her memory last week) was not the devil himself, most assuredly she was the very next thing to it; to wit, a woman who was no real woman, but undertook, within a fair form, to stuff all sorts of ugly male vices — pride, violence, and the getting of money — frightfully dealing in coals, and lead, and other sordid soul-smearing articles (considering she had no necessity for it), and being a sort of legitimate female Chartres, a money-lender, indulging her senses, which somehow is worse than being illegitimately so; for it adds the shield of law to the dagger of licence.

Here, then, is Bess of Hardwick, Countess of Shrewsbury, dealer in marine stores, money-lender, coal-merchant, farmer, builder, and the wife of four husbands — "proud, furious, selfish, and unfeeling" — sitting in a high-backed chair of state, with her caskets and carcanets before her, her stomacher crusted with jewels, her ruff of the richest Flanders lace, her bosom making horrible pretensions to be feminine, and her face hideously handsome, that is to say, smooth, well proportioned, sensual, haughty, pertinacious — a sort of mask. Look at her! Who does not long to take her up, chair and all (as Johnson did the insolent man from the side-scenes into the pit), and toss her into the river? Who does not rejoice that he is not one of her four husbands, especially the last; nor one of her maids, nor her footman, nor her physician (it must have been shocking to be her physician), nor her coal-heaver, nor her cow-driver, nor the man who came to consult her about dilapidations, nor her chaplain, nor her debtor, nor her creditor, nor the child of whom she was jealous, nor the heir whom she grudged her money? Look at her well. There is always something wrong and not handsome in these sort of handsome faces — either a devil in the eye, or too much nose, or too little, or a huge mouth, or a very small one, or an immense jowl and cheeks, or all face and no skull, or all forehead and no lips. It is not so well proportioned a face as we first took it for; or, if it is, the proportion is so complete, that the expression is in an unfeeling state of neutrality, except when passion moves it. The soft feelings of humanity have no more effect on it than summer air upon the face of a statue.

Yet how came she by that face and its want of feeling? She did not make it. She was not her own father and mother. She did not nurse herself, nor choose her instructors, nor predispose her circumstances, nor cause the follies and mistakes of all the preceding generations which caused the existence of all the people that contributed to hers. She was not her grandfather, who perhaps had that willful cheek of hers; nor her great-grandmother, who gave her the eye; nor the uncle, that was accountable for the transmission of the family chin; nor was she the rich man who spoilt his "heiress," nor the lady's maid who let her trample her toys in rage because they were "naughty toys," and "hurt pretty baby's hand." Again, neither was she her poor first husband, that flattered and called her an angel; nor the second, who extolled her wit and married her estate; nor was she the court or the city, or a parcel of sneaking footmen, nor a haughty-making aristocracy, nor a bowing mob. Oh, we must vindicate the conformation of poor, shocking Bess of Hardwick: lest we and our readers grow proud, and help to make future generations resemble her.

Voltaire, we forget where, traces some celebrated political event to the gift of a pair of gloves. The gift was resented by somebody, or had some stirring effect, we forget what; and then the feelings of others became implicated, and passions came in, and projects were concerted; and the event in question took place. Very mighty events have, undoubtedly, had sometimes no greater genealogies; so ignorantly have the many hitherto suffered the government of the world to depend upon the caprices of the few. The hint which the philosopher thus threw out for reflection was very useful; but far more useful is it to look into the first causes that modify the nature of the actors in these events, and that, while they excuse them as individuals, enable us to see how we may improve the species, — the race which they have hitherto contributed to spoil.

It begins to be pretty well understood that breeding and circumstances form individuals; and that, if ever it be necessary to punish, or even blame them, the necessity is to be regretted, as an evidence that society has not yet arrived at the wisdom of knowing how to generate better systems, and, consequently, a better species. But we shall do well, if, instead of contenting ourselves with assent to these doctrines, and letting charity and knowledge lazily make their way, we all make it a point to philosophise upon those causes with as much subtlety as we can, and to go as far back as possible to the first causes, individual as well as social. And "philosophising" has a grand sound, but is a very easy matter, if we are in earnest. We all, for instance, know well enough, that in breeding sheep or horses we shall improve or deteriorate the race in proportion as we match together suitable creatures, and make the right preparation for their existence and nurture; and yet, as if human creatures were of inferior consequence to cattle, and the whole well-being of the world did not depend upon as great a care in their generation and bringing up, a man shall go from a cattle-show or an agricultural board, where he has talked on the subject like an oracle, and marry his daughter to some old hack of a fellow, who has no more right to be paired with her than a hackney-coach horse with a young Arabian. Nay, less; for possibly he may originate some little, old-looking, perverse human being, ready made for disease and jealousy, and a precocious avarice. Or the same man, if he does not marry her to an old one, may induce her to marry somebody she has no real regard for — a fellow of bad passions and an unloving nature, who shall thus join in adding to the number of perverse, arbitrary, and unaffectionate beings, the tormentors of themselves and others, yet makers, perhaps, of our laws, and arbiters of our species! Haughty and stupid lords, new Countesses, like "Bess of Hardwick," — Nicholases of Russia. Nicholas himself is the son of a madman! Of a man, poor fellow, who ought not to have married at all! And yet it is on the proceedings of a son of this madman that the eyes of the civilised world have been lately fixed, to see what sort of fate it shall be pleased him to assign to myriads of his fellow creatures! We wish to be understood as speaking with great solemnity of all such human infirmities, and with reverence of their sorrows; but it is too much, surely, to expect of civilised nations that they should begin to think of the mistakes that occasion such preposterous evils; or that they should carry into the providence of their own homes, the care which they bestow on the rearing of the beasts of the field.

Our formidable Countess of Shrewsbury was, doubtless, the perverse result of some perverse parents or kindred, together with the follies they occasioned or overlooked in her bringing up. It is circumstances, not herself, that are to be accused. It is barbarous ignorance; it is to be lamented in the existence of a Nicholas of Russia. It is ignorant and selfish customs which we are to look to for the appearance in the world of Charles the Tenths, and Ferdinands, and Dukes of Angouleme. It is marriages of *old with young, money with money,* of *the averse with the unamiable,* &c.; and the innumerable unhappy marriages which are bound together for life in ignorance, and are miserable together for life in discord: — it is evil of *this* sort, and of our own daily committal, which keeps the world in a constant state of discord and lamentation, and perpetuates the breed of the perpetrators of evil.

But, it will be answered, we must grow wiser by dint of books, and the press, and the spread of knowledge! It is not to be expected that the passions in which we have been bred up should enable us suddenly to act well, even though we know them foolish. True; but then we must not be content with repeating the fact, and so encouraging ourselves to be more foolish than we need. We must look at the general necessity and our individual conduct together, and resolve to contribute *all that lies in our power* towards the *destruction* of those marriages of old with young, of money with money, of the averse with the unamiable, &c., and the better consideration of those innumerable unhappy marriages, which are bound together for life in ignorance, and are miserable together for life with discord.

April 6, 1834

We have not yet found time to search into the books, for want of which we postponed the conclusion of these articles on Chelsea; but it may be as well for the reader, and ourselves too, that we have not, for we fear there would have been no end of our inquiries. We therefore hasten to finish our walk by the help of such pleasant companions as we possess.

In our return towards London, down Cheyné-walk, we left off at old Shrewsbury-house, which formerly stood at the corner of Cheyné-row. The next point of interest to this was the palace of the Bishop of Winchester, which stood where the gap now is, near a gateway. The two prelates whose residence here is most worthy of notice, were Dr. Morley,[48] one of Ben Jonson's "sons" (as the poet used to call certain warranted favourites), and the famous Hoadley, the liberal Whig bishop, friend of Steele, and father of the author of the "Suspicious Husband." Morley is chiefly famous for having lived to a good old age, by dint of rising at five, going to bed at eleven, and eating but once a day. Early rising seems to be an invariable condition of longevity. Hoadley was an able, conscientious, generous, good-natured man; just the sort of prelate to delight Steele; who once having got the good Bishop to countenance a meeting of his Whig friends, where the bottle flowed a little too gaily, sent him the following distich the next morning. Hoadley was then Bishop of Bangor: —

> Virtue with so much ease on Bangor sits,
> All faults he pardons, though he none commits.

Next to Winchester Palace, and upon the site of the houses commencing with the one beautifully draperied with ivy and passion-flower, (the residence of the late Rev. Thomas Clare, who, we believe, dressed it in that graceful manner,) was the

Greater Manor-house, the history of which commenced with the times of Edward the Confessor, and which was successively the abode of the Abbots of Westminster; of the family Bray (who have monuments still existing in Chelsea church); of the Sandys family, a lord of which cuts so gallant a figure at Wolsey's banquet in Shakspeare; of Henry the Eighth; of Catherine[49] of Cleves, (the "Flanders mare," as he impudently called her,) who made so cool and truly Dutch a compromise with her awkward position, when she came over to England to marry the despot, and was content to receive a pension instead of his hand[50] (a good bargain by the way); of Catherine Parr, who had the luck to survive instead of being killed by him; of the Lord Admiral Seymour, who married her and made her a worse husband, some say poisoned her; of Elizabeth, when she was a girl under the care of Catherine Parr, and risked her reputation by "indiscreet familiarities" with Seymour; of Dudley, the intriguing Duke of Northumberland, who brought himself to the scaffold, as Seymour did too; of Stanhope (afterwards Lord Stanhope) of Harrington; of the Lord High Admiral, the Earl of Nottingham; of the Duke of Hamilton, who forfeited it to Parliament for his adherence to Charles the First; of Lord Douglas, who married one of the Duke's co-heiresses, and afterwards had his title; of the Cheyné family, who bought it of him, and gave their name to the walk; and, lastly, of Sir Hans Sloane, the physician and virtuoso, who bought it of the Cheynés. On the death of Sir Hans, it was pulled down, and the houses now standing subsequently built on its site. A mulberry tree, said to have been planted by Elizabeth's hands, is still, or was lately standing, though in great decay; and there are some elms, conveyed from the grounds of the late Winchester Palace, which are said to have been planted by Hoadley.

At all events, this is classic ground, not only on Hoadley's account, and that of the Queen, and of Shakspeare, and Spenser, but because Steele had a house in Cheyné-walk, though in what exact part is not known. He dates a letter from it to Lady Steele; and his house is rated in the parish-books at *fourteen pounds* per annum. It must have been a modest mansion for a member of parliament, even at the then rate of money. But Steele carried his elegancies with him, in his name and his nature.

Steele, in the *Tatler*, helped to give a merry celebrity to the public house in Cheyné-walk, still known by the name of "Don Saltero's Coffee-house," which was so called from the airs given himself, between buffoonery and earnest, by one Salter, who had been a servant of Sir Hans Sloane, and to whom Sir Hans made a present of some of the refuse of his collection of curiosities, in order to attract company to his tap. Some of Salter's curiosities (perhaps added by himself) were not of a very delicate description, and others not very reverent towards names in Scripture; for which reason, Steele thinks proper to conclude one of his pleasant recommendations of him with an intimation, that if he does not reform his collection in those particulars, "he may expect to have his letters patent for making punch superseded, be debarred wearing his muff next winter, or ever coming to London *without his wife.*" — *Tatler*, No. 34. "Salter," says a note to the *variorum* edition of the *Tatler*, "had an old grey muff, which he clapped constantly to his nose, and by which he was distinguishable at the distance of a quarter of a mile. His wife was none of the best, being much addicted to scolding; and Salter, who liked his glass, if he could make a slip to London by himself, was in no haste to return."

It is supposed, that on the site of Don Saltero's stood the old Chelsea coffee-house of the time of the Stuarts, to which Pennant says that his father had been often taken by a great uncle, on which occasion he used to see "poor Richard Cromwell,[51] a little and very neat old man, with a most placid countenance, the effect of his innocent and unambitious life." Why he is called "poor," considering his "most placid countenance," is a mystery that should give us pause.

Continuing eastward, the line of houses brings us to Paradise-row and Chelsea College; the former celebrated for the residence of the Duchess of Mazarin, one of the pensioned French

beauties of the court of Charles the Second, at whose house
St. Evremond used to spend the evenings of his old age in a
transport of venerable gallantry. The musical parties of the
Duchess are understood to have been the germ of the Italian
Opera. Here also lived a very diffident personage, Mrs. Mary
Astell, the seraphical friend of the Norrises, and other platonic
divines, and the subject of Swift's malicious but exquisite joke,
against Protestant nunneries, in one of the papers of the
Tatler.[52] It would seem, from the head under which their
Chelsea residences are mentioned in Faulkner, that in the
same row lived Nell Gwynne's son, the first Duke of St. Albans;
the first Earl of Sandwich (the admiral); Fletcher, Bishop of
London, father of the poet; and other persons of quality. The
houses in Paradise-row, though still what is called respectable,
have ceased to be occupied by the rich; but they are much
larger inside than they appear, and when first built, and in
possession of the prospect to the river which gave them their
name, would have been considered handsome dwellings, quite
fit for country lodgings for the courtiers in the neighbourhood
of town. The house still marked as "Ormond-house," next the
eastern corner, derives its name from having been the residence of the last Duchess of Ormond, whose husband was
obliged to fly the country for his adherence to James the
Second. The corner house of the row is occupied by Mr.
Faulkner, bookseller, the worthy historian of Chelsea, to whose
volumes we have been indebted for almost every fact of
importance or curiosity, on which we have made remarks.

We must keep some recollections of Chelsea Hospital and
Ranelagh for our next Sunday's article, being positively the
last (*Hibernice loquens*) on this everlasting subject.[53]

THE TOWNSMAN

March 23, 1834

In the very *darkest* ages streets had no lights at all.[1] People picked their way as they could through mud, slop, and occasional murder. Then came the darker ages, with a light and a wisp of straw strung here and there across a very grand street. The King's palace was approached under the magnificence of two wisps, and you heard his equipage lowing in their stalls. Then arose the dark ages, splendid with a lantern, and Madonna in a corner, throwing "mudshine" into the gutters. Torches, more or less, appeared in most times, according as the rich could afford them; and they prevailed till a late period, as may be seen by the mystic, trumpet-shaped appurtenances to the iron-work before great houses, in which the footmen, or "black-guard boys," were accustomed to thrust and put out their links. The rich no longer require these illustrious accompaniments, except in very great fogs, when the carriage-lights are insufficient, and when the links fly about in the public roads, flaring and smoking in seas of mists, amidst peril, and the cold, quiet, and calling voices.

Meanwhile had come up oil-lamps, now so despised. It is recorded of an envoy from some petty court (we believe Massa Carrara) that, when he entered the streets of London, and perceived a long line of oil-lamps on each side of him, he said, with an amazed gratitude and modest rapture, that "indeed he had been received in other places very kindly, but to find such a welcome as *this* — an illumination made expressly in his honour by so great a nation, was something that completely overpowered him."

There is a passage in Gay's "Trivia, or the Art of Walking the Streets of London," which, as lamps and torches are both mentioned in it, and every thing that Gay says has agreeable points, may be here quoted. It may be observed, that the term "blackguard-boy" above referred to, was first applied, we believe, to the little negroes whom it was the fashion to dress up in fancy attire, and make foot-boys of. It was then given, we suppose, ironically to the dirty urchins that offered their services with links; and these link-boys appear to have been such a turbulent and bad race, that at last the word "blackguard" came to mean any one who set at nought the decencies of life in a violent and abusive manner, and loved to have his way for its own sake, no matter through how much mud and dirt. There is a passage in Congreve (if we are not mistaken) that applies the metaphor somewhat ungallantly to ladies of violent and ostentatious claims upon one's admiration:

> Love is a gentle, generous joy

(we forget the next line) —

> *Her* Cupid is a blackguard-boy,
> That thrusts his link full in your face.

But to come to Gay:

> Though you through cleanlier alleys wind by day,
> To shun the hurries of the public way,
> Yet ne'er to those dark paths of night retire;
> Mind only safety, and contemn the mire.
> Then no imperious courts thy haste detain,
> Nor sneering alewives bid thee turn again.
> Where Lincoln's Inn, wide space, is rail'd around,
> Cross not with venturous step: there oft is found
> The lurking thief, who, while the day-light shone,
> Made the walls echo with his begging tone;
> That wretch, which late compassion moved, shall wound
> Thy bleeding head, and fell thee to the ground.
> Though thou art tempted by the link-men's call,
> Yet trust him not along the lonely wall;
> In the mid-way he'll quench the flaming brand,
> And share the booty with the pilfering band:
> Still keep the public streets, where oily rays
> Shot from the crystal lamp, o'erspread the ways.
> Happy Augusta! law-defended town!

Here no dark lanterns shade the villain's frown;
No Spanish jealousies thy lanes infest,
Nor Roman vengeance stabs th' unwary breast, &c.[2]

We need not quote any more. Our beloved countrymen are fond of complimenting themselves upon their freedom from the crimes of their neighbours; and certainly it cannot be said that in England we have much "*Spanish* jealousy" or "*Roman* vengeance." We have enough jealousy and vengeance, however, of our own to warrant a little more modesty in this matter — quite enough stabbings and poisoning of wives, husbands, and gentlemen in want of money. And more modest we are really becoming. It is not the fashion, as it used to be, in treatises and newspapers, to say every thing favourable of our own virtues and modesty, (a singular proof of the latter quality!) and every thing the reverse of French and Italians. We have found out that other nations have their good qualities as well as ourselves, and we have our faults as well as they; and the discovery is a blessing full of promise to all parties.

But "oily rays!" How we despise them now! And shot from a "crystal" lamp! It is fine poetic talking; but the old lamps appear any thing but "crystal," even in Grosvenor-square; where, in honour of the institutions of our ancestors, and contempt of the "light of the age," even in the article of lamps, they are still to be found. How grand! To refuse gas-light to the pavement, and insist upon blinking when every body else sees!

We remember well when the gas-lights first came up. People in general shook their heads at them, as much as the Grosvenor-square people do still, though from a different feeling. Strong was the suspicion, as usual, that they "would not do;" that they were a mere adventure — or innovation — something fantastic; and the hopes of the discoverer were laughed at and pitied. We fear that there was too much reason to pity him, unless he was a Sir Hugh Myddelton[3] in his way, and prepared to be a martyr; for we believe he was ruined by the difficulties he met with. It is a pity. We have not yet learnt the art of helping out nature thoroughly in her efforts to do us good; and individuals suffer in consequence; but the suffering is well warranted by the general benefit. Mr. Winsor's[4] ruin has been the means probably already of saving thousands of lives, certainly of pieces of property, and so contributing to the general sum of comfort, security, and good-will. The first exhibition of the lights, if we are not mistaken, was in Pall-mall. It was there, at any rate, we first saw it. What a sight it was! People walked up and down as if in a fairy day-light, and wondered whether it was possible that a lustre so beautiful could maintain itself, and become an ordinary utility.

We are forced to break off this week. The subject will be concluded next Sunday.

March 30, 1834

A defect is sometimes accompanied with an advantage. Far-sighted people seldom suspect that the near-sighted have a grander though not so clear a spectacle of the lamp-lights down a street. At a little distance the lamps merge into one thick and continuous stream of light on either side the way, whereas, to sharper eyes, they remain petty and distinct through the whole line, unless the street is a very long one; and in no case do they ever seem so large to the clear sight as to the dimmer one. It is the same with the moon and stars, and lights of every sort. We may here add, that near-sighted eyes have a more picturesque view of most objects. They see trees, for instance, in their masses of light and shade, as in a painting; and even faces lose with them the defects of their surface. Complexions, by day, have the same advantage with them as with others by candle-light; so that ladies who are doubtful of their perfections in that matter, ought to hail the sight of an eye-glass, when it is not in the act of being used. In that case the wearer is apt to make up for his defect, and to look closer than better eyes. They need not fear them, if he knows how to see truly, and their faces have soul as well as skin.

We confess, that with all our respect for new light of every kind, we do not care so much for gas on the pavement as gas in the shops; nor for its use even there, so much as its beauty. We could be content, as far as ourselves were concerned, to go on with the old oil. It was light sufficient for us, and it was an old acquaintance. Somebody—Plutarch or Pope, we cannot remember which—said he did not like to see even an old post removed, that he had been used to. Something of this feeling we had, when we saw the removal of the old lamp-posts; though with full acknowledgment of the right and good of removing them. And the rising generation will have as great a regard for the new ones, as we had for the others. In all tranquil displacings of old customs for better ones, little is lost, and much gained. But there was a softness, and somehow a congeniality with the night-time, in the oil-lamp, which is not the merit of the day-restoring gas; and for our parts, if the advantages of the latter did not far outweigh so nice an objection, we should not be for turning night into day, even on the pavement. We like the kindly interchange of times and seasons as they come round, and at night-time are content that it should be night-time, and dark too, provided we can reasonably see our way, and thieves are not excessively on the alert, or the mud savage.

The beauty of gas-light is seen in shops, theatres and illuminations. *Gas* means *spirit*, and is of the same stock as the words *ghost, ghaist, ghastly*. While we are writing this, there is a sudden and prodigious noise in our fire-grate, of fuming and splitting, which in the times of Dr. Dee,[5] or in some parts of the country still, might have been construed into objections on the part of the spirit of fire, to the liberties we are taking with his mystery. But all spirits are kindly to those who know how to discern their good qualities. We fear him not. Gas is the most beautiful emanation of light and fire that has yet risen on earth. Long before he became so public an acquaintance, did we know the playful evidences he gave of his presence, in his brilliant puffings from out the coal. Mr. Winsor got possession of him, as a magician does of his brethren in the books; and having prepared channels worthy for him to run through, and capable of showing him to advantage at their tops, forth came he, bright, and beauteous, and burning; now like a length of daylight in the lamps; now like a fiery tongue, or a leaf, a set of leaves, forming themselves with strenuous and ever-growing elegance into a fan, or very flower of fire, out of some brazen stem in a window; and now bursting into some floral orb, or basket of brilliance, in an opera-house chandelier, or fermenting with active and intensest glitter, the very sublimity of *neatness,* in the star of some house during an illumination.

Anon, if they did not take care of him, gas went out, and then he would show his tricks, like Robin Goodfellow; and make merry in the darkness, with goblin laughters of Ho! ho! and pretty shrieks of ladies.

Gas beats the oil lamps all to nothing in point of brilliancy of illumination. Those stars we speak of, in the front of illuminated houses, show it indeed like the very spirit of fire, and fire of the best kind, pure, fair, something almost heavenly. We could look at one of them for half an hour together, if the mob would let us, and no unheavenly-minded person asked us why we stopped up the way. Item, the gutters are inconvenient. Yet we cannot help thinking the oil-lamps retain a merit of their own; and look somehow like a soft mellow jewellery, by the side of those more surprising brilliants.

When will knowledge proceed far enough to make us honour publicly our *lasting* public men instead of fugitive ones, or at any rate in addition to them, and light up our houses on their birthdays with the names of Shakspeare, and Milton, and Algernon Sydney? Surely the theatres might set the example, especially now that there is such an opportunity of doing it in Shakspeare's own neighbourhood, and Mr. Knowles[6] is one of his own age's breed. Shakspeare's birth-day is coming soon. Why should not the Victoria Theatre take fire at the thought of it, and make the gas-lights tremble on its walls, as if with rapture to form his name?

A conflict of hostile or unpopular names on similar occasions would be little likely now-a-days, however the case might have been a few years back. On the night of the illumination for the Reform-bill, a wag had it in contemplation to put over the office of a daily paper the following query: —

> Sir Robert Peel,
> How do you feel?

Doubtless it would have "created a great deal of laughter at the time;" but it may have been as well that it was not done. Triumphs are better without flings at the vanquished, even of jokes. We do not recommend illuminations, except of kindness and joy. Light and beauty ought to represent nothing but what is pleasant. But then how much the more ought they not to glorify the names of the patriots, poets, and philosophers, who have made us partakers of light and beauty intellectual? We would have the names, among other places, put up in the streets in which the bearers of them were born; as in Lombard-street, for instance,

> ALEXANDER POPE,
> Born in this street, 1688.

In Cornhill,

> THOMAS GRAY,
> Born in this street, 1716.

In Bread-street, Cheapside,

> JOHN MILTON,
> Born in this street, 1608.

And so on; — Sir Thomas More in Milk-street, Bacon near Charing-cross, &c.

Meantime, will our brother enthusiasts in these matters oblige us by having no more transparencies? or by getting them a little better done? Jokes are particularly perilous through this medium, and seldom tell. But above all — and though they should abolish nothing else — will they have the kindness utterly to withhold and do away those cold and execrable common-places of Fame with a trumpet, and Britannia sitting dressed like a Roman Amazon by a Manchester bale of goods?

EXPLANATION AND RETROSPECTION. —
THE *EXAMINER* TWENTY YEARS AGO

October, 1837

Heartily wishing well to every body,[1] and believing that a
cause can be strenuously advocated without giving reasonable
offence to any (though we blame not such as conscientiously
fight it out, and have ourselves given and received as good
hard knocks as most people, in our time) we are sorry to find,
that the political article in our last number[2] has dissatisfied,
not indeed the usual *Repositorian* readers of the REPOSITORY,
(for that could not well be) but some who in return for our
good wishes to those who differ with us, wish well to ourselves,
and would fain have us agree with them in certain particulars.
A correspondent of the *Atlas* wonders how we could have
implied a doubt respecting the sincerity of Lord Durham. A
Whig friend is sorry that we differ as far as we do, with the
Whigs. And the editor of the *Brighton Patriot*, with a delightful, good-natured mixture of objection to us in various ways,
and willingness to be pleased, prefers the hotter tone of our
friend Tait, and accuses us of being very "lukewarm ond *philosophic.*"

Honour and glory to our friend Tait, and to all other able
men who are sincere and well-intentioned, whatsoever be
their opinions. Honour and glory to Lord Durham, and may
his Letter[3] turn out to have been what we said it most probably was, nothing but a momentary adaptation of tone to
circumstances, out of the best motives, and for the sake of the
cause to which it seemed "lukewarm." When the *Brighton
Patriot* accuses ourselves of being "lukewarm," well does it
remind us how we may think others so, and be mistaken.
(There is nothing for enlarging your charity, like wanting
a charitable construction for yourself!) But honour and glory

also to the *Brighton Patriot,* a paper of talent and tried honesty, and as ardent in the thick of the fight as ever.

Nay; hardly that either. For the thick of the fight was in old times, long before the 'Patriot' was born. Well do we remember it, for we are smarting this minute from head to foot with wounds given by it to our health, having been one among a very few who were left to sustain the battle by our friends the Whigs (without petulance be it said); and "the archers hurt" us; and calumny and poverty were upon us; and imprisonment was one of the least of our evils, though the iron entered into our *flesh.* Our "soul" it did not touch, for here we are, as hearty in the cause as ever, and as well able, after the measure of our faculties, to sustain it; albeit the sharp taste of suffering has rendered us less willing to inflict pain, and we have learnt to know that enemies may be as good men as others, and that the great point is, to lift the whole world if you can, and trample on nobody. If this is to be philosophic, we are glad of it; but "lukewarm!" Oh, that we never were. We do not think, that the sort of fighting is needed now that was at that time; nor perhaps at any time; but there is a warmth that has nothing to do with hostility, and this we have in our veins as fresh as ever, and far warmer; for the heat is unmixed. There was a good deal of mere antagonism in our former efforts; of the petulance and pride of the will, and of the shew of fancied superiority; and hence the good that suffering did us, in driving us from self-estimation into the arms of the good and beauty to be found any where, and every where, *else;* — a possession so infinite, that we have ever since been *hot* with a zeal to make every body partake of it.

We should apologise for referring thus personally to ourselves, did not some circumstances connected with the objections to our last article render it incumbent upon us to do so, and to do it still further, for the sake of justice both to ourselves and others. And to this end, we must explain how it is we came to write politics again, and to edit this magazine. We had thought (to confess the truth), that having done what

we could formerly to advance the good cause, and seeing that
the cause must continue to advance, however slowly, we had
a right to rest from our old labours, and work out our ordinary
salvation as well as we could, in directions more agreeable to
our private taste. But the late proprietors[4] of the REPOSITORY
having handsomely consigned the work over to us, in most
unworldly fashion, rather than receive money for it in quarters
where they were not sure of its being turned to reforming
account, we thought it our duty (as indeed we felt it to be
expected of us, though not insisted on, and the more binding
for that reason) to carry on the spirit of its politics, which
happened to be our own; and thus we again found ourselves
compelled to speak out, and of course with our old sincerity.
It was, on one account, very painful to us; for the personal
claims, which we conceive to have been given us upon a
reforming government by our pecuniary as well as other sufferings in the cause (not that we ever proposed, God knows,
to make a profit of those sufferings, or to complain of them,
if unrelieved; for old soldiers must not do that) had been met,
to a certain temporary extent, but at a moment of the greatest
importance to us, by the present ministry; and most unwillingly did we hazard the peril of being thought ungrateful by the
least reflecting of their friends, however erroneously. Such as
know how we have ever set up a principle against all personal
ideas of welfare, will not have mistaken us; and delightful is
it to feel assured, that those among the ministers themselves,
for whom we entertain the deepest respect (and very deep it
is) have ample regions in their own nature, in which to find
corners of scholarly and simple excuse for us; however simple
in a small as well as larger sense they may be induced to
think it, by a still more enlarged knowledge in such matters
than we fancy ourselves to have arrived at. The Whig friend,
alluded to at the commencement of this article, who is himself a man quite rich enough in heart and understanding, and
we will add, quite well enough acquainted with us, to give
us all the credit we demand in this instance, is nevertheless
led by the kind interest he takes in our welfare to fear that

we may do injury to the demands we still think we have the right of making on others. But all we can say in answer is, that his good opinion, and those of other honest men, is our best possession after all, and the best heir-loom, under providence, we can leave to others, where a sense of duty is in the way. It is no foppery in us to say so, for we do not partake the ordinary opinions held concerning merit and demerit, but look upon every man as the creature of circumstances and his kindred. And as to any expectations which it may ruin, court-wards or ministry-wards, it is undoubtedly possible that they may be ruined by circumstances over which individuals have less control than is supposed; but we shall not easily believe, that honourable and reflecting men will feel personally offended with the utterance of honest opinions expressed without discourtesy; and having nothing but the general good in view, their own included. Mistaken we may be in our mode of advancing it. Who may not be in *his*? But it is in any spirit, but that of a hostile one, that we entertain what difference of opinion we do with the men in power. We desire their prosperity so much, and respect more than one of them so affectionately, that it is out of the very impatience of love we long to see them rise triumphant above the fears and habits inferior to the best parts of their nature, and prove to us spectators, whose position enables us to discern them, how much better they can carry on the world's business, than we could pretend to do, if in theirs. For a critic does not of necessity assume that he could do better than the person criticised; and though we take the government of the world to be a far less terrible difficulty than is supposed, and are of opinion with Machiavel that the people, out of a general intinct of well-being, err less often in their judgment than the prince, different men are fit for different things, and we know well that our part lies more in the discernment of a general good, and the being able to suffer for it, than the canvassing it in detail or helping to carry it into execution. If suffering gives us any claim, or if the furtherance of that good in any respect, political or otherwise, gives us any claim, that claim, we conceive, should exist, not in less strength but in greater, in proportion to the consistency with which we prove it to have been an honest one; and it is not necessary surely for those who have a kindness for it, to demand that we shall always think as they do, or degrade sympathy into assentation. Co-operation, it is true, is desirable, and dissent should not be "frivolous and vexatious." But on the other hand, if you see a friend taking a wrong path, when the finger-post, according to your eyesight, manifestly points to a different one, you must tell him so by all the laws of help and reciprocity.

In short, we wish the Ministers so well, that in addition to what is good in themselves, we wish them whatsoever is good in their enemies and their emulators, — the fearless energy of the Tories, and the carrying out of the Reform Bill according to its first intention, or the principles of Lord Durham; for as to being *his* enemy; or wishing to throw an unhandsome and solitary doubt on his truthfulness, greatly indeed are we mistaken on that point also, and sorry are we that a just ardour of gratitude to his Lordship should have led the correspondent of the *Atlas* (for we have learnt who he is) to appear as if careless, or contemptuous, of our own feelings; which we have received his assurances that he did not intend to be. Deeply warranted do we feel ourselves to declare, that we have no such perversity in us as to object to a man because he is an "Aristides," or to grudge any man whatsoever, public or private, the credit which is due to him. But we are told there is not a shadow of "proof" for the doubts excited by Lord Durham's letter. Our answer is, that the proof of a thing's being doubtful is in the very doubts entertained of it, if they exist to a certain extent, and among honourable men; and that they do so, was our warrant for speaking as we did. But it should be recollected, that in a previous article we had defended his lordship against those doubts, or stated what ought in reason to be set off against them, and claimed for him the best construction, and the continuance of the public belief; and when we again alluded to the existence of the doubt, we had no intention of undoing that good construction, or of intimating that we did not hold to it. We simply put an hypothesis, as referring to a future contingency, and perhaps with a hope, that his lordship, if he happened to see our publication, might be moved by the effect which his letter had had upon some of his best wishers, to take some early step towards setting their minds at ease. For as to "looking down upon," and scorning, &c. (which our *Atlas* friend, though not meaning anything personal to ourselves, was moved out of the usual serenity of his reflections to think of in connexion with his noble friend and the doubt in general) a great and good man, in proportion to his greatness and goodness, looks down upon and scorns nothing. He knows his own weakness too well, as a man; and respects his fellow-creatures too much, as knowing the faculties and capabilities they share with him. It is a pity (not in this particular instance, for gratitude is a delightful virtue, and its ardour to adhere to a friend should be witnessed with regard, even when in its haste it treads on another's toes) but it is a pity that Lord Durham's friends in general assume this lofty tone for him, as if there were anything in a nobleman, or in any man, that should set him above the doubts even of those who are unwilling to doubt him. Ah! dear correspondent of the *Atlas*, thyself an instance, through what doubts, and far worse than doubts, are other honest innovators forced to make out their case in this world; and perhaps not succeed at last without being crippled in mind, body, and estate! what anxieties must they not bear, of every description! what obloquy not endure! what rage of enemies! what coldness of friends! what dread for the common wants of those who are dearest! what doubts of themselves, and of their own modesty or fitness! what sickness! what visitations of horror and astonishment, and all new and strange aspects of the moral phenomena of their own minds! valleys of the shadows of death, through which they are nevertheless expected to issue forth, patient, and modest, and charitable, upon pain of forfeiting the sympathy of the prudent, and the right of expecting some remote chance of the possibility of a resource. Justly too, we allow, in many respects: for every career has its pleasures as well as pains, has action, and hope in it, or the fancied right of complaint, or some other secret support of self-love; and the sense of doing one's duty is, above all, a payment that may suffice, and suffice well, for a man's self, provided the self be not distributed into other helpless selves, who share the misfortune of his career without having partaken the excitement that enlivened it.

Let it be permitted us to look back a moment at the period (some twenty years back) when the sacred fire of the cause of Reform was reduced to a few sparks so small, and left in the keeping of hands so little assisted, that the *Edinburgh Review,* in its witty despair, was for needs blowing them out, or swearing there were none at all. The writer of the present remarks was then editor of the *Examiner,* and, in divers formal articles on the subject, had to assert the very existence of the cause against the superior powers and jovial incredulity of the editor of the *Review,* at that time the reigning authority of the Whigs, and divider of public influence with the Tory press. Do we blame that excellent person for the opinion he held? No: no more than we value ourselves, in any arrogant sense, upon our own. Circumstances made us both see the case from different points of view; and had we been in his place, we should have come to his conclusion, though with less peril to our antagonist in the power of enforcing it. But what we mean by referring to the circumstance is, that we have a right of the oldest and most enduring kind to a considerate regard of any present difference of opinion which we may entertain with men whom we personally respect; and that if anything we say now may seem to militate against their notion of what is best for the cause, we were among the instruments, however humble, that helped to keep the cause itself alive for their very ascendancy. Let honest Reformers, Whig as well as Radical, look back at that period, and consider how very few were the public advocates of their cause. Cobbett was its most powerful upholder, though with a self-will that procured it enemies as well as friends. Bentham was secretly advancing his half- (though indeed a very *large* half-) philosophy in its support. Major Cartwright,[5] who has been accused of having but one idea in his head, had it however so strongly, urged it so like a missionary and a martyr, and was a man so above all suspicion of double-mindedness, that he had a thousand times the influence that far abler men have now. And such was the case with the *Examiner.* It had little political ability in detail, no statistics, nothing that Cobbett, for instance, had, except purpose and greater courage. We may say so without immodesty, or even self-reference; for one of its proprietors (if it be not an egotism in a brother to say so) was a man of an heroical nature, prepared for any sufferance, and proving it through sickness and trouble, by imprisonment on imprisonment, with tranquil readiness; for which he deserves well of his country. We never knew a fault in him but reserve, and a zeal for justice towards individuals so great, as sometimes made him not quite mindful enough of the claims of those whom he thought opposed to them. As to ourselves, with but half his courage (for, to give it no harsher term, which might be thought a vanity, we ever had a tendency to the luxurious and self-indulgent, which it required some excessive principle of friendship or *cosmopolity* to overcome), we had great animal spirits, an extraordinary equipoise of sick feelings and healthy, or levity and gravity; and between us both, the *Examiner,* by its combination of a love of literature with politics, and its undoubted honesty, introduced a regard for Reform in quarters that otherwise would not have thought of it, and became the father of many a journalist of the present day, especially in the provinces. It was the Robin Hood of its cause, plunder excepted; and by the gaiety of its daring, its love of the green places of poetry, and its sympathy with all who needed sympathy, produced many a brother champion that beat it at its own weapons. Hazlitt, in its pages, first made the public sensible of his great powers. There Keats and Shelley were first made known to the lovers of the beautiful. There Charles Lamb occasionally put forth a piece of criticism, worth twenty of the editor's, though a value was found in those also; and there we had the pleasure of reading the other day one of the earliest addresses to the public of a great man, who, with a hand mighty with justice, has succeeded in lifting up a nation into the equal atmosphere, which all have a right to breathe, — Daniel O'Connell. Let no friend, who ever mentions our having suffered for a "libel" (a word we hate) on the Prince Regent, forget to add, that it was occasioned by the warmth of our sympathy with that nation, and our anger at seeing the Prince break his promises with it. Well; such was the *Examiner* of that day, such as it was; and yet so great is the tendency of any cause to be acted upon by the common appearances of worldly prosperity, and to forget their own old soldiers, "famoused for fight," that a reform publication the other day complimented its present editor with having been the first to rescue the journalism of the cause from "contempt." How Cobbett's influence was "contemptible" we are at a loss to conceive; and we are at equal loss to conceive in what quarters, not contemptible themselves, the *Examiner* was despised, whatever tone to that effect may have been pretended towards it in others. The powers of its present editor[6] no man can appreciate with greater readiness than ourselves, or have oftener joined in praising. He is a wit of the times of Queen Anne, with greater political detail, though less general sympathies; and we always feel grateful to him for carrying on the reputation of the paper, which he does with far more political ability than its former editor; — but with more respectability in the eyes of the conscientious he could not, nor with greater encouragement from the respected. We enjoyed the good opinion of some of the greatest men among the present leading Reformers, Whig as well as Radical; the Tory government surely did not despise us, for they felt our blows, and were loud in complaint; and with respect to the great master, acknowledged by the publication in question, — Mr Bentham, — he did us the honour, like the really great man he was, with all his unpoetical drawbacks, of coming to see us and make our acquaintance, because we had taken his fancy by the ungrudging nature of our journal, and its love of fair play for its rivals.

But perhaps the "contempt" spoken of may be that of what is called "the circles;" a real power, we grant, in political matters, and in these times more visible than in most. But as this, we conceive, is not felt to be a contempt, "according to knowledge," or one that implies any thing like a feeling of it in quarters where opinion is of more reputable consequence, we shall say nothing further on the subject, except to express a regret that the esteemed author of the remark (if we guess him rightly) should have confounded his want of retrospective information with a matter of fact. And poor Sir Francis Burdett! Could not even he, the model of the "fine old English gentleman," rescue the cause he once advocated from the contempt of "the circles!" Poor, rich, indolent, busy, publicity-loving, solid-fame-never-acquiring Sir Francis! (as the good philosopher above-mentioned would have called him). *He* too ought not to be omitted in the list of the few who advocated the cause in its days of peril, though he is the only one, we think, who should dislike to be reminded of it. Poor, anxious, scornful old gentleman! What a noise did he not make by the mere show of a sympathy with the many, and a real earnestness in the love of that show! what zeal did he not beget in his followers! what confidence! what enthusiasm! what a roaring in the streets, and a credit for every virtue in private! If he had a reputation for gallantry, it was construed in the handsomest manner. He was a sort of Henry the Fourth with us, of whom no ill opinion was to be entertained, seeing that he wished "a fowl in every man's pot." How natural, we thought, that he who overflows with such love to his species, should not be able to restrain it towards the more loving portion. Alas! we now begin to fear that he never had any sympathies at all, erroneous or otherwise. The fowl in the pot he has left us to find how we may; and nobody meanwhile, it seems, ever saw the one in his own. His present zeal, during the interval of its direction against his old friends and Mr O'Connell, who is his "Mrs. Grundy,"* is all for ships and horses;

---

* "What will Mrs Grundy say?" the constant exclamation of the zealous old lady in the comedy of *John Bull*.

which to the disparagement of the infantry and the great guns, he calls the two thunder-bolts of war; or, not to defraud him of his scholarship, the *duo fulmina belli*. He is horribly excited at our not having ships enough to compete with the Czar of Muscovy, and at the notion of the royal stud's going out of the country, especially as it might be bought in for a "trifling consideration;" and he magnanimously hopes, that the glorious old nobility and gentry of England will "raise a subscription" for that purpose, rather than see his country so degraded. Dear, interesting Sir Francis! why doesn't he pay the two-pence himself? He is very rich, and his family has just had riches heaped upon riches. Why not himself make the country a present of the stud? We would stand by him during the bleeding of his purse, and help his old age from being overcome by the operation.

But enough of retrospection, and more than enough of apostasy. We shall conclude this not very definite article with briefly showing the whole amount of all that we intended to say in our last, either to Radical Reformers, or Whig: — all which, it is requested to be borne in mind, we say, not in our own person, which would be a presumption, but as belonging to a sincere, perhaps comparatively sequestered, but not altogether uninfluential body of Reformers, for in their connexion with books and the press, they help to influence opinion: and this opinion we would fain see heartily on the side of those who have got the cause in their hands, whether as ministers, or those who would fain assist ministers.

All we say then to the Radicals is, — *Get a leader. Exoriare aliquis.* Have enthusiasm enough to produce among you some one man, recognized and pre-eminent, who by a certain mighty weight of combined eloquence, and address, and sincerity, shall know how to consolidate your efforts, and bear them triumphantly upon your purpose.

All we say to the Whigs is, — *Prove to us that you wish to move onward.* Be you our leaders, if you will, but then be undoubtedly such; and do not pass another year in leaving the question unsettled. Do not confine your measures to governing Ireland well, and purifying the bench of Bishops; — excellent measures both, but dangerous to us by their very excellence, if they are to end in the mere ascendancy of Whiggism, and not in the advancement of the many. *Succeed in England as you have succeeded in Ireland, by fearing nothing, and doing justice.* The Tories fear nothing, and beget a show of formidableness in consequence, though in the wrong. Do you, who are in the right, fear not the Tories who are in the wrong, and down goes Toryism in the ring made for you by the hearty people of England, who love fair play, and whose majority is openly with you, and their minority secretly. Talk you of "convulsions," and of "real Tory power?" Who is to make the convulsion, if Ireland and Scotland and the great English towns are with you, together with the secret wishes of a peasantry under dictation? Tory power is made up of the assumption of it, and of the cold faces shewn you in the family; — those of your Tory kindred, and the clubs. Dare to vindicate the elder birthright of justice, and you are free and omnipotent. Dare heartily to *wish* it, and and you are free. Whatsoever the timid among you may think, coronets and crowns will be safe for quite enough centuries to come to re-assure all; for there is a good as well as bad side in men's minds, which loves to be led; but knowledge is spreading in the great human family, and the weaker brethren are growing strong, and wish to be really led, not to be dragged. If you fear to make as much haste with details as the Radicals desire, prove at all events that your notion of deliberateness does not consist in doing nothing; and while you are doing something for the detail, prove that your ultimate wishes are the right ones, by losing no further time in adopting some great plan of National Education. Do this; and we of the REPOSITORY, as belonging to one section of ardent Reformers, will take that great plan, accompanied with some real progress in other respects, for a final proof that you mean the nation the very best, and will stand by you, in all honest heartiness of the meaning, through thick and thin. We will blush to have doubted you; — will entreat you to believe that the doubt had never been of your kindly and handsome natures as men, but only that which is compelled by the corporate influences to which all men are liable; and will delightedly acknowledge that it was ourselves who were in the wrong, not you. What signifies? Whigs and Radicals will both have intended well; and what matters it which were most in the right, if the right be attained?

There is a Noble and Learned Lord, one of the greatest men of his age — the violence of his very enemies goes to prove it, — Lord Brougham. If it were wise to regret anything past, instead of looking to do the best in future, we would regret that he was not still with us in the House of Commons. But he is with us, wherever he is; for his genius is on the side of Time, to which he belongs. Why not institute a ministership which the wants of the age demand, — one of National Education, — and put him at the head of it?

Why not also bring Lord Durham's better part of the Reform Bill into play, and him along with it? That would be a stupefying blow for the Tories, — a settler; — and the country would be pleased at his showing them once for all, and notwithstanding the supposed coldness of his Letter, that there is no humour, in his own blood, Tory enough to realize the unjust fears of him created by such men as Sir Francis.

The BALLOT, HOUSEHOLD SUFFRAGE, and NATIONAL EDUCATION. Begin with the last instantly, — and show us that before the session is over you will do something for the rest, — and many a heart, like that of the REPOSITORY, will become, from an anxious friend, a delighted partisan.

TWELFTH NIGHT

January 1, 1854

For many reasons, new and old, the author of this article[1] is as happy to find himself writing in the present paper, as if he were within hearing of actual music, the circumstance of all others (a certain quiet kind of companionship excepted) under which he feels his thoughts flowing to their greatest comfort. "Advantage" he must not say, for reasons which may be too obvious; and people sometimes fail in doing their best out of a special desire to do it. But old and inherited friendships, the consciousness of being within the sphere of an art which he loves, and a subject to set his pen going like the one before us, the pleasure of all this may communicate some little bit of itself to the reader, if it do nothing more.

Hail then, royalest of the nights of Christmas! finish and climax of its holidays! night of King and Queen; night of Characters; night of Twelfth Cake! night on which that brilliant phenomenon rises like another moon; rises indeed like what it is, the sublunary moon of the season; round, and fair, and glittering; accompanied also by worlds of other moons, the clusters in a thousand shops, as though the moon itself were beheld through pieces of cut glass, and so turned into multitudes of its like.

Thee, O most illustrious and attractive of cakes, all the little Galileos of the streets contemplate through the glasses of the shop windows, —

> At evening, on the top of Finsbury,
> Or in Belgravia, to descry new sweets
> (Not to be theirs) beneath thy spot of snow.*

---

* Vide Milton, of Galileo looking at the moon; —
> At evening from the top of Fiesole,
> Or in Valdarno, to descry new lands,
> Rivers, or mountains, in her spotty globe.

[*Paradise Lost*, I, 289-291.]

In thee the maturer youth sees all his enjoyments of the coming evening, — his friend Smith, and his friend's sister, and his own song, and his character, which he hopes will be that of some high court officer, or at least of some *quizzer*, rather than *quizzee*. In thee, by like anticipation, Miss Smith responds to the royal aspirations of Blinkinsop, not without fear of being made a fright of a character. In thee, mothers, discerning a little too far, as astronomers do into lunar volcanos, behold doubts of the paints, and dreads of the demands of third slices; pleased nevertheless to think that the children will be more admired than found wanting. In thee, finally, besides antiquaries their lores, and poetical readers their quotations, and all people their greetings of the good custom, the oldest of old boys will see the Twelfth Nights of former days, and comfortably shake their heads with one another at the falling off of the present, happy at the same time to think that they have reached another new year, and secure of reaching many more, as long as they can discern cake from crumpet, and there is one single person in existence who is older than themselves. Pleasing privilege of old age! and as pleasing to others as to themselves, if there is a single person living whom they love and are loved by, and who will take care to help them to a slice of the cake, before younger ones are served.

It is a great addition to the pleasure of doing a good thing, to consider that everybody, who can, is doing it at the same moment. (Those who cannot, we must think of before and afterwards, but not at the same moment; otherwise we shall embitter every morsel we taste, and so destroy the pleasure that we would diffuse.) Yes, — all the genial people in Christendom who can afford a Twelfth Cake to-night, will be having it — from the buyers of the cake that costs guineas, down to those who are glad to get the humblest sixpenny imitation of it; and all these people, we may rest assured, will be enjoying it more or less in the same way; for "everybody," as the philosopher said, "is more like than unlike everybody else;" and customs which are universal, resemble one another among different ranks a good deal more than people suppose. The cost is not the point, but the individual's good sense, health, and companionability. Besides, the highest life does not differ from the humblest life so much as certain would-be great people imagine. It knows its comforts too well, and does not care what pretenders may think of it. While the upstart is fidgeting about his "urn" and his "footman," the marquis is probably taking the kettle off the drawing-room fire, to help the countess, who is making tea, and if there is anything of which we are as sure at this moment as we are of the existence of sense and good-nature, it is that the greatest personage in the kingdom will be as blithe over her Twelfth Cake with her husband and children, as the best village housewife in her dominions. And the housewife will be as blithe as she.

Two questions are sometimes asked respecting Twelfth Night: first, what it is; and second, what is the best way of keeping it. It is curious that people should ask what a thing is which they are all doing; though, to be sure, if we were as candid as we are ignorant, we should all find ourselves putting the same question about a hundred common-places. It is not the poorest people only, who stand in need of the late new suggestion of philanthropy — the recommendation of a knowledge of "common things." There will be thousands of rooms to-night in the greatest houses, which will endanger the health of the joyous and accomplished inmates, for want (even after all that has been said and written on the subject) of a little common knowledge of ventilation; a case which we instance for the seasonable prevention of faintings away, and the better digestion of the cake and turkey. The teacher of common things would also do a great deal of good on the like occasions, if he went about ripping up the bodices of tight-lacers, and laying his embargo on green teas, and acidulated drops of vitriols. But we must not be growing didactic on holidays. Twelfth Night is not a time for preaching. Sir Andrew Aguecheek was not so inconsiderate a jolly fellow as he wished to be thought, when being asked on Twelfth Night whether he would have "a love song, or a song of good life," said the love song, for he "cared not for good life."

Twelfth-Night, so called from its being the conclusion of the twelve days of Christmas, is one of the Christian versions of those natural winter holidays, which have prevailed from times the most ancient, and which are the instinctive result of the necessity which is felt for a double portion of joy and sociality at so inclement a time. Greeks and Romans had their Kings of the Feast, and their drawing of lots for imaginary dominions; the Christians of the middle ages converted into these kings the "wise men of the East," who are described as bringing presents to the infant Jesus; the cake and its ornaments (formerly called among us the Baby Cake) were the presents which they brought; the Characters of Twelfth-Night arose out of the imaginary court-officers and their ladies who were appointed to wait on the king and queen; and the wassail-bowl was the wine or other liquor, which was drunk at their coronation. To this jumble of Pagan and Christian ideas nobody now, of any creed, adheres. Devout believers, of course, retain their opinion of the circumstance on which it is founded; but in the cake, the king and queen, and the characters, &c., nobody now sees any thing but the merriment of a winter custom; and the devotion would be thought ill-timed that should hazard the confusion of serious and jocose by bringing church and such state together.

As to the best way of keeping Twelfth-Night, it must depend on the habits and inclinations of the parties concerned. Any way is bad, which thinks more of the form than the spirit; and any way is good, which is innocent, hearty, and successful. Some, who look at the custom from the antiquarian point of view, would do nothing on the occasion which was not done by their ancestors; a principle, which if their ancestors had acted upon it, would have carried them up to *their* ancestors, and so on through Greek and Egyptian till they came to Adam; whose Christmas at present would hardly be very comfortable. Others, who have a vulgar horror of doing any thing which they think vulgar, that is to say, of what is done by persons not so well off as themselves (an absurdity, which as we have before intimated, prevails the less in society, the higher in it we go) will have no Christmas, and no wassail bowl; because the former, they think, may commit their dignity; and the latter, they have heard, is made of such vulgar things as ale and roasted apples. Now the wassail-bowl is made of ale (and a very good drink it is) only where no wine is to be had. You might make it of Tokay, if you were rich enough; and very sorry people would ladies and gentlemen of the anti-vulgar description feel themselves to be, if they found themselves travelling in the region where Tokay is produced, and were obliged to put up before the landlord with a wine less costly; for costly it is, even there. The roasted apples, formerly called lamb's wool when thus mixed with the wassail drink, are despised by these gentry, because they are to be had at a half-penny apiece. As if any one who knew copper from clay, would buy the finest of their fine notions for half so much!

A good hearty peasant's or workman's Twelfth-Night is composed of an ale wassail bowl, a cake however homely (the best may be bought by co-operation) and as much king and queen, and character, as he feels inclined to throw in. Such would have been the Twelfth-Night of Burns, had he kept it; and who that has lived long enough, would not be proud to have passed such "a night with Burns?" No man could have done more justice to the part of a King of Good Fellows; and as for Characters, who could desire a better set than would have been furnished by the author of Tam o'Shanter? But ale, in order to be qualified for the wassail-bowl, must be sugared, and have nutmeg in it, and the aforesaid roasted apples; one of which, or a portion of it, is to be taken into each of the glasses in which the ale is served; and if all this does not sufficiently elevate the drink into something "genteel," or must be thought for the most part rather to degrade it, the aspirant may substitute for the ale the wine as above mentioned, and then he need not be ashamed to invite the dullest of his acquaintances to the potation. Besides, ale, it must be granted, whether spiced or otherwise, is not pleasant to every palate; whereas Burns himself, with all his eulogies of it, would gladly have partaken of the wine, provided the possessor had wit enough of his own to warrant the asking him to his party.

In old times a bean and a pea used to be put into the Twelfth-cake, the bean for the king's lot and the pea for the queen's. At present, the royal as well as the other characters are chosen by coloured engravings, folded up, and handed round to the company. The drawing commences any time between tea and supper, and the characters are supported till the meal. They may continue however during it, or after it, if they be so disposed; and the king and queen should always occupy the head of the table. Modes have varied in these, as they do in every thing, at different periods; and we suspect that nothing is absolutely indispensable to Twelfth-Night, but a cake, and drink of some sort, and merriment. In Shakspeare's play of that name, there is no allusion even to the cake; unless we are to suppose it implied in the immortal question respecting "cakes and ale;" which it probably is; especially as the two are mentioned together.

Sir Toby (to the Steward). "Dost thou think, because thou art virtuous, there shall be no more cakes and ale?"

Clown. "Yes, by Saint Anne; and ginger shall be hot in the mouth too."

Anne was the saint who bestowed the means of rich living; and ginger was an indispensable ingredient in the cake. The Clown, it seems, loved a good deal of it. In the Masques, or Court Entertainments, of Ben Jonson, several of which were brought out on Twelfth Nights, there is no mention of the Cake but once.

We should be rash, however, if we concluded that a great deal of it was not eaten, the court of his Majesty King James, who came from the Land of Cakes, being famous for eating and drinking of all sorts. The Puritans attempted to put down Christmas altogether; the consequence of which was, that it revived with a new excess under Charles the Second, whose "Beauties" (if such their foolish faces must be called) ate their cake, and played at forfeits, with all the pretended simplicity and real silliness of a parcel of underbred school-girls.

The best among them was Nell Gwyn, who had no breeding
at all, but who retained her good heartedness. If we possessed
Fortunatus's wishing-cap, and could partake, at our will and
pleasure, and on one and the same evening, the enjoyment of
the four main kinds of Twelfth Night, which are to be found
in Her Majesty's dominions, those of the agricultural class,
of the mechanical, of the commercial, and the aristocratical,
we should go, for a taste of the first, to the remotest one we
could find, as that which was likely to be the most primitive;
— some cottage in which the oldest country customs were to
be met with: — for the second, we should seek the pleasantest
person we could hear of who was an attender at a Mechanics'
Institution[2] and a Singing Class, as we should take him to be
the man of his class of society the most likely to be a person
of natural refinement: — for the third, we should join the
party of that man of business who knew how to enjoy money
as well as to get it, and who loved to see around him the faces
which it made happy: — and for the fourth,[3] we should wish
ourselves into the circle of one of those large-hearted, therefore wisest and pleasantest statesmen, who have come forward
of late years to lecture at the institutions just mentioned, and
whose homes are likely to furnish the best evidences of that
enjoyment perfected by intelligence, which they are so justly
anxious to diffuse.

Mighty talking this, for a man who is too ailing if not too
old, to visit his next door neighbour! But the imagination
which books and Twelfth-Nights have helped to cultivate,
is a great paymaster. We sit here, by our fire-side, and think
of all the nights of this description which we have enjoyed;
and very young and robust are we, while so thinking. We see
the whole evening's entertainments, proceeding with a kind
of involuntary order, the natural consequence of pleasures
growing out of one another. First, there is the tea, which
makes a quieting and refreshing interval between dinner and
the enjoyments to come; then rises the talk of what is coming,
and of old Twelfth-Nights as well as new (provided old faces
have not been too newly missed); then out of this talk naturally

grow references to books and poets (already lying near us on a table, in case we would read aloud, or our memory wants assistance); then music is suggested by the poetry (for all records of Twelfth-Night abound in music, and no pleasure is to be baulked, which any of us desires, and which all approve); then dancing must needs come (for now the mirth begins to grow eager, stimulated by some Laughing Trio, or other triumphant strain); then the Cake itself makes its consolidating appearance, hailed by the clapping of the hands of the little boys (in which the grandfathers join), and ushered in perhaps to the strain of "See the conquering hero comes" (for what will not sweets conquer?) then follow the drawing of king and queen, and of the characters, whether court-characters or otherwise, that is to say, characters in court-offices, or taken indiscriminately from existing manners; then is established the maintenance of these parts till supper aforesaid, or as late as you please; then comes the supper itself, with songs and glees, &c., after it, whether accompanied or not; — then, past midnight, we don't say how long, are muttered some remote hints of going away; and then perhaps, — eh? — yes, we have seen such things, and have survived them these four and thirty years, — there makes its appearance, breakfast; yea, breakfast at dawn; breakfast on St. Distaff's day; for that is the day next after Twelfth Night; the day on which we all ought to be spinning our jennies or our brains; — by which same token of breakfast, though we have mentioned the circumstance before, but it is a great circumstance, and will bear repetition, — we partook once of a Twelfth Night, which has been ever since called, by way of eminence, *the* Twelfth Night,[4] and which closed with that same victorious meal at daylight, when an assemblage of some of the finest eyes in the world, looked, by the acknowledgment of all present, as if they were still untired. The night, like Shakspeare's Twelfth Night, began with music; an accomplished musician set it going; it rolled on with music, amidst wits, poets, and beauties; and when the company broke up after breakfast, and the door was opened to let them forth, they were not only saluted by the morning rays, but there suddenly, and like enchantment, struck up the trumpets of a troop of horse, as if on purpose to greet them, and do honor to the lovely victors.

We do not say to the reader, Go and do likewise. That must depend upon a hundred circumstances of time, place, and occasion. The party in question did not do it themselves on purpose. They never even did it again. Circumstances carried most [of] us in different directions: and had the case been otherwise, the particular impulse might not have occurred. We only mentioned it, because the subject, like the occasion, transported us. Besides, health is to be considered; and we heartily join in the advocacy of good hours. All that we have desired to do in these remarks on a social custom, is to furnish those who might desire it with such a knowledge of the custom as we possessed; to recommend to them as much or as little use of the knowledge as would best meet the ideas of enjoyment in their own circles; and to partake with them, in imagination, a harmless pleasure.

CHRISTMAS DAY DIVIDED BETWEEN TWO WORLDS

OR, FRAGMENT OF A DAY-DREAM OF THE FIRST HEAVEN.

1857

The reader must not suppose, from the heading of this article,[1] that the object of it is to start questions in theology, or to oppress him with a feeling of seriousness too great for his Christmas enjoyments. Hearty and merry may his enjoyments be, as full of a very forgetfulness of the serious as becomes duties discharged, and the Source of all enjoyments thanked. The moment he has done what he can for others, and it is time for his festivities to begin, let him give thought itself to the winds, and turn his happy and happy-making face to nothing but the pleasures before him.

As the feelings, however, on which Christmas itself was founded were of a religious, though at the same time cheerfully religious nature; as nothing befits truly religious feeling better at most times than cheerfulness; and as those who are best constituted to make their friends happy have moments nevertheless in the midst of their most social enjoyments — nay, by very reason of those enjoyments — in which the faces are missed that will never join them more, and the shadow of another world thus falls as if in rebuke on the brightness of this (or if not in rebuke, yet with a sudden and horrible sense of difference, and of loss irretrievable), — it is proposed in this fragment of a religious, but very happy, and indeed half-earthly and whole-Christmas vision, to complete the round of Christmas sympathies furnished by the current number of this publication, and fill up the little gap, not unnaturally left by the livelier and more seasonable portions of it, with a thought or two of comfort against the chances of those exceptional pangs.

The article is called a fragment, because it is literally such of a larger account of the dream contemplated by the writer, should he have life and strength left him for its completion. The dream arose, not from meditations on any received religious opinion, but from a domestic sorrow[2] which occurred to him some years ago, and which no subsequent trouble, however surprising or vexatious, has hindered from daily presenting itself to his thoughts, often as a corrective to other sorrows, always in the midst of reflections more cheerful. The power, however, to reflect cheerfully at all, especially on matters connected with religion, is a blessing inestimable; and as dreams have had allowed and great influence in such matters, he would fain give his readers the benefit of certain seasonable portions of a dream, in unison both with religious and with cheerful reflections.

As the peculiar nature of it, however, would produce awkwardness in the narration if continued in the third person, the first person proceeds to speak accordingly.

I imagined myself, then, last Christmas Day in the act of dying, and at the same instant found myself living again, wonderfully light and strong, in a remote region outside our planet, which presented, nevertheless, to my enraptured eyes a spot containing the ideal of an earthly home, such as I had often pictured it to my mind. It had trees about it, birds, and a hive of bees. A beautiful stream of water, with a boat on it, was at the door. The door was open, disclosing a room containing books, pictures, and musical instruments; and by the threshold, with a book in his hand and his back towards me, sate a young man, who, with an archness in his face of a kind which I had never witnessed before, and containing a wonderful mixture of consideration, tenderness, and joy, turned slowly round; and I beheld — whom shall I say? I have never yet had courage enough to utter his name with my lips, and I now would rather not write it. Let "tears such as fathers shed" speak his importance to me. He afterwards, on a particular circumstance being called to mind, which I lamented, threw himself into my arms; when a most extraordinary thing occurred, and a sensation equally extraordinary possessed me. He disappeared, and yet never seemed to have been so intensely present. I seemed at once to be celestially filled with his very self, and yet I did not embrace him at all, or even behold him. Finding him nevertheless somehow so surely with me, I asked him how it was; when I was answered by a voice out of my own lips, bidding me "look in the water." I did so, and beheld my son's face in my own, so completely was one being absorbed in the other. But the unusual transport was too much for a spirit which had been loosed from earth, not entirely and by death, like his own, but only in the temporary separation of a dream; and he resumed his individuality, and tenderly begged my forgiveness. He had supposed I was dead. Adding the words, "One moment," he again disappeared, not as before, but in separation; yet had scarcely done so but was again visible, and standing in the same spot. He had been as anxious as a blessed spirit could be that the dream which had thus brought me to him should not be disturbed; and in that moment of time, with a speed which our electric-telegraphs will render credible without depriving it of its wonder, he had been twenty-six millions of miles from where he stood, in order to look on my sleeping body, and squeeze a heavenly poppy on the bed. O, if you can believe any thing, believe it of heaven and love!

I now found that I was in the First Heaven, or that to which (as I imagined) blessed spirits first go after passing through certain stages of the earth's atmosphere, where they halt for greater or less portions of time during their transit. And this First Heaven was the planet Venus. The Second Heaven is the planet Mercury; and the "Third Heaven," of the ecstasies in which we have heard so much, I thus for the first time understood in respect to its number, for it is the Sun; which, omitting satellites, the retainers only of other orbs, is the third orb from the earth, the greatest heaven in our system, and the origin of all the terms implying thrice blessed. This Third Heaven, so called in relation to earth, is the first heaven of heavens in relation to the general universe of stars, and the great agent, under God, of all the life and beauty of our portion of it, though itself subordinate to that second and greater heaven of heavens (the next first of how many!), towards which, or round which, it is now speeding with all our planets about it, as if with eagerness to know some new divine purpose. What a speeder, and what a paradise! made of paradises unnumbered, whose hints of themselves on earth are love and flowers. And how well may its attendant orbs roll with a like eagerness around it, being all, though they know not why, bound and borne along on the same heavenly journey, and all partaking of a circulation like that of the very blood of heaven itself!

But upon these mightiest marvels I must not touch farther; nor can I enter at present, hard as it is to withhold myself, into accounts of other spirits who soon joined us, each in the reverse order of its date of departure from earthly life. Love and reverence, full of memories yearning to speak, would not allow me to say little; and the space to which this fragment must be limited allows not even that. Suffice to observe at present, that in each of the successive heavens, to the first of which my dream had brought me, the inhabitants combine in their natures the choicest portions of the natures from which they have made progression, and some participation of those to which they are to attain. In other words, they bring with them the best portions of their human nature, its form and aspect included, and receive in addition an advanced nature, including portions of that which prevails in the heaven to which they will go next. Indeed, so to speak, the First Heaven is nothing but another and diviner earth, composed of all which it was best and noblest to have and to desire in this. Therefore in part it is humanly perfected, and in part angelically gifted.

The inhabitants lead the same lives, live in the same houses, walk in the same gardens, and behold the same skies, landscapes, and other sights, great and small, as they did on earth; but all of so perfected a kind, that no earthly objection, great or small, could by human being be made to them; and as they possess a share of the gifts, mental and bodily, which are attributed to angels, who are the inhabitants of the next, or Second Heaven (the planet we call Mercury), they are for the most part the real angels, or semi-angels, who visit and comfort earth; adding, by reason of their human experience, this special, though it must be considered inferior, sympathy to their graver ones, — that they enter into the pleasures as well as pains of the human societies in which they lived; enjoy, in a certain superior sense, the hearing of their conversations, and sight of their very pastimes; nay, have, like them, their favourite earthly holidays — one of which is the anniversary of the birth of Christ, our — Christmas Day.

The reader is not to suppose that any thing which is said in this article is intended to advocate such an absurdity as (I blush to introduce the word into it) *spirit-rapping*, or other like mechanical pretensions to the supernatural, which confuse and debase the spiritual standard, and refute themselves by their inconsistency and vulgarity. If the spirits thus introduced to us can rap, why can they not speak? if talk to us with such material things as knuckles, why not with tongues? — things which are also the more spiritual of the two, or at least more conversant with spiritual discourse.

But not to waste the reader's time on that clumsy contrivance, I return to my beloved people of the First Heaven. They divide the holidays to which I have alluded between heaven and earth; and such was the one I passed with them last Christmas Day — the day on which I dreamt that I had died. Such was that never-to-be-forgotten day, and such is the day, if their visits of my dreams prosper, which I hope to pass with them on the Christmas Day now at hand. The whole time was spent in alternately enjoying the identical old Christmas, — not even optimised (as far as they could help it) in heaven, — and in darting down, they and my spirit with them, to the Christmas on earth, smiling at some of the same music, rejoicing even in the good-natured and happy jests, and whispering consolation to "survivors" (*survivors!!*) when tender recollections mingled melancholy with their joy, and awoke sighs which Heaven is pleased to hear: for the softest and longest-drawn sighs, or rather the wishes within them (for the sighs themselves are but sorry travellers), can reach heaven at all times with speed inconceivable; and the spirits for whom they sigh can be with them on earth as instantaneously.[3]

O, enchanting beyond expression was that day to me, with the beloved household faces, young and old, — once supposed lost, now found, and known to be possessible for ever, — once breaking up habits and almost the heart with them, now restoring them, never to be broken, — once producing the doubt whether, if ever we could see them again, it would yet be possible for us to see them as they were — see them with the same lineaments, the same smiles, the same emotional aspects and manners throughout, with which we used to sympathise in joy and in sorrow, to laugh and to shed tears, to question and be questioned, and to interchange a hundred domestic nothings, all great somethings to us; and here now all again realised, never be so again mourned!

There is nothing great or little in nature, except as the heart makes it such; and therefore nobody must wonder that in heaven as well as on earth the commonest enjoyments of a Christmas Day could be repeated. God made laughter as well as tears, and mirth itself, when it is good, as well as the divine portions of melancholy. All else is owing to the dullness and hardness of the material through which He works, — material necessary and unmalignant, though producing transient effects that appear otherwise, but ending in flowers and fruits as beautiful as their roots appear black. With a wish, therefore, on that day (for as there is no depravity of will in heaven, every wish that can be realised in the particular sphere is indulged), — with a wish on that day, the room in which we sate became, first cold with frost, then warm and bright with a fire, then brighter with lights, then warmer with curtains, then lustrous with the glistening holly and its glowing berries. Even the mistletoe was not forgotten: and as there are death-less little children in heaven, there were veritable Christmas-boxes for them. I wish I could stop to describe them. No princes ever had the like; and yet they were like the good old Christmas-boxes, too.

Very joyous were those Christmas hours in the skies, and hardly less so those which we divided with them, and passed in the Christmas-keeping home on earth, — at one moment being those twenty-six millions of miles above the surface of the earth, singing earthly songs with earthly-sounding though celestial voices; and at another, mingling unseen with the earthly company below, while grace and love made *their* voices semi-celestial too; and the very want of the perfect celestialness made us feel over again the sweetest of earthly pities. Even I, assuming the privileges of the party I came with, ventured to kiss here and there a face that drooped awhile over some tender anxiety for myself; and though I could not suggest the thought as they did, of being perhaps present with those whom I consoled, I too, with spiritual lips, unfelt though not unrelieving, took away a portion of the tears that consoled my own trials.

THE OCCASIONAL
Nos. XIII, XIV

YOUNG OLD STATESMEN.

Lord Palmerston and Lord John Russell — Characterization of Lord Palmerston by the Times *— Longevity of the present age — Instances of its fitness for active government in five noble Lords — Defects and merits of the Premier, and numerous causes of his success.*

July 9, 1859

The question which has so often been put of late,[1] whether old men ought to remain at the head of governments and not give way to younger, appears likely to be set at rest for the present, not merely by the return of Lords Palmerston and John Russell to power,[2] (which might be regarded, however unjustly, as nothing but one of the old exclusive alternations between Whig and Tory,) but by the busy public life which Lord John has been leading for some time past, ever ready to write and to speak, always to the purpose, and particularly by the address which Lord Palmerston has just made to the students of the London University,[3] full of the energy which it recommends, and genially inculcating the addition of general to particular knowledge. Lord John, it is true, in these days of increased longevity, can hardly be called old at sixty-three, old as he is considered by younger men, and responsible as he is held for his age by the takers of the youthful side of the question; but Lord Palmerston, at seventy-five, has attained to a time of life which, in consequence of the dictum of a reverend Hebrew text, is still considered no small advance beyond the allotted period of existence; yet here, says the *Times*, in a fit of congenial vivacity, he is: —

Here is Lord Palmerston, still gay; still winning friends; still open to conviction; still learning; and, besides governing the nation, able to make a good speech for anybody that wants one. Here we have him distributing prizes at the University College, surrounded by some of the chief educationists of the country, and surpassing them on their own ground, even while, with his wonted good nature, he is reminding people of their good sayings. Well, tell us how this is, you jolly young fellows who think the fun of life must be over at thirty, and that at forty a man is a confirmed old fogey, good for nothing under the sun, except, perhaps, to make money and leave it to his betters. Your Premier is twice this age; beat him, if you can. Run a tilt with him anywhere. Cross rapiers at a table, put on the gloves with him at St. Stephen's, draw a bow with him for a set speech on an important subject, and you will find him your better, — better for hand, and for eye, and for stamina. How is it, think you? What virtue or what vice of our system still brings this man to the top of us all? He is only an Irish Peer; he has enough for his position, but no more; he pretends neither to much religion nor to none; he is not even an orator, for he is incapable of a philippic, a tremendous argument, or an overpowering climax. The old idea of the man who wields a fierce democracy or commands the applause of a senate is scarcely fulfilled in him who again and again becomes by common consent the first man in the nation. There is a mystery to be solved in a result of which the means are so wanting to the end. It is a mystery of nature and of art; and when Lord Palmerston comes before a throng of young aspirants for fame and advancement, and tells them the right way to get on, we hail him not merely as a man who has just got up some views on education, but as one who has solved in his own case a great secret of life, and now tells us how he has done it.[4]

This secret, or rather one of the great secrets, — "*a great secret,*" according to the *Times,* consists in perseverance in the pursuit fixed upon by the student, accompanied (as before mentioned) by the aids and refreshments to it resulting from the cultivation of general knowledge. For with regard to the noble Lord's success as an individual, apart from causes communicable to student minds, our contemporary intimates, that the chief of these are "the social qualities — a capacity for friendship, a real interest in worthy persons and objects, and a good-natured indifference to the petty animosities of the vulgar"; in other words, "a good and generous disposition"; a thing, which it justly as well as pleasantly tells us, a man might find it almost as vain to recommend where it does not exist, as to advise his students "to stand five feet ten in their shoes." Perseverance, therefore, refreshed and invigorated as aforesaid, is the one great impartable secret of success in life; and of this secret the noble Prime Minister is the great teacher and example.

Assuredly the fact of his Lordship's success in life nobody can deny; and as little will the proximate cause of it be denied by anybody who knows the untiring energy of his career, and his indomitable attention to business. Whether, at the same time, the power to persevere in the like degree, or sometimes in any degree, may not be a condition of success as difficult of communication to the youthful nature as the "good and generous disposition," is a point not touched upon by our contemporary, nor perhaps is it required of his object. Most British natures are remarkable for having some kind of energy; and it is therefore reasonably presumable, that such of them as have no particular predilection for pursuits that run counter to success in the ordinary or extraordinary acceptation of the word, which is not likely to be the case with many, may profit by having their wits encouraged to their tasks by such a teacher of prosperity as Lord Palmerston.

All this however does not suffice to explain the wonder of his lordship's nature, how it is that at seventy-five he is the man he is; nor what is the cause of the like if not the identical wonders in other men, which appear to have settled the question whether old age disqualifies people for the government of their countries. We believe that many old men might always be found thoroughly qualified; especially in these longævous times, when the arts of prolonging life have come to be better understood; when cheerfuller views of life itself, and less gloomy ones of futurity, have prevailed among a "reading public"; and when such men of seventy-five as have had the good fortune not to be born of intemperate blood, and who possess brains enough of their own to be reasonable in their enjoyments, are to be accounted perhaps no older than men used to be at fifty-five, or even fifty, a hundred or two years ago. For readers of books are surprised to find, how often in former days fifty was regarded as what we call "age," and a medium between fifty and sixty old age. Drinking and other bad habits may have caused this premature decline, and life may have lasted longer in the country than in town, as was the case in the extremest instances of longevity, such as those of Old Parr and Henry Jenkins;[5] nor was the greater amount of life which now prevails, ever wanting in individuals here and there among the inhabitants of towns. Its general duration, however, was undoubtedly inferior to what it is now. At no time in English history does there appear to have flourished such a contemporary cluster of green old ages as we now possess in the persons of Lord Palmerston, Lord Derby, Lord Lyndhurst, Lord Brougham, and Lord Campbell; all of them were exhibiting as much of the spirit of life as its experience; some of them more; and all rendering the boldest and most eloquent of their juniors cautious how they provoke them. Where is the man living, who paying laborious attention to his profession, is so ready to put forth a book for his amusement as Lord Campbell?[6] Where a man combining such a variety of knowledge with such indefatigable public zeal as Lord Brougham? Where such an oracle of the fastidious and aristocratical house in which he speaks, as the son of the American artist (Copley), Lord Lyndhurst?[7] Where a man so triumphant with life and oratory over his gout, as Lord Derby,[8] or one (if we are not misinformed) who so triumphs over his gout and his aristocracy itself, by giving his friends (absit common place) the most jovial thumps on the back? Finally, as to Lord Palmerston, here, as the *Times* exclaims, he is: "beat him, if you can." The next to his lordship, in regard to age, though at a considerable distance, is his colleague Lord John Russell, who beats him, we conceive, in many things, depth of sentiment for one; which the Premier, we suspect, confounds with sentimentality; a mistake, at the root of which lay that non-estimation, perhaps non-perception, of the feelings of the country, which occasioned his last ejection from office. But as a brilliant and effective sum total, beat him certainly nobody does. The *Times* says he is no orator, "for he is incapable of a

philippic, a tremendous argument, or an overpowering climax."
Perhaps so: for he appears to take nothing seriously to heart,
but success itself; and if he can do this with light weapons,
why should he try weightier? Mr. Disraeli is a master of grave
as well as light sarcasm; yet both came to nothing, nay, left
their master reduced to silence, when, exasperated by the
noble lord's indifference to his attacks, and remonstrating with
him on what he described as their parliamentary want of
propriety, he was answered, in a tone of good-natured regret,
that he (Palmerston) was *sorry he could not be more angry*
with the Right Honourable gentleman; that he would willingly
be so, if it became him; but that really he found it out of his
power." No heaviest blow, aimed by exasperation, could be
more effective than the sweeping of a feather across the face
like this.

A multitude of causes, all fortunate, have contributed to
make Lord Palmerston the man he is. In the first place, he
comes of a talented family. Then he must have received a good
constitution, or very good reasons for taking care of it, from
his parents. His male progenitors, up to the sixth generation,
probably higher if we knew the dates of anterior deaths, were
with one exception, all long lived persons. His means were
always above want, yet not affording encouragement to idleness. He received an unbigoted education. His birth and political opinions, combined with address, rendered him a favourite,
though not a slave, of the aristocracy; a certain openness at the
same time, real or apparent, to freer opinions, always keeping
the democracy in hopes of him, as with some exceptions they
are doing at this moment, though he is still putting off reform.
He has been accused, with equally lucky amounts of absurdity,
of selling himself to foreign powers, and doing nothing but
setting them by the ears; charges, which naturally make reasonable people of all parties willing to defend him. He has
encountered enough trouble from time to time to give his
prosperity some of the benefits of adversity. He has even succeeded, by dint of a certain pleasantness and heartiness of
manner in general, in saving himself from the most dangerous

of all perils to a prosperous man, that of allowing his prosperity to tempt him into airs of self-sufficiency, if not of contempt, towards persons whom he takes for inferiors. He is even said to have been able to convert such persons from enemies into friends. He has been considered handsome; is still of an engaging presence; and above all he has animal spirits, and a constitutional love of action. These two characteristics are the habits of his life, and they have kept him what he is; though he could no more have acquired them for himself than he could have been his own father and mother, or than he could impart them by admonition to the students of London University.

But so much remains to be said on Young Old Leading Men, that the reader's indulgence for the conclusion of this article must be begged for next week.

July 30, 1859

The inculcation of a love of general knowledge, as a help as well as ornament to knowledge, particular and professional, was mentioned in our remarks of last week * as the main leading point, next to perseverance, in Lord Palmerston's address to the students of the London University. Another important one remains to be noticed, in the quotation which he made from the great, good-natured statesman, Charles James Fox, to the effect, that failures in first instances, if followed up by unflagging endeavour, often afford better auguries of eventual success, than those attending success at once. The success at once (though it hardly might have been thought prudent, or even just, to say so) is indeed sometimes owing to the absence of qualities that retard victory by the multiplicity and anxiety of their number. It might have been thought still less proper to add, that immediate success is not seldom perilous to the modesty and perseverance of the succeeder, by inducing him to suppose that he has nothing further

---

* Now two weeks back. The appearance of the article has been twice delayed by the pressure of more immediate topics.

to acquire. And most imprudent and indelicate, indeed impossible it would have been on such an occasion to observe, that the arbiters and bestowers of college laurels are not always qualified to estimate the heads that most deserve them. Every tutor is not possessed of the self-knowledge or magnanimity of Johnson's Dr. Adams, who considered the future lexicographer as "above his mark." Swift obtained his degree at college, not as a right, but as a favour. And in the certificate of character and qualifications given to the first Napoleon, on his leaving the military college in which he was educated, he was described as a docile good sort of person, who would make an "excellent seaman."[9]

The good of associating general with particular knowledge, — of historical and biographical reading, for instance, with mechanics or mathematics, — might have been illustrated in connexion with perseverance, by the well-known but always welcome anecdote of Robert Bruce, who was encouraged to maintain his almost despairing efforts against the English by the sight of the spider, who, notwithstanding downfalls that seemed as if they would never end, persisted in climbing up again towards his point, till he gained it. (If the Chinese, who are great believers in ancestral influences, had been aware of this anecdote of the Scottish hero, perhaps they would not have been so astonished the other day as they were, in seeing his descendant, Lord Elgin, persist in sailing up their rivers, and bearding their forts.) We are tempted to add a less famous anecdote of the same prince, because it deserves to be equally popular, and because it shows, after its fashion, the same determination to let no obstacles prevent a man's doing what he thinks right; not even conventionalism, or usages of fashionable worlds. Furthermore we hold the anecdote eminently becoming "a prince and a gentleman." King Robert had just gained one of his victories, and was resuming his progress in triumph round a conquered country, when he heard the cry of a woman in distress.

"What is that?" said the King, drawing bridle.

"Oh, nothing, sir," answered an attendant, smiling.

"What is your nothing, sir?" returned the King, a little angrily.

"May it please your Majesty," (we substitute modern parlance for ancient, in order to hinder spirit from being disturbed by letter,) "may it please your Majesty, it is nothing but a soldier's wife, — in fact, the laundress of a regiment, — who is about to be confined, and whom the moving of the army perplexes, because she is not quite settled to the matter."

"Halt!" cried King Robert to his army. The army halted, boot, saddle, trumpets, triumph, and all; and King Robert saw the poor woman comfortably bedded and waited on, before it stirred again.

"Nothing but a soldier's wife!" said the King. "What are we all here but soldiers? and who shall talk of any wife of ours, and call her 'nothing'?"

The trumpets resumed their victorious progress; and tender were the strong hearts of the soldiers towards King Robert.

But to return to the other portion of our subject — the question, whether men in years ought to be administrators of Government. There is an essay on this question in the "Morals" of Plutarch; [10] and very angry is the good heathen statesman and clergyman — (for such was Plutarch, holder of various offices under Trajan, chief magistrate in Cheronæa, priest of Apollo at Delphi, and protester, equally liberal and devout, against the unworthy fables told of the gods by the poets) — very angry is Plutarch at the notion that age was to prevent a man from retaining one of the best habits of life, for which experience itself had served to qualify him, and which was at once his business, his glory, and his enjoyment. He looks upon that state as the best governed, which has young men for its hands, and old men for its brains. He insists that the soul does not of necessity decay like the body; nay, that age does not always imply even bodily incapacity for work; that the desire of honour never grows old; that for a man to be expected to retire to a country life after governing a state is like requiring him to make a clown of himself, or to lead the life of an old horse; and that, for his part, he shall do no such thing, but continue to serve his country and his fellow-creatures, and to do all the good he could, as long as he could prove his right to do so by the retention of the power to do it.

These arguments are accompanied by cases in point; as that of Pericles, who was never more vigorous in governing than when he was old, inducing the Athenians to fight or not fight, just as it pleased him; those of Phocion, Masinissa, and Cato,[11] who themselves led armies to victory in old age; and that of Agesilaus, of whom Xenophon cries out in a transport, "What youth ever existed that surpassed his old age? that was more terrible to his enemies, caused them greater joy when he died, or was more missed by his friends?" Masinissa, Plutarch informs us, having been in a great battle when he was near ninety, was seen next day in front of his tent eating a piece of brown bread; and though he died not long afterwards, he left a son that was but four years old which beats fine old Sir Stephen Fox,[12] the founder in age of the Holland and Ilchester families; and Coke of Norfolk,[13] who not long since, at the age of eighty, gave us another noble family of Leicester.

See a number of the like examples of excellent old statesmen and generals in Cicero's treatise on "Old Age."

The truth is, as Plutarch observes, that the whole real point in this question about young and old governors is not a matter of age, but of individual strength and fitness; and that you might with as much reason take a simpleton for a leader merely because he was young, as refuse a wise man for one, on no other ground than that of his years. What have the Austrians just profited from having been led by an emperor, young enough to be Louis Napoleon's son?[14]

We shall conclude this article with an anecdote of a septuagenarian, possessed of a profound legislative repute, not because it is most apposite or even most amusing, but because it is quite Palmerstonian, we conceive, both in the matter of life of mind, and the personal retention of youth and movement. It is of Montesquieu, author of the "Spirit of Laws," and is related in the "Life of Lord Charlemont," who during his travels about a century ago, and in company with another gentleman, visited the illustrious old Frenchman at his seat near Bordeaux. They were so anxious to avail themselves of his willingness to see them, that they called before he was up, and were shown by the servant into his library.

The first object of curiosity that presented itself was a table at which he had apparently been reading the night before, a book lying upon it open, turned down, and a lamp extinguished.

Eager (says his Lordship) to know the nocturnal studies of this great philosopher, we immediately flew to the book. It was a volume of Ovid's Works, containing his Elegies, and open at one of the most gallant poems of that master of love. Before we could overcome our surprise, it was greatly increased by the entrance of the President (Montesquieu was President of the Parliament of Bourdeaux), whose appearance and manner was totally opposite to the idea which we had formed to ourselves of him. Instead of a grave, austere philosopher, whose presence might strike with awe such boys as we were, the person who now addressed us, was a gay, polite, sprightly Frenchman, who, after a thousand genteel compliments, and a thousand thanks for the honour we had done him, desired to know whether we would not breakfast; and upon our declining the offer, having already eaten at an inn not far from the house, "Come, then," says he, "let us walk: the day is fine, and I long to show you my villa, as I have endeavoured to form it according to the English taste, and to cultivate and dress it in the English manner." Following him into the farm, we soon arrived at the skirts of a beautiful wood, cut into walks, and paled round, the entrance to which was barricaded with a moveable bar about three feet high, fastened with a padlock. "Come," said he, searching in his pocket for the key; "it is not worth our while to wait for the key: you, I am sure, can leap as well as I can, and this bar shall not stop me." So saying, he ran at the bar, and fairly jumped over it; while we followed him with amazement, though not without delight, to see the philosopher likely to become our playfellow.[15]

Lord Charlemont frequently afterwards met the philosopher in society, and was astonished with the inexhaustible grace and gaiety of his manners and conversations, particularly in the company of ladies: though he adds, that on reflection it was not surprising, considering that the profound author of the "Spirit of Laws" had written also the "Persian Letters" and the truly gallant "Temple de Gnide."

We do not imply by this extract, that Lord Palmerston's reading lies in the direction of "Ovid's Epistles." We know not what he reads, and should not expect it to lie much in any poetical direction. Neither should we look at his hands for another "Spirit of Laws." But here is a prototype of the eternally young old statesman; of the able statesman too; of the man charming in company, ever ready of speech, and never failing in spirits; and one who, though he beats Montesquieu's age at that time by five years, rides out a hunting with Emperors, and does not baulk, of course, a five-barred gate.

APPENDIX

THE OCCASIONAL

LEIGH HUNT

September 3, 1859

The readers of this journal need hardly be informed that they now see the heading of "The Occasional" for the last time.[1] The hand which has furnished all of the papers under that title, from time to time during the present year, even to so late a date as this day fortnight, now lies beneath the earth; the genius of Leigh Hunt can no longer animate the pages of the *Spectator*; and it is fit that the name of the particular division in which we are now writing should pass away with him who originated and sustained it. It is also thought fitting not to allow it to cease without some word of farewell, uttered, as it were, over the grave of the departed.

The writer to whom has been assigned the mournful task of pronouncing that farewell had many opportunities of seeing Leigh Hunt in his most domestic moments, and is therefore, perhaps, so far better qualified to speak of the complete being — author and man — than those who only knew him through his books. This twofold knowledge is particularly necessary in the case of one who put so much of his own personality into the productions of his pen. Sincerity and sympathy were the two central principles of the whole of Leigh Hunt's writings and actions. They were the secret of the love which he inspired in all who knew him; and they were at the same time the cause of the misapprehensions with respect to him which at one time prevailed, but which time has brushed away. His sense of truth was so strong that he could not, as most period-ical writers do, sink his own identity in the identity of the paper for which he might be working; nor would he equivocate

with any opinion which he held. He was therefore pinned
down, as indeed he desired to be, to the letter of everything
he wrote; and people who did not like the writings vented
their dissatisfaction on the man. But, if this entailed a penalty,
it also brought a blessing. No author has so frequently inspired
in his readers a feeling of personal regard, and a wish for
friendly intercourse; no one so completely realized in private
life the ideal suggested by his works. For many years he drew
his house, as to a place of pilgrimage, visitors from all parts
of England, Scotland, Ireland, and even America; and bashful
young verse-writers from the provinces have not unfrequently
thrown themselves on the kindness and allowance of the
veteran poet of *Rimini*.

It has been sometimes objected that the writings of Leigh
Hunt are not sufficiently dogmatic — that they are too prone
to leave questions undecided, and, mooting all conceivable
possibilities, to leave everything unsettled. The assertion is
merely an exaggerated form of stating what in truth is the
most valuable characteristic of his works — or rather of his
later works, for his earlier are certainly not wanting in hard
blows, strenuously and skilfully directed against the enemies
of progress and of liberal opinion. As the heat of the contest
abated, the natural kindness and geniality of the writer trium-
phed over the battle-sternness he had often been compelled to
assume; and thenceforth the writings of Leigh Hunt became
conspicuous for the depth and largeness of their charity. To
those who would rather they had retained their original
character, it is sufficient to say, without disparaging that kind
of writing (which is really necessary in the rough work of the
world), that plenty of it may be found in our standard literature, plenty in the columns of the daily and weekly press,
plenty in the utterances of the pulpit. It is surely an advantage,
a gain, a something special, fresh, and original, to have a series
of works, of which the animating soul is a belief in the divine
possibility of goodness under all forms of evil. We have smiters
and denunciators out of number; the glowing and generous
dogmatism of Carlyle has called up a host of imitators, who,

while quite as positive as their master, possess neither his brain nor his heart: let us also accept and reverence the Apostle of Charity — the man whose poems and essays were all written in the anticipation of a Future of love and wisdom, such as many have dreamt of, but few believed in and worked for with such constancy as he. There is not too much of sentiment in the world; there is no excess of faith, as a vital principle distinct from orthodox routine; nor are men likely in this commercial land to forget the realties of life for the graces of fancy. Certainly they will find no teaching with that object in the writings of Leigh Hunt. But they *will* find what is most necessary and healthful as a counterpoise to the hardening effects of the ordinary intercourse of business; — a love of beauty, as one of the tangible revelations of God; a love of Love, as the higher, intangible revelation, uttered perpetually to the human heart; a belief in the perfectability of the species; a proneness to make allowances for others, as the only means by which we can earn the right to make allowances for our own short-comings and many errors; a reverence for the truly religious duty of cheerfulness, as a golden clue through the darkness and perplexity of sorrow; a disposition to recognize friendship and self-sacrifice as the first of duties, and a regard for Nature, and for the amenities of books and art, as the first of pleasures. Various as were the writings of Leigh Hunt — wide as was their range over many departments of literature — we have summed up in that sentence the leading principles which run through all. Of what other writer could the same things be said, with such complete applicability? And is it not an advantage, even to the affluent literature of England, to have received the addition of a domain at once so novel and so noble in its characteristics?

Leigh Hunt was neither a partisan in his politics, nor a bigot in his religion, nor a mere author in his writings. In whatever he did he had the good of the human race at heart, as the first and chief consideration. It was this tendency, as shown even in the early days of the *Examiner*, which attracted to him the friendship of Shelley. The journalist suffered for many years on account of that friendship; for the phalanx of Tory writers chose to identify him with the whole of Shelley's opinions, though it was known that he dissented from some, while on all points recognizing the noble nature of the poet of the *Cenci*. But he always regarded it as a privilege to suffer on behalf of such a man; and it was a fitting close to his life that the last words he wrote in public should have been in vindication of his dead friend from what he regarded as a misapprehension, and that the very last words of any kind to which he put his pen should have been a letter also having reference to Shelley. That letter was written no longer ago than Thursday week — less than three days before his death.

One characteristic of Leigh Hunt, for which few gave him credit, was his great capacity for work. His writings were the result of immense labour and painstaking; of the most conscientious investigation of facts, where facts were needed; and of a complete devotion of his faculties towards the object to be accomplished. Notwithstanding his great experience, he was never a very rapid writer. He corrected, excised, reconsidered, and elaborated his productions (unless when pressed for time), with the most minute attention to details. The habit increased as he grew older; and some of his later poems are as near perfection as anything human can be.

A week ago, Leigh Hunt was still gladdening the hearts of his friends, who, though they had some cause for fearing the worst, could hardly believe that the end was so near. But, though they can never again answer the grasp of the true hand, nor meet the cordial eyes, let them not forget that the world is endowed with the legacy of his genius, and those who knew him with the memory of his life.

E[DMUND] O[LLIER]

NOTES

ON THE SEPARATION OF RUSSIA FROM
THE BRITISH INTEREST

1. "Political Examiner," No. 1, *Examiner* (Jan. 3, 1808), pp. 1-2.

2. Alexander I (1777—1825), Emperor of Russia, 1801—1825. Fearing the strength and ambition of Napoleon, Alexander had thrown the weight of his armies against France. In 1805, he had suffered a crushing defeat at Austerlitz, and in 1807, another at Friedland. Forced to seek terms of peace, Alexander negotiated with Napoleon at Tilsit in 1807, without the Ministers of either country being present. The settlement was considered reasonably fair and honorable to the Russians, but severe strictures were included against England, a former Russian ally, should she refuse to accept the terms of the new agreement. By 1812, however, Napoleon's war with Russia had begun.

3. Eleonora Galigai, the wife of the Marquis d'Ancre, marshal of France, was convicted of sorcery and executed in 1617. Maria de Médicis was the queen of Henry IV of France.

4. By the Tilsit treaty, Russia secretly agreed to arouse Sweden, Denmark, and Portugal against England should the latter object to the terms of the treaty. Canning became informed of the agreement, attacked Copenhagen in Sept. 1807, and carried off the Danish fleet. The British action was severely criticized by most of Europe, and was also protested against in both Houses of Parliament.

5. Armand Augustin Louis, Marquis de Caulaincourt (1773—1827), was a French diplomat to whom Napoleon assigned many important commissions. In 1807 Caulaincourt was sent as an Ambassador to St. Petersburg.

A LETTER OF STRONG ADVICE TO HIS ROYAL HIGHNESS
THE PRINCE OF WALES ON HIS CHARACTER AND
CONNECTIONS

1. Bolingbroke, *Works* (London, 1753—1783), X, *Letters on the Spirit of Patriotism: On the Idea of a Patriot King: and On the State of Parties . . .* , 209, 211-212.

2. "Political Examiner," No. 34, *Examiner* (Aug. 21, 1808), pp. 529-531. One of Hunt's earliest articles on the Prince of Wales.

3. Edward Young, *Love of Fame, Satire II*, 282.

4. Elizabeth Billington (1768–1818), famous English singer.

5. Confidential adviser to the Prince of Wales. See Hunt's article on Sheridan at the time of his death in 1816; reprinted in *Leigh Hunt's Literary Criticism*, ed. by L. H. and C. W. Houtchens (Columbia University Press, 1956).

DELIVERANCE OF EUROPE

1. "Political Examiner," No. 37, *Examiner* (Sept. 11, 1808), pp. 577-579.

2. Francis II (1768-1835), the last Holy Roman Emperor; ruled as Francis I, Emperor of Austria, 1804–1835. His daughter, Maria Louisa, married Napoleon in 1810.

3. Frederick William III (1770–1840), King of Prussia, 1797–1840, witnessed the defeat of his armies by the French at Jena and Auerstedt in 1806 and the reduction of his kingdom by the treaty of Tilsit in 1807.

4. Frederick VI (1768–1839), King of Denmark, 1808–1839.

5. Pope Pius VII (1742–1823), Luigi Barnaba Chiaramonti, crowned Napoleon in Paris in 1804, but later opposed him. On Feb. 2, 1808, Rome was occupied by General Miollis, and the Pope lost several of the papal states.

6. Following the invasion of Spain by the French under Murat, Charles IV (1748–1819) was forced to abdicate in favor of his son Ferdinand VII (1784–1833). During 1808–1813, Ferdinand was held prisoner by Napoleon, and Napoleon's brother Joseph ruled in Spain.

7. William Windham (1750–1810), in William Pitt's Cabinet as Secretary for War, 1794-1801.

8. John Whitelocke (1757-1833), lieutenant general in the British army. He was involved in a famous military scandal, tried, and cashiered in 1808.

FRANCE AND ENGLAND

1. "Political Examiner," No. 97, *Examiner* (Nov. 19, 1809), pp. 737-739.

2. Pope, "Elegy to the Memory of an Unfortunate Lady," l. 14.

3. Charles XII (1682-1718), King of Sweden (1697-1718), known as the "Alexander of the North" and the "Madman of the North."

4. Gaspar Melchor de Jovellanos or Jove-Llanos (1744–1811), Spanish statesman and author.

5. Ferdinand I (1751–1825), King of the Two Sicilies; King of Naples (1759–1806, 1815–1825) as Ferdinand IV.

6. In 1809 England sent an expedition to capture Antwerp. The result was disastrous. Four thousand British soldiers died of fever in the swamps of Walcheren. On this event, Hunt published in the *Examiner* (Jan. 7, 1810), p. 7, the following poem which is omitted from the Oxford edition of Hunt's poetry:

WALCHEREN EXPEDITION: OR,
THE ENGLISHMAN'S LAMENT FOR THE LOSS OF HIS COUNTRYMEN

1.

Ye brave, enduring Englishmen,
 Who dash thro' fire and flood,
And spend with equal thoughtlessness
 Your money and your blood,
I sing of that black season,
 Which all true hearts deplore,
  When ye lay,
  Night and day,
Upon Walcheren's swampy shore.

2.

'Twas in the summer's sunshine
 Your mighty host set sail
With valour in each longing heart
 And vigour in the gale;
The Frenchman dropp'd his laughter,
 The Fleming's thoughts grew sore,
  As ye came
  In your fame
To the dark and swampy shore.

3.

But foul delays encompass'd ye
 More dang'rous than the foe,
As Antwerp's town and its guarded fleet
 Too well for Britons know:
One spot alone ye conquer'd
 With hosts unknown of yore;
  And your might
  Day and night,
Lay still on the swampy shore.

4.

In vain your dauntless mariners
 Mourn'd ev'ry moment lost,
In vain your soldiers threw their eyes
 In flame to the hostile coast;

The fire of gallant aspects
     Was doom'd to be no more,
          And your fame
          Sunk with shame
In the dark and the swampy shore.

5.

Ye died not in the triumphing
     Of the battle-shaken flood,
Ye died not on the charging field
     In the mingle of brave blood;
But 'twas in wasting fevers
     For full three months and more,
          Britons born,
          Pierc'd with scorn,
Lay at rot on the swampy shore.

6.

No ship came o'er to bring relief
     No orders came to save;
But DEATH stood there and never stirr'd,
     Still counting for the grave.
They lay down, and they linger'd,
     And died with feelings sore,
          And the waves
          Pierc'd their graves
Thro' the dark and the swampy shore.

7.

Oh England! Oh my Countrymen!
     Ye ne'er shall thrive again
Till freed from Councils obstinate
     Of mercenary men.
So toll for the six thousand
     Whose miseries are o'er,
          Where the deep,
          To their sleep,
Bemoans on the swampy shore.

DINNER IN HONOUR OF "THE IMMORTAL PITT"

1. "One wreaks ruin on a city and its hapless homes, that he may drink from a jewelled cup and sleep on Tyrian purple." *Virgil, with an English Translation* by H. Rushton Fairclough (London, 1922), I, 151.

2. "Political Examiner," No. 125, *Examiner* (June 3, 1810), pp. 337-339. The preceding year, Hunt referred to the Pitt dinner as the "most gross, most inefficient of all political farces," where the

guests "still sought anxiously for that great man's memory where it was so often drowned — at the bottom of the sixth bottle." *Examiner*, (June 4, 1809), p. 355. William Pitt died on Jan. 23, 1806. For Hunt's characterization of Pitt in the *Tatler* (Aug. 27, 1831), see our text, p. 437, n. 13.

3. George Canning (1770–1827) refused office in Perceval's Cabinet; Richard le Poer Trench, second Earl of Clancarty and first Viscount Clancarty (1767–1837); Henry Dundas, first Viscount Melville (1742–1811), member of the Privy Council, and for almost thirty years the most powerful politician in Scotland; Sir Vicary Gibbs (1751–1820), Attorney General, 1807–1812; Charles Philip Yorke (1764–1834), First Lord of the Admiralty.

4. John Scott, first Earl of Eldon (1751–1838), Lord Chancellor; Sir Henry Phipps, first Earl of Mulgrave, first Viscount Normanby, third Baron Mulgrave (1755–1831), resigned as First Lord of the Admiralty in May, 1810, became master of the ordnance, and kept his seat in the Cabinet; Francis-Hervey Mountmorres, Viscount Mountmorres (1756–1833); Sir Charles Price (1747?–1818), representative in Parliament for the city of London; (?) Rev. Sir Charles-John Anderson (1767–1846), prebendary of Thorngate, in Lincoln Minster, and rector of Lea; Sir James Murray (afterwards Murray-Pulteney), seventh Baronet of Clermont (1751?–1811), general, M.P. for Weymouth, 1790–1811; Sir William Curtis (1752–1829), M.P. for London, 1790–1818.

5. Pope, "The First Satire of the Second Book of Horace, Imitated," l. 128.

6. William Thomas Fitzgerald (1759?–1829).

7. William Mellish, M.P. for Middlesex.

PROPOSED MONUMENT TO LOCKE

1. "Political Examiner," No. 126, *Examiner* (June 10, 1810), pp. 353-354. John Locke was buried in the churchyard at High Laver. In 1866 Christ Church restored his tomb and enclosed it in a railing.

2. Spencer Perceval was Prime Minister, Oct., 1809–May, 1812. His Cabinet was Tory.

3. Brother of the Prime Minister.

CONTINENTAL PRINCES

1. "Political Examiner," No. 140, *Examiner* (Sept. 23, 1810), pp. 593-594.

2. Paul I (1754–1801), Emperor of Russia, 1796–1801.

3. Christian VII (1749–1808), King of Denmark and Norway, 1766–1808.

4. Gustavus IV (1778–1837), King of Sweden, 1792–1809.

5. Maximilian I (1756–1825), became Elector of Bavaria in 1799; assumed title of King in 1806.

6. Maria I (1734–1816), Queen of Portugal, 1777–1816; John VI (1769–1826), Regent, 1799–1816, and King, 1816–1826.

7. Charles XIII (1748–1818), ruler of Sweden, 1809–1818; for the last eight years, King in title only.

8. "If the King of Spain, or rather the late King of Spain, is stripped of his dominions in Europe, ought not his dominions in America to be preserved for him? . . . few things would afford us more satisfaction, than that a throne should be erected in South America, first for the aged ex-monarch of Spain, and then for his son. . . ." "Lettre aux Espagnols-Americains," *Edinburgh Review*, XIII (Jan. 1809), 299-300.

ON CERTAIN TERMS MAGNANIMOUSLY APPLIED TO THE FRENCH RULER

1. "Political Examiner," No. 141, *Examiner* (Sept. 30, 1810), pp. 609-610.

2. Johann Buckholdt (c. 1508–1536), Dutch Anabaptist fanatic; became leader of the Anabaptists in Münster in 1534; established a theocracy or kingdom of Zion with himself as king.

3. Perkin Warbeck (1474–1499), pretender to the British throne; claimed to be Richard, Duke of York, son of Edward IV.

4. Marcus Didius Salvius Julianus (c. 133–193), Roman Emperor from March to June, 193. He purchased his throne when the praetorian guards offered it to the highest bidder.

5. Giacomo or Muzio Attendolo (1369–1424) peasant condottiere, who took the name of Sforza. From him were descended the famous Sforza family of Milan.

6. Hyder Ali (c. 1722–1782), became virtual ruler of Mysore.

7. Count Aluigi Zenobio (d. 1818) "is a Venetian Nobleman [and a prince of the House of Austria], who not chusing to acquiesce in the new order of things in his native country, left his large estates at the mercy of his enemies, and took up his residence in England, where he still lives, much respected, I believe, for his manners and good intentions." *Examiner* (July 22, 1810), p. 449.

CHANCELLORSHIP OF THE UNIVERSITY OF CAMBRIDGE

1. "Political Examiner," No. 165, *Examiner* (Mar. 24, 1811), pp. 177-179. See also "Chancellorship of the University of Oxford," *Examiner* (Nov. 12, 1809), pp. 721-723.

2. On Sept. 9, 1810, Hunt wrote in the "Political Examiner" concerning Napoleon's abolishing freedom of the press:

One of the first of our constitutional maxims is the necessity of a free-press; this is acknowledged by us all, unwillingly indeed by some, but without reserve by the great majority: — "The Freedom of the Press: it is the air we breathe: without it we die" — such is the standing toast of our Constitutional men; and the Ministerialists confess it to be true, though they do not toast it. Now here is a man, who after talking and doing so much from a professed love of freedom, and after having an opportunity of making so glorious a conclusion in its favour, has helped to banish the very name of liberty from France, — who condemns men without trial, who is above all law, and who, in the opinion of Englishmen, deprives his subjects of their political existence: — he takes away the air they breathe, and of course they die; they are no longer, in our opinion, any more than so many inanimate bodies, in which, like the disturbed dead of whom we read in romances, a cursed spirit walks abroad to harass and betray mankind . . . . no man who values the freedom of the press for the life and spirit it bestows can confine its necessity to any one country; the French have at times been free, and we have been slaves, according as the two nations have or have not breathed the common air of political right. The statesman, the conqueror, or whatever else he may be, who deprives his country of this political being, never does it but for a bad purpose; and the certain effect, sooner or later, is corruption and decay: — he does it, as a man commits murder, either from bad passion, for plunder, or for *security*; and the consequence is as destructive of the body politic, and as damning to the destroyer.

. . . . Bonaparte, elevated to the summit of power, surrounded by dependent chiefs, and fortified by his conquests, by French vanity, and by the terror of his name, is yet afraid of the very shadow of political liberty: he cannot conceal his fear: he proclaims it by the most jealous and minute decrees; and while he shows us what would be our fate in case of conquest, he teaches us how inviolably we ought to maintain a freedom so formidable in his eyes and so indispensably necessary to our existence.

— "Final Enslavement of the French Press," *Examiner*, p. 562.

3. William Wyndham Grenville, Baron Grenville (1759–1834), elected chancellor of Oxford University, Dec. 14, 1809; installed, Jan. 10, 1810.

4. John Henry Manners, fifth Duke of Rutland (1778–1857), was a recorder of Cambridge, Grantham, and Scarborough.

5. Two days later, William Frederick, the second Duke of Gloucester (1776–1834), was made chancellor. On the occasion of his installation, Hunt wrote,

It may be argued, that the Chancellor of an University has no great concern in its management; that he never interferes with its mode of instruction; and that the students are at liberty to form what notions and views they please, whether agreeable to his own or not. True: but still, as he is a man of rank and consequence in the state, he is sure to gather round him a particular interest, and to have a certain right in influencing the predominant politics of the place he governs; and therefore it is highly desirable that this interest and this weight should be on the side of what is liberal and public-spirited, rather than auxiliaries to courtly encroachment and a time-serving pliability in speaking and thinking. They who have been at any kind of public school must recollect the peculiar tone and fashion given to early opinion by the prevailing politics of the rulers, and what an excommunicating face was set against all romantic little boys, who in conformity with the great authors they studied, took it into their heads to think for themselves. It is the same, in its degree, with schools for men and with all other public institutions; so that to have any constituted authority endued with a proper spirit and fond of encouraging an independent way of thinking, is a blessing as rare as it is useful, and at once an honour to the nation in which it exists, and one of the best securities for keeping the nation honourable. *Examiner* (July 7, 1811), p. 417.

NAPOLEON, – HIS PRESENT ASPECT AND CHARACTER

1. "Political Examiner," No. 187, *Examiner* (Sept. 1, 1811), pp. 555-557. Bonaparte may have seen this and other *Examiner* articles about him. He is said to have "kept Mounier and twelve clerks at work, extracting, translating, and abridging the pamphlets and newspaper notices that were launched against him from England, and the compositions of the caricaturists were regularly transmitted to him, rousing him to transports of fury." S. Baring-Gould, *The Life of Napoleon Bonaparte* (London [c. 1908]), p. 426.

2. On Apr. 5, 1818, Hunt wrote concerning India:

The plain truth is, we have been playing the same game there for which we objected so violently and hypocritically to BONAPARTE in Europe; and we have been playing it with less excuse; for he was a conqueror educated in our own military institutions, – provoked, in addition to his love of power, by our inveterate hostility and our passion for doting old despotisms, – and more warranted in endeavouring to dictate his notions of improvement to Europe, because it was already at variance with its own prejudices, and he and its inhabitants were all of the same family. But, with the exception of one or two just interferences with custom and tyranny, we have been encroaching, and conquering, and usurping in India, whether we were wanted or not, or provoked or not, or whether we were or were not of any use whatsoever; nay, we have preserved some of the very despotisms against which we pretended to exclaim, with this aggravation of them, — that in addition to the exactions already made upon their subjects, we drain fresh exactions for ourselves, and turn the single despots into double ones. But we exclaim against French egotism, and then think that wherever we go, and whatever we do, we must do good. . . . Observers, who have been in India, have long been aware of the dangerous situation of our unwieldy power there; and from what we have heard them say, setting aside even all books on the subject, we would not give tenpence for the continuance of our sovereignty there, if a few skilful leaders should rise up to head a willing soldiery and population.

Examiner (Apr. 5, 1818), p. 216.

3. Jean Sarrazin (1770–c. 1840), French general and traitor.

4. Joseph Fouché, Duke of Otranto (1759–1820), powerful French statesman; Minister of the Interior; dismissed by Napoleon in 1810.

5. Michel L'Hôpital or L'Hospital (c. 1505–1573), Chancellor of France.

THE LATE MR. HORNE TOOKE

1. "Political Examiner," No. 217, *Examiner* (Apr. 5, 1812), pp. 209-211. Corrections noted in the *Examiner* (Apr. 12, 1812), p. 226, have been made here. John Horne Tooke died on March 18, 1812. In *The Town* (1848), Hunt characterized him as "perhaps, the hardest-headed man that ever figured in the union of literature and politics; meaning, by that epithet, the power to discuss, and impenetrability to objection." *The Town* (London: Gibbings & Co., 1893), p. 353.

2. Augustus Henry Fitzroy, third Duke of Crafton (1735–1811), statesman.

3. William Henry Cavendish Bentinck, third Duke of Portland (1738–1809), Prime Minister, 1807–1809.

4. John Wilkes (1727–1797), twice expelled from the House of Commons for libel; Lord Mayor of London, 1774; City Chamberlain, 1779–1797.

5. See Tooke's denunciation of James Paull (1770–1808) in the pamphlet *A Warning to the Electors of Westminster*, 1807.

6. *The Dictionary Historical and Critical of Mr. Peter Bayle*, 2nd edition (London, 1737), IV, 216-224.

7. James Harris (1709–1780), politician, author of *Hermes; or A Philosophical Inquiry concerning Universal Grammar*, 1751.

8. Part of the title of Tooke's *Diversions of Purley*, 1786, 1798.

THE MANUFACTURERS

1. "Political Examiner," No. 222, *Examiner* (May 10, 1812), pp. 289-290.

2. Late in 1806 Napoleon instituted the "continental system" or system of blockade to prevent England from trading with the Continent. In February, 1811, the United States revived its non-intercourse act with Great Britain.

3. The workers considered the introduction of machinery as the source of the depression and of unemployment; consequently, they were rioting, and smashing frames in the factories. The military had been called out to subdue the uprisings.

4. Burdett's speech to which Hunt refers was made in Parliament on May 1, 1812. See *Examiner* (May 3, 1812), p. 280.

5. Spencer Perceval, the Prime Minister, was assassinated the day after this article appeared.

6. The question under discussion was whether £90,000 should be granted for the erection of new barracks in Liverpool, Bristol, and Mary-le-bone Park. Perceval favored the grant.

7. George Rose (1744-1818), vice-president of the Board of Trade and Treasurer of the Navy, 1807–1812. On April 27, 1812, Mr. Rose was accused in the House of Commons of having said that, regarding obstruction of trade, England and the United States "were in the situation of two men whose heads were in a bucket of water; and the struggle was, which of the two could remain longest in that situation without suffocation." *Examiner* (May 3, 1812), p. 278.

TO THE RIGHT HONOURABLE LORD ELLENBOROUGH ...

1. "Political Examiner," No. 249, *Examiner* (Dec. 6, 1812), pp. 769-771. At the time of Lord Ellenborough's death, Hunt said of him:

Upon the whole, LORD ELLENBOROUGH seems to have been neither a man of genius, nor emphatically speaking, of virtue: he left the law not quite so good as he found it, at least in point of reputation: he was worldly, passionate, and apparently gross in his appetites: — he was a flatterer of those above him, and a dogmatist to those beneath; — he shook the sacred judgment seat with the bad passions of the court. But he was unquestionably a man of talent: — if he was ill-tempered, and violent, and overbearing, and even servile, he was at least not miserly, nor hypocritical, nor a bigot. *Examiner* (Jan. 10, 1819), p. 18.

2. Lloyd Kenyon, first Baron Kenyon (1732–1802), preceded Lord Ellenborough as Lord Chief-Justice of England.

FRENCH FASHIONS

1. Samuel Butler, "Satyr upon our Ridiculous Imitation of the French," ll. 1-12, 57-64.

2. *Examiner* (Sept. 4, 1814), pp. 572-574.

3. Matthew Prior, "Henry and Emma," l. 430.

CHRISTMAS AND OTHER OLD NATIONAL MERRY-MAKINGS CONSIDERED . . .

1. "Political Examiner," Nos. 506, 507, 508, *Examiner* (Dec. 21, and 28, 1817), pp. 801-803, 817-819, and (Jan. 4, 1818), pp. 1-2. Reprinted in the Manchester *Weekly Times* (Dec. 24, 1869). For other essays by Hunt on Christmas, see: "Christmas Enjoyments," *Examiner* (Dec. 20, 1818), pp. 801-802; "An English Christmas in 1819," *Examiner* (Dec. 26, 1819), pp. 817-818; "Keeping Christmas," *New Monthly Magazine* (Dec. 1825), n.s. XIV, 514-518; "Christmas Day," *Tatler* (Dec. 25, 1830), pp. 253-257 of our text: "Christmas Eve and Christmas Day." *Leigh Hunt's London Journal* (Dec. 24, 1834), reprinted incompletely in *A Day by the Fire and Other Papers by Leigh Hunt* (1870); "Inexhaustibility of the Subject of Christmas," *Monthly Repository* (Dec. 1837), reprinted in *The Seer* (1840); "Christmas and Italy," prefatory essay in Hunt's *A Jar of Honey* (1847); "Christmas Day Divided between Two Worlds," *National Magazine* (1857), pp. 391-397 of our text. See also the poem "Christmas," *New Monthly Magazine* (Dec. 1836), reprinted in the Oxford edition of Hunt's poems.

The quotations are from *The Taming of the Shrew*, Ind., ii, 137-138; *Christmas, His Masque,* opening lines; and Herrick's "A New-yeares gift sent to Sir Simeon Steward," ll. 27-29, 33-34, 37-40, 49-50.

2. *Iliad*, III, 23 ff.

3. *King John*, III, iv, 110.

4. Dr. Nathan Drake, *Shakspeare and His Times* (London, 1817), I, 206, fn.

5. *Ibid.*, p. 202. Thomas Tusser, not Tasser.

6. See *ibid.*, pp. 127-128. The incident is narrated in Geoffrey of Monmouth, VI, 12.

7. "A Paranaeticall, or Advisive Verse, to his friend, M. John Wicks," ll. 1-4, 7-12, 15-18, 28-35.

8. Beltane is the Celtic name for the first of May; Old May-Day.

9. The signature used by a correspondent in this issue of the *Examiner*. She congratulates Hunt on his Christmas articles and tells him how she has restored the old customs in her own home.

DISTRESSED SEAMEN, AND DISTRESS OF THE POOR IN GENERAL

1. "Political Examiner," Nos. 509, 510, 511, *Examiner* (Jan. 11, 18, and 25, 1818), pp. 12-13, 33-34, 49-50. Hunt deals here with a problem which received little systematic attention until near the end of the nineteenth century. See Elmo P. Hohman, "Seamen," *Encyclopaedia of the Social Sciences* (1937), XIII in VII, 615-616. One cannot be sure how much effect Hunt's articles had in helping the plight of the seamen, but the *Examiner* for Feb. 1, 1818 (p. 78) reports the action taken in their behalf. Among other benefits, seven ships were made available to them — six for the healthy seamen, and one for the ill.

2. Sir James Alexander Gordon (1782–1869), who was later made admiral of the fleet.

3. Sir Matthew Wood (1768–1843), Lord Mayor of London, 1815–1817.

4. Sir James Shaw (1764–1843), M.P. for the city of London.

5. Thomas Cochrane, later tenth Earl of Dundonald (1775–1860), attacked abuses of the admiralty; in 1817, assumed command of the Chilian navy; and later at various times was an admiral for Brazil, Greece, and Great Britain.

6. "*Droits of Admiralty*: certain rights or perquisites, as the proceeds arising from the seizure of enemies' ships, wrecks, etc. . . ." *N.E.D.*

7. Robert Blake (1599–1657), admiral and general at sea. His body was interred in a vault in Westminster Abbey. After the Restoration, it was removed and cast into a pit on the north side of the abbey.

8. James Gambier, first Baron Gambier (1756–1833), naval commander.

9. "The Neglected Tar," stanzas 1, 6, 7. See *The Universal Songster; or, Museum of Mirth* (London, 1829), II, 346. A copy of this song is in the Allen A. Brown Collection of Music at the Boston Public Library.

ON THE INTELLECTUAL INFERIORITY OF PARLIAMENT TO THE DEMANDS OF THE AGE

1. "Political Examiner," Nos. 513, 514, 515, *Examiner* (Feb. 8, 15, and 22, 1818), pp. 81-82, 97-98, 113-114. See also "House of Lords. — Origin of the Titles of Our Dukes and Marquisses," *Examiner*, (Aug. 17, 1828), pp. 532-535.

2. William Pleydell-Bouverie, Viscount Folkestone, later third Earl Radnor (1779–1869), M.P. for Salisbury, 1802–1828.

3. George Tierney (1761–1830), leader of the opposition party, 1817–1821.

4. Henry Bathurst, third Earl Bathurst (1762–1834), secretary for war and colonies in Liverpool's cabinet.

5. John Philpot Curran (1750–1817), Irish judge.

6. Henry Grattan (1746–1820), Irish orator and statesman; William Conyngham Plunket, first Baron Plunket (1764–1854), Irish statesman, later lord chancellor of Ireland.

7. John Nicholas Fazakerley (1787–1852), M.P. for Lincoln at this time.

8. Oliver was a spy who reported to Lord Sidmouth on the progress of the insurrection at Manchester in 1817. Oliver is also believed to have promoted the insurrection.

9. William Lowther, second Earl of Lonsdale (1787–1872), M.P. for Westmoreland in 1818; on the treasury board, 1813–1826.

10. Thomas William Coke, later first Earl of Leicester (1752–1842), agriculturist and statesman; M.P. for Norfolk, 1807–1832.

11. Nicholas Vansittart, later first Baron Bexley (1766–1851), chancellor of the exchequer, 1812–1823.

12. Sir William Curtis (1752–1829), M.P. for London, 1790–1818.

CAUSE OF THE INFERIORITY OF PARLIAMENT TO THE DEMANDS OF THE PRESENT AGE

1. "Political Examiner," No. 516, *Examiner* (Mar. 1, 1818), pp. 129-130.

DEATH AND CHARACTER OF THE QUEEN

1. "Political Examiner," No. 551, *Examiner* (Nov. 22, 1818), pp. 737-739. Charlotte Sophia (1744–1818), Queen of George III. Hunt defended his stand in this article the following week in "A Few More Words on the Late Queen," adding that "the Queen, who was bred up at one of those petty German Courts that have become proverbial for pride and narrowness, had most probably a very bad education, as hollow, as low and as dry as a chalk-pit. This is the best thing that can be said for her want of better reputation." *Examiner* (Nov. 29, 1818), p. 753.

2. A long article on the Queen from the *Times* of the preceding Wednesday is reprinted in this issue of the *Examiner*.

3. The Prince Regent, from whom Sheridan had become estranged, was erroneously thought to have left him to die in poverty.

4. Romilly committed suicide shortly after the death of his wife.

See Hunt's editorial in the *Examiner* on Romilly's death (Nov. 9, 1818), pp. 705-707.

5. A play by Arthur Murphy, first acted in 1761.

6. Georg Joachim Zollikofer (1730—1788), German preacher, poet, and hymn writer.

7. See Hunt's comment in "A Ramble in Mary-le-bone," p. 294 of this text.

CROWDING OF CONVICTS IN PRISON-SHIPS

1. "Political Examiner," No. 564, *Examiner* (Jan. 31, 1819), pp. 65-67.

2. Hon. Henry Grey Bennet, Earl of Tankerville (1777—1836), M.P. for Shrewsbury, 1811—1826.

3. Lawrence Hynes Halloran or O'Halloran (1766—1831), a miscellaneous writer rumored to have been an imposter in the church. He was indicted in 1818 for having counterfeited a frank, and was sentenced to seven years' transportation. According to the Old Bailey report in the *Examiner* (Sept. 13, 1818), p. 589, Halloran, "otherwise *Gregory*," was a "Doctor in Divinity of King's College, Aberdeen." See also *Examiner* (Oct. 4, 1818), p. 637. After being transported, Halloran successfully established a school in Sydney, New South Wales.

4. Charles Bragge, afterwards Bragge-Bathurst (c.1754—1831), Chancellor of the Duchy of Lancaster, 1812—1823.

5. Robert Henry Clive (1754—1839), Under Secretary of State for the Home Department, 1818—1822; M.P. for Ludlow, 1818—1832.

6. *Aeneid*, I, 686. "... amid the royal feast and the flowing wine...." *Virgil*, trans. by Fairclough, I, 289.

7. Sir Thomas Byam Martin (1773—1854), comptroller of the navy, 1816—1831; M.P. for Plymouth, 1818—1831.

8. The report for the House of Commons, May 11, 1809, in the *Annual Register*, p. 159, states: "In the last general election, Mr. Quintin Dick purchased a seat in that house for the borough of Cashell, through the negotiation of lord Castlereagh .... on a recent occasion of great importance ... lord Castlereagh intimated to that gentleman the necessity of his either voting with the government, or resigning his seat in that house .... Mr. Dick, sooner than vote against principle and conscience, made choice of the latter alternative."

MR. COBBETT, AND WHAT IS WANTED IN PARLIAMENT

1. "Political Examiner," No. 622, *Examiner* (Mar. 12, 1820), pp. 161-163. Cobbett failed at this time to be elected to Parliament, but became M.P. for Oldham in 1832. On January 18, [1853], Hunt wrote,

The only associate I should object to is Cobbett; because, though he suffered, he assuredly did not know "how to suffer;" and though he "fought," he assuredly *did* know how to run away, and though he beat me hollow as a political journalist, and I believe also did good to the cause of reform, it is to be doubted whether he was ever earnest in anything but selling his journal and finding fault.

HUNT, *Correspondence* (London, 1862), II, 331.

2. John Cam Hobhouse, later Baron Broughton de Gyfford (1786–1869), statesman and friend of Byron.

3. Arthur Thistlewood (1770–1820) and a group of about thirty conspirators, angered by governmental repression of the reformists, met in a stable in Cato Street in 1820 and there plotted to assassinate the Cabinet members at a Cabinet dinner. The plot was discovered and the leaders were executed.

4. *Much Ado about Nothing*, II, iii, 250.

THE LATE QUEEN OF ENGLAND, HER FUNERAL, &c.

1. "Political Examiner," No. 697, *Examiner* (Aug. 19, 1821), pp. 513-516. Hunt's defense of Queen Caroline reflects the ardor with which popular sentiment championed her at the time of her trial in 1820, and her death on August 7, 1821. For a full account of this incident, see Spencer Walpole, *A History of England from the Conclusion of the Great War in 1815* (London, 1900), II, 13-82. Hunt's enthusiasm can be attributed partly to his hatred of persecution and partly to his distaste for George IV.

2. Some indication of the Prince's reluctance to enter into the marriage, as well as his clever bargaining, is shown in the following statement from the *Dictionary of National Biography*, III, 1059-1060: "Hard pressed on all sides, the prince consented, on condition of the liquidation of his debts, and a large addition to his income, to marry his cousin, then twenty-six years old. He stipulated that his income was to be raised from 60,000 *l* to 125,000 *l* per annum, of which 25,000 *l* per annum was to be set aside to pay his debts, which at that time amounted to 630,000 *l*. Besides this he was to receive 27,000 *l* for preparations for the marriage, 28,000 *l* for jewels and plate, 26,000 *l* for the completion of Carlton House, and 50,000 *l* per annum as a jointure to her royal highness."

Almost ten years previously, the Prince had married Mrs. Fitz-
herbert, probably the only woman he really loved.

3. Queen Caroline tried unsuccessfully to force an entrance into
Westminster on the Coronation Day of George IV, July 19, 1821.
The Government denied her appeal to be crowned with the King.

4. The Prince Regent, in 1818, sent a secret commission to the
Continent to collect evidence against her for a divorce.

5. Crowds compelled the funeral cortege to pass through London. The Queen was buried at Brunswick by her own request.

ON THE KEEPING OF TWELFTH NIGHT

1. *New Monthly Magazine* (Jan. 1829), n.s. XXV, 59-61. The
editor was Thomas Campbell. Twelfth Night was one of Hunt's
favorite topics. See, for example, "Twelfth Night — A Street Portrait — Shakspeare's Play — Recollections of a Twelfth Night,"
Leigh Hunt's London Journal (Jan. 7, 1835), II, 1-2, reprinted in
The Seer (1840), and elsewhere; and "Twelfth Night," *Musical
Times, and Singing Class Circular* (Jan. 1, 1854), pp. 382-390 of our
text.

2. For Hunt's explanation of these Twelfth Night customs, see
his 1854 essay mentioned above. For a more general account, see
John Brand, *Observations on the Popular Antiquities of Great
Britain* (London, 1895), I, 21-34.

3. Perhaps Mrs. Vincent Novello, a good friend of the Hunts,
who was famed for her "foaming wassail-bowl." See Charles and
Mary Cowden Clarke, *Recollections of Writers* (New York, 1878),
p. 23.

4. Hunt reviewed William Hone's *Year Book* (Part I for Jan.
1831) in the *Tatler* (Jan. 7, 1831) with long excerpts from Hone
concerning Twelfth Night.

We conclude [wrote Hunt] with laying before our readers, a Twelfth
Night Dramatic Sketch, which was suggested, by passing a very pleasant evening, a few years back, when the company took it in their heads
to speak blank verse, and the drawing of a Twelfth-cake, was turned
into a mock-heroic upon royalty. The conversion of Twelfth Night characters into the members of a Court, is an obvious and natural mode of
playing the pastime; and the lovers of poetry, if they took courage,
would find it an easier thing than they imagine to convert their prose
into blank verse.

King and *Queen* sitting crowned. *Lords, Ladies,* the *General,* the *Arch-
bishop, Chief-Justice, Chief Cook,* the *Master of the Horse, Fool, &c.*
   King. Give us our cup. Soh! — now, my vassals all,
Lords, ladies, mighty (foolish) General,
Chief Judge, Chief-Cook, Right Reverends, and Wrong Reverends,

(If such there be, which is impossible)
Horse (Master of the), you; (henceforth to be
Called Horse, for shortness' sake, and to do honour
To this our index-like and shrewd parenthesis)
Fool, you, you fool; and you, my lord Archbishop;
My lady Giggle, and my lady Glum,
And Maids of Honour with your several children,
A health to all.

    All.   Wassail, my liege, and thanks.
    King (rising in anger.) Now by the Gods —
    All (rising).   Good God, Sir, what's the matter!
    King. Now by the Gods, as I before observ'd,
The bowl's too hot. See that the cook be slain.

                    (Chief-Cook faints.)

Take him away; first handing me his watch.

          (They take away the Cook to execution.)

    Archbishop. So perish all our sovereign's enemies!
    Chief Justice. And handed be their watches.
    General.   Sire, methinks
A general massacre of all the cooks
Would not be wrong, by way of hint in future.
    King. We'll think on't after Christmas. Meanwhile sit,
And sparkle all: — be merry on the spot.
    Chief Justice. How witty!
    Archbishop.   How divine!
    Lady Giggle.   How irresistible!
O heavens! For God's sake, Sir! I cannot bear it.
    King (aside). Giggle's a girl of infinite discernment,
I'll be in love with her.
    All.   The Queen is fainting!   *(Queen faints.)*
    King. How! Fainting in this inconvenient manner!
Take her away, and order a divorce.
    Queen (aside) Fainting was wrong, I see: but having fainted,
I must faint on. If he show any tenderness,
I'll have a fit, if not — the General.

               (The Queen is carried out.)

    King. What think ye, lords and ladies? Said I right?
    Ladies. Particularly so.
    King.   Delightful sex!
Henceforth all womankind shall be my wife.

         (All look enchanted, but Giggle.)

    Giggle. (Aside, and recovering herself). Well; be it so. To be
        his wife is little,
But to be Queen is much. Prodigious monarch!
    1st Lady. Wonderful!
    2nd Lady.   Awful!
    3rd Lady.   Dreadful!
    4th Lady.   Superhuman!

5th Lady. So fat, for a thin man!
6th Lady.   Decisive character!
Giggle. And then so gentle, not to kill the Queen!
Archbishop. A cheek like Phœbus!
Chief Justice.   Flaxen hair so black!
King. Nay, there you flatter.
Chief Justice.   Pardon me, great Sir,
Tis, as the poet says, "Dark with excess
Of light:" I never saw so black a snow.
    King. Well; lawyers I've been told, can make black white;
But never did I feel them right till now.
Move wassail! Hand the cake! Lords, you eat nothing.
Eat instantly and much, or we shall feel
Ourself disgraced. Archbishop, by the way,
A word with you: you need not stretch your ear:
'Tis long enough. I doubt if we can say
Ourself: 'tis wrong, is't not?
    Archbishop. It has been hitherto, may it please your Majesty,
But can be so no longer.
    King.   Good. We did
Remember some such saying in our youth,°
But we are young no longer.
    Chief Justice.   Ah, dear Sire,
Who *is* young?
    King.   But I've lost my teeth!
    Archbishop. (*shewing his teeth*).   And, Sire,
Who *has* teeth?† Teeth and all those sort of things,
Went from this world to keep their sovereign company.
What seems a tooth is none.
    King.   Alas!
Nor yet what seems a king. Slave to will,
I find, at last, he has no will at all,
Nor yet can will himself to feel no will;
So I will reign no longer. — Call the games;
And let us change our diadem for *Bob.*

                                        Tatler, II, 430-431.

    5. Mahmoud II.
    6. In the harbor of Navarino, Greece, the Turkish-Egyptian fleet
was defeated by the English-French-Russian fleet on Oct. 20, 1827.
    7. Henry Fielding's play, 1730.

    ° It was said by a French gentleman to a lady, who was expressing a fear
that she had spoken a word not to be found in his language. "It is not,
Madam," said he; "but it ought to be."

    † Said by a Cardinal (with good teeth) to Louis the Fourteenth.

CHRISTMAS DAY

1. *Tatler* (Dec. 25, 1830), I, 385-386.
2. William Gunter, *Gunter's Confectioner's Oracle, containing receipts for desserts* . . . (London, 1830).
3. Evelyn praises the virtues of the elder in "Acetaria: A Discourse of Sallets," but does not specifically mention elder wine. See *The Miscellaneous Writings of John Evelyn, Esq. F.R.S.*, ed. by William Upcott (London, 1825), pp. 740, 803. Evelyn's highest praise is given to cider. See the prefatory remarks to his "Pomona" appended to *Sylva.*
4. Lamb, "A Farewell to Tobacco," l. 55.
5. Milton, "Epitaphium Damonis," ll. 47-48.
6. See *A Tale of a Tub: The Prose Works of Jonathan Swift, D.D.*, ed. by Temple Scott (London, 1898—1908), I, 141.
7. *Ibid.*, p. 62.

THE WISHING CAP. NO. III. UNDUE INEQUALITIES IN SOCIETY . . .

1. *Tait's Edinburgh Magazine* (May, 1833), III, 141-148. Hunt published a series of "Wishing Cap" papers in the *Examiner,* Mar. 28, 1824—Aug. 7, 1825. He continued the series in *Tait's,* Jan., 1833 —Sept., 1833.
2. Charles Grey, second Earl Grey (1764—1845), Whig Prime Minister, 1830—1834.
3. Lord John Russell, later first Earl Russell (1792—1878), a framer of the 1832 Reform Bill and member of the Cabinet, 1831—1834; as Prime Minister, 1846—1852, assisted Hunt in securing a pension. Hunt was entertained at his residence in Downing Street in 1851.
4. William Russell, Lord Russell (courtesy title) (1639—1683), Whig leader known as "The Patriot"; beheaded for treason, but his attainder was reversed under William and Mary.
5. Brougham had threatened, in Nov., 1830, to introduce into Parliament a plan for reform which would extend the franchise to every householder, leaseholder, and copyholder and take one member from each rotten borough. To conciliate Brougham and stem his ambitions as a Radical reformer, the Whigs made him Lord Chancellor and elevated him to the peerage during that same month. He retained the Chancellorship until 1834 and effected notable legal reforms. Over twenty years previous, Brougham had successfully defended Leigh Hunt and his brother against a charge of libel in 1811; and unsuccessfully defended them in 1812 for libellously attacking the Prince Regent.

6. Seat of the Lord Chancellor in the House of Lords.

7. In April 1833, Parliament passed an Irish coercion bill to control terrorism in Ireland. As a partial conciliation, the Irish Church temporalities bill was introduced in Feb., 1833, and passed in Aug., 1833. For an account of these, see Geo. C. Brodrick and J. F. Fotheringham, *The History of England from Addington's Administration to the Close of William IV's Reign (1801–1837)*, Vol. XI of *The Political History of England*, ed. by W. Hunt and R. L. Poole (London, 1906), pp. 320-325.

8. The Irish archbishoprics were to be reduced from four to two, and the bishoprics from eighteen to ten, as vacancies occurred.

9. The Milesians were the sons or followers of Miledh, fabulous ancestor of the Irish.

10. John Jeffreys Pratt, second Earl and first Marquis of Camden (1759–1840); appointed Lord Lieutenant of Ireland in 1795; opposed remedial legislation for Ireland and maintained a policy of repression which led to the rebellion of 1798.

11. Chief Secretary for Ireland, 1798–1801; falsely charged with ordering inhuman punishments during the conspiracy of the United Irishmen; succeeded in getting the Irish parliament to pass a bill for the union of Great Britain and Ireland in 1800.

12. Pope, *Moral Essays*, I, 206-207.

13. George Townsend (1788–1857); *Plan for Abolishing Pluralities and Non-Residence*, 1833.

THE WISHING CAP. NO. VII.
ANSWER TO A SINGULAR ARGUMENT OF THE TORIES ...

1. *Tait's Edinburgh Magazine* (July 1833), III, 417-421. This is No. V, incorrectly numbered.

2. John Graham of Claverhouse, Viscount Dundee (1649?–1689), Scottish Royalist and Jacobite.

3. Lord Francis Leveson-Gower (later Francis Egerton), first Earl of Ellesmere (1800–1857), published a poor translation of *Faust* in 1823. He omitted from Goethe's prologue the dialogue between the Lord and Mephistopheles derived from the Book of Job, because he considered the "tone of Familiarity on both sides ... revolting in a sacred subject." *Faust*, trans. by Lord Francis Leveson Gower (London, 1823), p. 19. Lord Gower held various offices, being Lord of the Treasury in 1827 and Secretary at War in 1830.

4. Butler, *Hudibras*, Part I, Canto I, 197-198.

5. Second to None. Hunt suggests the translation "Worse than Nothing." See *A Book for a Corner* (London, 1849), II, 64.

6. The Birmingham Political Union had recently denounced the Ministry and called a meeting in Coldbath Fields. A proclamation by the Ministry forbidding the meeting had been ignored, and the police had charged the crowd. In the fight a policeman had been killed.

THE TOWNSMAN.
NOS. II, III, IV. A RAMBLE IN MARY-LE-BONE

1. Published in three parts in the London *Weekly True Sun* as "The Townsman. No. II. A Ramble in Mary-le-bone" (Sept. 8, 1833); "The Townsman. No. III. Ramble in Marylebone Continued" (Sept. 15, 1833), "The Townsman. No. IV. Ramble in Marylebone Concluded" (Sept. 22, 1833). Hunt lived at 8 York Buildings, New Road, Marylebone, during 1818–1819, and at 5 York Buildings in 1832.

2. A reference to Robert Owen's manufacturing community at New Lanark.

3. John Elwes or Meggott (1714–1789), a well-known and very wealthy miser.

4. *The Year Book*, ed. by Wm. Hone (London, 1845 [preface dated 1832]), V, 501–502.

5. Thomas Pennant, *Some Account of London*, 5th ed. (London, 1813), p. 181.

6. *Ibid.*, 170.

7. Gay, *The Beggar's Opera*, III, xiii, Air LXVII.

8. See the *Spectator*, No. 125. The incident concerned St. Anne's Lane.

9. Mrs. Elizabeth Montagu (1720–1800), society leader.

10. Stephen Storace (1763–1796); wrote the music for Prince Hoare's *No Song, No Supper*, 1790.

11. Dr. Alexander Geddes (1737–1802), biblical critic.

12. Giuseppe Marc' Antonio Baretti (1719–1789), miscellaneous writer.

13. James Ferguson (1710–1776).

14. Thomas Holcroft (1745–1809), dramatist and novelist.

15. Robert W. Elliston (1774–1831), actor; Richard Cosway (1740–1821), painter.

16. Thomas Tyrwhitt (1730–1786), critic.

17. James Barry (1741–1806).

18. Richard Cumberland (1732–1811), dramatist.

19. Cecilia Davies (1750?–1836). William Barclay Squire in the *Dictionary of National Biography* says of her: "She died, forgotten and deserted, at 58 Great Portland Street, on 3 July 1836. The

funeral of this fine singer, who had taught the queens of France, Spain, and Naples, was followed only by an old nurse and a faithful servant, and no notice of her death was taken by the daily newspapers."

20. Mrs. Spencer. See *The Autobiography of Leigh Hunt,* ed. by J. E. Morpurgo (London, 1948), p. 11.

21. An interesting point for biographers of Hunt.

22. John Nash (1752–1835).

23. All Souls' Church.

24. Joanna Southcott (1750–1814), a religious fanatic who stirred London by announcing that she would give birth to Shiloh, the second Christ.

25. See Hunt's essay, "A Visit to the Zoological Gardens," *New Monthly Magazine,* n.s., XLVII (Aug. 1836), 479-491, reprinted in *Men, Women, and Books* (1847).

THE TOWNSMAN. NO. V. NEWMAN STREET — MR. IRVING — MR. STOTHARD — RECOLLECTIONS OF MR. WEST AND HIS HOUSE

1. *Weekly True Sun* (Sept. 29, 1833).

2. Mrs. Benjamin West was aunt to Leigh Hunt's mother, who, with her husband, lived with the Wests for a short time. Hunt makes numerous references to the Wests in his *Autobiography.*

3. Edward Irving (1792–1834), a Presbyterian preacher.

4. See Hunt's *Autobiography,* ed. by Morpurgo, p. 287.

5. Thomas Stothard (1755–1834). Biographers appear to have overlooked Hunt's personal acquaintance with Stothard. He was a subscriber to Hunt's *Juvenilia* (1801). See also Hunt's "Prints from the Designs of Mr. Stothard. — Lord Byron's Works," *Examiner* (Aug. 20, 1815), pp. 538-539; Hunt's sonnet to Stothard (1818), Oxford edition of Hunt's poems, p. 248; and his article on the death of Stothard, *Leigh Hunt's London Journal* (May 7, 1834), reprinted in *Table-Talk* (1851).

6. See the conclusion of "A Nearer View of Some of the Shops," *Indicator* (June 7, 1820), reprinted in *The Indicator and the Companion* (1834); and also the "Sale of the Late Mr. West's Pictures," *Indicator* (June 14, 1820), reprinted in *A Day by the Fire* (1870).

7. At another time Hunt wrote that

Our dress was of the coarsest and quaintest kind, but was respected out of doors, and is so. It consisted of a blue drugget gown, or body, with ample skirts to it; a yellow vest underneath in winter-time; small clothes of Russia duck; worsted yellow stockings; a leathern girdle; and a little black worsted cap, usually carried in the hand.

HUNT, Autobiography, ed. by Morpurgo, p. 60.

8. In his Autobiography, Hunt speaks of the

two screens by the fireside, containing prints (from Angelica Kauffmann, I think, but I am not sure that Mr. West himself was not the designer) of the Loves of Angelica and Medoro, which I could have looked at from morning to night. Angelica's intent eyes, I thought, had the best of it; but I thought so without knowing why. This gave me a love for Ariosto before I knew him. I got Hoole's translation, but could make nothing of it. Angelica Kauffmann seemed to me to have done much more for her namesake. She could see farther into a pair of eyes than Mr. Hoole with his spectacles.   — Ibid., p. 88.

Angelica Kauffmann (1741—1807) was a well-known historical and portrait painter.

9. Corrected in "The Townsman. No. VI. City Churchyards and Trees" (Oct. 6, 1833):

Before we proceed with our present subject, we must correct an error of the press in our last number, in which we were made to say, that the butler of our venerable friend, Mr. West, imitated his master's "absurdities!" God forbid we should so speak of anybody we so much respected. The word should have been "amenities." The poor butler was absurd enough in his imitation; but the amenities of his master were any thing but ridiculous. They were the very flower and fragrance of the gentleness of his heart, — of the tranquillity in which he cultivated the sweet gardens of painting.

Later, in his Autobiography, Hunt recalled the butler:

Even the butler, with his little twinkling eyes, full of pleasant conceit, vented his notions of himself in half-tones and whispers. This was a strange fantastic person. He got my brother Robert to take a likeness of him, small enough to be contained in a shirt-pin. It was thought that his twinkling eyes, albeit not young, had some fair cynosure in the neighbourhood. What was my brother's amazement, when, the next time he saw him, the butler said, with a face of enchanted satisfaction, "Well, sir, you see!" making a movement at the same time with the frill at his waistcoat. The miniature that was to be given to the object of his affections, had been given accordingly. It was his own bosom!

Autobiography, p. 89.

10. Sir Peter Francis Bourgeois (1756—1811), appointed landscape-painter to George III.

11. Sir Thomas Lawrence (1769—1830), the celebrated portrait painter. See Hunt's sonnet "To Thomas Lawrence, Esq. R.A., on his Portrait of Mr. President West," Examiner (June 23, 1810),

reprinted in the Oxford edition of Hunt's poems, p. 739. Lawrence had been a subscriber to the *Juvenilia*.

12. William Beckford (1759–1844), best known today as the author of *Vathek*.

13. Raphael Lamar West (1769–1850), elder of West's two sons.

THE TOWNSMAN. No. XI (ET SEQ.)
A WALK TO CHELSEA

1. Published under "The Townsman" in the London *Weekly True Sun* as follows: No. XI, "A Walk to Chelsea" (Nov. 10, 1833); No. XII, "Names of Streets. – A Walk to Chelsea (Continued)" (Nov. 17, 1833); No. XIII, "Local Honours to Genius and Virtue. – Continuation of a Walk to Chelsea" (Nov. 24, 1833); No. XIV, "Acknowledgments to the Greenwich Gazette. – Walk in Chelsea Continued" (Dec. 1, 1833); No. XV, "Walk in Chelsea Continued – Swift's Memorandums on the Place" (Dec. 8, 1833); No. XVI, "Chelsea Church" (Dec. 15, 1833); No. XIX, "Greenwich Gazette. – Walk in Chelsea Resumed. Dr. Johnson a Manufacturer of China. Character of Smollett" (Jan. 5, 1834); (unnumbered) "Chelsea Continued. – Cheyne Walk. – Times of Steele and Addison. – Shrewsbury House and Its Subterraneous Passage. – Character of Elizabeth, Countess of Shrewsbury, A Four-Times Married Fury" (Jan. 12, 1834); (unnumbered) "A Word or Two More on the Character of the Countess of Shrewsbury, and a Deduction Therefrom to These Times" (Jan. 19, 1834); (unnumbered) "A Walk in Chelsea. – (*Continued*)" (Apr. 6, 1834). While Hunt was writing "The Townsman," he lived at 4 Upper Cheyne Row, Chelsea.

2. Mrs. Brooke's *Rosina*, first performed at Covent Garden, Dec. 12, 1782; Isaac Bickerstaffe's *Love in a Village*, first performed at Covent Garden, Aug. 12, 1762.

3. Lucia Elizabeth Mathews (1797–1856), actress; lessee of the Olympic (from 1831). See Hunt's description of the Olympic Pavilion in the *Tatler* "Play-Goer," (Jan. 4, 1831), reprinted in *Leigh Hunt's Dramatic Criticism, 1808–1831*, ed. by L. H. and C. W. Houtchens (Columbia University Press, 1949), p. 335.

4. Vincent Novello, Hunt's intimate friend.

5. Edward Wynne (1734–1784); *Eunomus; or, Dialogues concerning the Law and Constitution of England* (1767), 4 vols.

6. Richard Bentley (1662–1742).

7. George Morland (1763–1804), painter.

8. Alexander Stephens (1757–1821).

9. *Merchant of Venice*, V, i, 85.

10. Sir Hans Sloane (1660–1753).

11. Letitia Elizabeth Landon (1802–1838), popular poetess known as L.E.L.

12. *Love for Love*, II, ix.

13. In the *Tatler* (Aug. 27, 1831), III, 197, Hunt praised Mr. Chantrey's statue of Pitt, and asserted:

We look upon Mr. Pitt as one of the most common-place ministers, upon a grand scale, that ever existed; and he continued in power so long as he did, because English feeling was at that period in its most common-place condition, and had a sovereign that represented it. . . . Pitt was the tool of English prejudice and common-place. He was compounded of its self-love, its contemptuousness, its homeliness, its want of sympathy, and its faculty for the counting-house. . . .
. . . To us, he always appeared the son of his father's hauteur, crossed into something of a more mechanical aristocracy on the side of his other parent. . . . His person was gaunt, his face powerful but mechanical; he carried a large turned-up nose in the air; and he had a flow of words, from which posterity cannot find a single thing worth quoting. He was the sublime of commonness; the deification of a clerk in the Bank!

In the *Tatler* (July 23, 1831), III, 79, Hunt described briefly the statue of Major John Cartwright (1740–1824), the parliamentary reformer.

14. Sir Arthur Gorges (d. 1625).

15. Mary Eleanor Bowes, Countess of Strathmore (1749–1800). W. E. A. Axon, in his article on her in the *Dictionary of National Biography*, describes the brutal treatment she received from her husband.

16. The story of the maidservant shared as a mistress by Addison and Steele is unsupported by the standard biographers of these two writers. According to Willard Connely, Steele's illegitimate daughter — known as Elizabeth Ousley, later Mrs. Aynston — was born in 1701 and was probably the daughter of Elizabeth Tonson, daughter of the publisher Richard Tonson. See W. Connely, *Sir Richard Steele* (New York, London, 1934), pp. 51, 56, 126. In 1708 Steele, who had been recently married to "Dear Prue," visited Addison at Sandford Manor House, Sandy End, when Addison was standing for Parliament. See *ibid.*, p. 128.

17. See "The Townsman" for Nov. 17, 1833, p. 314 of this text. Allan Cunningham was publishing serially in the *Athenaeum* his *Biographical and Critical History of the Literature of the Last Fifty Years*. On November 16, 1833, he included this paragraph:

Leigh Hunt has scarcely obtained such fame as his talents deserve. His "Rimini," though not without affectation, has high merit, both in conception of character, and conduct of story; there is a singular ease and richness of expression, a quick sensibility, and a ready feeling for beauty, both of nature and life; he drops in, now and then, as if by accident, a homely but expressive phrase, which awakens many fine associations. His prose is gossiping, graceful, and searching, and charms many readers.   — *Athenaeum* (1833), p. 772.

See also note 40 below.

18. Dr. Benjamin Hoadly (1706–1757); *The Suspicious Husband* was first performed at Covent Garden, Feb. 1747.

19. Lady Elizabeth Hastings (1682–1739). Congreve praises her under the name of Aspasia in the *Tatler*, No. 42.

20. Hortensia Mancini, Duchess of Mazarin (1646–1699), mistress of Charles II.

21. Nikolaus Ludwig, Count von Zinzendorf (1700–1760).

22. Henry Constantine Jennings (1731–1819).

23. Rejected by modern biographers. For a fairer interpretation of More, see E. M. G. Routh, *Sir Thomas More and His Friends (1477–1535)* (London, 1934); R. W. Chambers, *Thomas More* (New York, 1935); Algernon Cecil, *A Portrait of Thomas More, Scholar, Statesman, Saint* (London, 1937). Hunt's remarks here and in "The Townsman XVI" are an expression of the revival of interest in More during the English Romantic period. See Rev. Alfred H. Deutsch, O.S.B., *The Vogue of Thomas More between 1790 and 1830*, M.A. thesis, University of Illinois, 1942.

24. William Cecil, first Baron Burghley or Burleigh (1520–1598), Lord High Treasurer under Elizabeth I.

25. Thomas Sackville, first Earl of Dorset and Baron Buckhurst (1536–1608).

26. Inigo Jones (1573–1652), famous English architect. For a sketch of this gate, see J. Alfred Gotch, *Inigo Jones* (London, 1928), p. 126.

27. "On Beaufort House Gate at Chiswick."

28. Mary Astell (1668–1731), author of a *Serious Proposal to Ladies,* 1694, urging the erection of a monastery or "Religious Retirement" for ladies.

29. Charles de Marguetel de Saint-Denis, Seigneur de Saint-Évremond (1610?–1703), French courtier and writer.

30. Sir John Danvers (1588?–1655).

31. Thomas Wharton, first Marquis of Wharton (1648–1715).

32. John Martyn (1699–1768), edited the *Georgics* in 1741.

33. Hunt makes many omissions in quoting the *Journal*. See *The Journal to Stella* in *The Prose Works of Jonathan Swift, D.D.*, ed. by Frederick Ryland (London, 1908), II, 163-171, 177, 188-189, 205.

34. The rest of this paragraph is partially obliterated in the only copy of the *Weekly True Sun* that we have been able to find.

35. Edward Lawrence (1633–1657), son of Henry Lawrence, Puritan statesman; Milton's pupil.

36. Edward Chamberlayne, LL.D. (1616–1703), English Ambassador to the Low Countries; author of *The Present State of England,* 1669. His lengthy epitaph, outlining the chief events of his life, is translated from the Latin in Thomas Faulkner's *Historical and Topographical Description of Chelsea and Its Environs* (Chelsea, 1829), I, 243. Hunt appears to be using this edition, revised from the original edition of 1810.

37. Philip Miller (1691–1771).

38. See note 23 above.

39. 1690. See Faulkner, *Historical and Topographical Description of Chelsea and Its Environs,* I, 246.

40. In the two preceding issues of "The Townsman" (Dec. 22 and 29, 1833), Hunt had vigorously responded to Allan Cunningham's accusation that he had shown poor taste in publishing *Lord Byron and Some of His Contemporaries* (1828). See *Leigh Hunt's Literary Criticism,* ed. by L. H. and C. W. Houtchens, pp. 664–665. "The Townsman. No. XVII" had concluded:

Mr. Cunningham should confine himself to his ballads, and sea songs, and small Scottish poems, in which, when he does not hamper himself with too many words or fine images, he sometimes makes a capital hit. He has a pleasant taste for landscape and bonny lasses, can relate anecdote agreeably, or manage a piece of pictorial biography, where no great gusto for the art is required; and he will make a good editor for Burns (as far as the poetry goes), both out of a national and fellow-feeling with him, in some respects, and because Burns, though a great poet of his class, requires nothing further in his critic than a sympathy with flesh and blood, and a hearty acknowledgment of natural and simple emotion. But our *Athenaeum* friend should not seat himself in a chair of state to criticise all England, nor meddle with any thing that requires depth of thought or sublimity of apprehension.
— *Weekly True Sun* (Dec. 22, 1833).

Unfortunately, half of the only copy of "The Townsman. No. XVIII" that we could obtain is obliterated. It includes, however, the following passage about Shelley:

I am *not* an ungrateful man, nor ever showed an atom of ingratitude, either in a great way or a small. My love for Mr. Shelley alone would prove it; for he indeed *heaped* me with obligations of every kind — and instead of thinking them a burden, or wincing in the least degree under a sense of any part of them, they have ever constituted my glory and my delight. He was the man of all men I was most obliged to; yet he was the man I ever loved best, whose name I have most on my lips, whose obligations of me I have proclaimed and never cease to talk of, and whose memory I so worship, that the having known him seems to me the next thing to having known and conversed with an angel. Are these the feelings of a man who has not a due sense of obligation? If I were of an ungrateful disposition, my ingratitude would have been in proportion to the favours conferred on me; or, at any rate, the height of my voluntary affection would never have been in that proportion. But observe the difference. Mr. Shelley conferred all his noble and real obligations out of the flowing fullness of his heart, and because he loved to do good, and to see your face happy. He had the most exalted notions of the duties of friends to each other; delighted to undo his own superiority, that he might be happy with you on the level of mutual kindness.   — *Weekly True Sun* (Dec. 29, 1833).

41. Alexander Stephens (see note 8), of whom G. LeGrys Norgate says in the *Dictionary of National Biography*, "As a biographer he was painstaking, accurate, and scrupulously fair." The passage as Hunt quotes it is almost as it appeared in Alexander Stephens' posthumous "Stephensiana. No. I." *Monthly Magazine* (Oct. 1, 1821), LII, 231. The information about Dr. Johnson seems authentic. See N.Q., "Varia," *New Rambler*, publication of the Johnson Society of London, No. 5 (July, 1944), pp. 19-20.

42. *Faerie Queene*, I, xii, 38, 4.

43. See Hunt on Smollett in *Table-Talk* (1851), reprinted from "Smollett and Mr. Cruikshank," *Tatler* (Sept. 21, 1831), III, 281-283.

44. Hunt was a great admirer of Fielding and praised *Joseph Andrews*, his "favourite novel," for its characterization. See "Joseph Andrews," *Tatler* (Jan. 19, 1832), IV, 61. *Tom Jones*, he believed

by universal consent, is reckoned the completest novel in the language. It is admirable for its description of manners, hardly less so for character, and truly epic (as the author delighted to think it) in the conduct and development of its plot. There are novels superior to it, in some one or two particulars, and many a late romance of intenser interest; but not one work of prose fiction that we are acquainted with, so complete altogether, and connecting all the little streams of interest into one final purpose.

— "Fielding and Tom Jones," *Tatler* (Dec. 6, 1831), III, 537.

45. *A Midsummer Night's Dream*, II, i, 10.

46. *As You Like It*, II, i, 48-49.

47. Inexact. According to the *Dictionary of National Biography*, Elizabeth Talbot, Countess of Shrewsbury, was born in 1518 and died on 13 Feb., 1608.

48. George Morley, D.D. (1597—1684), bishop of Winchester.

49. Anne of Cleves.

50. They were married, but the marriage was dissolved.

51. Richard Cromwell (1626–1712), third son of Oliver Cromwell, and Lord Protector of England, 1658–1659.
52. See *Tatler*, No. 32.
53. "The Townsman" for Apr. 13, 1834, was the final number and did not cover Chelsea.

THE TOWNSMAN.
STREET-LIGHTS, GAS, AND ILLUMINATIONS

1. Published in two parts (unnumbered) in "The Townsman," *Weekly True Sun* (Mar. 23 and 30, 1834).
2. Hunt quotes Book III, 127-148.
3. Sir Hugh Myddelton or Middleton (1560?–1631), promoter of the New River, a canal to supply London with water. He was impoverished but not ruined by his activities.
4. Frederick Albert Winsor (1763–1830), one of the first promotors of gas-illumination. The exhibition in Pall-Mall occurred in 1807.
5. John Dee (1527–1608); acquitted of the charge of practicing sorcery against Queen Mary (1555); astrologer and mathematician.
6. James Sheridan Knowles (1784–1862), dramatist and actor.

EXPLANATION AND RETROSPECTION.
THE *EXAMINER* TWENTY YEARS AGO

1. *Monthly Repository* (Oct. 1837), series 3, I, 225-235. Not long after this essay appeared, Julian Harcourt published the following description of Hunt in the first of a series of nine articles entitled "Personal Sketches of Eminent Men of the Day":

Mr. Grant's non-talkative nature reminds us of an observation made by Leigh Hunt to a friend of mine who remarked to that gentleman that he thought a passage in Cowley a very fine one, which drew the distinction between the solitude of a man, and that of other creatures. "Cogitation," says Cowley, "is that which distinguishes the solitude of a man from the solitude of a wild beast."
"It may be so," was Mr. Hunt's reply; "only you don't know what the wild beast is thinking about."

◦ ◦ ◦

Mr. Leigh Hunt, the politician and poet, (and there is no man living who has attained an equal celebrity in both these departments of literature), is in his fifty-fourth year. He is tall of stature, five feet eleven, or six feet, and of moderate sturdiness of proportion; though I recollect seeing him some ten years ago, and he was much stouter than he was when I last had that pleasure. His hair is of a jet black, and curls in ringlets; his complexion is also extremely dark, and his eyes, which we have before mentioned as singularly fine and expressive, are also tinged with a watchfulness and melancholy which persecution has put into them, but which have not dimmed the cheerfulness with which the heart and mind ever light them up. There is this melancholy also, at times, in his voice, but usually it has a lively tone, and is always musical, and impressive of the opinion or feeling which he wishes it to convey to your mind. Mr. Hunt's head is singularly small, as Shelley's and Byron's were; and as we believe that of the late inimitable Charles Lamb was. His face is not handsome, the upper lip is too long and large, and the other features are out of proportion; though full of care, its care is softened by its benignity, and the eyes put the genius into it. Mr. Hunt's manners are full of politeness, according to Swift's definition* of that very ill-used substantive: they have the gentleman's self-possession, his absence of all assumption of superiority or an ill-timed and improper inferiority, and the dignity imparted to them by a constant consciousness of rectitude and good endeavour. Mr. Hunt's scholarship, his sparkling conversation, his exquisite taste in singing, and his pianoforte playing constitute him the very life and soul of a convivial party, although he is an abstemious *winer*, and the worst hand in the world to enter into the merits of his host's dinner, paying his addresses to a very few of the innumerable attractions provided, and those of the simplest nature he can discover. Mr. Hunt is a good dresser, though by no means a Brummel in the art. His only peculiarity in this particular exists in the looseness of his neckerchief, and the nonelaborate inequality of his dexter and sinister shirt-bib, the one generally being up, and the other down, according to "their own sweet will." His walk is generally quick, and he carries himself upright, and his head generally thrown slightly backwards, with an eye-glass very often scientifically *hitched* into his eye, — for like a great many clever men, (paradoxical as it would seem), he is extremely short-sighted. Mr. Hunt has many children and grandchildren. He is beloved and deeply esteemed by all who know him.

— *Literary and Pictorial Repository* (1838), first series, pp. 51-52.

This article should be added to Professor Landré's bibliography.

2. "Result of the Elections, and Defects of the Reformers," *Monthly Repository* (Sept. 1837), series 3, I, 145-152. Hunt maintained in this article that the Reformers had no satisfactory leaders. At the general election, the Whigs had remained in power. The Cabinet at this time consisted of Viscount Melbourne, Prime Minister and First Lord Treasurer; Lord Cottenham, Lord Chancellor; the Marquis of Lansdowne, Lord President of Council; Viscount Duncannon, Lord Privy Seal; Lord John Russell, Home Secretary;

---

* "Politeness," says the Dean, "is the art of making people easy in your society." — I quote by memory.

Viscount Palmerston, Foreign Secretary; Lord Glenelg, Secretary for War and Colonies; the Earl of Minto, First Lord of Admiralty; T. Spring Rice, Chancellor of Exchequer; Sir J. C. Hobhouse, President of Board of Control; C. Poulett Thomson, President of Board of Trade; Lord Holland, Chancellor of the Duchy of Lancaster; Viscount Duncannon, First Commissioner of Woods and Forests; and Viscount Howick (later Earl Grey), Secretary at War.

3. John George Lambton, first Earl of Durham (1792–1840), statesman of the Liberal Party; Ambassador to St. Petersburg, 1835–1837; Governor General of Canada in 1838. His letter to the electors of North Durham developed the following theme: "I wish to rally as large a portion of the British people as possible around the existing institutions of the country — *the Throne, Lords, Commons, and the Established Church.* I do not wish to make new institutions, but to preserve and strengthen the old." Hunt, "Lord Durham and the Reformers," *Monthly Repository* (Aug. 1837), series 3, I, 75.

4. William J. Fox had sold the *Monthly Repository* in 1836 to R. H. Horne, who had become both the proprietor and the editor. From July, 1837, to April, 1838, when the magazine ceased publication, Leigh Hunt was the editor.

5. John Cartwright (1740–1824), parliamentary reformer; brother of the famous inventor, Edmund Cartwright.

6. Albany Fonblanque (1793–1872).

TWELFTH NIGHT

1. *Musical Times, and Singing Class Circular* (Jan. 1, 1854), V, 313–316. Joseph Alfred Novello, son of Vincent Novello, was the publisher of the *Musical Times*, to which Hunt contributed several essays in 1853–1854.

2. On the mechanics institutes, see A. E. Dobbs, *Education and Social Movements, 1700–1850* (London, 1919), Vol. I, chap. v.

3. Here Hunt asked to have "inserted the following words in a parenthesis (*next after one or two that we could name*) but not in italics.

"I am afraid," he added," the omission of these words might *possibly* hurt the feelings of one or two admirable persons. But everything of course must give way to printer's necessities." Letter to Alfred Novello, L. A. Brewer, *My Leigh Hunt Library: The Holograph Letters* (University of Iowa Press, 1938), p. 392. Letter dated Hammersmith, Dec. 29, [1853], State University of Iowa Library catalog card.

4. Hunt describes this in more detail in his 1835 essay on

Twelfth Night, *Leigh Hunt's London Journal* (Jan. 7, 1835), II, 1-2, reprinted in *The Seer* (1840). See also a letter from Hunt to Mary Shelley in Italy, Mar. 9, 1819: "[Walter] Coulson is a good deal here; so are Hogg and Peacock, besides the Novellos, and a very nice couple, friends of theirs, a Mr. and Mrs. Gliddon. We had a most glorious twelfth-night, with *tea in the study at half-past six* (in the morning), and the women all sparkling to the last." Hunt, *Correspondence*, I, 127-128. The "accomplished musician" to whom Hunt refers in this essay was probably Vincent Novello. See also a letter to Hunt from Mary Sabilla Novello, Oct. 19, 1823, *ibid.*, I, 210.

CHRISTMAS DAY DIVIDED BETWEEN TWO WORLDS

1. *National Magazine* (1857), I, 195-197.
2. The death, in 1852, of Hunt's son Vincent. On Dec. 2, [1857], Hunt wrote to Charles Ollier, mentioning the present article on Christmas.

The reason [continued Hunt] why the date of the most melancholy of days was not present to me, when I wrote to you a little time since, was, that whenever October comes round, I take pains to hinder myself from becoming aware of it, by ceasing to note the dates of the days for weeks previous.

God bless you, my dear Ollier, and may loss on earth only mean increase of gain to us in another world; — as I believe, thank God, it does. So let us live on as cheerfully as we can in that belief . . . .
— L. A. BREWER, *My Leigh Hunt Library. The Holograph Letters*, p. 112.

See also "On the Death of his Son Vincent," Oxford edition of Hunt's poems, p. 281, and *Letters to Leigh Hunt from His Son Vincent with Some Replies*, ed. by A. N. L. Munby (Storey's End, Cambridge, 1934).

3. See Leigh Hunt, *The Religion of the Heart*, "Of Spirits and the Invisible World" (London, 1853), pp. 74-76, also pp. 43-44; and "Reflections of a Dead Body," Oxford edition of Hunt's poems, pp. 267-269.

YOUNG OLD STATESMEN

1. "The Occasional. No. XIII. Young Old Statesmen . . . ," *Spectator* (July 9, 1859), XXXII, 715-716; "The Occasional. No. XIV. Subject of 'Young Old Statesmen' Concluded. Perseverance in spite of failures — Tutors themselves not always discerning — Robert Bruce, the spider, and the laundress — Plutarch's advocacy of the

right of old men to be statesmen — Instances adduced by him to that effect — Anecdote of Montesquieu in his seventieth year," *ibid.* (July 30, 1859), 787-788. Published in Hunt's seventy-fifth year.

2. Lord Palmerston formed his second administration on June 30, 1859. Lord John Russell was Foreign Secretary.

3. The speech was given on July 2, 1859, on the occasion of the distribution of prizes to the students. For a report of the event and Lord Palmerston's speech, see the *Times* (July 4, 1859), p. 4.

4. Quoted from an editorial in the *Times* (July 5, 1859), p. 8.

5. Thomas Parr (1483?–1635). Henry Jenkins (d. 1670) claimed to have been born (c.) 1501.

6. John Campbell, first Baron Campbell (1779–1861), legal biographer.

7. John Singleton Copley, Baron Lyndhurst (1772–1863) had served three times as Lord Chancellor and was an eloquent speaker.

8. The Earl of Derby, known as the "Rupert of debate," had just gone out of office as Prime Minister. Disraeli had been Chancellor of the Exchequer under Lord Derby.

9. In 1782, two years before Napoleon left the military school at Brienne, he was recommended for the navy by a school inspector. A new inspector in 1783, however, opposed the recommendation.

10. See Plutarch's *Moralia,* "Whether An Old Man Should Engage in Public Affairs," trans. by H. N. Fowler (Harvard University Press, 1936), X, 77-153.

11. Cato did not lead an army to victory in his old age.

12. Sir Stephen Fox (1627–1716) by his first marriage (c. 1654) had ten children; by his second marriage (1703) had four children.

13. Thomas William Coke, Earl of Leicester, had six children by his second marriage, which took place when he was sixty-nine.

14. Emperor Francis Joseph I of Austria was defeated in the Franco-Austrian War of 1859.

15. See Francis Hardy, *Memoirs of the Political and Private Life of James Caulfield, Earl of Charlemont,* 2nd ed., (London, 1812), I, 62-63.

THE OCCASIONAL. LEIGH HUNT

1. *Spectator* (Sept. 3, 1859), XXXII, 905-906. Hunt died on Aug. 28, 1859.

INDEX

essays on, 423n; at Christ's Hospital, 7-8; Civil List pension, 31; and Cobbett, 63-66; and Allan Cunningham, 439-40n; death, 445n; description by Julian Harcourt, 441-42n; and divine right, 37; dramatic critic for John Hunt's *News*, 8; editor of *Companion*, 28-29, of *Indicator*, 27, of *Leigh Hunt's London Journal*, 29-30, of *Liberal*, 27-28, of *Monthly Repository*, 30, 443n, of *Reflector*, 34, of *Tatler*, 29; editorials addressed to voters, 32-33; on Lord Ellenborough, 422n; empiricism, 37 ff.; on Fielding's novels, 440n; financial difficulties, 25-26; on French Revolution, 46; on geopolitics, 46; humanitarianism, 27, 51-52; imagination, 67-69; imprisonment, 26; informations against, 10-17, 21, 51; on Irish Catholics, 20; in Italy, 27-28; and Keats, 36; and legal dangers, 12-14; liberalism, 37-43; and limited monarchy, 37 ff.; literary achievements, 31; loss of interest in politics, 27-28; military reform, 10; and military flogging, 16; on morality, 44-45; on Napoleon, 46; obituary, 409-12; Oriental elements in satire, 68-69; and partisanship, 32-33; on "Party," 31; on "philosophical spirit" in political writing, 31-32; as "Political Examiner," 8; political independence, 90-91; political reality, lack of imagination concerning, 66; political verse, 61; political views and writing, 31-36, 369 ff.; pragmatism, 40 ff.; praise of great men, 48-49; and Prince Regent, 18 ff.; on "profligacy," 44; on racial differences, 46; reading, of English history, 6, of English literature, 7; on reform in male-female relationships, 241; and reform of parliament, 34; residence, in Chelsea, 436n, in Marylebone, 433n; resignation of clerkship in War Office, 3; retirement from *Ex-*

aminer, 27; romanticism, 40-41, 43-53; schoolboy friendships, 7-8; sentence and imprisonment, 25-26; and Shelley, 36, 411-12, 439-40n; on slave trade, 10; Southey's advice on transportation of, 35; support, of Robert Owen, 40, of Utilitarianism, 40-42; as "Theatrical Examiner," 9; translations by, 46; trials, 10-17, 20-25, 147-53, 431n; on tyranny, 39-40; vision of Heaven, 392 ff.

Hunt, Leigh: *Examiner*, v, 3-71 *passim*; early days of, 369-81; financial control lost; form of, 61-69; purpose and principles of, 31-36; sales rise, 22; significance of, 70-71; style of, 61-69

Hunt, Leigh: Writings: "Account of the Remarkable Rise and Downfall of the Late Kan of Tartary," 69; *Autobiography*, 7, 39, 44, 47, 62, 434n, quoted, 434-35n, 435nn; *Book for a Corner, A*, 432n; *Captain Sword and Captain Pen*, 30; *Correspondence*, 444n; *Day by the Fire, A*, 434n; "Deliverance of Europe," 69; "Dogs, The," 28; "Final Enslavement of the French Press", 419n; *Foliage*, 57; "French Fashions," 47; *Holograph Letters*, 15, 24, 51, 443n, 444n; "House of Lords.—Origin of the Titles of Our Dukes and Marquises," 424n; *Indicator and the Companion, The*, 434n; *Juvenilia*, 8, 434n, 436n; "Late Mr. Sheridan, The," 55; *Legend of Florence, A*, 31; *Leigh Hunt's Autobiography: The Earliest Sketches*, 7; *Leigh Hunt's Dramatic Criticism*, v, 436n; *Leigh Hunt's Literary Criticism*, v, 55, 62, 438n; *Leigh Hunt's London Journal*, 29-30, 41, 428n; letter to Charles Ollier, quoted, 444n; letter to Alfred Novello, quoted, 443n; *Lord Byron and Some of His Contemporaries*, 24, 54, 439-40n; "Lord Durham and the Reformers," 443n;